DEFINING DOCUMENTS
IN AMERICAN HISTORY

Reconstruction Era
(1865-1877)

DEFINING DOCUMENTS
IN AMERICAN HISTORY

Reconstruction Era
(1865-1877)

Editor

Michael Shally-Jensen, PhD

SALEM PRESS

A Division of EBSCO Information Services

Ipswich, Massachusetts

GREY HOUSE PUBLISHING

Library of Congress Cataloging-in-Publication Data

Publisher's Cataloging-In-Publication Data
(Prepared by The Donohue Group, Inc.)

Reconstruction era : (1865-1877) / [edited by Salem Press]. -- [First edition].

   pages ; cm. -- (Defining documents in American history)

   Includes bibliographical references and index.
   ISBN: 978-1-61925-487-9

   1. Reconstruction (U.S. history, 1865-1877)--Sources. 2. Industrialization--United States--Sources. 3. United States--History--1865-1898--Sources. I. Salem Press.

Cover photo: Charles Sumner on Reconstruction and the South, 1866 ©Gilder Lehrman

E668 .R436 2014
973.8

Table of Contents

Black Codes and White Lives

Extreme Reactions

Reconstruction Moves Ahead

An Ambiguous Legacy

APPENDIXES

Publisher's Note

The *Defining Documents in American History* series, produced by Salem Press, consists of a collection of essays on important historical documents by a diverse range of writers on a broad range of subjects in American history. *Defining Documents in American History: Reconstruction Era (1865-1877)* surveys key documents produced during the Reconstruction era, organized under the following broad themes:

- Debating Reconstruction
- Communities in Need
- Acts of State
- Black Codes & White Lives
- Extreme Reactions
- Reconstruction Moves Ahead
- An Ambiguous Legacy

Historical documents provide a compelling view of this unique period of American history. Designed for high school and college students, the aim of the series is to advance historical document studies as an important activity in learning about history.

Essay Format

Reconstruction Era contains 40 primary source documents – many in their entirety. Each document is supported by a critical essay, written by historians and teachers, that includes a Summary Overview, Defining Moment, Author Biography, Document Analysis, and Essential Themes. Readers will appreciate the diversity of the collected texts, including journals, letters, speeches, political sermons, laws, government reports, and court cases, among other genres. An important feature of each essay is a close reading of the primary source that develops evidence of broader themes, such as author's rhetorical purpose, social or class position, point of view, and other relevant issues. In addition, the chapter themes highlight major issues in the period, many of which extend across eras and continue to shape American life. Each chapter begins with a brief introduction that explains the questions and problems underlying the subjects in the historical documents. A brief glossary, included at the end of each document, highlights keywords important in the study of the primary source. Each essay also includes a Bibliography and Additional Reading section for further research.

Special Features/Appendixes
- **Chronological List** of all documents by year.
- **Web Resources** is an annotated list of web sites that offer valuable supplemental resources.
- **Bibliography** lists helpful articles and books for further study.

Contributors

Salem Press would like to extend its appreciation to all involved in the development and production of this work. The essays have been written and signed by scholars of history, humanities, and other disciplines related to the essay's topics. Without these expert contributions, a project of this nature would not be possible. A full list of contributor's names and affiliations appears in the front matter of this volume.

Editor's Introduction

Reconstruction refers, of course, to the period in U.S. history immediately following the Civil War, extending from 1865 to 1877. Some historians suggest that the Reconstruction era began earlier, in 1863, with President Lincoln's Emancipation Proclamation (Foner 1988). In any case, by the end of the war the South was in a state of ruin and changes of historic proportions were required of it. Battles with Union forces, and the advance of the Union Army across the region, had produced massive physical damage throughout the land. Slavery had been abolished, and with it the old social and economic order sustaining the South. Although the North was by no means unaffected by the war, the most urgent problems lay with the Confederate states. Those states now had to be brought back into the Union; functioning state governments had to be established, under wholly new conditions. Moreover, millions of former slaves—freedmen—had to be accommodated within Southern society.

Given the grand scope of this undertaking, it is not surprising that Reconstruction has been viewed differently by different observers over the course of time. When the first scholarly histories of the subject came out in the early 20th century, the prevailing view was that the radical Republicans of the winning side (i.e., the most liberal faction of the party of Lincoln) had imposed a punitive military regimen on the South. Republican-led state governments set up during Reconstruction were said to exhibit unconcealed hostility toward Southern Democrats and Southern ways and traditions. They set out a Northern-style rule across the South that promoted corrupt practices and did not properly address underlying social and economic problems. Reconstruction, in this view, was regarded as a tragic blunder, a big mistake. The South, in turn, was portrayed as fighting again for a noble cause, the preservation of its heritage. Instead of healing wounds left by the war, these writers argued, Reconstruction only caused further rifts between the North and the South (Baker 2007; Smith and Lowery 2013).

Another school of thought, emerging in the mid- to late-20th century and largely accepted today, states that it was, above all, the racism of the South that prevented Reconstruction from succeeding. The radicals and their idealism, it is argued, should be acknowledged as having struggled to advance the rights of the freedmen and as contributing to the restoration of the Southern economy. Most historians writing today hold that the radical state governments produced some worthy legislative achievements, including provisions for the education of blacks as well as poor whites. It is believed that Republican governments were no more corrupt than the governments preceding or succeeding them (whether Democratic or not). Lingering racism is identified as the principle reason why Reconstruction faltered—and why, once federal troops were pulled out at the end of Reconstruction, the rights of blacks were immediately extinguished (*ibid.*; Foner 1988).

Reconstruction Plans under Lincoln

After proclaiming the emancipation of slaves in January 1863, President Lincoln began planning for the postwar period. Later that year, for example, he developed a basic Reconstruction plan for the defeated Confederate state of Louisiana. Similar plans were introduced the following year in Tennessee and Arkansas. In beginning this process, Lincoln hoped to start the work of healing the damage done to the Union and to the South, and also to build up the Republican party in the former Confederate states. Thus, in a December 1863 decree, Lincoln offered amnesty and assistance toward reconstruction for all Confederate areas occupied by Union forces. Referred to as the Ten-Percent Plan, the decree provided a pardon to any Confederate who pledged allegiance to the Constitution and loyalty to the Union. It stated that a Confederate state could return to the Union when 10 percent of its voters (as of 1860) took the required oath and established a government that accepted emancipation.

Lincoln's Ten-Percent Plan caused the radicals in Congress to worry publically that it would grant the Southern aristocracy—the old planter society—a victory, of sorts, in that the bar for re-entry to the Union had been raised too low and ways would be found to get around or soften the requirements and lower expectations. In response, the radicals passed the Wade-Davis Bill (in July 1864), requiring 50 percent of a state's voters to take a solemn oath stating that they had not voluntarily acceded to the Confederate cause. Lincoln used the gambit of a pocket veto—a delay in signing a bill that causes it to expire—to prevent the Wade-Davis Bill from becoming law. Instead, he pursued his own plan, without great success. Several states (Louisiana, Arkansas, Tennessee, and Virginia) undertook the required course of action, but when the time came Congress refused to accept the Senators and Representatives elected from those states. Matters were at an impasse when news came of Lincoln's assassination.

Reconstruction Plans under Johnson

Andrew Johnson, successor to Abraham Lincoln, initially satisfied the radicals with talk of breaking up the planter class and punishing the Confederate states. In an amnesty proclamation of May 1865, Johnson instituted harsher retributions than did his predecessor. He sought to make the property of owners of large plantations subject to confiscation, and to disenfranchise both those owners and all former military and civil officers of the Confederacy. The main objective was to unseat the planter class, destabilize its control of politics, and return state government to small farmers, traders, and artisans.

Johnson took advantage of a congressional recess (April to December, 1865) to roll his plan out in the South. He appointed a series of provisional governors, under whom the Southern states held conventions to set up new governments and new government policies. They elected new legislatures, voided or repealed their prewar ordinances of secession, abolished slavery, and did away with Confederate debts (except South Carolina). They ratified the Thirteenth Amendment guaranteeing freedom for African Americans (except Mississippi, which only ratified it in 1995). By the end of 1865, every former rebel state except Texas had reconstituted their governments.

On the societal front, however, things were a little different. Whites reasserted their dominance over blacks, principally by enacting Black Codes, or statutes meant to severely restrict the rights of the blacks and the freedoms they could enjoy. Such laws, for example, limited the ability of blacks to own land and to work as free laborers. They denied African Americans most of the civil and political liberties enjoyed by whites. Worse yet, many of these laws came about because offices in the new governments had been won by ostensibly disenfranchised Confederate leaders, i.e., those who were supposed to have been barred from office. Rather than ordering new elections, however, President Johnson granted blanket pardons.

In the North, an outraged public came to feel that Johnson was squandering his chance to impose a victor's justice. When Congress reconvened in early December 1865, it declined to admit the newly elected

Senators and Representatives from the South. Not able to abide this, Johnson openly attacked Republican leaders and turned to vetoing their subsequent Reconstruction measures. Johnson's efforts had the effect of pushing moderate Republicans toward the side of the radicals. Thus, legislators passed, over the president's veto, the Civil Rights Act of 1866, intended to protect African Americans against harmful legislation such as black codes; and the Freedmen's Bureau Bill, granting that organization (the Freedman's Bureau) more time to do its work. When questions arose regarding the constitutionality of the Civil Rights Act, the radicals worked to incorporate many of its provisions into the Fourteenth Amendment (ratified 1868), making them permanent.

Relatively early on in the process (April 1866) the Joint Committee on Reconstruction issued a report stating that the ex-Confederate states were in no condition to conduct their own legislative affairs or to represent their citizens in the national government. These states had not held, nor could they be expected to hold, valid elections. The committee also proposed that Reconstruction was a matter for Congress to attend to, not the executive branch. Elections held in 1866 served to solidify the radicals' hold in Congress. Thus, when the Fourteenth Amendment failed to be ratified by the rebel states (except Tennessee), the time had come in the radicals' eyes for sterner measures to be introduced.

Reconstruction in Practice

The reconstruction of the South got under way on a large scale following the enactment, in March 1867, of the Reconstruction Act. According to it, and to three supplemental acts, the South (except Tennessee) was to be divided into five military districts, each led by an army commander whose authority reined over most matters of state. President Johnson, balking at this and other congressional measures, sought to remove the radical Secretary of War, Edwin M. Stanton, even though such a maneuver violated the Tenure of Office Act. The latter was itself authorized by Congress over a presidential veto. Thus, when Johnson aimed his guns at Stanton, the House of Representatives moved to impeach him (February 1868). In the end, the vote in the Senate for conviction of the president fell one short, but by then Johnson's ability to rule was virtually nil.

One of the first priorities under the Reconstruction Acts was the writing of new state constitutions in the South. This was done, and in mid-1868 six states (Arkansas, North Carolina, South Carolina, Louisiana, Alabama, and Florida) were readmitted to the Union, having duly ratified the Fourteenth Amendment as required by federal law. The four remaining, "unreconstructed" states (Virginia, Mississippi, Texas, and Georgia) were readmitted in 1870, after ratifying both the Fourteenth and Fifteenth amendments, the latter of which guaranteed the right to vote for adult African American males.

In Southern state capitals, radical Republican governments worked to address the grave problems left by the Civil War and the destruction of slavery. These state legislatures were led by a mix of 1) Northerners who settled in the South, i.e., so-called carpet-baggers; 2) Southern whites in the Republican party, known as scalawags; and 3) freedmen (former slaves) along with free blacks. Together these men labored to reorganize the Southern economy and reconstitute Southern society. Trade was restored, the production of food and fiber (cotton) was brought back online, infrastructure was rebuilt, the financial system (including a redistributive tax) was revised, and educational programs were established for blacks and impoverished whites. For the first time, blacks were allowed to participate in the civil and economic life of the South, now that their political rights were guaranteed.

The majority of Southern whites continued in the postwar period, however, to reject the idea of treating former slaves as full and equal members of society. This is the period when the Ku Klux Klan, a vigilante or hate group, arose. Its threats and acts of violence kept African Americans and many white Republicans from enjoying their civil liberties, including the right to vote. Revelations of corruption in the radical Republican governments further fueled animosities, and eventually caused the fall of those governments. Now gone from the scene, too, were many of the old-guard radicals in Congress, such as Thaddeus Stevens, who died while in office. In relatively short order, the administration of Ulysses S. Grant was implicated in a corruption scandal of its own and could no longer devote its attention to a flagging Reconstruction effort in the South.

The End of Reconstruction
Eighteen seventy-six was an election year. At that time, only three states—Florida, South Carolina, and Louisiana—remained under Republican control. The Republican presidential candidate that year, Rutherford B. Hayes (Ohio), proclaimed that the South would fare better under his administration. His Democratic opponent, Samuel J. Tilden (New York), was winning support in the South, as were other Democrats on the ballot. Inside the three holdout states concerted efforts were afoot to overturn the Republicans. Come the election, one of the most controversial in history, the results were indeterminate. Tilden won in the popular vote, but in the electoral vote both candidates claimed victory based on state tallies. To resolve the matter a compromise was struck, the Compromise of 1877, which awarded the disputed electoral votes—and the presidency—to Hayes in return for withdrawing federal troops from the South.

The withdrawal order was given on May 1st, 1877. The action effectively ended Reconstruction and returned the Southern states to Southerners, principally to white Southerners. Whites once again became politically dominant, as a "solid South" formed around the Democratic party. Blacks were promptly disenfranchised through new "Jim Crow" laws and other means, thus losing most of the civil and political rights they had won along with their hopes for economic prosperity. For the next eighty or ninety years, African Americans remained, as Frederick Douglass characterized it, "not yet quite free." Douglass wrote about the phenomenon in his autobiography:

> Though slavery was abolished, the wrongs of my people were not ended. Though they were slaves, they were not yet quite free. No man can be truly free whose liberty is dependent upon the thoughts, feeling, and actions of others, and who has himself no means in his own hands for guarding, protecting, defending, and maintaining that liberty. Yet the Negro after his emancipation was precisely in this state of destitution... He was free from the individual master but the slave of society. He had neither money, property, nor friends. He was free from the old plantation, but he had nothing but the dusty road under his feet. He was free from the old quarter that once gave him shelter, but a slave to the rains of summer and the frost of winter. He was in a word, literally turned loose, naked, hungry, and destitute to the open sky. (Douglass 1882, 458-59)

Michael Shally-Jensen, PhD

Bibliography and Additional Reading

Baker, Bruce E. *What Reconstruction Meant: Historical Memory in the American South.* Charlottesville: University of Virginia Press, 2007.

Current, Richard N. *Those Terrible Carpetbaggers: A Reinterpretation.* New York: Oxford University Press, 1988.

Douglass, Frederick. *Life and Times of Frederick Douglass.* Hartford, CT: Park Publishing, 1882.

Foner, Eric. *Forever Free: The Story of Emancipation and Reconstruction.* New York: Knopf, 2005.

Foner, Eric. *Reconstruction: America's Unfinished Revolution, 1863–1877.* New York: Harper & Row, 1988.

Ford, Lacy K. *A Companion to the Civil War and Reconstruction.* Malden, MA: Blackwell, 2005.

Smith, John David, and J. Vincent Lowery. *The Dunning School: Historians, Race, and the Meaning of Reconstruction.* Lexington, KY: University Press of Kentucky, 2013.

Contributors

Michael P Auerbach
Marblehead, MA

Adam J. Berger, PhD
Princeton University

Amanda Beyer-Purvis, MA
University of Florida

Steven L. Danver, PhD
Mesa Verde Publishing
Washougal, Washington

Tracey DiLascio, Esq., JD
Framingham, Massachusetts

Kevin E. Grimm, PhD
Beloit College

Bethany Groff, MA
Historic New England

Jennifer D. Henry, MEd
Lancaster, PA

Donald E. Heidenreich, Jr., PhD
Lindenwood University
St. Charles, Missouri

Ashleigh Imus, PhD
Ithaca, NY

Mark S. Joy, PhD
Jamestown College

Laurence W. Mazzeno, PhD
Alvernia University

Vanessa E. Vaughn, MA
Chicago, Illinois

Donald A. Watt, PhD
McGovern Center for Leadership
and Public Service

Madeline Weissman, MA
California State University
Los Angeles, California

DEFINING DOCUMENTS
IN AMERICAN HISTORY

Reconstruction Era
(1865-1877)

DEBATING RECONSTRUCTION

At the end of the Civil War, about the only thing that had been resolved definitively was that slavery was over. Beyond that there was still much to be decided. Where would the freed slaves fit in the new society of the South? Were whites and blacks to be regarded as equals in every respect, or would things go more smoothly if, initially at least, former slaves were granted legal rights and protections but less than full citizenship? Should those rights and protections include, for example, the right to vote and to hold elective office? How would such matters be decided, given that most of the former Confederate states had yet to be readmitted to the Union? The issue of whether these states were ready and able to be readmitted needed to be examined, many argued, before the U.S. Congress simply threw open its doors and allowed former rebel representatives to hold forth. In contrast, others argued that any delay would only breed resentment and complicate matters further: the Southern states should all be readmitted posthaste.

In this section we take a look at these questions and others, focusing on the early shaping of the landscape of Reconstruction. There were matters of legal rights and governance to be debated, along with questions regarding the enforcement of those rights and the creation of those (state) governments. How were these to be accomplished? Would the individual states bear the brunt of the costs and other responsibilities, or were these best left to the federal government (whose plan included "reconstruction" in the first place)? Some questions asked at the time might not even occur to us today, given our present understanding. People in the mid-nineteenth century needed to be reassured, for example, that blacks were capable of managing their own affairs and working toward their own betterment. What, people wondered, were the short- and long-term prospects in that regard? What role did education play, and what role did honest toil and practical experience play?

The period was also one of continued political conflict inside the halls of government. President Andrew Johnson, a Democrat, was of a mind to speed Reconstruction along and yield power to the states in getting the task done. One of his fiercest opponents (although he had many), the great Thaddeus Stevens, was a leading radical Republican who favored a strong federal role in Reconstruction and a careful, managed approach. (Clearly these were different parties from those of today.) Another of Johnson's opponents, Charles Sumner, pointed to the emergence of so-called "black codes" in the postwar South as evidence that defeated Southerners were going to do everything in their power to resist change, particularly when it came to the freed slaves, or freedmen. Frederick Douglass, speaking on behalf of his own strong constituency as a public intellectual and former slave, feared that without the federal government a not-so-subtle process of "re-enslavement" would occur. In many cases questions continued to be asked even as Reconstruction policies took shape and, more importantly, got under way on the ground.

■ "The Absolute Equality of All Men before the Law, the Only True Basis of Reconstruction"

Date: October 3, 1865
Author: William M. Dickson
Genre: speech

Summary Overview

Delivered in the Northern town of Oberlin, Ohio, William M. Dickson's speech on the course he believed the tentatively reunified United States should take in the wake of the bitter years of the Civil War reflects the key challenges with which Northern leaders and thinkers then grappled. Dickson, a Cincinnati Republican with personal ties to former president Abraham Lincoln, had shown himself willing to support racial equality through his leadership of a local African American volunteer unit during the Civil War. After the war, he continued to speak out in favor of the restructuring of US policies to bring about true racial equality across the North and South. Dickson argues that the key to achieving this goal is assuring African Americans the right to vote, thus giving freedmen a say in the operations of new Southern state governments and granting them equality before the law.

Defining Moment

On October 10, 1865, Ohio voters went to the polls to select a new governor. During the recently ended Civil War, Ohio had been a battleground of public opinion as the home both of fervent Republican and Union support and of the Northern Democratic "Copperhead" movement led by Ohio statesman Clement Vallandigham. Vallandigham's virulent anti-Lincoln and antiwar speeches had earned him the hatred of the pro-Union majority, but he remained a key voice for Southern sympathy in the North even after he was banished to the Confederacy as punishment for his antiwar activities. Ohio Democrats nominated Vallandigham *in absentia* for the office of governor in 1863, but he was defeated by a National Union Party candidate put for-

ward by a coalition of Republicans and pro-war Democrats. However, the 1865 gubernatorial campaign took place in the immediate postwar era; the coalition Union Party again put forward a candidate against a Democratic contender, former Union officer George W. Morgan, but the issues at hand had changed. Union victory had practically proved the value of fighting the Civil War. Yet Reconstruction loomed ahead.

By this time, Andrew Johnson—a Tennessee native and War Democrat—had become president following Lincoln's assassination. Johnson's plan for Reconstruction was a relatively mild one that showed little interest in securing civil rights for the millions of recently freed African Americans in the South. Although Johnson did require states of the former Confederacy to ratify the Thirteenth Amendment to the US Constitution, which barred slavery, his policies did not allow for the involvement of freedmen in the rebuilding of state governments. However, in Congress's eyes, no state had formally won readmission to the Union under Johnson's plan. Leaders across the Union and former Confederacy debated the question of whether Southern states should honor their war debts. In late 1865, neither the Fourteenth Amendment, guaranteeing birthright citizenship regardless of race, nor the Fifteenth Amendment, affirming black male suffrage, had yet been proposed.

At the time of Dickson's speech and the Ohio gubernatorial election, therefore, the status of Reconstructed America was far from settled. Opinions regarding African American rights were especially diverse, even within political parties. Supporters of the Radical Republican wing in the US Congress wished to ensure that freedmen enjoyed true political, social, and economic equality, even as more conservative politicians, including both candidates for Ohio's governorship, opposed the extension of voting rights to African Americans. For, although Northern states had abolished slavery before the Civil War, racism and racial discrimination remained widespread across the region. Dickson's arguments were thus made in an environment of great debate and disagreement over what kind of nation the United States was—and what kind of nation it would be in future.

Author Biography

William M. Dickson was a prominent Republican lawyer and judge from the border city of Cincinnati, Ohio. His wife was a cousin of Mary Todd Lincoln, and Dickson corresponded with Lincoln both about personal matters and about the political climate in Ohio during the 1860 presidential campaign. As the Civil War raged in the fall of 1862, Union Army leaders asked Dickson to organize the hundreds of African American conscripts who had been set to constructing fortifications to protect the city from a feared Confederate attack, despite a ban on African American enlistment in the military. Before Dickson took command, local officials ordered the arrest of the lawbreakers, and white police

treated the black conscripts harshly. Dickson, however, reversed the policy by forming two volunteer regiments and, in a then-unheard-of, but highly successful move, allowed this Black Brigade of Cincinnati to be run by African American officers. His leadership enhanced his reputation, and Dickson remained a local activist for racial equality after the war's end.

When the Civil War officially ended in April 1865, the nation's attention turned toward the vexing questions of how to reunify the sundered nation and "reconstruct" the states of the former Confederacy. While this address on Reconstruction was delivered by William M. Dickson (a lawyer, judge, and informal advisor to President Lincoln) at Oberlin College in December 1865, it is included here as an example of the national debate about the central questions of the early Reconstruction period: how to readmit the former Confederate states to the Union and whether to extend suffrage to the emancipated slaves. Barnum also spoke publicly in support of "Negro suffrage" in May 1865. While Dickson turned out to have been overly optimistic in some of his predictions, these excerpts from his speech reflect a moment in US history when the answers to profound questions about government and citizenship were not entirely clear.

HISTORICAL DOCUMENT

Fellow Citizens:—The long war with its destruction of precious life, its fearful waste, its harrowing anxieties, is now happily over. It has not been a failure. The object for which it was waged, has been completely attained. The rebellion is suppressed, and the territorial integrity of the Union is secure. The Constitution and laws made in pursuance thereof, are every where supreme. All this, too, has been accomplished without any degrading or embarrassing compromise. The original purpose, in this respect, of loyal men has been carried out to the letter. The rebellion has gained nothing by its violation of law, nothing by its appeal from the decision of the ballot-box to the trial by battle. Its results hold out no premium for a future one; and it is a precedent not likely soon to be followed. . . . let us rejoice that the war has not indeed been a failure, that the rebellion is suppressed, and that the national authority is every where re-established.

But, my friends, our work is only half done; reconstruction remains.

Force produces physical unity; this is not the basis of our institutions. We may not, with safety to ourselves, maintain permanently military control of rebel States. Pro-consular Governments are often alien to our system. Yet the rebels have invoked the war power; it is not for them to say when or how we shall lay it aside. We may not do this until the public safety permits. War powers are the defensive armor of a free people, to be put on in times of danger, but to be laid aside as soon as the danger is past. All patriots must desire that the eleven seceding States, shall, as speedily as the public safety will permit, become in fact as well as in form, members of our common body politic, equal in right with the other members and clothed with the powers of self-government. How this shall be done is the problem of our politics, that now presses for solution.

...The fact is, and we might as well look it squarely in the face, with a few unimportant exceptions, the Southern whites yield sullenly and reluctantly to the decision of the sword. They are conquered, not converted.

Do not mistake me; I ask them of no unmanly self-abasement. I would not have them otherwise than proud of the prowess they have exhibited in the contest. But before I would give them a voice in the affairs of the nation, a vote to control your and my concerns, I would have a guaranty that this voice and this vote would be directed to the common good, that these would not be merely new and more dangerous weapons in their hands, to carry on the war against the Union.

Is it wrong that I should require this guaranty? It is contrary to the laws of human conduct, that these mortified and embittered and unconverted men should use their voices in the national councils, rather in the direction of their desires and special interests than in behalf of the common good? For example, many of these men are largely interested in the rebel debt. Can it be expected that they will vote for the repudiation of this debt and the payment of the National debt, incurred in their coercion? Nay, would not their fifty-eight votes in the House of Representatives, almost one-fourth of the whole number, and their twenty-two in the Senate, nearly one-third of the whole number, be a constant quantity for repudiation.... Our free institutions cannot permanently survive so gross a breach of faith, as the repudiation of our war debt. I would not give these eleven States a vote in the National councils, unless I had a guaranty that this vote would not be for this breach of faith.

These rebel men have been accustomed all the days of their lives to eat their bread by the sweat of another's face; to make this condition of things perpetual, they have imbrued their hands in a brother's blood. They have failed; henceforth they must share the common doom of the sons of Adam. They must work. The slave is free; and the immortal proclamation pledges the public faith, by the most sacred of obligations, to the maintenance of his freedom. Now may we rationally expect these men to labor faithfully, to make this pledge good? Yet the Republic can not permanently survive the breach of this plighted faith. I would not give them power in this matter, until I had a guaranty that this power would not be

used for this breach of faith. But what then? Will you forever exclude these States? If not, what guaranties do you want? Upon what conditions would you admit them? Fortunately these questions can be satisfactorily answered.

At the commencement of this war, it was a common declaration of those who were in sympathy with the rebels, that the rebellion could not be put down; that history did not furnish an example of eight or ten millions of people determined on independence being conquered. These opinions were generally held by the rulers of Europe. But there was one important element left out of the calculation, namely, nearly one half of the population of the rebel States, were the determined enemies of the rebellion, and this half constituted the laboring class. This half neutralized, in the long run, the other half.

While I am not one of those who place the bravery of the negro soldiers above that of the white, it is a fact which will hardly denied, that but for the opposition of the entire negro population to the rebel cause, We could scarcely have succeeded; surely, had this force been added to the rebel side, we could not. Mr. Lincoln's proclamation of emancipation, derided at the times as a Pope's Bull against the comet, was death blow of the rebellion.

This loyal half still remains; they, who never in a single instance failed the Union cause, are now as loyal and faithful as ever. We have seen that this half of the southern population neutralized the other half in the war. I would have it continue this good work. I would so reconstruct the Southern States, that while I gave to the disloyal half their full equality before the law, I would paralyze their disloyal purposes by giving a like equality to the loyal half. What wrong is there is this? I give to the men who, for four years have been to destroy the nation full rights--the same which you and I have. The only condition imposed, is, that their loyal follow citizens shall have the problem of reconstructions is full harmony with the representative principle and all our institutions. It will in a brief time remove pro-consular governments, and restore the normal condition of all the States. The country can then rest satisfied that a full guaranty against any efforts of the rebels to do injury, under a restored government. This solution introduces no new element, no new principle into our government. It is but the complete application of the principles of our fathers, set forth in the declaration of independence.

The exception which they reluctantly permitted against the negro is removed. It gives representation to those whom we subject to drafts and taxes. It rests upon the golden rule of right. It is but doing unto others what we would that they should do unto us.

Why shall it not be adopted? And here the false theory of State rights is again thrust forward, by certain parties, in the precise same sense, and for the same purpose with which it was introduced at the beginning of the war, to support the proposition that the government had no right to defend against rebellion. Then the Government had no power to resist those who sought its life! Now these being captured, it has no power to require them to give bonds to keep the peace! Here again the true relation of things is perverted. Grant indeed, not Lee, has surrendered; the Union forces, not the rebels, have been disarmed.

…The rebels well knew, when they appealed to the tribunal of the sword, what the judgment must be, if the decision should be adverse to them. By the universal laws of war, the conquering power may impose such conditions of settlement, looking to its own safety and welfare, as it pleases; only these must not be in violation of the laws of humanity. This principle clearly gives the Government power to adopt the plan of reconstruction proposed. Surely it is not variance with the laws of humanity. This power also, maybe deprived from the present condition of the rebel States, and the peculiar structure of our Government….

…What other objection is there to the plan of reconstruction under consideration?

It is said there is a deeply rooted antagonism between the black and white races, forbidding their remaining together in the same country. If this is a fact, it is a very sad one; but it would not furnish an objection, specially against the plan of reconstruction under consideration. It would seem to apply equally to all plans. It is rather the statement of an insurmountable difficulty, than the solution of one. It is as if one were to complain of the light of the sun, or of the alternation of the seasons. For this is not a question of introducing four millions of negroes here; they are here now, and all plans that have ever been suggested for effecting their separation are purely chime-

rical. They cannot be separated, and yet, the declaration is, they cannot remain together. The ease would seem to be hopeless. But happily this declaration is not true. The prejudices between these races are not different in character from other prejudices. There are prejudices between Irishmen and Englishmen; between Catholics and Protestants: between Christians and Jews. These have often been very violent and wars have grown out of them. Not, however, because of their differences but because one race sought to subordinate to itself another, or one sect sought to impose its tenets upon another. Peace prevailed when each race and each sect attended to its own business. When our fathers framed our Constitution, they understood these principles and applied them. They the different races and sects, by securing to each absolute equality before the law. They, however, expected the negro race, it being then in slavery, and they seeing no way of securing its freedom, permitted this violation of their principles to remain. But now we have the opportunity of applying these principles to this race and of thus removing the last exception. I would make the application. Prejudice yields to power and interest. The votes of the black men will be too valuable to be slighted.

It is said, however, that the blacks could only vote at the point of the bayonet, that the Southern whites would not otherwise permit them. Then the rebellion is not subdued; we have a truce, not lasting peace. If this is the case, the sooner we know it the better; at least it were better to know it before we disband our armies. But I do not believe this; doubtless the masters are averse to the negroes voting; not any more however, than they were to their freedom. They profess to acquiesce in the latter, they will also in the former. The rebels are not now in a condition to fight the United States and the freedmen at the polls. And in a short time the soldiers of the Government can be safely removed. Every day the negro will acquire knowledge and power, all of which will be respected at the polls. This thing of fighting is an easy matter to the armed dominant party over his unarmed subordinate. But between equals, it is a very different affair. Men count the cost. The capacity to do this is attained at a very early age. My son, said a father the other day in my hearing to his little boy in his first breeches, "why didn't you strike Sam?" "Well, father," replied the urchin, "wouldn't he have hit me back?" In those rebel States in which the negroes are the more numerous, the whites will be slow to provoke a contest. They will, everywhere, rather endeavor in a different way to control the negro votes; they will seek them by kindness. Such is human nature. I expect to see the day when a Southern Democrat, will be seen "carrying" arm in arm to the polls, two negro voters. For the white race has no monopoly of worthless men. They belong to all races.

Again, it is objected, that the Southern negro is ignorant and unfit to vote. He seems to have been intelligent enough to be loyal, which was more than his master was. But I do not deny the ignorance; their condition of slavery forbids that it could be otherwise. Yet they share this ignorance in common with the poor whites; and I would be willing to apply to both these classes an educational test. Still I would not recommend this. Freedom is the school in which freemen are to be taught, and the ballot-box is a wonderful educator.

We cannot too constantly keep in our minds, that this is not a question as to the policy of introducing into our country four millions of ignorant negroes. They are here, are to remain with us in the indefinite future. We cannot escape if we desired, their influence upon our civilization. Were it possible for them to remain with us, and yet be so excluded from us, that they could have no influence upon the common welfare, then we might selfishly put them into such imaginary condition, and relieve ourselves of all further trouble concerning them. But we cannot do this. Their force must enter as one of the constituent elements in the formation of our American civilization.... As the force of the negro must enter into the formation of our civilization, it is to the interest of the white man not less than of the black man, that this force should be for good. It cannot be, however, unless the negro is moral, intelligent and industrious. How can we give him these desirable characteristics? We have only to consider the conditions under which white men have become moral, intelligent, and industrious, and apply these to the black man.

Our proposition thus becomes very simple; we must educate him and place before him the rewards of good conduct and the penalties of bad conduct. We must give him entire equality before the law and all these things will follow. Let not the law be a respecter of persons. The humbler the man the greater the necessity that the law should not oppress him. The rich and great can take care of themselves. With all the opportunities of equal laws, the poor man's lot is hard enough. He requires the protection of the law and the self respect which an equality of right before the law engenders. In a country where equality is the rule, we cannot have an exception founded on caste. The ballot is here the evidence of manhood; when we deny it to a race we at once degrade that race in the respect of others, and what is of greater consequence, in its own respect. Every man, the humbler he is the more, requires the right of suffrage for his protection. And the negro, as the most unprotected of all, needs it most of all. We must educate him, and give him the condition of self-respect, if we would have his influence for good upon our civilization.

But while we thus see the necessity of giving to the negro equality before the law, even upon the assumption that his presence is a necessary evil, let us not forget that this is indeed far from the truth. We need his labor in the South and we need the protection of his ballot against the ballot of his former traitorous master.

And further, if we educate him and place him in a position in which he will respect himself, we may expect the most gratifying results to the common good. In an economic view this is a matter of the greatest moment. The increased production of an intelligent, self-respecting and industrious population can hardly be estimated. In the South thrift will take the place of waste; voluntary labor directed by an enlightened self-interest will take the place of compulsory labor directed by the lash; provident abstinence will save for a reserved fund, that which has heretofore been lost in careless expenditure. Fixed capital will thus arise; towns will spring up; the industrial arts will be cultivated; and prosperity and wealth will abound where want and poverty have prevailed. That rich southern soil with its generous climate, is a mine of untold wealth. It needs but the hand of free industry to bring it forth. All this would greatly contribute to lightening the load of our debt. These grateful people would gladly aid in the payment of the ransom for their redemption.

My friends, every consideration which ought to influence human conduct, requires that the ballot should be given to the black man.

The protection of the black man himself requires it; gratitude for his devoted loyalty requires it; the protection of our civilization from the influence of a degraded and barbarous element requires it; the protection of ourselves from the insidious rebel ballot requires it; the speedy restoration of the rebel states to their proper relation to the General Government requires it; the fundamental principles of our Government require it; the Golden Rule of our most holy religion commanding us to do unto others as we would that they should do unto us, requires it. Can we withhold it?

My friends, when I leave here should you think of what I have said, remember that I have not proposed to take anything from any man,—no, not even from the rebels. I indeed propose to them, their full restoration to all the rights of citizenship, as fully as we possess them our selves. I seek nothing which need be offensive to them; nothing which is unknown to their own history. In their better days, before slavery became their absorbing thought, free black men voted in many if not all the Southern States. While we are in the way of restoring the forfeited rights of the rebels, let us give to the loyal black man, now free, his ancient right to vote—a gift that costs no one anything, but the withholding of which from him makes him poor indeed. Nay, it is for the interest of

the South far more than of the North that this should be done. There is no safety between absolute slavery and absolute freedom. If this plan of reconstruction is adopted a great and happy and prosperous future is open to the South. But if the contrary course is taken; if the negro is to continue a poor and despised being, with no rights which a white man is bound to respect; if he is to be the subject of insult and outrage, with no other protection than the strength of his arm, —then indeed the future of the South is very dark. The negro will soon know too much, know his strength too well, to submit.

Our fathers, yielding to the embarrassments of the day permitted negro slavery to remain, with the expectation, it is true, that it would soon pass away. Alas, what a fearful mistake! This action has been the cause of all our woe. Shall we repeat this mistake? Shall we learn no lesson from this sad experience? God grant that it may be otherwise. Let us catch the inspiration of our Martyr President at the field of Gettysburgh; let us join in his prayer "That this nation, under God, shall have a new birth of freedom, and that Government of the people, by the people, and for the people, shall not perish from the earth."

GLOSSARY

caste: a social system based on graded status groups; a rigid social hierarchy

Golden Rule: the biblical idea that one should treat others as one wishes to be treated in turn

plighted: promised, sworn, or pledged

Pope's Bull: papal bull, a formal proclamation by a pope

Pro-consular Government: government by persons who exercise authority without necessarily holding office; used broadly to refer to outside interference

Document Analysis

Coming at a time of national uncertainty about the shape of the United States to come, Dickson's speech essentially rejects the more modest reforms supported by President Johnson, Democrats, and conservative Republicans in favor of the sweeping reorganization of American society called for by the Radical Republicans. At the same time, it calls on Ohio's voters to reject the Democratic candidate for governor and the weight

of wartime policies that he carried as that party's representative. Dickson is clear that the choice was vital to creating a unified nation that could endure the test of time; despite the Civil War's end, he argues, "our work is only half done; reconstruction remains."

Dickson dedicates much of his speech to decrying the Democratic Party's history of Southern sympathies and arguing that the election of a Democratic candidate would threaten the achievements made during the war. In rejecting Copperhead candidate Clement Valladingham in 1863, Dickson tells his listeners, Ohio voters had helped assure that the division of the country would not endure. Again lending their electoral support to the Unionist candidate would, therefore, propel the nation toward a lasting reunification that guaranteed the end of Confederate influence and the beginning of a society based on racial equality.

Equally, Dickson argues that Reconstruction must require the former Confederacy to accept the new order. A sign of this acceptance would be the expansion of civil rights to the freedmen, who comprised half of the South's overall population and without whose consistent support, Dickson believes, the Union could not have prevailed. Johnson's program, Dickson maintains, is good enough, but certainly could have been better. Just as the Constitution provides for the equality of members of differing religious or national groups, it could and should assure racial equality across the nation. Its very successes, Dickson argues, showed the flaws in contemporary arguments for racial segregation.

Key to this goal was the expansion of suffrage to freedmen. Former Confederates had already swallowed the abolition of slavery and could certainly stand another bitter pill in the form of black suffrage. Although Dickson acknowledges the arguments against this proposal, especially the freedmen's lack of education, he argues that this state should not use this as an excuse to deny the vote. "Freedom is the school in which freemen are to be taught, and the ballot-box is a wonderful educator," he declares. Expanding liberties, Dickson claims, costs those who already have them nothing and give those lacking them a great and necessary benefit, which would in turn contribute to the political, economic, and moral betterment of the society at large.

Essential Themes

By calling for "absolute equality," Dickson proposes a bold move away from centuries of institutionalized discrimination in favor of expanded universal liberty. These arguments did not find immediate favor with all Americans. The candidate whom his speech supported, Union gubernatorial nominee Jacob D. Cox, had far different viewpoints, including opposition to African American suffrage and support for the creation of a large, segregated region of the South, to which all freedmen could settle and exclusively control political and economic affairs. Although nearly all political leaders of the day agreed that Cox's plan was impractical,

his inferred support for white supremacy and racial segregation reflected the opinions of a majority of Ohioans, let alone former Confederates. Whereas Dickson believed the vote would help ensure African American freedom, Cox believed that it would exacerbate racial tensions and ultimately lead to conflicts that would be incredibly damaging to African Americans. In this sense, Dickson's pro-equality statements represented a minority viewpoint.

Yet other holders of that minority viewpoint managed to gain control of the federal government for a time. In reaction to restrictive laws passed in some former Confederate states, Radical Republicans established military governments that, in conjunction with the Freedmen's Bureau, ratified amendments and created policies supporting racial equality across the South. The Freedmen's Bureau educated former slaves, registered them to vote, and oversaw measures to allow them to transition toward economic independence. With African American voters at the polls, South Carolina elected a majority black state legislature, and both Mississippi and South Carolina sent black representatives to the US Congress.

Dickson's arguments against the Democratic Party reflect a more widely held political viewpoint. Republicans of all stripes and Unionists alike agreed that the restoration of Democratic leaders to state governments carried the threat of undoing the difficult work of the war. This prediction proved, to a degree, a prescient one. With the end of Reconstruction in 1877, Southern white leaders embarked on political campaigns to effectively bar African American suffrage and restore Democratic state governments. These governments passed laws that restricted black civil rights, established legal segregation, and forced many Southern African Americans into a condition little better than enslavement.

—*Vanessa E. Vaughn, MA*

Bibliography and Additional Reading

Brown, William Wells. *The Negro in the American Rebellion: His Heroism and His Fidelity*. Boston: Lee, 1867. Print.

Foner, Eric. *Forever Free: The Story of Emancipation and Reconstruction*. New York: Knopf, 2005. Print.

Foner, Eric. *Reconstruction: America's Unfinished Revolution, 1863–1877*. New York: HarperCollins, 2011. Print.

Sawrey, Robert D. *Dubious Victory: The Reconstruction Debate in Ohio*. Lexington: UP of Kentucky, 1992. Print.

Prospects of the Freedmen of Hilton Head

Date: Late 1865
Author: Martin R. Delany
Genre: series of articles

Summary Overview

Celebrated by many as the father of black nationalism, Martin Robison Delany is among the leading black thinkers and leaders of the nineteenth century. Like his colleague Frederick Douglass, Delany achieved great things as he led the fight against slavery and created new opportunities for freedmen, including serving as the first black major in the Union army, writing scores of influential articles and books, gaining acceptance to Harvard Medical School, participating in conventions, meeting President Lincoln, and traveling to Africa. Yet Delany's celebration of black identity and his support of freedmen's emigration to Africa distinguish him clearly from leaders such as Douglass. At times, Delany dedicated his efforts to integration in the United States, but his personal experiences and frustrations with the persistence of racism led him, at other times, to call for separatism. Criticized by leaders during his time, Delany's prophetic vision as expressed in articles such as "Prospects of the Freedmen of Hilton Head" nonetheless planted the seeds for the Black Power movement that emerged in the second half of the twentieth century.

Defining Moment

The year 1865 marked the end of the U.S. Civil War and promised great hope but also great uncertainty. General Robert E. Lee's capitulation to Union commander Ulysses S. Grant on April 9, 1865, was the first major surrender and clearly signaled the war's impending conclusion. The war's end, however, did not immediately resolve the issue of slavery, in part because Lincoln's Emancipation Proclamation of 1863 had declared freedom only for slaves in the Confederacy. This exempted the slave-holding border states of Delaware, Kentucky, Maryland, and Missouri and the Union-controlled state of Tennessee as well as some other areas controlled by federal troops in parts of Louisiana and Virginia. It was only in December, 1865 that Congress formally abolished slavery by passing the Thirteenth Amendment to the Constitution. These events ushered in the period known as Reconstruction, which in part aimed to define the legal status and rights of freed slaves and to manage the former Confederate states' transition to self-government and the status of their leaders. During Reconstruction, Congress passed numerous acts and constitutional amendments addressing these issues and created the Bureau of Refugees, Freedmen, and Abandoned Lands (the Freedmen's Bureau) to establish the necessary institutions and resources for these transitions.

Martin Delany was the first black major in the Union army and later worked as an officer for the Freedmen's Bureau, but he knew that establishing political and economic opportunity for freed slaves required not only new laws and agencies but also a profound shift in culture. Southern planters would have to respect freed slaves as equal citizens with the right to contract fair labor, and building this respect would entail uprooting society's deep-seated ideology of white supremacy. Confronting the difficulty of changing this poisonous belief system, Delany wrote the seven articles of "Prospects of the Freedmen of Hilton Head" while he was working for the Freedmen's Bureau in Hilton Head, South Carolina in late 1865, just before the passage of the Thirteenth Amendment. Addressing both the cultural and practical challenges that lay ahead, the articles brilliantly reflect the high hopes and deep uncertainty of this moment in U.S. history in which legal and institutional ground shifted fundamentally in the context of profound cultural aspirations and resistance.

Author Biography

In his long and restless life of 73 years, Martin Robison Delany worked tirelessly for the cause of freedom and achieved countless distinctions. Born in 1812 in Charles Town, Virginia, to a free mother and an enslaved father, Delany moved to Pennsylvania in the 1820s with his mother when she fled authorities who tried to imprison her for educating her children. Delany studied with abolitionist leaders in Pittsburgh during the 1830s and began his distinguished career. Over the next two decades, he established his own medical practice, attended conventions, and became a prolific writer. His achievements during this time include editorial work with Frederick Douglass on the *North Star*, a highly influential African American newspaper, and his brief attendance at Harvard Medical School, which was cruelly cut short after white students protested his and other black students' presence.

Partly in response to his rejection at Harvard and to the Compromise of 1850, which strengthened the Fugitive Slave Act, Delany then wrote The Condition, Elevation, Emigration and Destiny of the Colored People of the United States, which promoted black emigration to Central and South America. In subsequent years, Delany backed up his words by organizing a convention for emigration, and he himself moved to Canada in 1856, where he consulted with abolitionist John Brown on a possible slave insurrection. In the late 1850s, he began to promote black emigration to Africa and even visited the Niger Valley, signed a treaty to establish a settlement in West Africa, and went on a speaking tour in England to raise funds for the effort. In 1859-1861, Delany published a novel and an account of his experiences in Africa, but he abandoned the emigration project after the king with whom he had signed the treaty reneged.

During the Civil War, Delany redirected his attention to the United States. He recruited black troops for the Union forces, became the army's first black major, and gained notoriety for meeting President Lincoln. He subsequently worked with the Freedmen's Bureau in South Carolina during Reconstruction, continued to write, and even ran for lieutenant governor of the state. Yet, as the failures of Reconstruction became increasingly clear in the 1870s, a disillusioned Delany once again began to promote emigration to Africa, and his late writings underscore a "Pan-African pride in blacks' historical, cultural, and racial ties to Africa" (Levine 2). This emphasis chiefly contributes to his place in history as the father of Black nationalism.

HISTORICAL DOCUMENT

I.

PROSPECTS OF THE FREEDMEN OF HILTON HEAD.

Every true friend of the Union, residing on the island, must feel an interest in the above subject, regardless of any other consideration than that of national polity. Have the blacks become self-sustaining? and will they ever, in a state of freedom, resupply the products which comprised the staples formerly of the old planters? These are questions of importance, and not unworthy of the consideration of grave political economists.

That the blacks of the island have not been self-sustaining will not be pretended, neither can it be denied that they have been generally industrious and inclined to work. But industry alone is not sufficient, nor work available, except these command adequate compensation.

Have the blacks innately the elements of industry and enterprise? Compare them with any other people, and note their adaptation. Do they not make good "day laborers"? Are they not good field hands? Do they not make good domestics? Are they not good house servants? Do they not readily "turn their hands" to anything or kind of work they may find to do? Trained, they make good body servants, house servants, or laundresses, waiters, chamber and dining-room servants, cooks, nurses, drivers, horse "tenders," and, indeed, fill as well, and better, many of the domestic occupations than any other race. And with unrestricted facilities for learning, will it be denied that they are as susceptible of the mechanical occupations or trades as they are of the domestic? Will it be denied that a people easily domesticated are susceptible of the higher attainments? The slaveholder, long since, cautioned against "giving a nigger an inch, lest he should take an ell."

If permitted, I will continue this subject in a series of equally short articles, so as not to intrude on your columns.

II.

This subject must now be examined in the light of political economy, and, for reasons stated in a previous article, treated tersely in every sentence, and, therefore, will not be condemned by the absence of elaboration and extensive proof.

America was discovered in 1492 — then peopled only by the original inhabitants, or Indians, as afterwards called. No part of the country was found in a state of cultivation, and no industrial enterprise was carried on, either foreign or domestic. Not even in the West Indies — prolific with spices, gums, dye-woods, and fruits — was there any trade carried on among or by the natives. These people were put to labor by the foreigners; but, owing to their former habits of hunting, fishing, and want of physical exercise, they sank beneath the weight of toil, fast dying off, till their mortality, in time, from this cause alone, reached the frightful figure of two and a half millions. (See Ramsay's History.)

The whites were put to labor, and their fate was no better — which requires no figures, as all are familiar with the history and career of Thomas Gates and associates at one time; John Smith and associates, as colonists in the South, at another; how, not farther than Virginia, — at most, North Carolina, — they "died like sheep," to the destruction of the settlements, in attempting to do the work required to improve for civilized life. Neither whites, as foreigners, nor Indians, as natives, were adequate to the task of performing the labor necessary to their advent in the New World.

So early as 1502 — but ten years after Columbus landed — "the Spaniards commenced bringing a few negroes from Africa to work the soil." (See Ramsay's History.) In 1515, but thirteen years afterwards, and twenty-three from the discovery of America, Carolus V., King of Spain, granted letters patent to import annually into the colonies of Cuba, Ispaniola (Hayti), Jamaica, and Porto Rico, four thousand Africans as slaves — people contracted with to "emigrate" to these new colonies, as the French, under Louis Napoleon, attempted, in 1858, to decoy native Africans, under the pretext of emigrating to the colonies, into French slavery, then reject international interference, on the ground that they obtained them by "voluntary emigration."

Such was the success of this new industrial element, that not only did Spaniards and Portuguese employ them in all their American colonies, but so great was the demand for these laborers, that Elizabeth, the Virgin Queen of England, became a partner in the slave trade with the infamous Captain Hawkins; and, in 1618, her successor to the throne, and royal relative, James I., King of England, negotiated for and obtained the entire carrying trade, thus securing, by international patent, the exclusive right for British vessels alone to "traffic in blood and souls of men," to reap the profits arising from their importation.

Was it the policy of political economists, such as were then the rulers and statesmen of Europe, to employ a people in preference to all others for the development of wealth, if such people were not adapted to the labor designed for them? Would the civilized and highly polished, such as were then the Spanish, French, and Portuguese nations, together with the English, still have continued the use of these people as laborers and domestics in every social relation among them, if they had not found them a most desirable domestic element? Would, after the lapse of one hundred and sixteen years' rigid trial and experience from their first importation, the King of England have been able — whatever his avarice as an individual — to have effected so great a diplomatic treaty, as the consent from all the civilized nations having interests here to people their colonies with a race if that race had been worthless as laborers, and deficient as an industrial element? Would, in the year of the grace of Jesus Christ, and the light of the highest civilization, after the lapse of two hundred and twenty years from James's treaty, the most powerful and enlightened monarchy have come near the crisis of its political career in its determination to continue the system, and for two hundred and forty-seven years the most powerful and enlightened republic that ever the world saw have distracted the harmony of the nations of the earth, and driven itself to the verge of destruction by the mad determination of one half of the people and leading states, to perpetuate the service of this race as essential to the development of the agricultural wealth of the land? After these centuries of trial and experience, would these people have been continually sought after, had they not proven to be superior to all others as laborers in the kind of work assigned them? Let political economists answer.

V.

As shown in my last article, these people are the lineal descendants of an industrious, hardy race of men — those whom the most powerful and accomplished statesmen and political economists of the great states of Europe, after years of trial and rigid experience, decided upon and selected as the element best adapted to develop in a strange and foreign clime — a new world of unbroken soil and dense, impenetrable forests — the industry and labor necessary to the new life. This cannot and will not be attempted to be denied without ignoring all historical authority, though presented in a different light — and may I not say motive? — from that in which history has ever given It.

These people are of those to retain whom in her power the great British nation was agitated to the point, at as late a period as 1837-8, of shattering the basis of its political foundation; and, within the last four years, the genius of the American government was spurned, assaulted, and trampled upon, and had come well nigh its final dissolution by full one half of the states, people, and statesmen inaugurating a civil war, the most stupendous on record, for no other purpose than retaining them as laborers. Does any intelligent person doubt the utility of such a people? Can such a people now be worthless in the country? Does any enlightened, reflecting person believe it? I think not.

But this is an experiment. Have we no precedent, no example? What of the British colonies of the West Indies and South America? Let impartial history and dispassionate, intelligent investigation answer. The land in the colonies was owned by wealthy capitalists and gentlemen who resided in Europe. The "proprietors," or planters, were occupants of the land, who owned the slaves that worked it, having borrowed the capital with which to purchase them at the Cuba markets or barracoons and supply the plantations. In security for this, mortgages were held by those in Europe on "all estate, real and personal," belonging to the planters, who paid a liberal interest on the loans.

When the opposition in the British Parliament, led by Tories, who were the representatives of the capitalists, yielded to the Emancipation Bill, it was only on condition of an appropriation of twenty millions of pounds sterling, or one hundred millions of dollars, as remuneration to the planters for their slaves set free. This proposition was so moderate as to surprise and astonish the intelligent in state affairs on both sides of the ocean, as the sum proposed only amounted to the penurious price of about one hundred and twenty dollars apiece, when men and women were then bringing at the barracoons in Cuba from five to six hundred dollars apiece in cash; and the average of men, women, and children, according to their estimate of black mankind, were "worth" four hundred and fifty dollars. Of course the tutored colonial laborer would be worth still more.

After the passage of the Act of Emancipation by the Imperial Parliament, the complaint was wafted back by the breeze of every passing wind, that the planters in the colonies were impoverished by emancipation, and dishonest politicians and defeated, morose statesmen seized the opportunity to display their duplicity. "What will become of the fair colonial possessions? The lands will go back into a wilderness waste. The negroes are idle, lazy, and will not work. They are unfit for freedom, and ought to have masters. Where they do work, not half the crop is produced on the same quantity of land. What will the whites do if they don't get servants to work for them? They and their posterity must starve. The lands are lying waste for the want of occupants, and the negroes are idling their time away, and will not have them when offered to them. The social system in the West Indies has been ruined by the emancipation of the negroes." These, and a thousand such complaints, tingled upon the sensitive ear in every word that came from the British colonies, as the key-note of the pro-slavery British party, till caught up and reechoed from the swift current of the southern extremity of Brazil to the banks of the Potomac, the northern extremity of the slave territory of the United States. But alive to passing events, and true to their great trust, the philanthropists and people soon discovered, through their eminent representatives and statesmen in Parliament, that the whites in the colonies had never owned the lands nor the blacks which they lost by the Act of Emancipation. And when the appropriation was made by Parliament, the money remained in the vaults of the banks in Europe, being precisely the amount required to liquidate the claims of the capitalists, and to satisfy the mortgages held by those gentlemen against "all estates" of the borrowers in the colonies, both "real and personal."

The cause of the cry and clamor must be seen at a glance. The money supposed to be intended for the colonists, small as it was, instead of being appropriated to them, simply went to satisfy the claims of the capitalists who resided in Great Britain, not one out of a hundred of whom had ever seen the colonies. And the lands being owned in Europe, and the laborers free, what was to save the white colonists from poverty? All this was well known to leading pro-slavery politicians and statesmen in Europe as well as America; but a determination to perpetuate the bondage of a people as laborers — a people so valuable as to cause them, rather than loose their grasp upon them, to boldly hazard their national integrity, and set at defiance the morality of the civilized world in holding them — caused this reprehensible imposition and moral outrage in misleading to distraction their common constituency

VI.

Mr. Editor: This is my sixth article on the subject of the "Prospects of the Freedmen of Hilton Head" Island, which you have so generously admitted into the columns of The New South, and for which liberality towards a recently liberated people, I most heartily thank you. The time may come when they, for themselves, may be able to thank you. I hope to conclude with my next.

After what has been adduced in proof of their susceptibility, adaptation, and propensity for the vocations of the domestic and social relations of our civilization, what are their *prospects?* for that now must be the leading question, and give more concern to the philanthropist,

true statesman, and Christian, than anything relating to their fitness or innate adaptation, since that I hold to be admitted, and no longer a question — at least with the intelligent inquirer.

What should be the prospects? Will not the same labor that was performed by a slave be in requisition still? Cannot he do the same work as a freedman that he once did as a slave? Are the products of slave labor preferable to free? or are the products of free labor less valuable than slave? Will not rice and cotton be in as great demand after emancipation as before it? or will these commodities cease to be used, because they cease to be produced by the labor of slaves? All these are questions pertinent, if not potent, to the important inquiry under consideration — the prospects of the freedmen of Hilton Head.

Certainly these things will be required, in demand, and labor quite as plentiful; but not one half of the negroes can be induced to work, as was proven in the West Indies, and is apparent from the comparative number who now seek their old vocations to those who formerly did the same work.

Grant this, — which is true, — and is it an objectionable feature, or does it impair the prospects of the freedman? By no means; but, on the contrary, it enhances his prospects and elevates his manhood. Here, as in the case of West India emancipation before emancipation took place every available person — male and female — from seven years of age to decrepit old age (as field hands) was put into the field to labor.

For example, take one case to illustrate the whole. Before liberated, Juba had a wife and eight children, from seven to thirty years of age, everyone of whom was at labor in the field as a slave. When set free, the mother and all of the younger children (consisting of five) quit the field, leaving the father and three older sons, from twenty-five to thirty years of age, who preferred field labor; the five children being sent to school. The mother, now the pride of the recently-elevated freedman, stays in her own house, to take charge, as a housewife, in her new domestic relations — thus permanently withdrawing from the field six tenths of the service of this family; while the husband and three sons (but four tenths) are all who remain to do the work formerly performed by ten tenths, or the whole. Here are more than one half who will not work in the field. Will any one say they should?

And this one example may suffice for the most querulous on this subject. Human nature is all the same under like circumstances. The immutable, unalterable laws which governed or controlled the instincts or impulses of a Hannibal, Alexander, or Napoleon, are the same implanted in the brain and breast of page or footman, be he black or white, circumstances alone making the difference in development according to the individual propensity.

As slaves, people have no choice of pursuit or vocation, but must follow that which is chosen by the master. Slaves, like freemen, have different tastes and desires — many doing that which is repugnant to their choice. As slaves, they were compelled to subserve the interests of the master regardless of themselves; as freemen, as should be expected and be understood, many changes would take place in the labor and pursuits of the people. Some who were field hands, among the young men and women of mature age, seek employment at other pursuits, and choose for themselves various trades — vocations adapted to their tastes.

Will this be charged to the worthlessness of the negro, and made an argument against his elevation? Truth stands defiant in the pathway of error.

VII.

I propose to conclude the subject of "THE PROSPECTS OF THE FREEDMEN OF HILTON HEAD" with this article, and believe that the prospects of the one are the prospects of the whole population of freedmen throughout the South.

Political economy must stand most prominent as the leading feature of this great question of the elevation of the negro — and it is a great question — in this country, because, however humane and philanthropic, however Christian and philanthropic we may be, except we can be made to see that there is a prospective enhancement of the general wealth of the country, — a pecuniary benefit to accrue by it to society, — the best of us, whatever our pretensions, could scarcely be willing to see him elevated in the United States.

Equality of political rights being the genius of the American government, I shall not spend time with this,

as great principles will take care of' themselves, and must eventually prevail.

Will the negroes be able to obtain land by which to earn a livelihood? Why should they not? It is a well-known fact to the statisticians of the South that two thirds of the lands have never been cultivated. These lands being mainly owned by but three hundred and twelve thousand persons (according to Helper) — one third of which was worked by four millions of slaves, who are now freemen — what better can be done with these lands to make them available and unburdensome to the proprietors, than let them out in small tracts to the freedmen, as well as to employ a portion of the same people, who prefer it, to cultivate lands for themselves?

It is a fact — probably not so well known as it should be — in political economy, that a given amount of means divided among a greater number of persons, makes a wealthier community than the same amount held or possessed by a few.

For example, there is a community of a small country village of twenty families, the (cash) wealth of the community being fifty thousand dollars, and but one family the possessor of it; certainly the community would not be regarded as in good circumstances, much less having available means. But let this amount be possessed by ten families in sums of five thousand dollars each, would not this enhance the wealth of the community? And again, let the whole twenty families be in possession of two thousand five hundred dollars each of the fifty thousand, would not this be still a wealthier community, by placing each family in easier circumstances, and making these means much more available? Certainly it would, And as to a community or village, so to a state; and as to a state, so to a nation.

This is the solution to the great problem of the difference between the strength of the North and the South in the late rebellion — the North possessing the means within itself without requiring outside help, almost every man being able to aid the national treasury; everybody commanding means, whether earned by a white-wash brush in black hands, or wooden nutmegs in white: all had something to sustain the integrity of the Union. It must be seen by this that the strength of a country — internationally considered — depends greatly upon its wealth; the wealth consisting not in the greatest amount possessed, but the greatest available amount.

Let, then, such lands as belong to the government, by sale from direct taxation, be let or sold to these freedmen, and other poor loyal men of the South, in small tracts of from twenty to forty acres to each head of a family, and large landholders do the same, — the rental and sales of which amply rewarding them, — and there will be no difficulty in the solution of the problem of the future, or prospects of the freedmen, not only of Hilton Head, but of the whole United States.

This increase of the wealth of the country by the greater division of its means is not new to New England, nor to the economists of the North generally. As in Pennsylvania, many years ago, the old farmers commenced dividing their one hundred and one hundred and fifty acre tracts of lands into twenty-five acres each among their sons and daughters, who are known to have realized more available means always among them — though by far greater in numbers — than their parents did, who were comparatively few. And it is now patent as an historic fact, that, leaving behind them the extensive evergreen, fertile plains, and savannas of the South, the rebel armies and raiders continually sought the limited farms of the North to replenish their worn-out cavalry stock and exhausted commissary department — impoverished in cattle for food, and forage for horses.

In the Path Valley of Pennsylvania, on a single march of a radius of thirty-five miles of Chambersburg, Lee's army, besides all the breadstuffs that his three thousand five hundred wagons (as they went empty for the purpose) were able to carry, captured and carried off more than six thousand head of stock, four thousand of which were horses. The wealth of that valley alone, they reported, was more than India fiction, and equal to all of the South put together. And whence this mighty available wealth of Pennsylvania? Simply by its division and possession among the many.

The Rothschilds are said to have once controlled the exchequer of England, compelling (by implication) the premier to comply with their requisition at a time of great peril to the nation, simply because it depended upon them for means; and the same functionaries are reported, during our recent struggle, to have greatly annoyed the Bank of England, by a menace of some kind, which immediately brought the institution to their terms.

Whether true or false, the points are sufficiently acute to serve for illustration.

In the apportionment of small farms to the freedmen, an immense amount of means is placed at their command, and thereby a great market opened, a new source of consumption of every commodity in demand in free civilized communities. The blacks are great consumers, and four millions of a population, before barefooted, would here make a demand for the single article of shoes. The money heretofore spent in Europe by the old slaveholders would be all disbursed by these new people in their own country. Where but one cotton gin and a limited number of farming utensils were formerly required to the plantation of a thousand acres, every small farm will want a gin and farming implements, the actual valuation of which on the same tract of land would be several fold greater than the other. Huts would give place to beautiful, comfortable cottages, with all their appurtenances, fixtures, and furniture; osnaburgs and rags would give place to genteel apparel becoming a free and industrious people; and even the luxuries, as well as the general comforts, of table would take the place of black-eye peas and fresh fish, hominy and salt pork, all of which have been mainly the products of their own labor when slaves. They would quickly prove that arduous and faithfully fawning, miserable volunteer advocate of the rebellion and slaveholder's rule in the United States, — the London Times, — an arrant falsifier, when it gratuitously and unbidden came to the aid of its kith and kin, declaring that the great and good President Lincoln's Emancipation Proclamation would not be accepted by the negroes; 'that all Cuffee wanted and cared for to make him happy was his hog and his hominy;" but they will neither get land, nor will the old slaveholders give them employment. Don't fear any such absurdity. There are too many political economists among the old leading slaveholders to fear the adoption of any such policy. Neither will the leading statesmen of the country, of any part, North or South, favor any such policy.

We have on record but one instance of such a course in the history of modern states. The silly-brained, foolhardy king of France, Louis V., taking umbrage at the political course of the artisans and laborers against him, by royal decree expelled them from the country, when they flocked into England, which readily opened her doors to them, transplanting from France to England their arts and industry; ever since which, England, for fabrics, has become the "workshop of the world," to the poverty of France, the government of which is sustained by borrowed capital.

No fears of our country driving into neighboring countries such immense resources as emanate from the peculiar labor of these people; but when worst comes to worst, they have among them educated freemen of their own color North, fully competent to lead the way, by making

negotiations with foreign states on this continent, which would only be too ready to receive them and theirs.

Place no impediment in the way of the freedman; let his right be equally protected and his chances be equally regarded, and with the facts presented to you in this series of seven articles as the basis, he will stand and thrive, as firmly rooted, not only on the soil of Hilton Head, but in all the South, — though a black, — as any white, or "Live Oak," as ever was grown in South Carolina, or transplanted to Columbia.

GLOSSARY

barracoon: an enclosure or barracks used in the slave trade to confine slaves temporarily while they awaited transport to other locations

Black nationalism: a twentieth-century political and social movement emphasizing national identity on the basis of race, self-determination, and independence from European cultural, political, and economic control

Hannibal: a third-century BCE Carthaginian military leader who successfully invaded the Roman Empire but was ultimately defeated by the Roman leader Scipio Africanus

John Smith: English explorer who was one of the settlers in Jamestown, Virginia, in the early seventeenth century

Napoleon: Late eighteenth- and early nineteenth-century French emperor who ruled during the French Revolution and subjugated much of Europe during the conflicts known as the Napoleonic Wars

osnaburg: a heavy, course cotton fabric used for grain sacks and other utilitarian applications

political economy: a term for the relationship between economic production and its legal, cultural, and political contexts and institutions

Document Analysis

In August of 1865, Delany traveled to Hilton Head, South Carolina after a sudden change of plans. In May of that year, he had been ordered to begin recruiting men to serve in the 105TH regiment of the United States Colored Troops, but the military withdrew the order in June when the war ended. On August 7, 1865, Major Delany was commanded to report to the Freedmen's Bureau in Hilton Head for a three-year period of service. There, Delany served as an assistant commissioner and worked to organize and educate freedmen about their new rights and responsibilities and to help them obtain fair labor contracts. Delany's articles submitted to the newspaper *The New South* (five of the seven remain in print) were part of his strategy to defend the freed-

men and African Americans in general against certain criticisms and to promote his ideas for how to establish new labor structures in the South (Levine 396). The articles, however, reflect deep ambiguity about the nature of African Americans and their chances for progress. With impressive boldness, Delany asserts the notion of universal human nature and yet African American superiority, and his plan for the political and economic success of freed slaves expresses both belief in the possibility of integration and cynicism about whites' motivations. To be sure, Delany's life experiences inform the articles' contradictions, but it would be a mistake to dismiss these tensions as an intellectual flaw or the product of the writer's personal idiosyncrasies. Instead, we can best understand these inconsistencies as a vivid reflection of the deep ambivalence in the legal and cultural history of the nineteenth-century.

In the first article, Delany implies that he is responding to the charge that former slaves are not ready for freedom and have not demonstrated adequate self-sufficiency. He immediately acknowledges that freedmen are not yet self-sustaining but also points out their industriousness and desire to work. Then, he writes, "But industry alone is not sufficient, nor work available, except these command adequate compensation" (Rollin 230). With this, he announces his two primary concerns in the series: the worth of African Americans and the structures needed to organize fair labor. The first two articles address the nature and talents of his race in astonishing terms of "political economy," in which Delany argues that the Africans brought to America were in fact chosen because they were the only group capable of the backbreaking work in the New World. He begins with the date of 1492, describing America as a vast wilderness populated by Native Americans, who had not cultivated the land and thus could not survive the hard labor required when they "were put to labor by the foreigners" (Rollin 231). Here, Delany claims that two-and-a-half million Native Americans died "from this cause alone" (Rollin 231), i.e., inability to survive the working conditions imposed by the colonists. He then claims that white settlers suffered the same fate and cites the colonist John Smith as an example. The solution for the European colonists was to import African slaves, whose unique capabilities convinced Queen Elizabeth to invest in the slave trade. Delany goes on to argue that the African slave trade flourished and eventually provoked a Civil War because the Africans themselves had rare abilities unmatched by either whites or Native Americans. In this way, he transforms slavery from an issue of the weak oppressed by the strong to one of demand for rare talent, which effectively subverts racist notions of African inferiority and establishes the high value of the freedmen's labor. Nonetheless, this celebration of African identity reinforces the notion of racial separateness and partly accounts for Delany's legacy as a Black Nationalist.

In the sixth article, Delany addresses the question of industriousness against a more specific charge, but here he appeals to an egalitarian notion of "human nature." The issue is that many freed people refuse to work in the fields as they had done as slaves, prompting charges of laziness and unsuitability for freedom. Yet Delany describes the change as a natural consequence of freedom. If a family is no longer forced to work in the fields, then it is only natural that a mother might choose to stay home to run her household and to send her children to school, which accounts for the reduction in field labor. Delany thus defends the worth of blacks by declaring, "The immutable, unalterable laws which governed or controlled the instincts or impulses of a Hannibal, Alexander, or Napoleon, are the same implanted in the brain and breast of page or footman, be he black or white, circumstances alone making the difference in development according to the individual propensity" (Rollin 237). Here, people of African descent are characterized no longer as exceptional but as acting according to universal human nature—a nature that makes no distinction between the most prestigious leaders and the least-respected laborers.

An analogous contradiction emerges when Delany turns to the actual prospects of the freedmen in the seventh article. This time, the tension lies between hope for an integrated society and Delany's cynicism toward those who control the labor economy. The cynicism is immediately apparent when he chooses to frame his argument in terms of political economy because, he states, "however Christian and philanthropic we may be" (Rollin 238), no one will want to support the elevation of blacks unless they can offer "a prospective enhancement of the general wealth of the country" (Rollin 238). With this, Delany flatly rejects the idea that anyone will support freedmen as deserving human rights per se; wealth is the only true motivation for supporting the newly free people.

At the same time, however, Delany proposes a plan that implies strong hope and even belief in the possibility of an integrated labor economy that respects the ideal of the common good. Delany first points out the availability of land, as two-thirds of land in the South remains uncultivated. He then claims that only 312,000 people have been landowners in the South and, citing Pennsylvania as a positive example, argues that a greater number of owners would increase the wealth of the community overall. His specific proposal is that both the government and large landowners should either lease or sell to freedmen its lands in portions of 20 to 40 acres. These freedmen would then create great demand for farming supplies and other goods, thereby stimulating the economy. Delany declares his faith in such a plan by rejecting those sources (such as the *London Times*) that deny the practical feasibility of freedom. And yet, he also considers the possibility of failure when he states at the conclusion that if the government and plantation owners in the United States refuse to employ free blacks, educated freemen of the North would be willing to negotiate "with foreign states on this continent, which would only be too ready to receive them and theirs" (Rollin 241). Here, Delany refers to the possibility of emigrating within the North American continent, suggesting his doubts about the success of his own plan.

Delany's fascinating contradictions reflect larger tensions in the legal and cultural history of the nineteenth century. The legal and constitutional approach to slavery was long dedicated to preserving the union rather than to addressing slavery exclusively as a moral issue. For example, the Mexican-American War (1846-48) resulted in vast new territories for the United States, provoking the key issue of whether the new lands would allow slavery. After significant conflict and debate, Congress passed the Compromise of 1850, which was a series of bills intended to placate parties on both sides of the debate in order to preserve the union and maintain peace, not to address the issue of slavery as a moral or human rights issue. Accordingly, the Compromise pleased abolitionists by admitting California as a free state and by banning the slave trade in the District of Columbia, and it placated pro-slavery people by protecting the *practice* of slavery in the District of Columbia and by offering a harsher Fugitive Slave Act. This Act required runaway slaves to be returned to their owners and imposed heavy fines on negligent law-enforcement officials and both fines and imprisonment on those who aided runaway slaves. It also denied both slaves and free blacks trials and testimony, so that many free blacks became enslaved based on nothing more than a white person's affidavit. For these reasons, The Fugitive Slave Act of 1850 outraged abolitionists.

Likewise, the Emancipation Proclamation of 1863 was directed toward the cause of freedom, not least because it began to formalize what appeared to be the inevitable end of slavery, but it also strategically tolerated slavery for the sake of preserving the Union. The proclamation granted freedom to more than 3 million slaves in the Confederate states but denied it to hundreds of thousands of slaves in the border states, in Union-occupied Tennessee, and in other parts of federally controlled slave states. Lincoln's rationale for this partial gesture was that he needed the border slave states to remain in the Union so that he could garner as much support for the North as possible and weaken "the

Confederacy by holding out to irresolute Southerners the possibility that they could return to the Union with their property, including slaves, intact" (Foner 4). This does not mean that Lincoln did not want to abolish slavery; the proclamation was an important part of Lincoln's progressive evolution on the slavery issue and in part ensured that abolition would indeed occur. Rather, the proclamation's partial liberation reveals politics, rather than justice, as Lincoln's chief priority.

These political and legal compromises did in fact lead to justice, with the passage of the Thirteenth Amendment and subsequent constitutional amendments and laws that were part of Reconstruction, which lasted until 1877. In the early years of Reconstruction, progressive citizens and politicians achieved a great deal, establishing voting rights and citizenship for freed slaves, setting up integrated governments in the South, and establishing educational and other institutions for the new black citizens. Most scholars agree, however, that Reconstruction ultimately failed for many different reasons, including the devastating economic fallout from the war on the Southern economy and the international economic depression that began in 1873. Yet perhaps the most important cause of failure was the racist belief system that persisted despite the South's defeat and the new federal laws and institutions that supported the former slaves' freedom. By the early 1870s, conservatives replaced progressive governments throughout the South, and many conservatives staunchly opposed Reconstruction and tolerated or even encouraged widespread violence against African Americans. As reactionary conservatives took control of the South and the North began to lose interest in Reconstruction, the stage was set for the Jim Crow era, which established African Americans as an underclass in the United States for the next century.

Martin Delany lived to see the failure of Reconstruction, but he wrote "Prospects of the Freedmen" earlier, in 1865. Nonetheless, Delany clearly understood the distance between politics and justice and between the law and culture. He had witnessed this gap in the legal compromises prior to and during the war. He also experienced it in his own life from his earliest days: his family's move from Charles Town to Pennsylvania occurred after his mother, who was free, was persecuted for teaching her children to read and write; later, Delany was admitted to Harvard Medical School, but its racist culture defeated his right to attend. These realities of white resistance to the law deeply inform Delany's writings and help us to understand his desire to exalt African Americans while arguing for equal opportunity as well as his impulse to imagine economic structures that would facilitate success for freedmen even as he harbored doubts and cynicism about the motives of whites. His shrewd observation and experience taught him that culture had the power to defeat the law. Sadly, the failure of Reconstruction would justify the lesson. Yet, in 1865, he valiantly resolved to redefine prevailing beliefs and to frame them as part of an economic plan that he hoped and believed could succeed.

Essential Themes

In an attempt to lend objectivity to his arguments, Delany organizes both his characterization of African Americans and his practical proposals under the theme of political economy. Against the popular notion of the former slaves' childlike nature, laziness, and inability to be self-sufficient, Delany shockingly declares the African slave trade as a unique success in the face of previous failures based on the cultural (and implicitly racial) inferiority of whites and Native Americans. He uses this stance to elevate people of African descent based on the economic success that only they could provide to the New World settlers. He then uses this strategy to bolster his plan to promote the economic opportunity and welfare of freedmen: it is in the United States' interest to support this uniquely talented group that ensured the country's prosperity. Yet in arguing for equal opportunity, Delany can only take this claim so far, as demonstrated when he falls back on the notion of universal human nature to explain the reduced pool of field labor. Likewise, Delany proposes a plan that assumes the cooperation and integration of government, private landholders, and freedmen but that also reveals

cynicism and doubts about the plan's likelihood. These themes of separatism versus unity and hope versus cynicism mirror the deeper patterns of ambivalence and compromise that were so prevalent in the laws and culture of nineteenth-century slavery and its subsequent abolition.

Ashleigh Imus, Ph.D.

Bibliography and Additional Reading

Adeleke, Tunde. *Without Regard to Race: the Other Martin Robison Delany*. Jackson: UP of Mississippi, 2003. Print.

Foner, Eric. *Reconstruction: America's Unfinished Revolution, 1863-1877*. New York: Harper & Row, 1988. Print.

Foner, Philip S. and Robert James Branham, eds. *Lift Every Voice: African American Oratory, 1787-1900*. Tuscaloosa: U of Alabama P, 1998. Print.

Levine, Robert S. *Martin R. Delany: A Documentary Reader*. Chapel Hill: U of North Carolina P, 2003. Print.

Levine, Robert S. *Martin Delany, Frederick Douglass and the Politics of Representative Identity*. Chapel Hill: U of North Carolina P, 1997. Print.

Rollin, Frank A. *Life and Public Services of Martin R. Delany*. New York: Arno Press and the New York Times, 1969. Print.

Sterling, Dorothy. *The Making of an Afro-American: Martin Robison Delany 1812-1885*. Garden City: Doubleday, 1971. Print.

Ullman, Victor. *Martin R. Delany: The Beginnings of Black Nationalism*. Boston: Beacon Press, 1971. Print.

■ Thaddeus Stevens: Speech to Congress

Date: December 18, 1865
Author: Thaddeus Stevens
Genre: speech

Summary Overview

Thaddeus Stevens, Republican congressman from Pennsylvania, gave a speech before Congress that articulated his vision for the period following the Civil War, known as Reconstruction. Delivered only seven months after the war ended and on the same day that the Thirteenth Amendment, which abolished slavery, went into effect, Stevens's speech represented the view of a group in Congress known as the Radical Republicans. It portrayed a strident vision of the Reconstruction era, wherein the defeated Southern states were not welcomed back with open arms, and their rights would remain curtailed until Congress saw fit to restore them. Importantly, the speech placed Congress itself in charge of Reconstruction policy—a fact that galled President Andrew Johnson, who promoted a relatively simple reinstatement process for Southern states. The policy and personal disputes between Johnson and Stevens helped frame the Reconstruction era, mirroring the divisions present in the nation as a whole.

Defining Moment

The conclusion of the Civil War may have halted the direct warfare between the Union and Confederate armies, but disagreements among Northerners over what to do with the South were just beginning. Before the end of the war, President Abraham Lincoln had issued his Proclamation of Amnesty and Reconstruction, in which he outlined a generous plan that called for the readmission of any former Confederate states in which ten percent of the voters swore allegiance to the restored Union and amnesty for all but the highest-ranking Confederate military and political leaders. Lincoln may have been the only one who could have made this arrangement work, but he was assassinated in April 1865, leaving his vice president, Johnson, as the executive in charge of Reconstruction. As both a Southerner (who had remained loyal to the Union) and a Democrat, Johnson was hard-pressed to implement Lincoln's plan, especially in the face of a public discourse dominated by Thaddeus Stevens and the Radical Republicans.

In the immediate aftermath of the war, however, Congress was not in session, and Johnson did his best to implement Lincoln's plan in Congress's absence. Lincoln had already authorized reconstructed governments in Arkansas, Louisiana, Virginia, and Johnson's home state of Tennessee, and Johnson continued Lincoln's goal of quickly restoring local sovereignty to the states. Ensuring the rights of former slaves, now called freedmen, was, to Johnson, a matter for state governments—another important issue on which he and Stevens's Radical Republicans disagreed. Johnson's policies allowed many former Confederates to regain political power. To those white leaders, voting rights for the freedmen, as advocated by Radical Republicans, were out of the question. Many Southern states quickly passed what became known as the Black Codes—repressive laws that governed where and when freedmen could go, the conditions under which they would work, and the limits on their gathering together. Though many Northerners were ambivalent about African American suffrage, the Black Codes turned public opinion against Johnson and his moderate approach to Reconstruction.

By the time Congress arrived to begin its session in December 1865, a confrontation between the two opposing systems of Reconstruction, as well as Johnson and Stevens, was imminent. Stevens, who led the Radical faction in the House, along with Charles Sumner in the Senate, were determined both to ensure that the sacrifices made during the Civil War were not wasted by handing power back to the same Southern politicians who had driven secession forward four years earlier and to see that the freedmen's civil rights, including the right to vote, were guaranteed.

Author Biography

Thaddeus Stevens was a Republican congressman from Pennsylvania who became the face of the opposition to Abraham Lincoln and Andrew Johnson's lenient approach to the South after the Civil War. Stevens had a long history of opposition to slavery and was outraged over the secession of the South. Born in Danville, Vermont, in 1792, Stevens grew up poor, yet he graduated from Dartmouth College and became an attorney before entering politics in 1833. As the nation edged toward Civil War, Stevens, now living in Pennsylvania, was elected to Congress in 1849 as an antislavery Republican. During the war, as the powerful chair of the Ways and Means Committee, Stevens pushed Lincoln for emancipation of the slaves. Lincoln had called for reconciliation in his second inaugural and Gettysburg addresses, but Stevens disagreed vehemently, pushing for the punishment of the South—including the disenfranchisement of all Confederates—and full citizenship rights for the freed slaves. In 1868, he led the charge to impeach Johnson, who was narrowly acquitted in the Senate. Later that year, on August 11, Stevens died in Washington and was buried near his home in Lancaster, Pennsylvania.

HISTORICAL DOCUMENT

The President assumes, what no one doubts, that the late rebel States have lost their constitutional relations to the Union, and are incapable of representation in Congress, except by permission of the Government. It matters but little, with this admission, whether you call them States out of the Union, and now conquered territories, or assert that because the Constitution forbids them to do what they did do, that they are therefore only dead as to all national and political action, and will remain so until the Government shall breathe into them the breath of life anew and permit them to occupy their former position. In other words, that they are not out of the Union, but are only dead carcasses lying within the Union. In either case, it is very plain that it requires the action of Congress to enable them to form a State government and send representatives to Congress. Nobody, I believe, pretends that with their old constitutions and frames of government they can be permitted to claim their old rights under the Constitution. They have torn their constitutional States into atoms, and built on their foundations fabrics of a totally different character. Dead men cannot raise themselves. Dead States cannot restore their existence "as it was." Whose especial duty is it to do it? In whom does the Constitution place the power? Not in the judicial branch of Government, for it only adjudicates and does not prescribe laws. Not in the Executive, for he only executes and cannot make laws. Not in the Commander-in-Chief of the armies, for he can only hold them under military rule until the sovereign legislative power of the conqueror shall give them law. Unless the law of nations is a dead letter, the late war between two acknowledged belligerents severed their original compacts and broke all the ties that bound them together. The future condition of the conquered power depends on the will of the conqueror. They must come in as new states or remain as conquered provinces. Congress ... is the only power that can act in the matter.

Congress alone can do it.... Congress must create States and declare when they are entitled to be represented. Then each House must judge whether the members presenting themselves from a recognized State possess the requisite qualifications of age, residence, and citizenship; and whether the election and returns are according to law...

It is obvious from all this that the first duty of Congress is to pass a law declaring the condition of these outside or defunct States, and providing proper civil governments for them. Since the conquest they have been governed by martial law. Military rule is necessarily despotic, and ought not to exist longer than is absolutely necessary. As there are no symptoms that the people of these provinces will be prepared to participate in constitutional government for some years, I know of no arrangement so proper for them as territorial governments. There they can learn the principles of freedom and eat the fruit of foul rebellion. Under such governments, while electing members to the territorial Legislatures, they will necessarily mingle with those to whom Congress shall extend the right of suffrage. In Territories Congress fixes the qualifications of electors; and I know of no better place nor better occasion for the conquered rebels and the conqueror to practice justice to all men, and accustom themselves to make and obey equal laws....

They ought never to be recognized as capable of acting in the Union, or of being counted as valid States, until the Constitution shall have been so amended as to make it what its framers intended; and so as to secure perpetual ascendency to the party of the Union; and so as to render our republican Government firm and stable forever. The first of those amendments is to change the basis of representation among the States from Federal numbers to actual voters.... With the basis unchanged the 83 Southern members, with the Democrats that will in the best times be elected from the North, will always give a major

ity in Congress and in the Electoral college.... I need not depict the ruin that would follow. . .

But this is not all that we ought to do before inveterate rebels are invited to participate in our legislation. We have turned, or are about to turn, loose four million slaves without a hut to shelter them or a cent in their pockets. The infernal laws of slavery have prevented them from acquiring an education, understanding the common laws of contract, or of managing the ordinary business of life. This Congress is bound to provide for them until they can take care of themselves. If we do not furnish them with homesteads, and hedge them around with protective laws; if we leave them to the legislation of their late masters, we had better have left them in bondage.

If we fail in this great duty now, when we have the power, we shall deserve and receive the execration of history and of all future ages.

GLOSSARY

Electoral College: a body of electors chosen by voters who formally elect the president and vice president

Republican government: government by a body of representative citizens

Document Analysis

When Stevens rose to speak in the House of Representatives on December 18, 1865, his opposition to Johnson's Reconstruction plan was already well known. Simply allowing the Southern states to rejoin the Union upon the acceptance of federal sovereignty by ten percent of voters and ratification of the Thirteenth Amendment was not even close to sufficient for Stevens, who, like many in the North, held the Southerners completely responsible for four years of unprecedented bloodshed. However, his plan proved too radical for many war-weary Northerners.

Rather than debate the presidential plan, Stevens took a different tack, questioning the very propriety of having the executive branch direct Reconstruction policy. The states of the entire southern half of the nation had seceded, but they were again under federal jurisdiction after the Union victory. He argued that, since the Confederate states had divorced themselves from the Union, there was "no arrangement so proper

for them as territorial governments." Neither the president nor the judiciary had the power to create states out of unincorporated territories before the Civil War, nor should they have the power to do so now, according to Stevens.

As everyone within the government knew, Stevens was not amenable to allowing the Confederates to regain their role within the Union. Instead of seeking the quick reconciliation that Lincoln and Johnson promoted, Stevens was comfortable both with the process of Southern reintegration taking years and with Congress being the final arbiter of when each Southern state could rejoin the nation. To Stevens, the procedure by which a territory becomes a state was the logical blueprint for this process. The Southern territories could have non-voting representation, and it would be Congress, which would ensure that they could not exercise any power until Congress was convinced they would pose no further threat to the Union.

Finally, Stevens turned his attention to the plight of

the former slaves who, though free, were "without a hut to shelter them or a cent in their pockets." Rather than looking for Congress to help the Confederates, Stevens thought it more proper for Congress to shepherd the freedmen, providing them with the basic tools they needed in terms of education, legal protections, and security to establish themselves in their newfound freedom. In this, Stevens was zealous, but well outside of the mainstream of Northern opinion, a fact that would shape the mixed record of accomplishment and frustration that followed.

Essential Themes

Thaddeus Stevens was one of the most influential people in shaping public policy during the Reconstruction era, but not all of his ideas were implemented. Certainly many people shared his outrage and desire to see the former Confederates punished, but his particular bitterness ran counter to the feelings of many others who wanted to see a quick reconciliation with the South and who cared little about anything more than rudimentary freedom for former slaves.

Stevens successfully prevented the first few new state governments implemented under Lincoln and Johnson's Reconstruction plan from being recognized, refusing to seat the senators and representatives elected by those states. The Black Codes passed in those states to keep the freed slaves from exercising their new freedoms further angered the Radical Republicans—and even most moderate Republicans. These extreme measures allowed Stevens to push through the establishment of the Freedmen's Bureau, created to help former slaves, as well as the Civil Rights Act of 1866, which defined citizenship as including anyone born in the United States without regard to race (a provision enshrined a few years later in the Fourteenth Amendment to the Constitution). President Johnson's opposition to these measures created a schism between him and Stevens, and eventually led to the president's impeachment. The Civil Rights Act became the first major piece of legislation to be passed despite a president's veto.

Not all of the ideas Stevens voiced in his speech were implemented. Rather than making the South go through the process of territorial government, in 1867 and 1868, Congress passed the Reconstruction Acts, which divided the South into five military districts under the command of a general and provided clear criteria for readmission to the Union, including redrafting their state constitutions to include loyalty to the Union, ratification of the Fourteenth Amendment, and guaranteeing former slaves the right to vote.

Popular interest in punishing or governing the South, as well as in ensuring justice for freedmen, waned, however, as Northerners prioritized a return to prosperity. After Stevens's death in 1868, the Freedmen's Bureau was chronically underfunded, and although many African Americans held political office in the reconstructed states, the power of the former Confederates rose again through terrorist organizations such as the Ku Klux Klan.

— *Steven L. Danver, PhD*

Bibliography and Additional Reading

Brodie, Fawn. *Thaddeus Stevens: Scourge of the South.* New York: Norton, 1959. Print.

DuBois, W. E. B. *Black Reconstruction in America: Toward a History of the Part of Which Black Folk Played in the Attempt to Reconstruct Democracy in America, 1860–1880.* Rev. ed. New Brunswick, NH: Transaction, 2012. Print.

Foner, Eric. *Reconstruction: America's Unfinished Revolution, 1863–1877.* New York: Harper & Row, 1988. Print.

McPherson, James M. *Battle Cry of Freedom: The Civil War Era.* New York: Ballantine, 1989. Print.

Trefousse, Hans Louis. *Thaddeus Stevens: Nineteenth-Century Egalitarian.* Chapel Hill: U of North Carolina P, 1997. Print.

■ Alexander Stephens: "On Reconstruction"

Date: April 11, 1866
Author: Alexander H. Stephens.
Genre: speech

Summary Overview

Alexander H. Stephens, former vice president of the Confederacy, testified before the US Congress's Joint Committee on Reconstruction in April of 1866. This congressional committee was formed in 1865 to address the vexing questions that arose with the end of the Civil War. Stephens, who was a slave owner and believed in the natural mental and physical inferiority of black people, was asked to comment on whether Georgia would return to the Union if African Americans were given full citizenship and equal protection under the law, and if they would accept reduced representation in Congress based on subtracting the numbers of people who had been denied full citizenship. Stephens argued that Georgia's return to the Union should not be contingent on giving African Americans full citizenship rights—the key issue in the Fourteenth Amendment, then awaiting ratification by the states. He believed that once the states that had joined the Confederacy had given up the war, they should be freely admitted back to the Union with full representation.

Defining Moment

The Fourteenth Amendment to the US Constitution established that anyone born in the United States (including, by implication, African Americans) was a US citizen, entitled to equal protection under the law; this amendment was awaiting ratification by the states when Stephens testified before the Joint Committee on Reconstruction. Since before the end of the Civil War, Congress had hotly debated what the citizenship rights of former slaves should be when the Confederate states were returned to the Union; the issue of black suffrage was particularly thorny. If freedmen were not given the vote, but their numbers still counted toward a state's representation in Congress, the Southern states (mean-

ing Democrats) would gain significant political power over what they had before the war (when only three-fifths of the number of slaves in a state were counted toward that state's number of congressional representatives). If, on the other hand, freedmen were given full citizenship rights, including the right to vote, their votes would bolster the strength of the Republicans in Congress, who were driving Reconstruction. After much wrangling over this issue between congressional Democrats and Republicans, the final language of the Fourteenth Amendment stopped short of granting explicit voting rights to black men, instead establishing that if a state denied the vote to any subset of eligible adult men, that state's representation in Congress would be reduced proportionately.

The Joint Committee on Reconstruction was formed in 1865 to study how to readmit the states of the former Confederacy into the Union. It was this committee that drafted the Fourteenth Amendment and heard testimony and gathered evidence from a variety of sources about how best to reintegrate the former Confederacy into national politics and government. This committee interviewed Stephens to ascertain whether Georgia would be willing to accept the full citizenship of African Americans.

The Report of the Joint Committee on Reconstruction was issued on June 20, 1866, and urged caution in the readmission of representatives from the former Confederacy to Congress. The report did not make the recommendation that states needed to immediately give black men the vote, but stated instead that a state's representation in Congress could only be based on the total number of voters. The former Confederate states, while theoretically able to deny black men the vote, would only do so by giving up significant political power.

It was this trade-off that Stephens objected to in his testimony. He argued that the states of the former Confederacy should be readmitted to the Union with full representation as before the war, and then all the states could settle these vexing issues together. The Joint Committee disagreed, pointing out that relations between states that had rebelled and states that had not were vastly different than they were before the war and that people who had taken part in an active rebellion against the government should not immediately be allowed to resume positions of authority in that government. Before the states of the former Confederacy could be given full representation, the civil rights of black citizens needed to be protected. The issue of voting rights for black men was settled definitively with the Fifteenth Amendment, ratified in 1870, which states that the right to vote cannot be denied because of "race, color, or previous condition of servitude."

Author Biography

Alexander H. Stephens was born in 1812 in Crawfordville, Georgia. Despite a difficult childhood and an adolescence marked by illness and the death of both his parents, Stephens was a precocious student and passed the bar in 1834. During a successful career as a lawyer and politician, first in the Georgia House and Senate and then in the US House of Representatives, Stephens amassed considerable wealth and purchased slaves. In 1861, Stephens became a delegate to the Georgia Secession Convention, and he was elected vice president of the Confederacy in November 1861. During the Civil War, Stephens gave several speeches, in which he described slavery as the natural state of people of African descent. Stephens was briefly imprisoned in Boston in 1865; shortly after his release, he was elected senator for his home state of Georgia. He was not allowed to take his seat, however, because, at the time, there was a federal ban on rebel leaders holding office. He continued to believe in the inferiority of black people after the Civil War ended, arguing against black suffrage and civil rights. In 1873, Stephens was elected to the US House of Representatives, where he served until November 4, 1882, when he was elected governor of Georgia. He died less than a year later, in 1883.

HISTORICAL DOCUMENT

I think the people of the State would be unwilling do more than they have done for restoration. Restricted to limited suffrage would not be so objectionable as general or universal. But it is a matter that belongs to the State to regulate. The question of suffrage, whether universal or restricted, is one of State policy exclusively, as they believe. Individually I should not be opposed to a propose system of restricted or limited suffrage to this class our population. . . . The only view in their opinion that could possibly justify the war that was carried on by the federal government against them was the idea of the indisolubleness of the Union; that those who held the administration for the time were bound to enforce the execution of the laws and the maintenance of the integrity of the country under the Constitution. . . . They expected as soon as the confederate cause was abandoned that immediately the States would be brought back into their practical relations with the government as previously constituted. That is what they looked to. They expected that the States would immediately have their representatives in the Senate and in the House; and they expected in good faith, as loyal men, as the term is frequently used -- loyal to law, order, and the Constitution -- to support the government under the Constitution. . . . Towards the Constitution of the United States the great mass of our people were always as much devoted in their feelings as any people ever were towards any laws or people. They resorted to secession with a view of more securely maintaining these principles. And when they found they were not successful in their object in perfect good faith, as far as I can judge from meeting with them and conversing with them, looking to the future development of their country . . . their earnest desire and expectation was to allow the past struggle . . . to pass by and to co-operate with . . . those of all sections who earnestly desire the preservation of constitutional liberty and the perpetuation of the government in its purity. They have been . . . disappointed in this, and are . . . patiently waiting, however, and believing that when the passions of the hour have passed away this delay in representation will cease.

My own opinion is, that these terms ought not to be offered as conditions precedent. . . . It would be best for the peace, harmony, and prosperity of the whole country that there should be an immediate restoration, an immediate bringing back of the States into their original practical relations; and let all these questions then be discussed in common council. Then the representatives from the south could be heard, and you and all could judge much better of the tone and temper of the people than you could from the opinions given by any individuals. . . .

My judgment, therefore, is very decided, that it would have been better as soon as the lamentable conflict was over, when the people of the south abandoned their cause and agreed to accept the issue, desiring as they do to resume their places for the future in the Union, and to look to the arena of reason and justice for the protection of their rights in the Union -- it would have been better to have allowed that result to take place, to follow under the policy adopted by the administration, than to delay or hinder it by propositions to amend the Constitution in respect to suffrage. . . . I think the people of all the southern States would in the halls of Congress discuss these questions calmly and deliberately. And if they did not show that the views they entertained were just and proper, such as to control the judgment of the people of the other sections and States, they would quietly yield to whatever should be constitutionally determined in common council. But I think they feel very sensitively the offer to them of propositions to accept while they are denied all voice . . . in the discussion of these propositions. I think they feel very sensitively that they are denied the right to be heard.

GLOSSARY

common council: ordinary deliberations

indisolubleness: or indissolubleness: resistance to dissolution; permanence

Document Analysis

Stephens's replies to questions posed by the Joint Committee on Reconstruction illuminated the feelings that many Southerners had about the treatment they deserved at the end of the Civil War. Stephens stated that the citizens of Georgia were "unwilling [to] do more than they have done for restoration." He argued that the issue of universal versus limited suffrage in the South—that is, whether or not the vote would be extended to African Americans—should be "one of State policy exclusively," and not made a condition for readmission to the Union. Besides, if the reason for the Civil War was to bring the states back into the Union, then with the conclusion of the war, it was time to do just that—bring the states of the former Confederacy back as full political participants—and then these thorny issues could be settled in a proper way, with full participation and representation. "It would be best for the peace, harmony, and prosperity of the whole country that there should be an immediate restoration."

Stephens took the position that secession had happened in the first place, in part, because of the attachment of the people of the South to the Constitution. When they felt that their constitutional rights were being violated, they rebelled to protect these rights. Now that they were prepared to rejoin the Union, they once again stood ready to take their place in a government supported by the Constitution. Decisions could then be made by all states properly represented. Stephens chose his words carefully and did not directly attack the idea of the vote for black men. He argued instead that it was unfair for the former Confederate states to be shut out of the process of government decision-making.

Essential Themes

The primary issue in Stephens's testimony before the Joint Committee on Reconstruction was giving full citizenship rights to black men, including the vote and how this would affect the process of returning former Confederate states, such as Stephens's home state of Georgia, to the Union. With the Civil War over, a conflict ostensibly fought to reunite the country, many Southern states believed that they should be readmitted to the Union on the same terms they had left. The Republican-led Congress, however, had a vested interest in establishing legal rights and protections for former slaves before allowing states, such as Georgia, to have full representation. It was also not clear what full and fair representation would be, since, if slavery no longer existed, then the formula that states had used to count a percentage of their enslaved population in determining their representation no longer applied.

Stephens argued that voting issues could be determined only by states, and so holding these issues over the states' heads as a prerequisite to their return to the Union was unfair. Stephens argued against settling these issues through constitutional amendments without full Southern participation in the process, as this took away the ability of states to determine voting laws.

—*Bethany Groff, MA*

Bibliography and Additional Reading

Alexander, Danielle. "Forty Acres and a Mule: The Ruined Hope of Reconstruction." *Humanities* 25.1 (2004): 26–29. Print.

Foner, Eric. *Reconstruction: America's Unfinished Revolution, 1863–1877.* New York: Harper, 2011. Print.

Schott, Thomas E. *Alexander H. Stephens of Georgia: A Biography.* Baton Rouge: Louisiana State UP, 1988. Print.

"Stephens, Alexander Hamilton (1812–1883)." *Biographical Directory of the United States Congress.* US Congress, n.d. Web. 8 Jan. 2014.

Sterling, Dorothy. *The Trouble They Seen: The Story of Reconstruction in the Words of African Americans.* New York: Da Capo, 1994. Print.

■ Report of the Joint Committee on Reconstruction

Date: June 20, 1866
Author: Joint Committee on Reconstruction
Genre: report

Summary Overview

In April 1865, as the Civil War drew to a close, Abraham Lincoln was assassinated. Vice President Andrew Johnson inherited the mantle of leadership. With the nation reunited, the process of reintegrating the South into the larger whole had to be accomplished. Which branch of government would establish the rules for the Reconstruction of the South was at stake when Congress opened their regular session. In order to play the role its leaders believed was proper for the legislative branch, Congress appointed a Joint Committee to investigate the actions taken by Johnson and the leaders of the Southern states. After six months of study, this Report was written and delivered to both houses of Congress. The Report was a major challenge to President Johnson and a repudiation of virtually all he had done. The appointing of this Committee was the opening volley in the struggle between Congress and President Johnson as to whether the legislative or executive branch would hold the power in the postwar era.

Defining Moment

The Civil War had devastated the nation. In addition, the assassination of President Lincoln had shocked the people in the Northern states, coming when all but one of the major Southern armies had surrendered and the war was virtually over. Although a Democrat from the seceded state of Tennessee, Andrew Johnson had been chosen as vice president, in order to demonstrate Lincoln's desire for national unity. From the beginning, Republicans in Congress were uneasy about Johnson being on the ticket. Coming into the presidency when Congress was not scheduled to be in session for almost eight months, Johnson unilaterally moved ahead with plans for the Reconstruction of the South, rather than calling a special session to get Congressional input.

Congressional Republicans thought Johnson's plans for Reconstruction were too easy on the South, and so, as one of the first acts of the regular session in December 1865, they established a Joint Committee to study and report on Johnson's actions.

Although a major part of the split between Congress and President Johnson was the normal interparty/regional rivalry, the seriousness of the split went well beyond that. The effect of those differences should not be underestimated as to the division within the national government in 1865–66. However, in addition this split was a continuation of the problems created by the separation of powers established in the Constitution. During the Civil War, the executive branch, under President Lincoln, had acquired a substantial amount of power at the expense of Congress. Now that the war was over and the president's role as commander-in-chief was less important, members of Congress desired to reassert power over national programs and policy. This would have been true even if Lincoln were alive, but with the party and regional differences between Johnson and the majority of the members of Congress, it was magnified. Thus, the members of Congress wanted to make it clear that they would be in charge of Reconstruction and not the president.

The means for doing this was for a Joint Committee of the two houses (Senate and House of Representatives) to develop a basic plan, based on the situation seven months after the last hostilities between the Union and the Confederacy. This was the Committee charged with this important task. The report, with the attached proposal to amend the Constitution, was a step toward gaining control of the Reconstruction of the South. If Congress had not done this, Reconstruction would have been very different.

Author Biography

The Joint Committee on Reconstruction was composed of fifteen members, nine members of the House and six Senators. Republicans dominated the Committee, as they did each chamber, with seven House members and five senators from that party. These were the twelve men who signed the report. The other three members were Democrats, and they filed a minority report. The Committee itself was the result of a resolution introduced by Congressman Thaddeus Stevens and passed by both houses thirteen days after the start of the first regular session of the Thirty-ninth Congress. Stevens was appointed to the Committee, although Senator William Pitt Fessenden of Maine was the chairman. In the House, Stevens was a leader of the Radical Republicans, who believed that full equality should be given to African Americans and that a structure should be put in place to assist in this becoming reality. This wing of the party, totally opposed to President Johnson's Reconstruction plan, was to dominate national politics for the next few years.

HISTORICAL DOCUMENT

The resolution under which your committee was appointed directed them to inquire into the condition of the Confederate States, and report whether they were entitled to representation in Congress. It is obvious that such an investigation, covering so large an extent of territory and involving so many important considerations, must necessarily require no trifling labor, and consume a very considerable amount of time. It must embrace the condition in which those States were left at the close of the war; the measures which have been taken towards the reorganization of civil government, and the disposition of the people towards the United States; in a word, their fitness to take an active part in the administration of national affairs....

A claim for the immediate admission of senators and representatives from the so called Confederate States has been urged, which seems to your committee not to be founded either in reason or in law, and which cannot be passed without comment. Stated in a few words, it amounts to this: That inasmuch as the lately insurgent States had no legal right to separate themselves from the Union, they still retain their positions as States, and consequently the people thereof have a right to immediate representation in Congress without the imposition of any conditions whatever; and further, that until such admission Congress has no right to tax them for the support of the government. It has even been contended that until such admission all legislation affecting their interests is, if not unconstitutional, at least unjustifiable and oppressive.

It is believed by your Committee that these propositions are not only wholly untenable, but, if admitted would tend to the destruction of the government.

It must not be forgotten that the people of these States, without justification or excuse, rose in insurrection against the United States. They deliberately abolished their State governments so far as the same connected them politically with the Union as members thereof under the Constitution. They deliberately renounced their allegiance to the federal government, and proceeded to establish an independent government for themselves. In the prosecution of this enterprise they seized the national forts, arsenals, dock-yards, and other public property within their borders, drove out from among them those who remained true to the Union, and heaped every imaginable insult and injury upon the United States and its citizens. Finally, they opened hostilities and levied war against the government. They continued this war for four years with the most determined and malignant spirit, killing in battle, and otherwise, large numbers of loyal people, destroying the property of loyal citizens on the sea and on the land, and entailing on the government an enormous debt, incurred to sustain its rightful authority. Whether legally and constitutionally or not, they did, in fact, withdraw from the Union and made themselves subjects of another government of their own creation. And they only yielded when they were compelled by utter exhaustion to lay down their arms; and this they did, not willingly, but declaring that they yielded because they could no longer resist, affording no evidence whatever of repentance for their crime, and expressing no regret, except that they had no longer the power to continue the desperate struggle.

It cannot, we think, be denied by any one, having tolerable acquaintance with public law, that the war thus waged was a civil war of the greatest magnitude. The people waging it were necessarily subject to all the rule which, by the law of nations, control a contest of that character, and to all the legitimate consequences following it. One of those consequences was that, within the limits prescribed by humanity, the conquered rebels were at the mercy of the conquerors. That a government thus outraged had a most perfect right to exact indemnity for the injuries done, and security against the recurrence of such outrages in the future, would seem too clear for dispute.

It is moreover contended, and with apparent gravity, that, from the peculiar nature and character of our government, no such right on the part of the conqueror can exist; that from the moment when rebellion lays down its arms and actual hostilities cease, all political rights of rebellious communities are at once restored; that, because the people of a State of the Union were once an organized community within the Union, they necessarily so remain, and their right to be represented in Congress at any and all times, and to participate in the government of the country under all circumstances, admits of neither question nor dispute. If this is indeed true, then is the government of the United States powerless for its own protection, and flagrant rebellion, carried to the extreme of civil war, is a pastime which any State may play at, not only certain that it can lose nothing in any event, but may even be the gainer by defeat. If rebellion succeeds, it accomplishes its purpose and destroys the government. If it fails, the war has been barren of results, and the battle may be still fought out in the legislative halls of the country. Treason, defeated in the field, has only to take possession of Congress and the cabinet....

Your committee came to the consideration of the subject referred to them with the most anxious desire ascertain what was the condition of the people of the States recently in insurrection, and what, if anything, was necessary to be done before restoring them to the full enjoyment of all their original privileges. It was undeniable that the war into which they had plunged the country had materially changed their relations to the people of the loyal States. Slavery had been abolished by constitutional amendment. A large proportion of the population had become, instead of mere chattels, free men and citizens. Through all the past struggle these had remained true and loyal, and had, in large numbers, fought on the side of the Union. It was impossible to abandon them, without securing them their rights as free men and citizens. The whole civilized world would have cried out against such base ingratitude, and the bare idea is offensive to all right-thinking men.

Hence it became important to inquire what could be done to secure their rights, civil and political. It was evident to your committee that adequate security could only be found in appropriate constitutional provisions. By an original provision of the Constitution, representation is based on the whole number of free persons in each State, and three-fifths of all other persons. When all become free, representation for all necessarily follows. As a consequence the inevitable effect of the rebellion would be to increase the political power of the insurrectionary States, whenever they should be allowed to resume their position as States of the Union. As representation is by the Constitution based upon population, your committee did not think it advisable to recommend a change of that basis. The increase of representation necessarily resulting from the abolition of slavery was considered the most important element in the questions arising out of the changed condition of affairs, and the necessity for some fundamental action in this regard seemed imperative. It appeared to your committee that the rights of these persons by whom the basis of representation had been thus increased should be recognized by the general government. While slaves they were not considered as having any rights, civil or political.

It did not seem just or proper that all the political advantages derived from their becoming free should be confined to their former masters, who had fought against the Union, and withheld from themselves, who had always been loyal. Slavery, by building up a ruling and dominant class, had produced a spirit of oligarchy adverse to republican institutions, which finally inaugurated civil war. The tendency of continuing the domination of such a class, by leaving it in the exclusive possession of political power, would be to encourage the same spirit, and lead to a similar result. Doubts were entertained whether Congress had power, even under the amended Constitution, to prescribe the qualifications of voters in a State, or could act directly on the subject. It was doubtful, in the opinion of your committee, whether the States would consent to surrender a power they had always exercised, and to which they were attached. As the best if not the only method of surmounting the difficulty, and as eminently just and proper in itself, your committee came to the conclusion that political power should be possessed in all the States exactly in proportion as the right of suffrage should be granted, without distinction of color or race. This it was thought would leave the whole question with the people of each State, holding out to all the advantage of increased political power as an inducement to allow all to participate in its exercise. Such a provision would be in its nature gentle and persuasive, and would lead, it was hoped, at no distant day, to an equal participation of all, without distinction, in all the rights and privileges of citizenship, thus affording a full and adequate protection to all classes of citizens, since all would have, through the ballot-box, the power of self-protection....

With such evidence before them, it is the opinion of your committee:

I. That the States lately in rebellion were, at the close of the war, disorganized communities, without civil government, and without constitutions or other forms, by virtue of which political relations could legally exist between them and the federal government.

II. That Congress cannot be expected to recognize as valid the election of representatives from disorganized communities, which, from the very nature of the case, were unable to present their claim to representation under those established and recognized rules, the observance of which has been hitherto required.

III. That Congress would not be justified in admitting such communities to a participation in the government of the country without first providing such constitutional or other guarantees as will tend to secure the civil rights of all citizens of the republic; a just equality of representation; protection against claims founded in rebellion and crime; a temporary restoration of the right of suffrage to those who had not actively participated in the efforts to destroy the Union and overthrow the government, and the exclusion from positions of public trust of, at least, a portion of those whose crimes have proved them to be enemies to the Union, and unworthy of public confidence....

Before closing this report, your committee beg leave to state that the specific recommendations submitted by them are the result of mutual concession, after a long and careful comparison of conflicting opinions. Upon a question of such magnitude, infinitely important as it is to the future of toe republic, it was not to be expected that all should think alike. Sensible of the imperfections of the scheme, your committee submit it to Congress as the best they could agree upon, in the hope that its imperfections may be cured, and its deficiencies supplied, by legislative wisdom; and that, when finally adopted, it may tend to restore peace and harmony to the whole country, and to place our republican institutions on a more stable foundation.

W. P. FESSENDEN.

JAMES W. GRIMES.

IRA HARRIS.

J. M. HOWARD.

GEORGE H. WILLIAMS.

THADDEUS STEVENS.

ELIHU B. WASHBURNE.

JUSTIN S. MORRILL.

JNO. A. BINGHAM.

ROSCOE CONKLING.

GEORGE S. BOUTWELL.

GLOSSARY

abrogate: to do away with

advert: to draw attention to an item

inhered: inherent

viz: a short form of videlicet, meaning "namely," used to introduce a list

writ of habeas corpus: a legal order to bring a prisoner before a judge, which, in this case, would be a sign of the restoration of full Constitutional rights

Document Analysis

The Congress of the United States was very upset with President Johnson, due to his lack of consultation regarding Reconstruction. The Joint Committee investigated what steps had been, and were being, taken to reintegrate the South. The majority (all Republican) was appalled at what had been done and the promises that had been made. After numerous pages outlining the Committee's investigative work, the report offered ten statements/resolutions stating that the steps taken by the president had exceeded his authority and had also been generally worthless. The report went on to recommend that Congress take full control of Reconstruction, especially deciding when and by whom vacant Congressional seats could be filled. The report ended with a proposal for a Fourteenth Amendment to the Constitution (eventually passed and ratified) to strengthen the rights of all citizens, as an attempt to block, in the Southern states, what became called Jim Crow laws.

The Committee's investigation began by requesting records from the president regarding his actions and the official responses of the Southern states. The report states that these were not received in a timely manner, and what the Southern states had given the president was generally worthless. Only Tennessee seemed to be making an attempt to meet the spirit of the Reconstruction process, from the Committee's point of view. While the Committee appreciated the president's steps to restore order in the defeated states, the Committee concluded that if the president's plans were followed, the South would be given what they could not win through rebellion. The Committee did recognize that there needed to be a balance between punishing treason and rehabilitating the South. However, for the Committee, "civil equality" had to be developed to assure the freed slaves they would not only be free, but safe.

The ten statements/proposals made by the Committee noted that all the problems faced by the South were of their own making. They had withdrawn their representatives in Congress, they had tried to secede from the Union, they had begun the military conflict, and quit only when all their forces were totally defeated. For the South to complain they were being treated unfairly had no foundation, from the Committee's perspective. The fact that there had not been documented changes among the people or leadership of the Southern states meant, to the Committee, that the states were "not, at present, entitled to representation." The Committee believed only Congress could make this determination, and they would do so only when a secure society was in place for all citizens, North and South, white and African-American.

Essential Themes

Although the topic of the report was Reconstruction, a major portion of it dealt with the question of which branch of government had the authority and power to oversee and regulate the process. As might be expected, the Congressional Committee believed that this was Congress' right and responsibility. In outlining the weaknesses of President Johnson's Reconstruction plans, and their implementation, much of the focus was on the difference between the powers wielded by the president as commander-in-chief, versus the president as leader of a country at peace. In the latter circumstances, the Committee believed only Congress could set the rules for Reconstruction.

As to the structure of the Reconstruction process, the Committee dwelt at length on the role of the military provisional governors appointed by President Johnson. Congress accepted their presence as necessary to bring order to an area where the civilian government had been destroyed, but they did not accept as fact that the military governors (paid by the War Department; what would now be the Department of Defense) had the right to establish civilian government. This, in the Committee's view, could only be done by the nation's civilian leadership, Congress. Thus Congress had the responsibility for developing the regulations for Reconstruction and implementing them. This included a much stronger effort to create the conditions for the full equality of all people. If Congress accepted and acted on this report, they would have the responsibility of changing essential legal aspects of society to guarantee the "civil rights and privileges of all citizens in all parts of the republic." Although this desire to have full equality for African Americans in the South by the end of Reconstruction did not come to pass, this report, the Fourteenth Amendment, and related legislation, not only shaped events during Reconstruction, but formed the foundation for much of the civil rights legislation in the twentieth century.

—*Donald A. Watt, PhD*

Bibliography and Additional Reading

Franklin, John Hope and Eric Foner. *Reconstruction after the Civil War*. Chicago: University of Chicago Press, 2013. Print.

Kendrick, Benjamin B. *The Journal of the Joint Committee of Fifteen on Reconstruction*. New York: Columbia University, 1914. Google eBooks. n.d. Web. 20 March 2014.

Saxon, Rufus. "Testimony before Congress's Joint Committee on Reconstruction." *History of St. Augustine*. Ed. Gil Wilson. Dr. Bronson Tours. n.d. Web. 20 March 2014.

Smith, John David. *A Just and Lasting Peace: A Documentary History of Reconstruction*. New York: Signet Classics, 2013. Print.

United States Congress Joint Committee on Reconstruction. *Report*. Washington: Government Printing Office, 1866. Online University of Pittsburgh Library System. 28 Feb. 2009. Web. 20 March 2014.

■ "The One Man Power vs. Congress"

Date: October 2, 1866
Author: Charles Sumner
Genre: address

Summary Overview

After the assassination of Abraham Lincoln, Andrew Johnson became president and oversaw Reconstruction in the South. Unlike many Republicans in Congress, President Johnson was in favor of loosening restrictions on former Confederate states and pushed to quickly return them to the Union. Republican legislators, such as Charles Sumner of Massachusetts, felt that Johnson had overstepped the authority of his office by involving himself in state constitutions of the former Confederacy and in federal legislation governing Reconstruction. They also felt that he was undoing the hard, bloody work of the Civil War by allowing increased participation from Southern states in national government before those states had proven themselves to be supportive of Republican demands, such as citizenship rights for former slaves.

President Johnson came into conflict with the Republican-led legislature over many issues, and Charles Sumner articulated a few of these in an 1866 address. Johnson directed the states of the former Confederacy to gather conventions and hold elections; when they did so, many states elected men who had been leaders of the Confederacy. Many of these states also passed harsh "Black codes" that stripped free African Americans of their rights. Charles Sumner foresaw disastrous consequences in Johnson's haste to allow Southern states back into national government so quickly.

Defining Moment

When Charles Sumner addressed the Music Hall in Boston in 1866, Andrew Johnson had been president for a year and a half, and his handling of the readmission to the Union of the states of the former Confederacy had set him squarely at odds with Republicans in Congress. Johnson issued a series of proclamations after the war instructing Southern states to hold elections and reconstitute their state governments. When these elections returned federal legislators, who were former leaders of the Confederacy, to power and states passed harsh laws to restrict the rights of former slaves, Congress refused to allow these Southern delegates to take office and drafted legislation that would override the actions of Southern state governments. Johnson vetoed this legislation, and Congress overrode his veto. This established a pattern of antagonism that lasted throughout Johnson's presidency, resulting in his impeachment in the House of Representatives in 1868. He was narrowly acquitted by the Senate.

Johnson opposed the Fourteenth Amendment, which granted citizenship rights to "all persons born or naturalized in the United States," saying he believed that voting rights and requirements should be set up by individual states. Since the executive branch has no formal role in the ratification of constitutional amendments, his opposition was particularly galling to members of Congress. Johnson was willing to allow the return of Southern states to full political power without requiring the sweeping changes that most Northern Republicans demanded. Though at first it seemed that Johnson's lenient attitude toward the South would help the former Confederacy accept their defeat and implement progressive Reconstruction laws, it had the opposite effect, emboldening Southern states to enact laws restricting the movement of former slaves, allowing them to be arrested with little cause, and permitting them to be rented to white landowners. It was a far cry from the equal rights and full citizenship demanded by Radical Republicans in Congress, and it seemed that Johnson's conciliatory positions would undo the progress made, at great cost, during the Civil War. Johnson's unwillingness to force the South to accept these changes enraged Republicans like Charles Sumner, who believed that Johnson was greatly overstepping his authority by involving himself in legislation. When Johnson refused to allow the Freedmen's Bureau to continue its work assisting former slaves in the South and also vetoed the Civil Rights Act of 1866, even moderate Republicans broke with the president. The dislike was mutual. In 1866, Johnson gave a speech accusing several Republican senators, Sumner among them, of plotting his assassination and of being enemies of the Union.

Sumner's "The One Man Power vs. Congress" speech was given just one month before the pivotal election of 1866. Johnson was vigorously campaigning for Democrats and the few Republicans who still seemed to favor his policies, and Sumner embarked on a speaking tour to demand that the president leave the crafting of legislation to Congress. Speeches such as this one achieved their goal. Support for Johnson and his conciliatory attitude toward the former Confederacy gave way to widespread Republican control of Congress.

Author Biography

Charles Sumner was born on January 6, 1811, in Boston, Massachusetts. He was a lifelong abolitionist. Sumner was elected senator from Massachusetts in 1851, and he is perhaps best known for being beaten nearly to death on the floor of the Senate by South Carolina Congressman Preston Brooks in 1856, an act that further inflamed sectional tensions in the run up to the Civil War. Sumner continued to serve in the Senate throughout the war, championing emancipation, allowing black men to serve in the military, and advocating for creation of the Freedmen's Bureau, which would assist former slaves in finding housing and employment. During Reconstruction, Sumner proposed harsh restrictions on the former Confederacy, arguing that by being in a state of rebellion, they had given up their rights under the Constitution and should be treated as territories until they could prove themselves ready to rejoin the Union as states. Sumner continued to serve as a United States senator until his death in 1874.

HISTORICAL DOCUMENT

MR. PRESIDENT, More than a year has passed since I last had the honor of addressing my fellow-citizens of Massachusetts. I then dwelt on what seemed the proper policy towards the States recently in rebel lion, insisting that it was our duty, while renouncing Indemnity for the past, to obtain at least Security for the future; and this security, I maintained, could be found only in exclusion of ex-Rebels from political power, and in irreversible guaranties especially applicable to the national creditor and the national freedman. During intervening months, the country has been agitated by this question, which was perplexed by unexpected difference between the President and Congress. The President insists upon installing ex-Rebels in political power, and sets at nought the claim of guaranties and the idea of security for the future, while he denies to Congress any control over the question, taking it all to himself. Congress asserts control, and endeavors to exclude ex-Rebels from political power and establish guaranties, to the end that there may be security for the future. Meanwhile the States recently in rebellion, with the exception of Tennessee,

are without representation. Thus stands the case.

The two parties are the President, on the one side, and the people of the United States in Congress assembled, on the other side, the first representing the Executive, the second representing the Legislative. It is The One Man Power vs. Congress, Of course, each performs its part in the government; but until now it has always been supposed that the legislative gave law to the executive, and not that the executive gave law to the legislative. This irrational assumption becomes more astonishing, when it is considered that the actual President, besides being the creature of circumstance, is inferior in ability and character, while the House of Representatives is eminent in both respects. A President who has already sunk below any other President, even James Buchanan, madly undertakes to rule a House of Representatives which there is reason to believe is the best that has sat since the formation of the Constitution. Looking at the two parties, we are tempted to exclaim, Such a President dictating to such a Congress! It was said of Gustavus Adolphus, that he drilled the Diet of Sweden to vote or be silent at the word of command; but Andrew Johnson is not Gustavus Adolphus, and the American Congress is not the Diet of Sweden.

The question at issue is one of the vastest ever presented for practical decision, involving the name and weal of the Republic at home and abroad. It is not a military question; it is a question of statesmanship. We are to secure by counsel what was won by war. Failure now will make the war itself a failure; surrender now will undo all our victories. Let the President prevail, and straightway the plighted faith of the Republic will be broken, the national creditor and the national freedman will be sacrificed, the Rebellion itself will flaunt its insulting power, the whole country, in length and breadth, will be disturbed, and the Rebel region will be handed over to misrule and anarchy. Let Congress prevail, and all this will be reversed: the plighted faith of the Republic will be preserved; the national creditor and the national freedman will be protected; the Rebellion itself will be trampled out forever; the whole country, in length and breadth, will be at peace; and the Rebel region, no longer harassed by controversy and degraded by injustice, will enjoy the richest fruits of security and reconciliation. To labor for this cause may well tempt the young and rejoice the old.

And now, to-day, I again protest against any present admission of ex-Rebels to the great partnership of this Republic, and I renew the claim of irreversible guaranties, especially applicable to the national creditor and the national freedman, insisting now, as I did a year ago, that it is our duty, while renouncing Indemnity for the past, to obtain at least Security for the future. At the close of a terrible war, wasting our treasure, murdering our fellow-citizens, filling the land with funerals, maiming and wounding multitudes whom Death had spared, and breaking up the very foundations of peace, our first duty is to provide safeguards for the future. This can be only by provisions, sure, fundamental, and irrepealable, fixing forever the results of the war, the obligations of the Government, and the equal rights of all. Such is the suggestion of common prudence and of self-defense, as well as of common honesty. To this end we must make haste slowly.

States which precipitated themselves out of Congress must not be permitted to precipitate themselves back.

They must not enter the Halls they treasonably deserted, until we have every reasonable assurance of future good conduct. We must not admit them, and then repent our folly. The verses in which the satirist renders the quaint conceit of the old Parliamentary orator, verses revived by Mr. Webster, and on another occasion used by myself, furnish the key to our duty:

"I hear a lion in the lobby roar:

Say, Mr. Speaker, shall we shut the door,

And keep him there? or shall we let him in,

To try if we can turn him out again?"

I am against letting the monster in, until he is no longer terrible in mouth or paw.

But, while holding this ground of prudence, I desire to disclaim every sentiment of vengeance or punishment, and also every thought of delay or procrastination. Here I do not yield to the President, or to any other person. Nobody more anxious than I to see this chasm closed forever.

There is a long way and a short way. There is a long time and a short time. If there be any whose policy is for the longest way or for the longest time, I am not of the number. I am for the shortest way, and also for the shortest time. And I object to the interference of the President, because, whether intentionally or unintentionally, he interposes delay and keeps the chasm open. More than all others, the President, by officious assumptions, has lengthened the way and lengthened the time. Of this there can be no doubt.

From all quarters we learn that after the surrender of Lee the Rebels were ready for any terms, if they could escape with life. They were vanquished, and they knew it. The Rebellion was crushed, and they knew it. They hardly expected to save a small fraction of property. They did not expect to save political power. They were too sensible not to see that participants in rebellion could not pass at once into the co-partnership of government. They made up their minds to exclusion. They were submissive. There was nothing they would not do, even to the extent of enfranchising the freedmen and providing for them homesteads. Had the National Government taken advantage of this plastic condition, it might have stamped Equal Rights upon the whole people, as upon molten wax, while it fixed the immutable conditions of permanent peace. The question of Reconstruction would have been settled before it arose. It is sad to think that this was not done. Perhaps in all history there is no instance of such an opportunity lost. Truly should our country say in penitential supplication, "We have left undone those things which we ought to have done, and we have done those things which we ought not to have done."

Do not take this on my authority. Listen to those on the spot, who have seen with their own eyes. A brave officer of our army writes from Alabama :

> "I believe the mass of the people could have been easily controlled, if none of the excepted classes had received pardon. These classes did not expect anything more than life, and even feared for that. Let me condense the whole subject. At the surrender, the South could have been moulded at will; but it is now as stiff-necked and rebellious as ever."

In the same vein another officer testifies from Texas:

> "There is one thing, however, that is making against the speedy return of quietness, not only in this State, but throughout the entire South, and that is the Reconstruction policy of President Johnson. It is doing more to unsettle this country than people who are not practical observers of its workings have any idea of. Before this policy was made known, the people were prepared to accept anything. They expected to be treated as rebels, their leaders being punished, and the property of others confiscated. But the moment it was made known, all their assurance returned. Rebels have again become

arrogant and exacting; Treason stalks through the land unabashed."

This testimony might be multiplied indefinitely. From city and country, from highway and by-way, there is but one voice. When, therefore, the President, in opprobrius terms, complains of Congress as interposing delay, I reply to him: "No, Sir, it is you, who, by unexpected and most perverse assumption, have put off the glad day of security and reconciliation, so much longed for. It is you who have inaugurated anew that malignant sectionalism, which, so long as it exists, will keep the Union divided in fact, if not in name. Sir, you are the Disunionist."

Glance, if you please, at that Presidential policy so constantly called "my policy" now so vehemently pressed upon the country, and you will find that it pivots on at least two alarming blunders, as can be easily seen : first, in setting up the One Man Power as the source of jurisdiction over this great question; and, secondly, in using the One Man Power for the restoration of Rebels to place and influence, so that good Unionists, whether white or black, are rejected, and the Rebellion itself is revived in the new governments. Each of these assumptions is an enormous blunder. You see that I use a mild term to characterize such a double-headed usurpation.

Pray, Sir, where in the Constitution do you find any sanction of the One Man Power as source of this extraordinary jurisdiction? I had always supposed that the President was the Executive, bound to see the laws faithfully executed, but not empowered to make laws. The Constitution expressly says: "The Executive power shall be vested in a President of the United States of America." But the Legislative power is elsewhere. According to the Constitution, "All Legislative powers herein granted shall be vested in a Congress of the United States, which shall consist of a Senate and House of Representatives." And yet the President has assumed legislative power, even to the extent of making laws and constitutions for States. You all know, that, at the close of the war, when the Rebel States were without lawful governments, he assumed to supply them. In this business of Reconstruction he assumed to determine who should vote, and also to affix conditions for adoption by the conventions. Look, if you please, at the character of this assumption. The President, from the Executive Mansion at Washington, reaches his long executive arm into certain States and dictates constitutions. Surely here is nothing executive; it is not even military. It is legislative, pure and simple, and nothing else. It is an attempt by the One Man Power to do what can be done only by the legislative branch of Government.

GLOSSARY

Gustavus Adolphus: king of Sweden

Mr. Webster: Daniel Webster (1782–1852), senator from Massachusetts

set at nought: count as nothing; disregard

Document Analysis

Charles Sumner was a lifelong advocate of abolition, then full citizenship for African Americans. He fully expected that after the Confederacy was defeated, laws would be passed that would protect newly freed slaves' rights and that the South would be made to accept a diminished role until they had proved themselves able to protect these rights. In his 1866 speech at the Music Hall in Boston, Sumner expressed his shock and disappointment that the president was willing to allow Southern states back into the Union while they returned former Confederate leaders to power and enacted laws that returned freedmen to a state of near-slavery.

Sumner began his speech by pitting the president against Congress: "The President insists upon installing ex-Rebels in political power. . . . Congress endeavors to exclude ex-Rebels from political power." The exclusion of former Confederates is key to "security for the future," in Sumner's opinion. The president, by disregarding the will of Congress in these matters, is disregarding the will of the people. To make matters worse, Sumner argues that the president is outmatched intellectually by Congress. He is not only overstepping his authority, but he is also "inferior in ability and character," while the House of Representatives is "the best that has sat since the formation of the Constitution."

Sumner states his belief that all of the gains made during the war are in imminent danger of being lost. "We are to secure by counsel what was won by war," but if the president is allowed to continue his conciliatory policies toward the South, "the Rebel region will be handed over to misrule and anarchy." If Congress prevails and is allowed to control the pace of Reconstruction, the South will become a model of peace and justice. The primary duty of the government is to protect the rights of former slaves. This can only happen if there are "provisions, sure, fundamental, and irrepealable, fixing forever the results of the war, the obligations of the Government, and the equal rights of all." Southern states can only be allowed back into the Union when they can prove that they will behave themselves and be productive members of government, which to Sumner includes supporting the right of African American men to vote. Once the states of the former Confederacy are allowed back into the Union, they will not be removed again, and the chance that the government has to shape the future of the South and to protect the rights of all its citizens will be gone. Sumner therefore urges caution.

Essential Themes

Debate over the proper way to return Confederate states to the Union began while the war was still being fought. There were those in the South who felt that they should be allowed to rejoin just as they had left. On the other side, men like Charles Sumner believed that states in rebellion had given up their right to participate in national government until they could prove that they were committed to protecting the rights of black citizens. The primary theme of this speech is the outrage that many members of Congress felt at the way the South was being treated by President Johnson, whose leniency toward the former Confederacy had encouraged opposition to full citizenship rights for black men. If allowed to continue his "One Man Power," said Sumner, Johnson would undo the gains made by a painful and protracted war.

—*Bethany Groff, MA*

Bibliography and Additional Reading

Donald, David H. *Charles Sumner and the Coming of the Civil War. 1960.* Naperville: Sourcebooks, 2009. Print.

Foner, Eric. *Reconstruction: America's Unfinished Revolution, 1863–1877.* 1988. New York: Harper, 2002. Print.

Gordon-Reed, Annette. *Andrew Johnson.* New York: Times Books, 2011. Print.

Sumner, Charles. "Charles Sumner on Reconstruction and the South, 1866." *Gilder Lehrman Institute of American History.* Gilder Lehrman Institute of American History, n.d. Web. 22 Jan. 2014.

_____. *The One Man Power vs. Congress! Address of Hon. Charles Sumner, at the Music Hall, Boston, October 2, 1866.* Boston: Wright and Potter, 1866. Internet Archive.

Frederick Douglass: "Reconstruction"

Date: December 1866
Author: Frederick Douglass
Genre: essay

Summary Overview

In the December 1866 edition of *The Atlantic Monthly*, abolitionist and author Frederick Douglass warned that, if left intact, the state governments of the South could allow for re-enslavement of the region's recently freed black population. In the article, Douglass questioned whether the Civil War had really resulted in freedom and liberty for all Americans, including black people. He called upon Congress to pass the Civil Rights Act and the Fourteenth Amendment to the Constitution. However, he also understood that even with federal mandates for equality among African Americans and whites, the federal government's power to enforce the rights of individuals in every state was limited. Douglass, therefore, pushed for empowering African Americans with the right to vote. Such a policy, he said, would enable Southern black men to be involved in and even change the political system, fostering a truly equitable environment for all races within each state.

Defining Moment

In 1841, three years after he escaped slavery via the Underground Railroad, Douglass attended an antislavery meeting on the island of Nantucket, off the coast of Massachusetts. The meeting was hosted by famed abolitionist William Lloyd Garrison, who was so inspired by an impromptu set of comments by Douglass that he recruited the former slave as a lecturer in his American Anti-Slavery Society. Douglass gained national prominence in 1845 when he penned his autobiography, *Narrative of the Life of Frederick Douglass, an American Slave*. That text, which was seen by audiences as not only a highly personal account of a life of slavery, but also as an indictment of this practice, would fuel the fire of the abolitionist movement.

Douglass was unabashed in his goals. He sought a permanent end to slavery in the United States. He also looked to instill in the American political system a framework in which racism would be eradicated and equality among all Americans would be promoted. Over time, Douglas became an international figure—a symbol of the antislavery movement. He developed a reputation as an inspiring orator, giving thousands of speeches to audiences in both the United States and abroad. He was also an accomplished writer, using his pen as a weapon against slavery and racism in the United States. Furthermore, Douglass edited three newspapers, including one of the most prominent black newspapers of the early nineteenth century, the *North Star*.

When the Civil War broke out in 1861, Douglass seized upon it as an opportunity to accomplish his goals. He helped promote the Union cause and even recruited black soldiers to fight on the Union's behalf. His relationship with President Abraham Lincoln helped his pursuits even further. However, Douglass was, by most accounts, a radical, adhering to the notion that all of humanity should be treated equally, while Lincoln was more of a pragmatist. Still, with Lincoln struggling to win reelection in 1864, the president turned to Douglass to help bring more African Americans into the Union Army to help push toward a victory in the war. The two leaders were on decidedly different pages (prior to the war, Lincoln looked for the abolition of slavery within one hundred years, for example), but their eventual friendship proved beneficial to the pursuit of both individuals' ultimate goals.

Still, before and after the Civil War, Douglass faced a daunting reality: White Americans (even a large number of abolitionists) saw black men and women as inferior to whites. After the war, Douglass felt the need to impress upon American political leaders an imperative to prevent the return of slavery and reconstruct the political system in such a way that black people would find themselves on an equal social, economic, and political footing with their white counterparts.

Author Biography

Frederick Augustus Washington Bailey was born a slave in Maryland around February of 1818. In 1838, he escaped to the North, moving to New Bedford, Massachusetts (where he changed his name to Frederick Douglass). He married Anna Murray, a free black woman whom he had met in Maryland and with whom he would have five children. Following the success of his *Narrative of the Life of Frederick Douglass, An American Slave* (1845), Douglass became a prominent orator and writer. He and his family moved to Rochester, New York, where he edited two black newspapers and wrote his second autobiography, *My Bondage and My Freedom* (1855). Some years after the Civil War, he moved to Cedar Hill, an estate in the Washington, DC, neighborhood of Anacostia. In 1881, he published his third autobiography, *Life and Times of Frederick Douglass.* Douglass was a vice presidential candidate for the unsuccessful Equal Rights Party in 1872 and later served as minister and consul to Haiti, among a number of other government appointments in the postwar years. In 1882, his wife Anna died; he remarried, to Helen Pitts, in 1884. Douglas died at Cedar Hill on February 20, 1895.

HISTORICAL DOCUMENT

The assembling of the Second Session of the Thirty-ninth Congress may very properly be made the occasion of a few earnest words on the already much-worn topic of reconstruction.

Seldom has any legislative body been the subject of a solicitude more intense, or of aspirations more sincere and ardent. There are the best of reasons for this profound interest. Questions of vast moment, left undecided by the last session of Congress, must be manfully grappled with by this. No political skirmishing will avail. The occasion demands statesmanship.

Whether the tremendous war so heroically fought and so victoriously ended shall pass into history a miserable failure, barren of permanent results,—a scandalous and shocking waste of blood and treasure,—a strife for empire, as Earl Russell characterized it, of no value to liberty or civilization,—an attempt to re-establish a Union by force, which must be the merest mockery of a Union,—an effort to bring under Federal authority States into which no loyal man from the North may safely enter, and to bring men into the national councils who deliberate with daggers and vote with revolvers, and who do not even conceal their deadly hate of the country that conquered them; or whether, on the other hand, we shall, as the rightful reward of victory over treason, have a solid nation, entirely delivered from all contradictions and social antagonisms, based upon loyalty, liberty, and equality, must be determined one way or the other by the present session of Congress. The last session really did nothing which can be considered final as to these questions. The Civil Rights Bill and the Freedmen's Bureau Bill and the proposed constitutional amendments, with the amendment already adopted and recognized as the law of the land, do not reach the difficulty, and cannot, unless the whole structure of the government is changed from a government by States to something like a despotic central government, with power to control even the municipal regulations of States, and to make them conform to its own despotic will. While there remains such an idea as the right of each State to control its own local affairs,—an idea, by the way, more deeply rooted in the minds of men of all sections of the country than perhaps any one other political idea,—no general assertion of human rights can be of any practical value. To change the character of the government at this point is neither possible nor desirable. All that is necessary to be done is to make the government consistent with itself, and render the rights of the States compatible with the sacred rights of human nature.

The arm of the Federal government is long, but it is far too short to protect the rights of individuals in the interior of distant States. They must have the power to protect themselves, or they will go unprotected, spite of all the laws the Federal Government can put upon the national statute-book.

Slavery, like all other great systems of wrong, founded in the depths of human selfishness, and existing for ages, has not neglected its own conservation. It has steadily exerted an influence upon all around it favorable to its own continuance. And to-day it is so strong that it could exist, not only without law, but even against law. Custom, manners, morals, religion, are all on its side everywhere in the South; and when you add the ignorance and servility of the ex-slave to the intelligence and accustomed authority of the master, you have the conditions, not out of which slavery will again grow, but under which it is impossible for the Federal government to wholly destroy it, unless the Federal government be armed with despotic power, to blot out State authority, and to station a Federal officer at every cross-road. This, of course, cannot be done, and ought not even if it could. The true way and the easiest way is to make our government entirely consistent with itself, and give to every loyal citizen the elective franchise,—a right and power which will be ever present, and will form a wall of fire for his protection.

One of the invaluable compensations of the late Rebellion is the highly instructive disclosure it made of the true source of danger to republican government. Whatever may be tolerated in monarchical and despotic governments, no republic is safe that tolerates a privileged class, or denies to any of its citizens equal rights and equal means to maintain them. What was theory before the war has been made fact by the war.

There is cause to be thankful even for rebellion. It is an impressive teacher, though a stern and terrible one. In both characters it has come to us, and it was perhaps needed in both. It is an instructor never a day before its time, for it comes only when all other means of progress and enlightenment have failed. Whether the oppressed and despairing bondman, no longer able to repress his deep yearnings for manhood, or the tyrant, in his pride and impatience, takes the initiative, and strikes the blow for a firmer hold and a longer lease of oppression, the result is the same,—society is instructed, or may be.

Such are the limitations of the common mind, and so thoroughly engrossing are the cares of common life, that only the few among men can discern through the glitter and dazzle of present prosperity the dark outlines of approaching disasters, even though they may have

come up to our very gates, and are already within striking distance. The yawning seam and corroded bolt conceal their defects from the mariner until the storm calls all hands to the pumps. Prophets, indeed, were abundant before the war; but who cares for prophets while their predictions remain unfulfilled, and the calamities of which they tell are masked behind a blinding blaze of national prosperity?

It is asked, said Henry Clay, on a memorable occasion, will slavery never come to an end? That question, said he, was asked fifty years ago, and it has been answered by fifty years of unprecedented prosperity. Spite of the eloquence of the earnest Abolitionists,—poured out against slavery during thirty years,—even they must confess, that, in all the probabilities of the case, that system of barbarism would have continued its horrors far beyond the limits of the nineteenth century but for the Rebellion, and perhaps only have disappeared at last in a fiery conflict, even more fierce and bloody than that which has now been suppressed.

It is no disparagement to truth, that it can only prevail where reason prevails. War begins where reason ends. The thing worse than rebellion is the thing that causes rebellion. What that thing is, we have been taught to our cost. It remains now to be seen whether we have the needed courage to have that cause entirely removed from the Republic. At any rate, to this grand work of national regeneration and entire purification Congress must now address itself, with full purpose that the work shall this time be thoroughly done. The deadly upas, root and branch, leaf and fibre, body and sap, must be utterly destroyed. HisThe country is evidently not in a condition to listen patiently to pleas for postponement, however, plausible, nor will it permit the responsibility to be shifted to other shoulders. Authority and power are here commensurate with the duty imposed. There are no cloudflung shadows to obscure the way. Truth shines with brighter light and intenser heat at every moment, and a country torn and rent and bleeding implores relief from its distress and agony. If time was at first needed, Congress has now had time. All the requisite materials from which to form an intelligent judgment are now before it. Whether its members look at the origin, the progress, the termination of the war, or at the mockery of a peace now existing, they will find only one unbroken chain of argument in favor of a radical policy of reconstruction. For the omissions of the last session, some excuses may be allowed. A treacherous President stood in the way; and it can be easily seen how reluctant good men might be to admit an apostasy which involved so much of baseness and ingratitude. It was natural that they should seek to save him by bending to him even when he leaned to the side of error. But all is changed now. Congress knows now that it must go on without his aid, and even against his machinations. The advantage of the present session over the last is immense. Where that investigated, this has the facts. Where that walked by faith, this may walk by sight. Where that halted, this must go forward, and where that failed, this must succeed, giving the country whole measures where that gave us half-measures, merely as a means of saving the elections in a few doubtful districts. That Congress saw what was right, but distrusted the enlightenment of the loyal masses; but what was forborne in distrust of the people must now be done with a full knowledge that the people expect and require it. The members go to Washington fresh from the inspiring presence of the people. In every considerable public meeting, and in almost every conceivable way, whether at court-house, school-house, or cross-roads, in doors and out, the subject has been discussed, and the people have emphatically pronounced in favor of a radical policy. Listening to the doctrines of expediency and compromise with pity, impatience, and disgust, they have everywhere broken into demonstrations of the wildest enthusiasm when a brave word has been spoken in favor of equal rights and impartial suffrage. Radicalism, so far from being odious, is now the popular passport to power. The men most bitterly charged with it go to Congress with the largest majorities, while the timid and doubtful are sent by lean majorities, or else left at home. The strange controversy between the President and Congress, at one time so threatening, is disposed of by the people. The high reconstructive powers which he so confidently, ostentatiously, and haughtily claimed, have been disallowed, denounced, and utterly repudiated; while those claimed by Congress have been confirmed.

Of the spirit and magnitude of the canvass nothing need be said. The appeal was to the people, and the verdict was worthy of the tribunal. Upon an occasion of his own selection, with the advice and approval of his astute Secretary, soon after the members of Congress had returned to their constituents, the President quitted the executive mansion, sandwiched himself between two recognized heroes,—men whom the whole country delighted to honor,—and, with all the advantage which such company could give him, stumped the country from the Atlantic to the Mississippi, advocating everywhere his policy as against that of Congress. It was a strange sight, and perhaps the most disgraceful exhibition ever made by any President; but, as no evil is entirely unmixed, good has come of this, as from many others. Ambitious, unscrupulous, energetic, indefatigable, voluble, and plausible,—a political gladiator, ready for a "set-to" in any crowd,—he is beaten in his own chosen field, and stands to-day before the country as a convicted usurper, a political criminal, guilty of a bold and persistent attempt to possess himself of the legislative powers solemnly secured to Congress by the Constitution. No vindication could be more complete, no condemnation could be more absolute and humiliating. Unless reopened by the sword, as recklessly threatened in some circles, this question is now closed for all time.

Without attempting to settle here the metaphysical and somewhat theological question (about which so much has already been said and written), whether once in the Union means always in the Union,—agreeably to the formula, Once in grace always in grace,—it is obvious to common sense that the rebellious States stand to-day, in point of law, precisely where they stood when, exhausted, beaten, conquered, they fell powerless at the feet of Federal authority. Their State governments were overthrown, and the lives and property of the leaders of the Rebellion were forfeited. In reconstructing the institutions of these shattered and overthrown States, Congress should begin with a clean slate, and make clean work of it. Let there be no hesitation. It would be a cowardly deference to a defeated and treacherous President, if any account were made of the illegitimate, one-sided, sham governments hurried into existence for a malign purpose in the absence of Congress. These pretended governments, which were never submitted to the people, and from participation in which four millions of the loyal people were excluded by Presidential order, should now be treated according to their true character, as shams and impositions, and supplanted by true and legitimate governments, in the formation of which loyal men, black and white, shall participate.

It is not, however, within the scope of this paper to point out the precise steps to be taken, and the means to be employed. The people are less concerned about these than the grand end to be attained. They demand such a reconstruction as shall put an end to the present anarchical state of things in the late rebellious States,—where frightful murders and wholesale massacres are perpetrated in the very presence of Federal soldiers. This horrible business they require shall cease.

They want a reconstruction such as will protect loyal men, black and white, in their persons and property; such a one as will cause Northern industry, Northern capital, and Northern civilization to flow into the South, and make a man from New England as much at home in Carolina as elsewhere in the Republic. No Chinese wall can now be tolerated. The South must be opened to the light of law and liberty, and this session of Congress is relied upon to accomplish this important work.

The plain, common-sense way of doing this work, as intimated at the beginning, is simply to establish in the South one law, one government, one administration of justice, one condition to the exercise of the elective franchise, for men of all races and colors alike. This great measure is sought as earnestly by loyal white men as by loyal blacks, and is needed alike by both. Let sound political prescience but take the place of an unreasoning prejudice, and this will be done.

Men denounce the negro for his prominence in this discussion; but it is no fault of his that in peace as in war, that in conquering Rebel armies as in reconstructing the rebellious States, the right of the negro is the true solution of our national troubles. The stern logic of events, which goes directly to the point, disdaining all concern for the color or features of men, has determined the interests of the country as identical with and inseparable from those of the negro.

The policy that emancipated and armed the negro— now seen to have been wise and proper by the dullest— was not certainly more sternly demanded than is now the policy of enfranchisement. If with the negro was success in war, and without him failure, so in peace it will be found that the nation must fall or flourish with the negro.

Fortunately, the Constitution of the United States knows no distinction between citizens on account of color. Neither does it know any difference between a citizen of a State and a citizen of the United States. Citizenship evidently includes all the rights of citizens, whether State or national. If the Constitution knows none, it is clearly no part of the duty of a Republican Congress now to institute one. The mistake of the last session was the attempt to do this very thing, by a renunciation of its power to secure political rights to any class of citizens, with the obvious purpose to allow the rebellious States to disfranchise, if they should see fit, their colored citizens. This unfortunate blunder must now be retrieved, and the emasculated citizenship given to the negro supplanted by that contemplated in the Constitution of the United States, which declares that the citizens of each State shall enjoy all the rights and immunities of citizens of the several States,—so that a legal voter in any State shall be a legal voter in all the States.

GLOSSARY

statute book: a book of laws

upas: a small, tropical tree, whose sap is poisonous

Document Analysis

"Reconstruction" provides an illustration of Frederick Douglass's idealism and relative political radicalism. Douglass was consistently an advocate of a simple agenda: equal treatment for all people in the United States, regardless of race. In the article, he calls upon Congress to appreciate the devastation and loss caused by the Civil War and, during the course of rebuilding US institutions, instill within them the mechanisms to prevent the reemergence of slavery and inequality. Without such action, Douglass warns, the war will have been fought in vain.

Douglass's opening in this article is a challenge to Congress. The Civil War, he says, was fought "heroically" in an effort to protect the Union. Much blood was shed, the nation's monetary resources were depleted, and the country was exhausted. After the war, Congress was tasked with rebuilding the country, bringing back into the fold the states that had been defeated, and healing the deep wounds that tore apart American society. However, Douglass argues, in its first session following the war, Congress offered very little with regard to these tasks. Now, he states, Congress must take visible and major action on these issues—failure to do so will mean that the Union's hard-fought victory "shall pass into history a miserable failure."

In Douglass's view, the most pressing task Congress must take up is to foster a culture that empowers each citizen equally. Racism and slavery, he says, are not just matters of public policy (laws that permitted slavery or the violation of nonwhite civil rights, for example); rather, they are born from "the depths of human selfishness." Over time, the law—along with religion and social tradition—evolved to validate them. Congress could pass laws forbidding slavery and the violation of black civil rights, Douglass says, but unless the federal government became a tyranny, wiping away all state rights, Congress could not destroy the desire to mistreat and/or enslave black Americans.

Then again, he says, if Congress gave the same power to every American that only white men had enjoyed—the power to vote and, thereby, protect one's individual interests—the culture of racism in the United States could be diluted and even overridden. The time has come, Douglass argues, for Congress to finally take up this issue. That Congress had stalled its action in the previous session was understandable but regrettable, he argues. After all, President Andrew Johnson had, in 1865, quickly moved to return the secessionist states

to the Union, while Congress was not in session, an action Douglass viewed as "treacherous" and "disgraceful." Congress returned, but did not overrule Johnson for the sake of national unity. Now, Douglass stressed, Congress had a clean slate, all of the information necessary to make a proper decision, and the moral imperative to take action.

To Douglass, how Congress worked to undo Johnson's actions (and undermine the hastily assembled state governments in the former Confederacy) was not his concern. His focus was on one goal: the establishment of a civil society that utilized the full participation of all of its citizens, regardless of race. The Constitution, he says, does not distinguish between a citizen of a state or the nation, nor does it distinguish between races. The governments of the newly reconstructed South, he states, should, therefore, be built upon the voting power of every citizen, each of whom enjoys the same rights under the Constitution.

Essential Themes

Douglass's "Reconstruction" provides an illustration of the famed abolitionist's perspectives as they compared to the political agenda of the post–Civil War federal government. To be sure, even before the war, Douglass was seen as a radical (a designation he accepted) whose only priorities were the complete and global eradication of the practice of slavery and the establishment of the equality of all peoples. During the war, his relationship with President Lincoln gave him an understanding of the risks of a headstrong attack on these issues. Lincoln's careful, pragmatic political approach to defeating slavery was frustrating to Douglass, but in "Reconstruction" (written in the year after Lincoln's assassination), Douglass saw that any heavier approach would have revitalized the rebellion and possibly facilitated a Confederate victory.

With the Union victory complete, however, Douglass saw an opportunity. Lincoln's successor, Johnson, had (in Douglass's opinion) run roughshod over Congress and the democratic process by attempting to quickly reintegrate the former Confederate states into the United States. Congress was now in a better position to create and enforce thoughtful policy that would achieve Douglass's goals without undermining the government or inciting a new rebellion. If Congress failed to do so now, however, then the war that had cost so many lives and resources would have been fought in vain.

Douglass also saw an opportunity to prevent a future rebellion, in addition to ending racism and slavery, through one simple act. Slavery had survived for generations because political systems were instituted to meet the needs of a dominant group of people, who had embraced racism and prejudice; the state governments of the South were no exception to this trend, he felt. Allowing state governments in the former Confederacy to continue to follow the lead of this elite class of white men could facilitate a return to slavery, Douglass said. By passing a single federal law that allowed for all American peoples to vote, the age-old traditions of racism and slavery could be defeated, he argued, and a new and more equitable political order would rise in its place.

—*Michael P. Auerbach, MA*

Bibliography and Additional Reading

"Black History, American History." *The Atlantic*. The Atlantic Monthly, 12 Feb. 1997. Web. 9 Jan. 2014.

Blight, David W. "Frederick Douglass, 1818–1895." *Documenting the American South*. U of North Carolina at Chapel Hill, 2004. Web. 9 Jan. 2014.

_____. *Frederick Douglass' Civil War: Keeping Faith in Jubilee*. Baton Rouge: Louisiana State UP, 1989. Print.

"Douglass Biography." *Frederick Douglass Papers Edition, Institute for American Thought*. Indiana University–Purdue University Indianapolis, n.d. Web. 9 Jan. 2014.

"Lincoln and Douglass Shared Uncommon Bond." *NPR Books*. NPR, 16 Feb. 2009. Web. 9 Jan. 2014.

McFeely, William S. *Frederick Douglass*. New York: Norton, 1995. Print.

Oakes, James. *The Radical and the Republican: Frederick Douglass, Abraham Lincoln, and the Triumph of Antislavery Politics*. New York: Norton, 2008. Print.

COMMUNITIES IN NEED

Descriptions by and about the people most affected by Reconstruction, the freedmen, can make for compelling reading. In some cases these took the form of letters written to members of the newly established Freedmen's Bureau, a federal agency charged with overseeing the progress of freed slaves. Many of the accounts involved complaints or enumerations of problems encountered while individuals and their families came to terms with their new lives, often under the aegis of federal or state authorities. The descriptions range from misbehavior and theft by outsiders—including Union soldiers nominally assigned to the protection of freedmen communities—to the denial of basic rights and other legal provisions that were supposed to have been accorded them. It is not always certain, given the nature of the situation (i.e., government bodies and voluntary groups overseeing complicated, multifaceted programs), that these individuals' complaints were satisfactorily addressed.

In this section we hear from the members of such communities as well as from persons involved in assisting them and from members of the public who had an interest in the subject. One of the clearest examples of a "relief" program instituted under the banner of Reconstruction was a concerted effort to provide educational opportunities to the freedmen and their offspring. Again, the issue of the scope and kind of education to be provided raised itself, and again the approach frequently taken was one that may strike today's reader as unfamiliar (involving, as it did, a blend of vocational training and the "three R's" along with a healthy dose of religious precepts). Overall, a tone of high morality prevailed. When, however, we hear the story from an actual teacher, particularly an African American teacher such as Edmonia Highgate, we can appreciate the reality of the time all the more. Highgate shows us that more was involved than simple pedagogy; there were problems of a life-or-death nature brewing outside the classroom as Southern whites sought to disrupt the effort.

"Sickness and suffering," a commonly used phrase of the nineteenth century, certainly applied to many of these early freedmen's communities—including the oldest and best known of them, Roanoke Island. We hear here more than once about Roanoke and its ills. In truth, many of the "communities" that formed during the Reconstruction era were nothing like Roanoke: they were not planned on idealistic principles but rather emerged on the basis of age-old principles of (free) human movement and economic opportunity. "Forty acres and a mule" was about as high-principled as many of them got. We also include in this section a look at another group, Native Americans, who were affected only indirectly by Reconstruction but whose plight was ultimately bound up with the same federal government as the one addressing the freedmen's concerns and whose own problems and complaints went largely ignored.

■ Letter from Black Soldiers of North Carolina to the Freedmen's Bureau Commissioner

Date: May 1865
Authors: Richard Etheridge and William Benson
Genre: letter

Summary Overview

Roanoke Island, North Carolina, became a haven for freed slaves following the Union Army's occupation in 1862. The Freedmen's Colony was established in May 1863, and by 1865, it housed nearly four thousand former slaves. Though the goal of the settlement was to become a self-sufficient community, many of the working-age men joined the army, and their families relied increasingly on paid work and food from the government, as well as pay that the soldiers were able to send home. William Benson and others brought news to the men serving in the army that their families were being mistreated and not given their proper pay and rations on Roanoke Island. Richard Etheridge wrote a letter, signed also by Benson, detailing the failure of the island's leadership to provide for the freed slaves living there. This letter details the hardships suffered by former slaves on Roanoke Island, particularly those with family members serving in the military.

Defining Moment

On May 22, 1863, the US Department of War issued General Order Number 143, which established the Bureau of Colored Troops. This order opened the Union Army to African American soldiers. Nearly 180,000 free blacks and former slaves served in the Union Army, and they were known as United States Colored Troops. They made up nearly one-tenth of the soldiers in the army by the end of the war. Many of the young men who had fled slavery for the relative safety of the Roanoke Freedmen's Colony enlisted in the "colored" regiments as a way to prove their fitness for freedom and provide for their families.

The Roanoke Freedmen's Colony was established in 1863, after the Union Army occupied the island and freed all the slaves living there. Former slaves from across the South quickly streamed onto Roanoke Island, and the government responded by seizing land and building settlements that were intended to transition to a self-sufficient colony. The government officials in charge of the colony were instructed to provide paid work for the residents until they were able to support themselves. Many former slaves were employed as cooks, cleaners, and laborers for the Union Army. Those who were able to join the army were promised rations for their families. A church was set up in the colony, along with schools and a sawmill.

The Roanoke Freedmen's Colony was supposed to be an example of successful transition from enslaved life to freedom for the many thousands of African Americans freed as a consequence of the war, and whose future was precarious and widely debated. It was one thing to free the slaves, but quite another to find a place for them within the Union. Problems, many of which are outlined in this letter, surfaced quickly at Roanoke. Men and women were not paid for their work, and their food rations were cut. Soldiers stationed on the island were able to steal from the inhabitants with impunity. At the end of the Civil War, the land seized to build the Freedmen's Colony was returned to its original owners. Within two years, the colony was disbanded, and its residents were transported off the island.

This letter illustrates a moment near the end of the Civil War when the Union Army was heavily reliant on African American troops, but was unable or unwilling to fulfill the promises made to their families and other former slaves on Roanoke Island. As slaves were freed throughout the South, the question of how they should be treated, what benefits they should receive, and how these benefits should be distributed continued to vex both the military and civilian government, and corruption and theft were rampant.

Author Biography

Richard Etheridge (spelled "Etheredge" in the letter) and William Benson both served in the Thirty-sixth US Colored Regiment, organized in February 1864 and stationed primarily in Virginia and North Carolina. Little is known about Benson, other than his enlistment in 1863 in the Thirty-seventh US Colored Regiment. He joined the Thirty-sixth after deserting the Thirty-seventh in August 1864.

Etheridge was born a slave in 1842 on Pea Island in the Outer Banks of North Carolina. He was taught by his master to read and write, and he joined the Thirty-sixth US Colored Regiment in 1863. The Thirty-sixth fought well in the September 1864 Battle of New Market Heights, Virginia, and two days later, Etheridge was promoted to sergeant. At the time that he wrote this letter, Etheridge was unmarried, but he had family on Roanoke Island. After the war, he was made the first black commander of the Pea Island Lifesaving Station, not far from where he was born a slave.

HISTORICAL DOCUMENT

Genl We the soldiers of the 36 U.S.Col Regt Humbly petition to you to alter the Affairs at Roanoke Island. We have served in the US Army faithfully and don our duty to our Country, for which we thank God (that we had the opportunity) but at the same time our family's are suffering at Roanoke Island N.C.

1 When we were enlisted in the service we were promised that our wifes and family's should receive rations from goverment. The rations for our wifes and family's have been (and are now cut down) to one half the regular ration. Consequently three or four days out of every ten days, thee have nothing to eat. at the same time our ration's are stolen from the ration house by Mr Streeter the Asst Supt at the Island (and others) and sold while our family's are suffering for some thing to eat.

2nd Mr Steeter the Asst Supt of Negro aff's at Roanoke Island is a througher Cooper head a man who says that he is no part of a Abolitionist. takes no care of the colored people and has no Simpathy with the colored people. A man who kicks our wives and children out of the ration house or commissary, he takes no notice of their actual suffering and sells the rations and allows it to be sold, and our family's suffer for something to eat.

3rd Captn James the Suptn in Charge has been told of these facts and has taken no notice of them. so has Coln Lahaman the Commander in Charge of Roanoke, but no notice is taken of it, because it comes from Contrabands or Freedmen the cause of much suffering is that Captn James has not paid the Colored people for their work for near a year and at the same time cuts the ration's off to one half so the people have neither provisions or money to buy it with. There are men on the Island that have been wounded at Dutch Gap Canal, working there, and some discharged soldiers, men that were wounded in the service of the U.S. Army, and returned home to Roanoke that Cannot get any rations and are not able to work, some soldiers are sick in Hospitals that have never been paid a cent and their familys are suffering and their children going crying without anything to eat.

4th our familys have no protection   the white soldiers break into our houses act as they please steal our chickens rob our gardens and if any one defends their-Selves against them they are taken to the gard house for it. so our familys have no protection when Mr Streeter is here to protect them and will not do it.

5th. Genl we the soldiers of the 36 U.S. Co Troops having familys at Roanoke Island humbly petition you to favour us by removeing Mr Streeter the present Asst Supt at Roanoke Island under Captn James.

Genl perhaps you think the Statements against Mr Streeter too strong, but we can prove them.

Genl order Chaplain Green to Washington to report the true state of things at Roanoke Island. Chaplain Green is an asst Supt at Roanoke Island, with Mr Holland Streeter and he can prove the facts. and there are plenty of white men here that can prove them also, and many more thing's not mentioned   Signed in behalf of humanity

Richard Etheredge

Wm Benson

GLOSSARY

Copperhead: A Northerner who sympathizes with the South

Document Analysis

This letter illustrates the uncertainties faced by former slaves, both those who had joined the Union Army and those who were left behind. The status of freedmen was in flux. Slaves had been declared contraband of war—which reinforced their status as property—then freed, but without full citizenship and uncertain of their rights. Many joined the army not only to provide for their families, but also to prove their fitness for citizenship. The general chaos of war added to the difficulties encountered by freed slaves, as their welfare was dependant on the willingness of military commanders to enforce the very rights that many commanders did not believe they possessed. When unsympathetic and corrupt commanders were placed in leadership positions, such as in Roanoke, the settlers were easily exploited and abused, even those whose relatives were serving in the army.

Etheridge and Benson begin their letter with a restatement of their service to their country and their gratitude for the opportunity, "for which we thank God." Despite this service, their families at Roanoke were suffering. The first charge leveled against the leadership at Roanoke is the violation of the promises made to these men when they enlisted, including that their families would receive rations, which had been cut in half. Furthermore, Etheridge and Benson charge that Holland Streeter, one of the assistant superintendants, was stealing supplies from the storehouses and selling them, while the residents of the colony go hungry "three or four days out of every ten." Streeter's personal politics were relevant to the argument. He, like many others in the Union Army, did not believe in the abolition of slavery, and the soldiers identified him as a "Cooper head," or Copperhead, a Northerner who supported slavery in the interest of ending the war. Horace James, Streeter's supervisor, and Colonel Lahaman (Theodore Lehman of the 103rd Pennsylvania), the commander of the entire island, were unwilling to rein in the flagrant abuse by Streeter and others like him. In the letter, Etheridge and Benson also implicate James for failing to pay former slaves, including sick and wounded soldiers, for their work. However, the petitioners request the removal of Streeter only, whose violations seem to have been particularly egregious.

The physical safety of the Roanoke Colony residents is also of grave concern to Etheridge and Benson. They charge that "our familys have no protection" and that soldiers have stolen their livestock and produce with impunity. If any of the residents defend themselves against the white soldiers, they are imprisoned. Without the protection of sympathetic and effective leadership, the former slaves of the Roanoke Colony were extremely vulnerable.

The letter also shows that there were many people on the island who were sympathetic to the plight of the African Americans and were willing to testify on their behalf. Chaplain Green was identified as assistant superintendant willing to testify against Streeter, and "there are plenty of white men here who can prove them [the facts] also." If the government was unwilling to accept the accusations leveled by black soldiers against white men, there were white men prepared to make the same accusations.

Essential Themes

The primary theme of this letter is the insecurity and vulnerability of former slaves during the Civil War, even the families of those serving in the Union Army. Hundreds of thousands of displaced people poured into army camps and refugee settlements, and how best to provide for them became the subject of heated debate. Roanoke Freedmen's Colony's initial goal was self-sufficiency for the freed African Americans. When most of its men of working age joined the army, their families were promised support, which was unevenly distributed and subject to the whims of corrupt officials. Many white soldiers, resentful that black soldiers received equal pay, felt that additional rations and subsidies to black families, even those who had no other means of support, were unfair. Even government officials debated if rations for freed slaves would make them "lazy" and less likely to work. Black soldiers often went unpaid for months and were thus unable to send wages home to their families; when the residents of the colony moved toward some measure of self-sufficiency, their gardens and livestock were unprotected from theft and their families were subject to violence. The soldiers of the Thirty-sixth US Colored Regiment sought protection for their families during an uncertain and turbulent time.

—*Bethany Groff, MA*

Bibliography and Additional Reading

Bryant, James K. *The 36th Infantry United States Colored Troops in the Civil War: A History and Roster. Jefferson,* NC: McFarland, 2012. Print.

"The Freedmen's Colony on Roanoke Island." *Fort Raleigh, North Carolina*: National Historic Site. National Park Service, US Department of the Interior, n.d. Web. 1 Dec. 2013.

Weidman, Budge. "The Fight for Equal Rights: Black Soldiers in the Civil War." *National Archives.* National Archives and Records Administration, 1997. Web. 28 Nov. 2013.

Wright, David. Fire on the Beach: Recovering the Lost Story of Richard Etheridge and the Pea Island Lifesavers. New York: Oxford UP, 2002. Print.

■ Address of a Convention of Negroes Held in Alexandria, VA

Date: August 1865
Author: Members of a convention of African American citizens of the Commonwealth of Virginia
Genre: address

Summary Overview

Many Southern slaves had been freed through one of the Confiscation Acts or the Emancipation Proclamation. This proclamation initially only affected slaves in the states in rebellion, but was later amended to extend to the entire nation. Many African Americans attempted to join the Union Army prior to the Emancipation Proclamation, but were denied enlistment. In addition to declaring free the slaves of the rebel states, the Emancipation Proclamation granted African Americans permission to join the United States Army to fight on the behalf of the Union. Many African Americans enlisted and fought alongside white Union soldiers. Despite this demonstration of loyalty, African Americans continued to be regarded as second-class citizens after being declared free. Their options were limited, and many were forced to live in squalid conditions. This address outlines the apparent hypocrisy of the decision to allow African Americans the right to enlist in the Army, while denying them basic rights enjoyed by whites. The Thirteenth Amendment was approved by the House of Representatives and the Senate prior to this address, but had yet to be ratified by every state.

Defining Moment

The address illustrates the conditions endured by African Americans following the Emancipation Proclamation and the passage of the Thirteenth Amendment by the House of Representatives and Congress. American citizens and members of Congress of the United States are the intended audience. It calls for action to address the fears and social and economic hardships faced by recently freed African Americans. It is acknowledged that they were effectively freed from slavery, however little else has changed. They still must live among the former slave owners of the South, believed to continue to embrace their racist beliefs. This address suggests that despite the constitutional amendment guaranteeing their freedom, African Americans believed that without greater protection and equal rights they could never truly be free. It highlights the lack of entitlement to protection of African Americans through laws because they did not possess citizen status. They feared revocation of their freedom, either through government intervention, or violent action taken by former participants of the rebellion. Some states had not yet ratified the Thirteenth Amendment, creating a sense of uncertainty. These sentiments, shared by many recently freed African Americans, were later addressed by the Fourteenth and Fifteenth Constitutional Amendments. The Fourteenth Amendment declares all individuals who are born in the United States citizens, regardless of race, thus offering the same protection by laws that white citizens had enjoyed exclusively. The Fifteenth Amendment granted all citizens, including African Americans the right to vote. Although this address did not directly contribute to the passage of these Constitutional Amendments, it clearly demonstrated the need for action beyond abolition, in order to protect African Americans. This address illustrates a government unable to pass legislation fast enough to keep up with a chaotic period of transition and rapid social change from the perspective of African Americans who were directly affected.

Author Biography

The names of the authors of this address are unknown. They were members of a convention of African American citizens of Virginia, who had previously been owned as slave laborers. These individuals, although anonymous, brought to the attention of citizens and Congress the difficulties recently freed African Americans were facing. They also effectively pointed out the hypocrisy of legislative actions that granted African Americans permission to enlist in the Army, while denying them the basic rights of citizenship.

HISTORICAL DOCUMENT

We, the undersigned members of a Convention of colored citizens of the State of Virginia, would respectfully represent that, although we have been held as slaves, and denied all recognition as a constituent of your nationality for almost the entire period of the duration of your Government, and that by your permission we have been denied either home or country, and deprived of the dearest rights of human nature: yet when you and our immediate oppressors met in deadly conflict upon the field of battle—the one to destroy and the other to save your Government and nationality, we, with scarce an exception, in our inmost souls espoused your cause, and watched, and prayed, and waited, and labored for your success.

When the contest waxed long, and the result hung doubtfully, you appealed to us for help, and how well we answered is written in the rosters of the two hundred thousand colored troops now enrolled in your service; and as to our undying devotion to your cause, let the uniform acclamation of escaped prisoners, *"whenever we saw a black face we felt sure of a friend,"* answer.

Well, the war is over, the rebellion is "put down," and we are declared free! Four fifths of our enemies are paroled or amnestied, and the other fifth are being pardoned, and the President has, in his efforts at the reconstruction of the civil government of the States, late in rebellion, left us entirely at the mercy of these subjugated but unconverted rebels, in everything save the privilege of bringing us, our wives and little ones, to the auction block. . . . We know these men—know them well—and we assure you that, with the majority of them, loyalty is only "lip deep," and that their professions of loyalty are used as a cover to the cherished design of getting restored to their former relations with the Federal Government, and then, by all sorts of "unfriendly legislation," to render the freedom you have given us more intolerable than the slavery they intended for us.

We warn you in time that our only safety is in keeping them under Governors of the *military persuasion* until you have so amended the Federal Constitution that it will prohibit the States from making any distinction between citizens on account of race or color. In one word, the only salvation for us besides the power of the Government, is in the possession of the ballot. Give us this, and we will protect ourselves. . . . But, is said we are ignorant. Admit it. Yet who denies we know a traitor from a loyal man, a gentleman from a rowdy, a friend from an enemy? The twelve thousand colored votes of the State of New York sent Governor Seymour home and Reuben E. Fenton to Albany. Did not they know who to vote for? . . . All we ask is an equal chance with the white traitors varnished and japanned with the oath of amnesty. Can you deny us this and still keep faith with us?

We are *"sheep in the midst of wolves,"* and nothing but the military arm of the Government prevents us and all the truly loyal white men from being driven from the land of our birth. Do not then, we beseech you, give to one of these "wayward sisters" the rights they abandoned and forfeited when they rebelled until you have secured our rights by the aforementioned amendment to the Constitution.

Trusting that you will not be deaf to the appeal herein made, nor unmindful of the warnings which the malignity of the rebels are constantly giving you, and that you will rise to the height of being just for the sake of justice, we remain yours for our flag, our country and humanity.

GLOSSARY

Japanned: lacquered or painted, usually black; used figuratively in this context to suggest white traitors are disguising themselves as patriots by taking an oath of amnesty

Document Analysis

This address is an appeal to Congress and citizens of the United States, urging them to recognize the limitations of abolition in the absence of protection, as well as the value of African Americans to the nation. It reminds them of their participation in the war, fighting the rebels on behalf of the Union, and calls Congress and citizens out on their selective views of equality. Conditions are described as only slightly improved from when African Americans were enslaved. A climate of hostility toward former slaves remained, and African Americans were relegated to less than desirable living conditions.

This address was intended to persuade Congress and citizens of the United States to consider taking action to protect recently freed African Americans. It outlined the harsh realities of life as a former slave, while portraying African Americans as patriots, humbly seeking a peaceful solution. Southern states passed laws which echoed many of the restrictions of slavery, called the Black Codes. The address describes the Black Codes as "all sorts of 'unfriendly legislation,' to render the freedom you have given us more intolerable than the slavery they intended for us." The Black Codes did, indeed, seek to maintain white supremacy and perpetuate the economy enjoyed by whites in the South prior to abolition.

The participation of African Americans in the war as part of the Union Army is cited as a demonstration of loyalty, and compared to the actions of the South, described in the address as "wayward sisters" whose "rights they abandoned and forfeited when they rebelled."

Fear for the safety of African Americans is expressed, primarily at the hands of Southern whites who still embrace the rebel cause. Safety of African Americans, the address asserts, cannot be guaranteed unless they are granted citizenship. The appeal goes on to challenge the popular belief among whites that African Americans are ignorant. The address demonstrates that this belief is invalid, illustrating a clear understanding of the hypocrisy evident in restoration efforts that favor the disloyal South to the detriment of the African Americans who remain patriotic in spite of the nation's failure to grant citizenship. The address argues in favor of voting rights for African Americans, defending their knowledge and awareness of circumstances, as well as their ability to judge character. A situation in which African Americans contributed to a poll in the North is cited to this end.

In addition to prompting the audience to recall the rebellion of the South for the Confederate cause, the authors describe the maltreatment African Americans continue to endure from former rebels. The rebels are portrayed as untrustworthy and dangerous as long as there are no laws that protect African Americans.

The address could be considered ahead of its time, as it calls for legislation that would come to fruition many years later.

Essential Themes

Of the themes in this address, of greatest importance may be the early recognition of African Americans that citizenship status and voting rights would be essential if the Thirteenth Amendment were to have any social significance. This address was made in August of 1865, the year following the Emancipation Proclamation and only months after the Thirteenth Amendment was passed by the Senate and House of Representatives. Some states had not even yet ratified the amendment. Despite its prematurity, this address implores Congress to consider passing laws addressing precisely the rights guaranteed by the Fourteenth Amendment and the Fifteenth Amendment, ratified in 1868 and 1870 respectively.

Another important theme of the address is the loyalty and patriotism of African Americans. Despite the tremendous maltreatment they had suffered as slaves, and the continued hardships they endured as freed people, the African Americans of the South demonstrated loyalty to the nation. Many African Americans served in the Civil War alongside white Union soldiers. Before the Emancipation Proclamation allowed them to enlist, free African Americans expressed interest in fighting the Confederacy, but were denied enlistment. They continued to contribute to the economy of the United States as workers before being granted citizenship and accept representation from a government that denied them voting rights.

The treatment of African Americans following their freedom from slavery is a prominent theme of the address. In addition to being denied rights, such as citizenship, African Americans were treated harshly in the South. Laws, known as 'Black Codes,' restricted the rights of African Americans and dictated where they could live and work. They also allowed whites to enter into binding contracts with African Americans, in which African Americans agreed to a level of servitude that had much in common with slavery. Vagrancy laws essentially permitted slavery by defining the unemployed African American as a "vagrant" and punishing this vagrancy with a period of unpaid labor.

—Jennifer D. Henry, MEd

Bibliography and Additional Reading

"Address of a Convention of Negroes Held in Alexandria, Virginia August 1865." *American History from Revolution to Reconstruction and Beyond.* University of Groningen, 2012. Web. 29 Mar. 2014.

"Constitution of the United States: Amendments 11–27." *National Archives.* National Archives and Records Administration. n. d. Web. 29 Mar. 2014.

Hacker, Louis M. and Benjamin Kendrick. *The United States Since 1865.* Rev. ed. New York: F. S. Crofts & Co., 1937. Print.

Kennedy, Stetson. *Jim Crow Guide to the U.S.A.: The Laws, Customs and Etiquette Governing the Conduct of Nonwhites and Other Minorities as Second-Class Citizens.* 2nd ed. Tuscaloosa, AL: University of Alabama Press, 2011. Print.

McConnell, John Preston. *Negroes and their Treatment in Virginia from 1865–1867.* Pulaski, VA: B.D. Smith & Brothers, 1910. Print

"The Southern Black Codes of 1865–66." *Constitutional Rights Foundation: Bill of Right in Action.* Constitutional Rights Foundation. Spring 1999. Web. 29 Mar. 2014.

Schultz, Kevin. *HIST2.* Vol 1. 2nd ed. Boston, MA: Wadsworth, Cengage Learning, 2012. Print.

■ "The Education of the Freedmen"

Date: February 10, 1866
Author: editorial staff of *Harper's Weekly*
Genre: essay

Summary Overview

"The Education of the Freedmen" appeared as an unsigned editorial in the February 10, 1866, edition *Harper's Weekly*, a popular illustrated serial publication printed by Harper & Brothers. It states that the North, recently victorious over the Southern rebellion, has a moral imperative to help former slaves adjust to their new status as American citizens. The essay also lays out a powerful practical argument for educating African Americans and praises the National Freedmen's Relief Association of New York, a charity working to improve the lives of former slaves.

On one level, the editorial is an appeal to support the so-called freedmen's aid movement, the general label given to a loose, overlapping network of charitable agencies dedicated to improving the social status of African Americans in the South. Considering the political climate of the day, though, the piece had a wider message. In praising those who put their private resources toward educating freed slaves, it implicitly supports the very controversial use of the federal government to improve race relations in Southern society, a process often known as Radical Reconstruction.

Defining Moment

On April 9, 1865, mere days before US president Abraham Lincoln was fatally shot, Confederate general Robert E. Lee surrendered to Union forces. A month later, on May 10, 1865, Confederate president Jefferson Davis was captured, thus ending the American Civil War. The ensuing peace was extremely fragile and the future of the nation was uncertain. In particular, there was debate over how the newly defeated Southern states should be treated by the reunited United States.

In the victorious North, there were two main schools of thought about how Reconstruction, as Lincoln called

the process of national reunification, should proceed. Many thought that the governments of the Southern states should be granted authority to continue more or less intact, after swearing loyalty to the US government and vowing never to engage in insurrection again. Others argued that the South should be treated as conquered territory and that Southern governments should not be reinstated without major systemic changes.

The abolition of slavery in the United States at the end of the Civil War complicated the process of Reconstruction. This, along with a series of constitutional amendments, created approximately four million new American citizens, largely concentrated in the former Confederacy, where attitudes toward African Americans were particularly hostile. The newly emancipated African Americans, known as "freedmen," struggled to fit into postwar society. Many citizens in Northern states felt it was the duty of the reunified nation to provide assistance to the freedmen, including housing, health care, and education.

In March 1865, the month before President Lincoln's assassination, the US government affirmed its commitment to helping former slaves by passing the Freedmen's Bureau Act, which mandated that an agency called the Freedmen's Bureau oversee the provision of improved health care, housing, education, and employment opportunities to freed slaves. Andrew Johnson, the centrist Democrat serving as president after Lincoln, rejected a congressional mandate to give the Freedmen's Bureau expanded resources, including military backing, when he vetoed the Second Freedmen's Bureau Act on February 19, 1866. A less radical version of the bill survived another presidential veto in July 1866.

The February 10, 1866, editorial, "The Education of the Freedmen," was published in *Harper's Weekly* just as the Second Freedmen's Bureau Act was being considered. The essay was an effort by the popular publication's editorial staff to raise public awareness of the issue of education among newly freed slaves and to praise those involved with charitable efforts to improve freedmen's education. Given the political context of the time, it was also a way of bolstering support for the federal government's involvement in reforming Southern society, which many Americans called Radical Reconstruction and President Johnson opposed.

Author Biography

"The Education of the Freedmen" was published without an author's name attached to it. Historians typically attribute it to an anonymous author or the editorial staff of *Harper's Weekly*. Exploring the latter attribution is useful, as *Harper's Weekly*, and the company that published it, played an important role in shaping public opinion during the Civil War and Reconstruction.

At the end of the seventeenth century, a Methodist carpenter named Joseph Harper was building a home for a Dutch farmer in Newtown, New York, when he fell in love with the landowner's daughter, Elizabeth Kolyer. The couple married and had four sons who survived childhood. When the eldest, James, became a young adult, he was sent to work for a Methodist-owned publishing house called Paul & Thomas in New York City.

He was soon joined by his brother John. In 1817, the two brothers started their own publishing company, J. & J. Harper, on Dover Street in lower Manhattan. They were joined by their two younger brothers, Joseph Wesley and Fletcher, and in 1833, the company was renamed Harper & Brothers.

In 1850, Harper & Brothers began printing *Harper's Monthly*, based on a newly emerging format of illustrated serial publication. It proved to be such a success that they launched *Harper's Weekly* in 1857. *Harper's Weekly* became famous for its reporting on the events of the Civil War, thoughtful editorials, and artwork by celebrated artists, such as political cartoonist Thomas Nast and painter Winslow Homer. By the end of the Civil War and the beginning of Reconstruction, *Harper's Weekly* was the most popular publication of its kind in the United States.

HISTORICAL DOCUMENT

"The Freedmen," said our martyr President, "are the Wards of the Nation." "Yes," replied Mr. Stanton, "Ward in Chancery." What is our duty to them as their guardians? Clearly, to clothe them if they are naked; to teach them if they are ignorant; to nurse them if they are sick, and to adopt them if they are homeless and motherless. They have been slaves, war made them freedmen, and peace must make them freemen. They must be shielded from unjust laws and unkindly prejudices; they must be instructed in the true principles of social order and democratic government; they must be prepared to take their place by-and-by in the great army of voters as lately they filled up the ranks in the great army of fighters. The superstitions, the vices, the unthriftiness, the loitering and indolent habits which slavery foisted on the whites and blacks alike, who were cursed by its presence in their midst, must be dispelled and supplanted by all the traits and virtues of a truly Christian civilization.

The North, that liberated the slave, has not been remiss in its duty to the freedman. The common school has kept step to the music of the advancing army. Willson's Readers have followed Grant's soldiers everywhere. Many of the colored troops on the march had primers in their boxes and primers in their pockets. They were namesakes, but not of the same family. Charleston had not been captured more than a week before the schools for freedmen and poor whites were opened there. It is proposed now to educate all the negroes and poor whites in the South—as a political necessity; in order that henceforth there may be no other insurrections, the result of ignorance, either on the part of the late slave or that late slaveholder. Ignorance has cost us too much to be suffered to disturb us again. In free countries it is not the intelligent but the ignorant who rebel. Ambitious men could never induce an enlightened people to overthrow a free Government. It was because there were over 600,000 white adults in the slave States, and 4,000,000 of slaves who could neither read nor write, that Davis and Toombs and Slidell had power to raise armies against the nation. Let us prevent all social upheavals in the future by educating all men now.

The National Freedmen's Relief Association of New York—of which Francis George Shaw is President and Joseph B. Collins Treasurer—has been the most active of the agencies in relieving the wants and dispelling the ignorance of the freedman. It has expended during the last four years three quarters of a million of dollars in clothing the naked; in establishing the freedmen on farms; in supplying them with tools; in founding orphan homes; in distributing school-books and establishing schools. They have over two hundred teachers in the South at this time. They support orphan homes in Florida and South Carolina. They teach ten thousand children, and large numbers of adults. They have instituted industrial schools to educate the negro women to be thrifty housewives. They are continually laboring, in brief, to make the negroes self-reliant and self-supporting. They appeal for additional aid. There are but a thousand teachers for freedmen in all the Southern States; whereas twenty thousand could find immediate employment. The National Relief Association could find pupils for 5,000. It has but 200. As the work is a good and great one, and as the officers of this Society are eminent citizens of New York, we heartily commend their appeal to the generosity of our readers.

GLOSSARY

Davis, Toombs, and Slidell: Jefferson Davis, Robert Toombs, and John Slidell, Confederate officials

Stanton: Edwin M. Stanton, secretary of War under presidents Lincoln and Johnson

Willson's Reader: a standard book of readings for students

Document Analysis

"The Education of the Freedmen" begins with an imagined conversation between Abraham Lincoln, described as "our martyr President," and Edwin Stanton, Lincoln's secretary of war. After Lincoln's assassination, Stanton continued to serve as secretary of war under Andrew Johnson, and his agency was initially put in charge of caring for freed slaves in the South. Stanton frequently disagreed with President Johnson's focus on cooperation with white Southern leaders and spoke out in favor of more radical intervention in race relations in the former Confederate states.

The editorial goes on to argue that it is the duty of the North, which recently "liberated the slave," to help freedmen with clothing, shelter, education, and health care in order to facilitate their assimilation into a new role as citizens of the United States. Just as many African Americans served with honor in the Union military during the Civil War, the editorial insists, they should be helped to "take their place by-and-by in the great army of voters." The editorial then asserts that education is the key to this transformation.

In fact, the editorial contends, education had always been a part of the Union strategy for victory in the South. It observes that common schools, as basic education facilities were called at the time, sprang up in the wake of advancing Union armies. Willson's Readers, the standard tool for teaching literacy, were distributed as the Confederate forces retreated.

The article then takes a very frank tone, stating that the reason for educating newly freed African Americans is very practical and of the utmost political importance. It notes that the elite white Confederate class was able to control Southern politics because they were educated and the slaves and poor whites were not. Providing education to all, it contends, is a prudent way to ensure that the white Confederate minority would never again be able to control Southern politics. Education, it emphasizes, is the best way to prevent future insurrections.

The author then praises the National Freedmen's Relief Association of New York—particularly its senior leaders, the well-known New York philanthropists Francis George Shaw and Joseph Collins—and describes how it spent over $750,000 (equivalent to some $12 million in 2013) to clothe, house, and educate freedmen. The editorial concludes by appealing for support from Harper's Weekly readers to help the organization expand to meet the demand for educational facilities in the South, saying that it employs two hundred teachers, but could use as many as five thousand.

Essential Themes

"The Education of the Freedmen" was an important public appeal for putting resources into educating freedmen in the South. Although it begins with an argument based on moral imperative, it quickly turns to a more practical tone. Namely, it notes that educating the freed population is a way to create informed African American voters to counter the political faction of Southern whites, who might renew their insurrection against the Union.

Education has always been an important theme within the history of slavery and its aftermath in the United States. Before the Civil War, most Southern states barred anyone from teaching slaves basic literacy. Such laws were practical measures to prevent slaves from organizing against or running away from their masters. Despite its illegality, some people did teach slaves to read and write, and clandestine schools for African Americans did exist, scattered throughout the South. However, black literacy rates were very low before the Civil War. Some historians estimate that only about ten percent could read and write at a basic level by the war's end.

A loose network of charitable organizations worked to educate African Americans in the South before, during, and after the Civil War. Perhaps the most important of these in the early days of the struggle was the American Missionary Association, an Albany, New York–based group that established schools for fleeing slaves as the Union forces advanced in the South. After the Civil War and Emancipation, the cause of African American education was joined by groups that were part of the so-called freedmen's aid movement. The National Freedmen's Relief Association of New York, mentioned in the editorial, was one of these.

Given the political climate when "The Education of the Freedmen" was published in February 1866, the editorial was implicitly a call for the US government to put resources into the cause. As the Northern military gradually suppressed the Southern insurrection, Secretary of War Edwin Stanton assumed responsibility for providing social services, including education, to the freedmen. The legislative branch, controlled by the Republican Party, pushed for a more permanent governmental entity to oversee the process, but Democratic President Andrew Johnson resisted the creation and funding of such a federal agency.

In the end, the Freedmen's Bureau was able to operate in the postwar South until it was closed due to lack of political support in 1872. In the time it was open, however, the Freedmen's Bureau and nongovernmental organizations representing the freedmen's aid movement managed to build thousands of schools to educate African Americans in the South. Teaching children during the day and adults at night and Sundays, these schools helped to transform Southern society, just as backers of Radical Reconstruction had hoped.

—*Adam J. Berger, PhD*

Bibliography and Additional Reading

Buchart, Ronald. *Northern Schools, Southern Blacks, and Reconstruction*: Freedmen's Education, 1862–1875. Westport: Greenwood, 1980. Print.

Exman, Eugene. *The House of Harper*. New York: Harper, 1967. Print.

Pohlmann, Marcus and Linda Whisenhunt. *Student's Guide to Landmark Congressional Laws on Civil Rights*. Westport: Greenwood, 2002. Print.

■ Letters from Louisiana

Date: February 8, 1866, and December 17, 1866
Author: Edmonia Highgate
Genre: letter

Summary Overview

Well before President Lincoln's Emancipation Proclamation in 1863 and the end of the Civil War, teachers and activists in both the North and the South began the arduous task of creating educational opportunities and institutions for freed slaves. This effort occurred as part of the legal and institutional changes that came with the end of slavery; for example, the Freedmen's Bureau, a relief agency, provided funds to set up schools and to compensate teachers in the South. Yet this educational project also occurred in spite of the government's woefully inadequate support and the resistance of racist groups who undermined and even terrorized teachers and students attending the new black schools. Edmonia Highgate's letters from Louisiana document a generation's attempt to negotiate this resistance. They also reveal the diversity of the communities where she worked as well as the talent and ambition of the teachers who sought to create a culture of education for freed slaves in a society that nonetheless denied Highgate and her peers equal opportunity.

Defining Moment

President Lincoln's Emancipation Proclamation of 1863, which freed slaves in the Confederacy, initiated a period of astonishing change for both Southerners and Northerners. To be sure, this change did not happen overnight as true freedom for the former slaves proved slow and daunting: the Civil War would not end officially until Confederate troops began to surrender in April of 1865, and in December of the same year, the Thirteenth Amendment to the Constitution abolished the institution of slavery and was formally adopted. In the years following, Congress enacted a series of reforms as part of the period known as Reconstruction (1865-1877). These reforms included the Reconstruction Acts of 1867 and 1868, which gave the vote to freedmen, required new constitutions for the states that had supported the Confederacy, and set up occupied military districts in the South to ensure compliance with the new laws. The Fourteenth Amendment, which acknowledged African Americans' rights to citizenship, was ratified in 1868, followed by the Fifteenth Amendment in 1870, which intended to eradicate racial restrictions to voting (Mjagkij xi-xii).

In addition to these legal reforms, important new educational opportunities emerged for newly freed slaves. During and after the Civil War, Northerners, including many women, traveled to the South to provide food, clothing, and medical care as well as to set up schools for millions of freedpeople. Northern churches and secular humanitarian groups initially sponsored these relief efforts and included the American Missionary Association, the Friends Associations of Philadelphia and New York, and other societies. In 1865, Congress created the Bureau of Refugees, Freedmen, and abandoned Lands, more commonly known as the Freedmen's Bureau, to assist the work begun by churches and other organizations. The Bureau provided over 5 million dollars for freedmen's education, including transporting and compensating teachers and providing educational supplies, buildings, and properties to set up schools. The American Missionary Association (AMA) sponsored its first teacher, Mary S. Peake, in Virginia in September 1861. In 1864, the Association sent Syracuse native Edmonia Highgate to her first teaching post in Norfolk, Virginia. She later taught in Louisiana, and her letters of February 8, 1866, and December 17, 1866, document the astonishing challenges she faced there and her formidable courage and success as a teacher and leader (Sterling 261 and Butchart 1).

Author Biography

Edmonia Goodelle Highgate was the first of six children born to Hannah Francis and Charles Highgate in 1844 in Syracuse, New York. Her mother Hannah was born in Virginia and may have been a slave. Charles Highgate hailed from Pennsylvania and worked as a barber. The Highgates lived in the black community of Syracuse, where Charles worked hard to ensure his children's education. Edmonia graduated with honors from Syracuse High School in 1861, evidently the only African American student in her class. Earning a teaching certificate but barred by racism from teaching in her hometown, she first taught in a black school in Montrose, Pennsylvania. After only term, she was hired as principal of another black school in Binghamton. In January of 1864, Edmonia applied to the American Missionary Association to teach freed slaves in the South. She was accepted and, after a brief period of fundraising for the National Freedmen's Relief Association, began teaching in Norfolk, Virginia. Exhausted after several months, she recuperated in Syracuse and took the opportunity to speak at a prestigious black convention held in the city (Butchart 3-11).

Edmonia returned to teaching in 1865, this time in Darlington, Maryland, where she organized a school and later brought her mother and sister Willela to run it. Once the school was established, Edmonia headed to New Orleans to organize another school for freed slaves and the Louisiana Educational Relief Association, an organization to support the education and general welfare of black people. After racial violence and rioting occurred, Edmonia moved to Lafayette Parish to continue teaching. Although there was violence there as well, she continued undaunted in her work and returned to New Orleans in 1867 to open yet another school. Early in 1868, Edmonia joined her sister Caroline in Mississippi and opened a new school in the town of Enterprise. Other Highgate family members joined the sisters to establish other schools. In 1870, Edmonia returned to the North to raise money for her school. During this time, she spoke at the Massachusetts Anti-Slavery Society and began publishing her letters in various journals. While preparing to return to Mississippi, Edmonia fell in love with a white man named John Henry Vosburg, with whom she became pregnant. Sadly, Vosburg was already married to another woman and betrayed Edmonia, who died from complications related to an abortion in the fall of 1870.

HISTORICAL DOCUMENT

When her brother died, Highgate placed her mother as teacher in Darlington, and she accepted a more rewarding position in New Orleans. That the "men in the rooms" acquiesced to her arrangement and continued to take an interest in her welfare is an indication of the esteem in which she was held. As she explained in her letter to the Reverend Strieby who had been her pastor in Syracuse before becoming an AMA official, New Orleans' schools were supported by the Freedmen's Bureau until a cutback in February 1866.

Reverend M.E. Strieby
February 8, 1866
New Orleans, [Louisiana]

Dear Friend:

The schools of New Orleans have been sustained without aid from northern Associations. But commencing with this month, the government has withdrawn its pecuniary assistance. While the Freedmen's Bureau still retains its supervision i.e. regulation of tuition fees, provision of school houses and school property, yet the colored people must compensate the teachers by making an advance installment of $1.50 per mo. for each child they send. This plan was proposed by Maj. Gen. Howard because the Bureau owes an arrearage on teacher's salaries of four months standing. Consequently the number of teachers in the city which up to Feb'y 1st was 150 has been reduced to twenty-eight. I need scarcely inform you that something like 3000 children have been shut out of our schools because their widowed mothers are "too poor to pay." Their fathers being among the numbers "who made way for Liberty and died."

There is a class mostly Creoles, who have for years, paid an educational tax to support the schools of the whites, themselves deriving no benefit there from. They cannot afford to pay that tax and teachers also. I refer now to the poorer class of Creoles. Of course some of them are wealthy but do not feel in the least identified with the freed men or their interest. Nor need we wonder when we remember that many of them were formerly slaveholders. You know the peculiar institution cared little for the ethnology of its supporters.

The question is this dear sir, can the American Missionary Association pay several teachers under the F. Bureau's supervision? The people's fees will not warrant the salary of even the twenty eight teachers retained. The Fred. Douglass school of which I am principal, numbered 800 pupils, now it has but 127. Board and other expenses are exorbitant here. We still draw rations from the Government yet those who have to wait for so long for their salary are reduced to sad straits. It may perhaps amuse you to know that the building in which I teach was formerly a slave pen but now conveniently fitted up as a graded school.

Very truly yours,

Edmonia G. Highgate

* * *

On July 30, 1866, white rioters attacked white and black Unionists who were holding a constitutional convention in New Orleans. Forty-eight men were killed and 166 wounded. After the riot, Highgate left the city to teach in a country parish some 200 miles away. Her letter is one of the few reports on the black Creoles of rural Louisiana.

Rev. M.E. Strieby
December 17th, 1866
Lafayette Parish, Louisiana

Dear Friend:

After the horrible riot in New Orleans in July I found my health getting impaired, from hospital visiting and excitement so I came here to do what I could and to get stronger corporally. I have a very interesting and constantly growing day school, a night school, and a glorious Sabbath School of near one hundred scholars. The school is under the auspices of the Freedmen's Bureau, yet it is wholly self supporting. The majority of my pupils come from plantations, three, four, and even eight miles distant. So anxious are they to learn that they walk these distances so early in the morning as never to be tardy. Every scholar buys his own book and slate &c. They, with but few exceptions are French Creoles. My little knowledge of French is put in constant use in order to instruct them in our language. They do learn rapidly. A class who did not understand any English came to school last Monday morning and at the close of the week they were reading "easy lessons." The only church of any kind here is Catholic and any of the people that incline to any belief are of the denomination.

There is but little actual want among these freed people. The corn, cotton and sugar crops have been abundant. Most of the men women and larger children are hired by the year "on contract" upon the plantations of their former so called masters. One of the articles of agreements is that the planter shall pay "a five per cent tax" for the education of the children of his laborers. They get on amicably. The adjustment of relation between employer and former slaves would surprise our northern politicians.

Most all of them are trying to buy a home of their own. Many of them own a little land on which they work nights and Sabbaths for themselves. They own cows and horses, besides raising poultry. The great sin of Sabbath breaking I am trying to make them see in its proper light. But they urge so strongly its absolute necessity in order to keep from suffering that I am almost discouraged of convincing them. They are given greatly to the sin of adultry. Out of three hundred I found but three couple legally married. This fault was largely the masters and it has grown upon the people till they cease to see the wickedness of it. There has never been a missionary here to open their eyes. I am doing what I can but my three schools take most of my time and strength. I am trying to carry on an Industrial School on Saturdays, for that I greatly need material. There are some aged ones here to whom I read the bible. But the distances are so great I must always hire conveyances and although I ride horseback I can seldom get a horse. There is more than work for two teachers yet I am all alone.

There has been much opposition to the School. Twice I have been shot at in my room. My night scholars have been shot but none killed. The rebels here threatened to burn down the school and house in which I board before the first month was passed yet they have not materially harmed us. The nearest military protection is two hundred miles distant at New Orleans. Even the F. M. B^{au} agt [Freedmen's Bureau Agent] has been absent for near a

month. But I trust fearlessly in God and am safe. Will you not send me a package of "The Freedmen" for my Sunday School? No matter how old they are for there has never been a Sunday School paper here.

Yours for Christ's poor

Edmonia Highgate

GLOSSARY

Creole: a person who has African and French or Spanish ancestors; also, a language based on French and that uses words from African languages

Frederick Douglass: an escaped slave who became a prominent activist, writer, and speaker for the cause of African American freedom

industrial school: in this context, a school to teach sewing

Northern associations: the American Missionary Association and other private religious and secular organizations that supported the establishment of schools in the South

parish: in Louisiana, a secular territory that corresponds to a county in other states

pecuniary: relating to or consisting of money.

Sabbath: for Christians, Sunday, which is observed as a day of rest and religious observance

slave pen: a holding area where slaves were kept to wait to be sold or transported to other trading locations

Document Analysis

We can best understand Edmonia Highgate's letters of February 8 and December 17, 1866, in the context of her entire career as a distinguished teacher as well as a speaker and writer whose impressive intellect attracted the attention of notable black thinkers. She first wrote to the American Missionary Association (AMA) on January 18, 1864, in a letter describing her desire to teach in the South or southwest, her experience of two-and-a-half years, her age of 20 years, and her good health. In this letter, Highgate also asserts her moral virtue, stating confidently, "I know just what selfdenial, selfdiscipline [sic] and domestic qualifications are needed for the work and modestly trust that with God's help I could labor advantageously in the field for my newly freed brethren" (Sterling 294). The courage, directness, and confidence in these words characterize Highgate's subsequent achievements.

She responded with total dedication to her first teaching assignment in Norfolk, which began in March 1864. There, she reported being moved beyond words by the joy and thirst for knowledge she observed in the newly freed people. By the end of that summer, however, Highgate suffered a breakdown from overwork and returned briefly to recuperate in Syracuse. While home, she was one of only two women to speak at the National Convention of Colored Men, a prestigious meeting attended by leading Black thinkers of the day, including Frederick Douglass, who introduced Highgate's lecture. This impressive accomplishment achieved at only 20 years old reveals Highgate's intellectual talent and ambition, qualities that she exercised in her subsequent work. To raise relief funds for freedmen, she traveled around upstate New York during the remaining months of 1864 and early 1865, earning money by delivering lectures about her experiences (Sterling 294-96).

In March of 1865, she returned under the auspices of the AMA to teach in Darlington, Maryland, but she soon communicated her intention to resign because she considered the position beneath her abilities: "I do not conceive it to be my duty to stay here in the woods and teach thirty four pupils when I have an opportunity of reaching hundreds" (Sterling 297). Highgate gave her position in Maryland to her mother and was then placed by the AMA in New Orleans. The organization's willingness to fulfill this request suggests the leaders' deep respect for this young, ambitious teacher.

Established in New Orleans, Highgate wrote on February 8, 1866, to Reverend Strieby, the family's church pastor in Syracuse and subsequently an AMA official. In this letter, Highgate reports the extreme challenges she faced in teaching the free people who were so desperate for education. With her customary directness, her letter dispenses with niceties and immediately reports the financial straits of the New Orleans schools. The situation was this: the northern missionary and secular humanitarian organizations that supported and staffed other new schools for freedmen in the South had not been supporting New Orleans schools because the Freedmen's Bureau, a government agency established for similar purposes, had done so. Beginning in February, 1866, however, the Freedmen's Bureau could no longer support the New Orleans schools because they had run out of funds and were four months' behind in paying teachers' salaries. As a result, even though the government bureau still supervised the schools by regulating tuition and providing buildings and property, families had to pay an advance installment of $1.50 for each child. This fee, explains Highgate, was impossible for many families, in part because the mothers were widowed after their husbands had died as soldiers in the war. Highgate estimates that due to inability to pay, "something like 3000 children" (297) were barred from attending school, and the number of teachers declined from 150 to 28. These numbers document the severe poverty of many of the freed people as well as the participation and profound sacrifice of the many former slaves who died defending their freedom.

Next, Highgate offers more detail about the financial struggle of, in her words, "a class mostly Creoles" (297). This group, she explains, were forced to pay an educational tax to support schools for whites, "themselves deriving no benefit there from" (297). Thus, the tax was not used to support any schools for the Creole people who paid it, and they were barred from attending the white schools. Moreover, the poorer Creoles were unable to pay both the tax and the advance installment required to send their children to the new schools. Interestingly, Highgate in this explanation distinguishes between the poor Creoles and their wealthy counterparts, whose role in slavery she does not hesitate to criticize when she declares that it is no wonder that the wealthy Creoles do not identify with the freed people at all "when we remember that many of them were formerly slaveholders. You know the peculiar institution cared little for the ethnology of its supporters" (297). In this fascinating statement, Highgate asserts that the institution of slavery did not discriminate on the basis of ethnicity among slaveholders, so that the white holders of power allowed Creoles (who are by definition partly of African ancestry) to own slaves. This is a notable fact given that the system of slavery in the United States was largely created and justified precisely on the basis of race and thus, to a significant degree, on ethnicity as well. In making this distinction, Highgate shows her understanding of the irrational nature of slavery as an institution and offers a rare glimpse of the diverse situations that occurred in practice.

In the final part of this letter, Highgate turns her attention to a specific request, asking whether the AMA might compensate several teachers, under the Freedmen Bureau's supervision. She again underscores the school's dire situation, reporting that her own school's enrollment has declined from 800 to 127, and she mentions the city's high cost of living and the "sad straits" (298) of those teachers who work without a salary. Yet her final sentence changes tone abruptly and reveals her courage and tenacity of spirit when she tells the Reverend that he might be amused to learn that her school building was once a slave pen. With this concluding remark, Highgate achieves several effects: First, she shows that she remains undaunted in the face of the serious financial and other difficulties presented by her teaching assignment. In fact, she celebrates the triumph of using a former slave pen as a schoolhouse: the very edifices of slavery have become the means of liberation. Second, this courageous, triumphant tone serves to support her request: she is not merely complaining but is making the best of a daunting challenge that deserves the attention and support of the American Missionary Association.

The following July in New Orleans, an integrated constitutional convention took place in New Orleans, but white racists began a riot and attacked the attendees, killing 48 and wounding 166 people. Edmonia Highgate decided it would be wise to leave the city, so she went to teach in Lafayette parish, 200 miles away. From there, she wrote again to Reverend Strieby on December 17, this time documenting a rather different situation for her students, but constant courage and dedication on her part (Sterling 298).

Highgate begins the letter by explaining her move from New Orleans to Lafayette Parish, stating that after the riot, "I found my health getting impaired, from hospital visiting and excitement so I came here to do what I could and to get stronger corporally" (298). What Highgate could achieve despite her compromised health was quite impressive, as she reports running essentially three schools, a day school, a night school, and "a glorious Sabbath School of near one hundred scholars" (298). She explains that the Freedman's Bureau supervises but does not fund the school, which is evidently supported by tuition paid by the students and by a tax on plantation owners (see below for explanation). She also later mentions needing cloth so that she might start a fourth "Industrial School" (299) on Saturdays, by which she means a school to teach sewing.

Highgate reports her students in Lafayette Parish to be more fortunate than those she taught in New Orleans. Most of them are "french Creoles" (298) from plantations anywhere from three to eight miles away, and they are so eager to learn that they rise early each morning and are never late. These former slaves are spared the abject poverty of most other freedpeople. Highgate writes that most of the adults and older children work as contract laborers on the plantations of the men who formerly owned them. Particularly interesting is the five-percent tax she mentions, which, according to the labor contracts, plantation owners had to pay for the education of their laborers' children. This partly accounts for the success of Highgate's school, but she also reports abundant corn, cotton, and sugar crops, which have allowed students to purchase their own books and slates; many families own land and livestock and plan to buy their own homes.

Highgate dedicates much of this letter to the cultural differences she must negotiate with her students. We learn that Highgate's own education included at least some French as she reports using it to communicate with her Creole students, who learn English quickly: one class of students with no knowledge of English progressed to an "easy" reader in one week's time. She discovers that the only Christian church in the area is Catholic and that many of her students insist on working on Sundays (which she calls "Sabbath breaking") to survive, frustrating her efforts to convince them otherwise. She also reports her dismay at the people's practice of adultery, by which she means intercourse between unmarried people (as opposed to extramarital intercourse), as she reports finding only three legally married couples out of 300 people. She reports doing what she can, but "there is more than work for two teachers yet I am all alone" (299).

As in her letter from February of the same year, Highgate follows this frank admission with a vivid portrait of her bravery. Despite her students' relative comfort, rebels continue to terrorize them and their teacher. In the final paragraph, Highgate reports that she has received death threats, has been shot at twice, and her night school students have also been shot at. The lack of protection from both the military and the Freedman's Bureau makes the situation all the more dire, but she remains undaunted. She concludes her letter by requesting Sunday school materials for her religious education efforts, once again communicating both the reality of the danger and her intentions to overcome it.

Highgate's letter seems primarily descriptive as she reports basic facts about her students and her ongoing struggle to teach despite the opposition of racist rebels. Nonetheless, her words occasionally reveal valuable context and subtext. When she mentions former slave owners, for example, she refers to them as "so called masters" (298), which represents a pointed effort to challenge the very notion of slave owners' dominance; with this phrase, Highgate rejects the notion that such owners were ever masters of other human beings, despite their legal ownership. This is not simply rhetoric; rather, it represents Highgate's confrontation with the shards of a dehumanizing institution and her determination to subvert its ideology of dominance, which lives on in her students' psyches. We see this confrontation again when she blames "the masters" (299) for the freed slaves' practice of adultery. Here, too, she signals that her task is nothing less than the construction of a new culture.

This level of awareness and ambition distinguishes Highgate as much more than a selfless schoolteacher with remarkable courage. Refusing to settle for the easy stereotype of "strong black woman," Highgate proves that she is a thinker and an activist. This is perhaps most notable in her comment about the amicable relations between the planters and former slaves: "The adjustment of relation between employer and former slaves would surprise our northern politicians" (299). The precise context of this comment is unclear, but Highgate implies that Northern politicians had doubts about the prospects for peaceful adjustment between former slave owners and slaves. With this statement, Highgate claims the right to educate privileged men about the facts on the ground and displays the intellectual prowess that earned her a distinguished reputation as speaker, writer, and teacher in her brief life.

Essential Themes

The learning, ambition, and courage that shine through Edmonia Highgate's letters represent the lives of many African Americans in the nineteenth century. As Butchart claims, the impressive achievement of both Edmonia and her sister Caroline "symbolized a widespread black thirst for knowledge" (3), which began prior to emancipation and increased rapidly. This desire for learning was remarkable given that emancipated people in other cultures frequently chose either to embrace ignorance or to exalt traditional forms of wisdom rather than formal learning (Butchart 2). This desire for learning prompted thousands of African American teachers, even before the end of the Civil War, to travel to the South to aid the freed slaves. As Highgate exemplifies, many of these teachers were not mere untrained volunteers but highly educated and qualified teachers, and they often endured financial and other hardships, including acts of terror.

It is unfortunate that these hardships also reveal betrayal as another central theme in African Americans' lives during this period. Highgate's letters show that, despite the legal progress that occurred with the Emancipation Proclamation and subsequent constitutional amendments, the government did not establish sufficient services for its newly freed people. The Freedmen's Bureau was a step in the right direction but proved inadequate for the task at hand and eventually lost its funding. Worse, when African Americans persisted despite lack of resources and set up their own schools, partly with the help of charitable organiza-

tions, white racists attempted to destroy their efforts and, in some cases, their lives. This attempt to undermine the building of new lives would endure long after Reconstruction as Jim Crow laws were established to maintain segregation and inequality. In these ways, Edmonia Highgate's life and her death, which occurred as a result of her white lover's betrayal, emerge as a powerful symbol of the social and political victories and losses of African Americans during and after Reconstruction

Ashleigh Imus, Ph.D.

Bibliography and Additional Reading

Butchart, Ronald E. "Edmonia G. and Caroline V. Highgate: *Black Teachers, Freed Slaves, and the Betrayal of Black Hearts.*" *Portraits of African American Life Since 1865.* Edited by Nina Mjagkij. Wilmington: Scholarly Resources, 2003. Print.

Butchart, Ronald E. *Schooling the Freed People: Teaching, Learning, and the Struggle for Black Freedom, 1861-1876.* Chapel Hill: U of North Carolina P, 2010. Print.

Clark Hine, Darlene and Kathleen Thompson. *A Shining Thread of Hope: The History of Black Women in America.* New York: Broadway Books, 1998. Print.

Enoch, Jessica. *Refiguring Rhetorical Education: Women Teaching African American, Native American, and Chicano/a Students, 1865-1911.* Carbondale: Southern Illinois UP, 2008. Print.

Hodges, Graham Russell, ed. *African American History and Culture.* New York: Garland, 1998. Print.

Mjagkij, Nina. "Introduction." *Portraits of African American Life Since 1865.* Edited by Nina Mjagkij. Wilmington: Scholarly Resources, 2003. Print.

Sterling, Dorothy, ed. *We Are Your Sisters: Black Women in the Nineteenth Century.* New York: Norton, 1984. Print.

Sernett, Milton C. *North Star Country: Upstate New York and the Crusade for African American Freedom.* Syracuse: Syracuse UP, 2002. Print.

■ Letter from Roanoke Island

Date: June 13, 1866
Author: Sarah P. Freeman
Genre: letter

Summary Overview

After the Roanoke Island Freedmen's Colony was established on Roanoke Island, North Carolina, in 1863 and became a haven for former slaves, missionaries from throughout the Union were sent to help the refugees there. By 1865, the colony housed nearly four thousand former slaves. Many of its residents were sick or injured, and those men of working age had joined the Union Army. After the end of the Civil War, property taken to establish the colony was returned to its owners, and the three forts on the island were disbanded, leaving the residents of the colony without protection. Sarah P. Freeman, a missionary from Maine, was one of several who stayed on the island after the war to try to help the people still living there, particularly the aged, ill, and orphaned, of which there were many. Her letter—published in the *National Freedman* on July 15, 1866, and written the previous month—outlines the struggles of the missionaries, who worked to provide the refugees with food, shelter, and education, as well as the confusion and uncertainty that followed the war for those who had been freed by it. Whether former slaves stayed on the island or left to find work elsewhere, they faced constant challenges to their lives and livelihoods.

Defining Moment

The Roanoke Freedmen's Colony was established in 1863 after the Union Army occupied the island, an important strategic location, and freed the slaves living there. Former slaves from throughout the South soon joined the population of Roanoke, and the government responded by seizing land and building settlements that were intended to transition into a self-sufficient colony. The government officials in charge of the colony were instructed to provide paid work for the residents un-

til they were able to support themselves. Many former slaves were employed as cooks, cleaners, and laborers for the Union Army. Those who were able to join the army were promised rations for their families. A church was established in the colony, along with schools and a sawmill.

Although the colony was supervised by an army chaplain, the Reverend Horace James, and initially administered as a military contraband camp, most of the daily care of its residents was provided by men and women supported by the American Missionary Association and the National Freedman's Relief Association (NFRA). One of the first relief workers to arrive at the island was Elizabeth James, a cousin of Rev. James and an experienced educator. Others followed, with more than twenty-five missionaries serving the colony in the three short years it was active. Like Sarah P. Freeman, many of those workers were from New England and wrote letters to the agencies that sponsored them, providing valuable information about the state of the colony.

At the end of the Civil War, the Union Army presence on Roanoke Island was removed, its forts disbanded, and the land on which the colony was built returned to its owners. Some relief agencies negotiated to purchase parcels of land from their former owners, but this effort was largely unsuccessful. Many former slaves returned to an uncertain future on the mainland, but some were unable or unwilling to do so, and relief work continued under dangerous conditions. The situation on the island, which had deteriorated quickly in the last year of the war, became critical. Food was in very short supply, disease was rampant, and the residents of the island were vulnerable to violence and exploitation. Many were afraid to leave the island, despite the deplorable conditions, because they had nowhere to go and did not believe that they could find work.

Freeman's letter illustrates the crisis faced by former slaves on Roanoke Island and also describes the uncertainty and danger they faced if they left the island. Freeman was one of many relief workers who stayed on after the war and tried to help this vulnerable population, but she and her colleagues were unable to prevent the demise of the colony and the suffering of its residents.

Author Biography

Sarah P. Freeman was a widow from Maine, the sister of a prominent South Freeport congregational minister. At about seventy years old, she was older than most of the other relief workers when she came to the Roanoke Freedmen's Colony with her daughter as a volunteer for the National Freedman's Relief Association. Freeman was an energetic and organized woman who made significant contributions to the colony. Like many NFRA volunteers, Freeman was primarily interested in the vocational and occupational, rather than religious, training of the colony residents. She was instrumental in founding a vocational school for women to learn quilting and straw braiding, along with sewing and knitting. In addition, Freeman wrote many letters to the National Freedman, the journal of the NFRA, beginning in 1864. These letters, many of which were published, shed light on life in the Roanoke Freedmen's Colony and the needs of its residents.

HISTORICAL DOCUMENT

Roanoke Island, N.C.
June 13, 1866

Dear Sir:—I find there is a great amount of sickness and suffering, which, I think, is the result of the scarcity of food. At one time, during my absence, so nearly did they approach to starvation, in consequence of not being able to get supplies here, that our ladies, besides giving all that they could spare from family stores, were obliged to give out damaged food, which I purchased for our pigs before I left. This the people cooked and ate, to save life.

Is it any wonder that sickness follows? Whose fault is this? Surely not the fault of any one here, for there was no means of transportation to bring food to the island till a boat came down to transport goods from a steamer which was wrecked on the coast. This was seized by our kind-hearted assistant superintendent, Capt. Goslin, and dispatched to Newbern for stores, but owing to a very violent storm, it was gone two long weeks, being eight days on her passage back, and obliged to be lightened by throwing overboard a part of her stores.

During this terrible time, the passengers of the ill-fated steamer, about sixty in number, among whom were the wife and children of the rebel Gen. Price, the private Secretary of Maximilian, and other celebrities, on their way to Mexico, arrived on the island, and having money, could procure food. A boat could also be sent to take them on their way, and every attention shown them. This was as it should be. But should these poor oppressed people, to whom our Government has pledged protection and aid, be left to perish?

Some may say they should leave the island, go into the interior and find employment.

They have been trying the experiment to some extent; but many who have not quite confidence enough yet in their former owners, have left their families, and been out to work, and look for a home for their families.

I have been collecting facts from some with whom I am well acquainted, and whom I advised last winter to go out and see what they could do. I will give a few of them. Kinohen Rennick, a house carpenter (whom the N.Y.N.F.R. Association employed in building industrial school and store, a smart man of middle age, having a family to support), left the island the 11th of February, has worked to the mount of $100 been paid only $15 in money, and was obliged to leave in debt, was called upon to pay poll tax of $1.50, and when he inquired what it was for, was told that it was for his freedom.

John Mills, without family, left at the same time, and has made on an average 4,000 shingles per week, which, at the stipulated price for manufacturing, amounts to $16 per week, and at his settlement, a few days since, found $10 due him, and that he could not get, and was obliged to work his passage to the island.

Alphonso Lenox, a smart young man, who served as a private during the war, went into Murden [Martin?]

County and engaged to work for fifty cents per day and found, during the days that he work; but on the Sabbath, he must either work or find himself; chose to do the latter; but after working two weeks found that it cost him nearly as much to keep him over the Sabbath as he could earn during the week, and concluded to return to the island. Employers keep supply stores, from which they pay their employees, selling them corn meal for $1.80 per bushel, when plenty can be bought in the vicinity with cash for ninety cents.

These facts speak for themselves.

In view of them, is it any wonder that the people hesitate about taking their families into the country?

One more case. Nelson Perkins went a few miles beyond Elizabeth City, engaged work, sent for his family, and got them nicely settled; but, while pursuing peacefully his avocation, was shot down in cold blood; reason assigned, that some time during the war he was serving as a Federal soldier, on picket line, not far from the place where he was at work. After his death, his family came back again to the island.

This is the second case of murder among those who have gone from the island, and yet nothing, so far as I can learn, has been done with the murderers.

Is it any wonder they hesitate about leaving a place of safety?

I hope the number of teachers for the coming autumn will be greatly increased.

In many places the people are doing all they can to prepare buildings, and sustain their schools.

At Rowell's [Powells] Point, near Currituck Court House, the colored people have built a schoolhouse, and promise to board a teacher, and supply fuel.

At Ben [Trent] River settlement, near Newbern, they have a school-house, and $75 subscribed for support of a teacher. I hope Mr. Pond will see to that when he returns.

There are calls from Hyde County and various other points. Those who go out into the country bring back with them very urgent appeals for teachers.

Say to the people: The harvest is ripe, send laborers.

GLOSSARY

Maximilian: emperor of Mexico, 1864–67

poll tax: a tax on the act of voting, used to discourage underprivileged voters

Document Analysis

Freeman's letter to the *National Freedman*, written in June of 1866 and published the following month, illustrates the hardships faced by former slaves on Roanoke Island and the relief workers who remained behind to assist them after the end of the war. She begins her letter to the *National Freedman* with the most pressing need and goes on to explain that people remaining on Roanoke Island were sick and starving, but were too frightened to leave—and for good reason. She concludes by asking for help in the form of "teachers," who could presumably provide not only educational but also material support.

Freeman's letter begins with an example of how dire the situation had become. She had left the island temporarily and came back to find that "damaged" food purchased for pigs had been eaten by the desperate population. Without the military infrastructure in place, it was nearly impossible to arrange for transportation of goods to the island, though when a steamer carrying wealthy passengers wrecked, they were able to find food and transportation quickly. This injustice outraged Freeman, who asks, "Should these poor oppressed people, to whom our Government has pledged protection and aid, be left to perish?"

Much of the remainder of the letter is a response to those who thought that the residents of the island should simply leave and find work. "I have been collecting facts from some with whom I am well acquainted, and whom I advised last winter to go out and see what they could do," Freeman writes. She catalogues the difficulties faced by the men who had set off from the island to find work. One had been paid only a fraction of what he was owed and returned to the island in debt. Another, who made shingles, was similarly underpaid and had to work off his passage back to the island. Many of these laborers were forced to buy food and supplies from company stores at greatly inflated prices, and one of Freeman's sources reported that it cost him more to feed himself on Sunday than he made in a week.

In addition to economic exploitation, there was the ever-present threat of violence. Freeman provides the example of a man who was murdered because he had served as a soldier in the Union Army near where he was employed. Freeman notes that this was the second such murder. "Is it any wonder they hesitate about leaving a place of safety?" she asks.

Freeman ends her letter with an urgent plea for help. Residents of the island had set up schools and were "doing all they [could] to prepare buildings, and sustain their schools." Teachers were also desperately needed on the mainland, as relief workers and the organizations that sponsored them were often the only resources available to former slaves.

Essential Themes

The primary theme of Freeman's letter is the hardship faced by both the residents of the former Roanoke Freedmen's Colony and those who had chosen to leave the island. Missionaries and relief workers, who were primarily educated women from New England, were forced to beg for supplies and support for a population in crisis. They faced a daunting choice: Fight for the survival of the sick and starving settlements on Roanoke Island, or encourage its residents to find work on the mainland, a prospect that was equally perilous. Though Freeman was clearly devoted to her cause, she was unable to provide for the basic needs of the people in her care and understood the crisis they were in, even as she sought to convince more people to join her. Her letter sheds light on an extremely dangerous and uncertain time for former slaves, even those who had found temporary refuge on Roanoke Island, and illustrates the difficulties faced by those who worked to help this vulnerable population.

—*Bethany Groff, MA*

Bibliography and Additional Reading

Click, Patricia C. *The Roanoke Island Freedmen's Colony*. Patricia C. Click, 2001. Web. 17 Jan. 2014.

_____. *Time Full of Trial: The Roanoke Island Freedmen's Colony, 1862–1867*. Chapel Hill: U of North Carolina P, 2001. Print.

"The Freedmen's Colony on Roanoke Island." National Park Service. US Dept. of the Interior, 4. Jan 2014. Web. 17 Jan. 2014.

Teele, Arthur Earle. "Education of the Negro in North Carolina, 1862–1872." Diss. Cornell U, 1953. Print.

■ The Sad State of Indian Affairs

Date: January 7, 1868; November 23, 1869
Authors: Members of the Indian Peace Commission (1868); Members of the Board of Indian Commissioners (1869)
Genre: government report

Summary Overview

Although both of these documents address concern for the fair treatment of Native American peoples, the two documents are considerably different. The excerpt from the report of the Indian Peace Commission proposes few specific reforms, but simply expresses dismay at the mistreatment of the Indians and the public's general disregard for Indian affairs. This report argues that, to many Americans, government Indian policy is aimed only at obtaining Indian land. The Peace Commission does recommend education of the Indians as a way of promoting peaceful co-existence between Indians and settlers.

The Report of the Board of Indian Commissioners lays out more specific policy proposals, including dealing with the corruption within the Office of Indian Affairs, advancing education, and promoting the allotment of reservation lands into individual land holdings for Indian families. Both documents envision the ultimate assimilation of the American Indians into the general society.

Defining Moment

In the late nineteenth century, the attitudes of many Americans toward the Native Americans began to change. While in the West—that is, in frontier and near frontier areas—there was still fear and mistrust of Indians, in the urban areas of the East, there was a new awareness that the Indians had been mistreated in numerous ways, and that the violence used against them was often unjustified. The Sand Creek Massacre in Colorado in 1864 and the Washita Massacre in the Indian Territory in 1868 both prompted strong outcries among people in the East. A new movement was rising that would eventually be known as the "Friends of the Indian." The Friends of the Indian was not an organization, although there were several organizations pushing for reform of Indian affairs in the post-Civil War era. Rather, the Friends of the Indian was an informal network of individuals who worked to change government policy toward tribal peoples. Although they had the best of intentions, the reformers—who were mostly middle class or wealthy white Americans—and, particularly, the reforms they advocated displayed an ethnocentrism that presumed the best course was assimilation, not co-existence or other alternatives.

For a brief time in the late 1860s and early 1870s, these reformers had some influence with the US government. All of the civilian members of the Indian Peace Commission and all of the men appointed to the Board of Indian Commissioners, were reform-minded individuals, who had previous experience in pushing for change in federal Indian policy. Many scholars have argued that throughout most of the nineteenth century, a kind of generic Protestantism was the "unofficial established religion" in the United States. Thus, these reformers had a strong faith in the significance of Christian missions and believed that converting the Indians to Christianity would be an important step toward assimilation.

In the long run, neither the Indian Peace Commission nor the Board of Indian Commissioners lasted very long; nor did either have much of an impact on Indian affairs. The Indian Peace Commission did succeed in negotiating the Medicine Lodge Treaties with some of the Southern Plains Tribes. Disputes between the Board of Indian Commissioners and the leadership of the Office of Indian Affairs led to the entire original membership of the board resigning in 1873. Bureaucratic inertia within the Office of Indian Affairs, as well as rampant corruption, limited any move toward real reform. Some of the ideas promoted by these reformers were adopted, but had tragic effects. "Allotment in Severalty," the idea of breaking up the reservations into individual homesteads for Indian families and selling land declared "excess" to non-Indian settlers, drastically reduced the amount of land controlled by native peoples.

Author Biography

The collective authors of these two documents are a varied group, but, in general, they represent reformers with an interest in Indian affairs. Congress created the Indian Peace Commission in 1867, headed by Nathaniel G. Taylor (a pro-Union lawyer and congressman from Tennessee), to try to put an end to Indian conflicts in the American West. The legislation creating the commission specifically appointed the four civilian members of the commission, all of whom had some experience in Indian affairs. The commission was also to have military members, who were appointed by President Andrew Johnson. One of these was General William T. Sherman; another was General William S. Harney. Both are remembered, in part, for campaigns against the Indians, and yet both also had an interest in working towards peace.

The Board of Indian Commissioners was created by President Ulysses S. Grant in April 1869. It consisted of nine members, all of whom were Republican men from the North prominent in Indian reform activities and active in their Protestant denominations. The board was to serve without pay, and was to investigate conditions among the Indians and make recommendations to the president on needed reforms.

HISTORICAL DOCUMENT

Report of the Indian Peace Commission

In making treaties it was enjoined on us to remove, if possible, the causes of complaint on the part of the Indians. This would be no easy task. We have done the best we could under the circumstances, but it is now rather late in the day to think of obliterating from the minds of the present generation the remembrance of wrong. Among civilized men, war usually springs from a sense of injustice. The best possible way, then, to avoid war is to do no act of injustice. When we learn that the same rule holds good with Indians, the chief difficulty is removed. But, it is said our wars with them have been almost constant. Have we been uniformly unjust? We answer unhesitatingly, yes! We are aware that the masses of our people have felt kindly toward them, and the legislation in Congress has always been conceived in the best intentions; but it has been erroneous in fact or perverted in execution. Nobody pays any attention to Indian matters. This is a deplorable fact. Members of Congress understand the Negro question, and talk learnedly of finance, and other problems of political economy, but when the progress of settlement reaches the Indian's home, the only question is, "how best to get his lands." When they are obtained the Indian is lost sight of. While our missionary societies and benevolent associations have annually collected thousands of dollars from the charitable, to be sent to Asia and Africa for purposes of civilization, scarcely a dollar is expended or a thought bestowed on the civilization of Indians at our very doors. Is it because the Indians are not worth the effort at civilization? Or is it because our people, who have grown rich in the occupation of their former lands—too often taken by force or procured by fraud—will not contribute? It would be harsh to insinuate that covetous eyes have possibly been set on their remaining possessions, and extermination harbored as a means of accomplishing it. As we know that our legislators and nine-tenths of our people are actuated by no such spirit, would it not be well to so regulate our future conduct in this matter as to exclude the possibility of so unfavorable an inference?

We are aware that it is an easy task to condemn the errors of former times, as well as a very thankless one to criticise those of the present; but the past policy of the government has been so much at variance with our ideas of treating this important subject, that we hope to be indulged in a short allusion to it.

The wave of our population has been from the east to

the west. The Indian was found on the Atlantic seaboard, and thence to the Rocky mountains lived numerous distinct tribes, each speaking a language as incomprehensible to the other as was our language to any of them. As our settlements penetrated the interior, the border came in contact with some Indian tribe. The white and Indian must mingle together and jointly occupy the country, or one of them must abandon it. If they could have lived together, the Indian by this contact would soon have become civilized and war would have been impossible…. What prevented their living together? First. The antipathy of race. Second. The difference of customs and manners arising from their tribal or clannish organization. Third. The difference in language, which, in a great measure, barred intercourse and a proper understanding each of the other's motives and intentions.

Now by educating the children of these tribes in the English language these differences would have disappeared, and civilization would have followed at once. Nothing then would have been left but the antipathy or race, and that too is always softened in the beams of a higher civilization…. To maintain peace with the Indian, let the frontier settler treat him with humanity, and railroad directors see to it that he is not shot down by employees in wanton cruelty. In short, if settlers and railroad men will treat Indians as they would treat white men under similar circumstances, we apprehend but little trouble will exist. They must acquaint themselves with the treaty obligations of the government, and respect them as the highest law in the land. Instead of regarding the Indian as an enemy, let them regard him as a friend, and they will almost surely receive his friendship and esteem. If they will look upon him as an unfortunate human being, deserving their sympathy and care, instead of a wild beast to be feared and detested, then their own hearts have removed the chief danger….

Respectfully submitted:

N.G. Taylor, President,

J.B. Henderson,

W.T. Sherman, Lieut. Gen.,

Wm. S. Harney, Bvt. Maj. Gen.,

John B. Sanborn,

Alfred H. Terry, Bvt. Maj. Gen., S.F. Tappan

C.C. Augur, Bvt. Maj. Gen. U.S.A.,

Commissioners.

Washington City, D.C., January 7, 1868

* * *

Report of the Board of Indian Commissioners
Pittsburg, November 23, 1869

The history of the government's connections with the Indians is a shameful record of broken treaties and unfulfilled promises. The history of the border white man's connection with the Indians is a sickening record of murder, outrage, robbery, and wrongs committed by the former as the rule, and occasional savage outbreaks and unspeakably barbarous acts of retaliation by the latter as the exception….

The testimony of some of our highest military officers of the United States is on record to the effect that, in our Indian wars, almost without exception, the first aggressions have been made by the white man…. In addition to the class of robbers and outlaws who find impunity in their nefarious pursuits upon the frontiers, there is a large class of professedly reputable men who use every means in their power to bring on Indian wars, for the sake of the profit to be realized from the presence of troops and the expenditure of government funds in their midst. They proclaim death to the Indians at all times, in words and publications, making no distinction between the innocent and the guilty….

Paradoxical as it may seem, the white man has been the chief obstacle in the way of Indian civilization. The benevolent measures attempted by the government for their advancement have been almost uniformly thwarted by the agencies employed to carry them out. The soldiers, sent for their protection, too often carried demoralization and disease into their midst. The agent, appointed to be their friend and counselor, business manager, and the almoner of the government bounties, frequently went among them only to enrich himself in the shortest time, at the cost of the Indians, and spent the largest available sum of the government money with the least ostensible beneficial result....

The policy of collecting the Indian tribes upon small reservations...seems to be the best that can be devised.... When upon the reservation they should be taught as soon as possible the advantage of individual ownership of property; and should be given land in severalty as soon as it is desired by any of them, and the tribal relations should be discouraged.... The titles should be inalienable from the family of the holder for at least two or three generations. The civilized tribes now in the Indian territory should be taxed, and made citizens of the United States as soon as possible.

The treaty system should be abandoned, and as soon as any just method can be devised to accomplish it, existing treaties should be abrogated. The legal status of the uncivilized Indians should be that of wards of the government; the duty of the latter being to protect them, to educate them in industry, the arts of civilization, and the principles of Christianity; elevate them to the rights of citizenship, and to sustain and clothe them until they can support themselves.

The payment of money annuities to the Indians should be abandoned, for the reason that such payments encourage idleness and vice, to the injury of those whom it is intended to benefit. Schools should be established, and teachers employed by the government to introduce the English language in every tribe. It is believed that many of the difficulties with Indians occur from misunderstanding as to the meaning and intention of either party. The teachers employed should be nominated by some religious body having a mission nearest to the location of the school. The establishment of Christian missions should be encouraged, and their schools fostered. The pupils should at least receive the rations and clothing they would get if remaining with their families. The religion of our blessed Saviour is believed to be the most effective agent for the civilization of any people....

Respectfully submitted.

Felix R. Brunot, Chairman.

Robert Campbell.

H. S. Lane.

W. E. Dodge.

Nathan Bishop.

John V. Farwell.

Vincent Colyer.

George H. Stuart.

Edward S. Tobey.

GLOSSARY

almoner: someone giving alms or dispensing benefits

antipathy: a feeling of aversion, dislike, or hostility; in this context, (racial) prejudice

border white man: a settler; someone living on the frontier

severalty: individual right of (land) ownership, as against collective ownership

Document Analysis

The 1868 report of the Indian Peace Commission did little in the way of making specific policy recommendations, but pointed to the causes of Indian conflicts and bemoaned the public's lack of concern about Indian affairs. Neither political leaders nor the general public showed much concern for the Indians. Even American churches and missionary groups seemed more interested in overseas efforts than in work among the Native Americans.

The commissioners believed that Indians and whites had to learn to live together peacefully. If the groups peacefully coexisted, it was believed the Indians would be civilized by this contact with white society. Of course, the commissioners viewed this ethnocentrically, and tended to define civilization as learning to live as white Americans did. Three problems are listed that had prevented this peaceful co-mingling: racial "antipathy" or prejudice, cultural differences, and the language barrier. The commissioners further state that, if the Indians had been taught English and educated in schools conducted by the government or by missionaries sanctioned by the government, all of these barriers could have been removed. Moving beyond stereotypes and treating individual Indians as friends is also mentioned. Despite the rather ethnocentric approach, the Commissioners do suggest that peace could be maintained if white settlers and railroad workers treated the Indians fairly, if nothing else. Thus, they reiterate that much of the violence in the West was being caused by the white man's mistreatment of the Indians.

The Board of Indian Commissioners laid down more specific proposals for reform. Like the Peace commissioners, the members of this Board admit that much of the trouble among Indians in the West was caused by whites. As solutions to these problems, the Board recommended several policy proposals, all of which were common among those pushing for reform of Indian affairs in this era. One was confining the Indians to reservations, where the tribal lands should, as soon as possible, be turned into individual allotments for Indian families, thus breaking down the communal bonds that hindered assimilation. The Indians should be considered wards of the government, but at the same time, they should be prepared to eventually receive American citizenship. Payment of cash annuities to the tribes should end, because this led to dependency rather than self-sufficiency. Treaty making should be ended, not only because previous treaties had failed to protect the Indians, but also so that Indians could be brought under the jurisdiction of the laws that applied to all other Americans. Finally, Christian missions and schools among the Indians should be encouraged. Indians generally had little interest in these proposals, but the paternalistic approach of the reformers led them to believe they knew what was best for the Indian better than the natives peoples themselves did.

Essential Themes

One of the most remarkable themes that is present in both of these documents is an admission that much of the Indian conflict in the West was due to mistreatment of the Indians by the government and white settlers. Even when the government had made formal treaties and established reservations, settlers often encroached on the lands that were supposedly "reserved" for the Indians. When native peoples attacked in retaliation against these intrusions, the military was sent to put down the uprising, and warfare was the result.

The members of both of these commissions were aware that regrettable mistakes had been made in the government's dealings with the Indians in the past, with tragic consequences. They genuinely wanted to bring about reforms to prevent recurrence of such tragedies. But their reform ideas were expressed in ethnocentric, paternalistic terms. They believed that the ultimate assimilation of the Indians into the general American society was the only alternative to the literal extinction of the native peoples. But convinced that they had the best interests of the Indians at heart and knew what was best for them, the reformers promoted policies that often had disastrous impact on the Indian's culture and ways of life. Education and allotment in severalty were preeminent examples of this. While many Indian parents wanted their children to learn something about the ways of the American people, they did not realize that, as these educational programs were implemented in the late nineteenth century, the goal would be to break down cultural attachments and traditional ways of life, and to virtually force assimilation on the native pupils. In a similar way, allotting reservation lands into individual homesteads for Indian families was also seen as a way to distance the native people from their tribal communal lifestyles; holding their land as private property was thought to be an incentive that would lead to assimilation. Because reservation lands declared "excess" were open to sale to non-Indians and because many Indians sold their land as soon as they were legally able to do so, allotment resulted in the loss of millions of acres of Indian-held land.

—*Mark S. Joy, PhD*

Bibliography and Additional Reading

Mardock, Robert Winston. *The Reformers and the American Indians*. Columbia: University of Missouri Press, 1971. Print.

Milner, Clyde A. and Floyd A. O'Neil, eds. *The Churchmen and the Western Indians, 1820–1920*. Norman: University of Oklahoma Press, 1985. Print.

Prucha, Francis Paul. *The Great Father: The United States Government and the American Indian*. 2 vols. Lincoln: University of Nebraska Press, 1984. Print.

ACTS OF STATE

In this section we encounter the various legislative acts that were developed to address the needs of the South as a whole and the freedmen in particular. Most of these laws went through fiery trials in the Capitol, as competing voices had their say even while in these early years of Reconstruction the radical Republicans held sway. In the first of the laws (or "bills," as the case may be) examined here, the Freedmen's Bureau is established—at a time when the war had yet to draw to a close. This bureau came to perform a noted role in bringing former slaves into the economic system and the wider sociopolitical arena, doing so by extending federal power at the expense of the states. It was, however, never a model of effective government and suffered from various problems that are discussed here and elsewhere in the book.

The Civil Rights Act of 1866, also discussed here, laid out some basic rights such as economic rights and a provision for equal treatment under the law. The latter provision, of course, is a Constitutional one, but in the 1866 law it is re-stated so as to apply to all persons regardless of race and regardless of prior status (such as having been a slave). The law, moreover, affirms that all persons born in the United States are citizens, regardless of any conditions.

Following the Civil Rights Act came the first and second Reconstruction acts, both of which imposed military controls on the South. These were wide-ranging laws that greatly expanded federal oversight, yet they were enacted, in part, because Southern resistance to the radical Republicans' agenda was already evident. Martial law, in one form or another, seemed the most direct measure to ensure that Reconstruction proceeded. It also prodded the former Confederate states that had not yet been readmitted to the Union to satisfy the requirements—such as ratifying the Fourteenth Amendment.

Political infighting is also on display in the present section, chiefly in the form of an analysis of the articles of impeachment against President Andrew Johnson. Johnson the Democrat was at odds with the Republican-controlled Congress throughout his tenure, and the battle came to a head in early 1868. Although he managed to escape conviction and serve out his term, in the presidential election later in 1868 Johnson saw the presidency fall back in the hands of the Republicans. Ulysses S. Grant succeeded him and went on to face problems of his own.

■ The Freedmen's Bureau Bill

Date: March 3, 1865
Main Authors/Supporters: Senator Charles Sumner (R-MA), Samuel Howe, James McKaye, Robert Owen
Genre: law, legislation

Summary Overview

Even before the fighting of the Civil War ended, Northern leaders began to plan for the postwar reconstruction of the Southern states. One of the biggest questions, of course, was what to do with millions of people who were exiting the condition of slavery. Especially important to many Republicans was preventing a return to a similar situation in which white Southerners dominated black Southerners politically, economically, and socially. While that unhappy result did, in the end, come to pass, before Reconstruction ended, there were many experiments, some at least partially successful, designed to give former slaves political and economic strength and an ability to determine their own future. The Freedmen's Bureau, created by this bill in early 1865, was one such attempt; and by providing economic, and, later, educational opportunities for Southern blacks, it helped lay some of the groundwork for black communities to consolidate and then hold together through the later dark days of Jim Crow and segregation. Therefore, the bill also showed that Reconstruction was not a badly flawed experiment in social change that was doomed to failure; rather, it showed, as historian Eric Foner argues in his influential book *Reconstruction: America's Unfinished Revolution: 1863-1877*, that the period was one, which witnessed remarkable successes and was, therefore, a worthwhile undertaking.

Defining Moment

While the spring of 1864 had seen the Union armies stalled before Atlanta and suffering massive losses in Virginia, by the end of the year, President Abraham Lincoln had been re-elected and the tide of the war was clearly moving in the direction of Northern victory. More thought could now be given to what the South would look like after the war ended. As slaves fled to Union lines throughout the war, Northern generals had to decide, on an individual basis, or at times with some limited direction from Washington, what to do with them. Sometimes, they were put to work on military fortifications, but as the trickle of people turned into a flood, other ideas appeared, such as that suggested by General William T. Sherman in January 1865 to offer 10,000 families plots of land and a mule on South Carolina's Sea Islands.

The Freedmen's Bureau Bill can, therefore, be seen as the latest and most wide-reaching instance of the North trying to determine a solution for how millions of former slaves would fit into a post-Civil War Southern society and economy. Of course, this time, the law was made at the federal level by a Congress dominated by pro-Union Republicans, since many Democrats had obviously left Congress when the war started. Congress was also often influenced by the Radical Republicans, a group who heavily supported deep federal involvement in the South after the war and who wanted to completely remake Southern society. While the bill's authors were not the most extreme of these radicals, they had been involved in the multiple social reform movements of the pre-war decades that spawned from the Second Great Awakening, including abolitionism.

Therefore, as the war appeared to be winding down, they made their recommendation for a postwar organization to aid former slaves—and loyal Southern whites—in a number of ways. Yet, as Eric Foner has pointed out in *Reconstruction*, the bill "reflected the tensions between the laissez-faire and interventionist approaches to the aftermath of emancipation" because, while the Freedmen's Bureau had extensive federal authority to seize and redistribute Southern land, it was also originally designed to last for only one year after the war ended (68–69). The question of the depth and length of Northern and federal commitment to African Americans in the South, therefore, still remained open, even after the Freedman's Bureau Bill seemed to provide a direct avenue for former slaves to become economically viable participants in a new postwar society and economy.

Author Biography

The main authors and supporters of the bill were Radical Republican Senator Charles Sumner of Massachusetts, assisted by the influential abolitionist George Curtis, and the three men who lead the American Freedmen's Inquiry Commission, Samuel Howe, James McKaye, and Robert Owen (Kennedy, Foner 68). The latter organization had been created in 1863, owing to the need for Union forces to determine what to do with thousands of ex-slaves, who were fleeing to Union lines. These men, as Foner notes in *Reconstruction*, also had firsthand experience of such events during the war. They were all strong proponents of the need for drastic and wide-reaching social changes in the South that would provide a solid economic foundation and future for Southern African Americans. However, not even all their ideas, radical for the time, made their way into the bill, let alone came to fruition during the Reconstruction period.

HISTORICAL DOCUMENT

An Act to establish a Bureau for the Relief of Freedmen and Refugees.

Be it enacted by the Senate and House of Representatives of the United States of America in Congress assembled, That there is hereby established in the War Department, to continue during the present war of rebellion, and for one year thereafter, a bureau of refugees, freedmen, and abandoned lands, to which shall be committed, as hereinafter provided, the supervision and management of all abandoned lands, and the control of all subjects relating to refugees and freedmen from rebel states, or from any district of country within the territory embraced in the operations of the army, under such rules and regulations as may be prescribed by the head of the bureau and approved by the President. The said bureau shall be under the management and control of a commissioner to be appointed by the President, by and with the advice and consent of the Senate, whose compensation shall be three thousand dollars per annum, and such number of clerks as may be assigned to him by the Secretary of War, not exceeding one chief clerk, two of the fourth class, two of the third class, and five of the first class. And the commissioner and all persons appointed under this act, shall, before entering upon their duties, take the oath of office prescribed in an act entitled "An act to prescribe an oath of office, and for other purposes," approved July second, eighteen hundred and sixty-two, and the com-missioner and the chief clerk shall, before entering upon their duties, give bonds to the treasurer of the United States, the former in the sum of fifty thousand dollars, and the latter in the sum of ten thousand dollars, conditioned for the faithful discharge of their duties respectively, with securities to be approved as sufficient by the Attorney-General, which bonds shall be filed in the office of the first comptroller of the treasury, to be by him put in suit for the benefit of any injured party upon any breach of the conditions thereof.

SEC. 2. *And be it further enacted,* That the Secretary of War may direct such issues of provisions, clothing, and fuel, as he may deem needful for the immediate and temporary shelter and supply of destitute and suffering refugees and freedmen and their wives and children, under such rules and regulations as he may direct.

SEC. 3. *And be it further enacted,* That the President may, by and with the advice and consent of the Senate, appoint an assistant commissioner for each of the states declared to be in insurrection, not exceeding ten in number, who shall, under the direction of the commissioner, aid in the execution of the provisions of this act; and he shall give a bond to the Treasurer of the United States, in the sum of twenty thousand dollars, in the form and manner prescribed in the first section of this act. Each of said commissioners shall receive an annual salary of two thousand five hundred dollars in full compensation for all his services. And any military officer may be detailed and assigned to duty under this act without increase of pay or allowances. The commissioner shall, before the commencement of each regular session of congress, make full report of his proceedings with exhibits of the state of his accounts to the President, who shall communicate the same to congress, and shall also make special reports whenever required to do so by the President or either house of congress; and the assistant commissioners shall make quarterly reports of their proceedings to the commissioner, and also such other special reports as from time to time may be required.

SEC. 4. *And be it further enacted*, That the commissioner, under the direction of the President, shall have authority to set apart, for the use of loyal refugees and freedmen, such tracts of land within the insurrectionary states as shall have been abandoned, or to which the United States shall have acquired title by confiscation or sale, or otherwise, and to every male citizen, whether refugee or freedmen, as aforesaid, there shall be assigned not more than forty acres of such land, and the person to whom it was so assigned shall be protected in the use and enjoyment of the land for the term of three years at an annual rent not exceeding six per centum upon the value of such land, as it was appraised by the state authorities in the year eighteen hundred and sixty, for the purpose of taxation, and in case no such appraisal can be found, then the rental shall be based upon the estimated value of the land in said year, to be ascertained in such manner as the commissioner may by regulation prescribe. At the end of said term, or at any time during said term, the occupants of any parcels so assigned may purchase the land and receive such title thereto as the United States can convey, upon paying therefor the value of the land, as ascertained and fixed for the purpose of determining the annual rent aforesaid.

And be it further enacted, That all acts and parts of acts inconsistent with the provisions of this act, are hereby repealed.

APPROVED, March 3, 1865.

GLOSSARY

clerk/class: administrative job grades or categories

per annum: per year; annually

per centum: percent

states declared to be in insurrection: Confederate states; insurrectionary states

Document Analysis

While several parts of the bill lay out the usual hierarchies of authority and annual salaries of newly created positions that are contained in any federal bill, the sections of the bill that expand the scope of federal authority are the most intriguing. They were also the most impactful in the history of Reconstruction. Within the Department of War, the bill not only created a new commissioner to head this organization, but also assistant commissioners to direct the bureau's operations in each of the ten states that had seceded from the Union. Therefore, the Republican-led Congress was already attempting to create structures to rebuild the South, evidenced most by the fact that the Bureau would be in place "during the present war of rebellion, and for one year thereafter," so even while the fighting raged on.

Overall, while the bill spoke of giving "provisions, clothing, and fuel" to "loyal refugees and freedmen," and, therefore, also included loyal Southern whites who might need help, the most important aspect of the bill was exactly how it provided for the future of these people, especially the former slaves. Each family would receive up to forty acres of land, at a low annual rental rate of six percent of the land's value, for a length of time that was guaranteed to be three years. After that time had passed, the renters could then purchase the land from the government. Therefore, the federal government was attempting to provide former slaves, and loyal whites as well, with a way to transition from serving a master to being their own individual small farmer.

Had hundreds of thousands of black families been able to use this bill successfully to move into the ranks of small freeholders, it would have been quite a transformation of Southern society. However, the rise of the sharecropping model, in which blacks became trapped in endless cycles of debt; the Democratic resurgence in the South; and the failure of Reconstruction in other respects all combined to prevent such a happy result. Still, in this bill and for a time during Reconstruction in general, the power of the federal government in the South was quite enhanced. For instance, the bill noted that the land to be provided to former slaves and loyal Southern whites was land "as shall have been abandoned, or to which the United States shall have acquired title by confiscation or sale, or otherwise." Essentially, any time a supporter of secession had left his farm or plantation, that land would be deemed "abandoned" and federal power would be expanded to confiscate and redistribute that land. In addition, the "otherwise" option left the door open to the further expansion of that sort of federal power in the future, and as Reconstruction progressed, some Radical Republicans would certainly push for such an expansion. Overall, the bill sought to provide a means of making a living for the millions of former slaves in the South and did so by legislatively expanding the reach and power of the federal government.

Essential Themes

One of the clearest themes in the history of the Freedmen's Bureau Bill was that of whether or not—and how far—to expand federal authority, especially regarding the political, economic, and civil rights of black Southerners. Since the original bill only authorized the Bureau to operate for a year after the end of the war, Congress had to pass the bill again in the early part of 1866. Although Andrew Johnson, who was president by then, vetoed the bill as an unconstitutional expansion of federal authority, his move united both moderate and Radical Republicans, who then passed the extension of

the Bureau over his veto. However, this same debate over the extent of federal involvement in the protection of black economic and civil rights was not resolved in 1866 and continued until enough Northerners decided essentially to abandon Southern African Americans in the Compromise of 1877, which ended Reconstruction and pulled the remaining army forces out of the South.

The Freedmen's Bureau Bill also touched on issues of black agency, meaning the ability of African Americans to shape their own history and to affect the context in which they found themselves. While relatively few African Americans actually obtained land in the South during Reconstruction, the Freedmen's Bureau played a large role in helping former slaves organize politically, protect themselves in court, expand their educational opportunities, and generally attempt to assert their economic and civil rights between 1865 and 1872. For instance, the Bureau founded Howard University in Washington, DC, and Bureau officials were often supportive of Union Leagues, which were political organizations of black Southern Republicans during Reconstruction (Kennedy 144). Therefore, the Freedmen's Bureau often provided an avenue for black Southern voices to be heard. In addition, the pressure that Union generals and politicians felt during the Civil War to do something with the increasing numbers of former slaves who were fleeing to Union lines during the war, as noted above, helped push Northerners to think about possible postwar solutions, including the Freedmen's Bureau. In this way, African Americans "voted with their feet" and did their own part in creating the post-Civil War history of the American South.

—*Kevin Grimm, PhD*

Bibliography and Additional Reading

Foner, Eric. *Reconstruction: America's Unfinished Revolution, 1863–1877*. New York: Harper & Row, 1988. Print.

Kennedy, Robert C. "On This Day: The Freedmen's Bureau." *HarpWeek*. The New York Times Company, 2001. Web. 3 April 2014.

■ Civil Rights Act of 1866

Date: April 9, 1866
Author: Thirty-ninth US Congress
Genre: law, legislation

Summary Overview

The Reconstruction Era in American history was the time when the political, economic, and social systems were rebuilt after the Civil War. A key part of this was the new role to be played by the freed slaves. As the first national civil rights law, the Civil Rights Act of 1866 sought to place African Americans on an equal footing with white Americans. Senator Lyman Trumbull, from Illinois, introduced the initial bill. In its final form, it had passed both houses of Congress by March 1866; was vetoed by President Johnson; and within two weeks, both houses voted to override the veto. Opposition to the bill was two-fold. Some did not believe that the Thirteenth Amendment gave Congress the power to pass a law dealing with affairs within a state, while others were against it because of racial prejudice. This was the first step in attempting to end racial discrimination in the United States.

Defining Moment

In 1863, as the Union forces were moving toward victory on the battlefield, the question of slavery moved to the forefront. The Emancipation Proclamation had freed slaves in the states that made up the Confederacy, but the legislation's post-war validity was uncertain. Various constitutional amendments to end slavery were proposed, with what was to become the Thirteenth Amendment being passed by Congress in January 1865 and ratified by enough states in December 1865. This led to concerns as to how the rights of African Americans might be secured. Since many believed that the Southern states would not grant equal rights to freed slaves, Congress acted to insure to them many of the economic and political rights necessary to be truly equal. Thus, this first civil rights law, although limited in scope, was passed with hopes that it would transform race relations.

At the close of the Civil War, how the Southern states would be re-integrated into the Union was a contentious topic, even within the North. This was one topic on which President Andrew Johnson and Congress strongly disagreed. Thus, when a Civil Rights Act was first proposed and passed in 1865, President Johnson vetoed it. When Sen. Trumbull introduced the bill in January 1866, he and his allies pressed hard to pass it with enough votes to override the anticipated veto. Upon doing this in April, the law became an important symbol. Part of it was incorporated into the Fourteenth Amendment, which specifically gave all citizens the constitutional protection of due process in legal matters as well as equal protection before the law. Many saw the Act to be of such importance that, after the ratification of the Fourteenth Amendment, they passed the law as part of the Enforcement Act of 1870, in order for it to have a stronger Constitutional foundation.

Although initially the Civil Rights Act had some limiting effect upon the actions of those seeking to oppress African Americans, this was soon whittled away by the courts and by terrorist actions of hate groups, such as the Ku Klux Klan. Thus, while the law's sponsors had expectations that it would be a force to move the country in a positive direction, as regarded racial equality, in the end, it was only of limited use in keeping the worst from happening. Although the provision dealing with "real" property was not always observed, this law has been the foundation for the legal barrier to racial and ethnic discrimination in housing and real estate transactions.

Author Biography

The Civil Rights Act of 1866 was passed by the Thirty-ninth Congress of the United States, which ran from March 4, 1865 to March 4, 1867. Although the Thirty-ninth Congress officially began on March 4, it met only until March 14 to organize and then adjourned until December 4, as was the norm at that time. The election for this Congress was the same one in which Abraham Lincoln was elected to his second term as president, and the Republicans outnumbered Democrats by more than three to one in both houses. However,

only a month into the term, Andrew Johnson became president due to Lincoln's assassination. Congress was not called back into a special session, and this was the source of many of the problems between Johnson and the Thirty-ninth and Fortieth Congresses. The sponsor of the bill, Lyman Trumbull, had originally been an anti-slavery Democrat, but had become a Republican.

HISTORICAL DOCUMENT

An Act to protect all Persons in the United States in their Civil Rights, and furnish the Means of their Vindication.

Be it enacted by the Senate and House of Representatives of the United States of America in Congress assembled, That all persons born in the United States and not subject to any foreign power, excluding Indians not taxed, are hereby declared to be citizens of the United States; and such citizens, of every race and color, without regard to any previous condition of slavery or involuntary servitude, except as a punishment for crime whereof the party shall have been duly convicted, shall have the same right, in every State and Territory in the United States, to make and enforce contracts, to sue, be parties, and give evidence, to inherit, purchase, lease, sell, hold, and convey real and personal property, and to full and equal benefit of all laws and proceedings for the security of person and property, as is enjoyed by white citizens, and shall be subject to like punishment, pains, and penalties, and to none other, any law, statute, ordinance, regulation, or custom, to the contrary notwithstanding.

Sec. 2. *And be it further enacted,* That any person who, under color of any law, statute, ordinance, regulation, or custom, shall subject, or cause to be subjected, any inhabitant of any State or Territory to the deprivation of any right secured or protected by this act, or to different punishment, pains, or penalties on account of such person having at any time been held in a condition of slavery or involuntary servitude, except as a punishment for crime whereof the party shall have been duly convicted, or by reason of his color or race, than is prescribed for the punishment of white persons, shall be deemed guilty of a misdemeanor, and, on conviction, shall be punished by fine not exceeding one thousand

dollars, or imprisonment not exceeding one year, or both, in the discretion of the court.

Sec. 3. *And be it further enacted,* That the district courts of the United States, within their respective districts, shall have, exclusively of the courts of the several States, cognizance of all crimes and offences committed against the provisions of this act, and also, concurrently with the circuit courts of the United States, of all causes, civil and criminal, affecting persons who are denied or cannot enforce in the courts or judicial tribunals of the State or locality where they may be any of the rights secured to them by the first section of this act; and if any suit or prosecution, civil or criminal, has been or shall be commenced in any State court, against any such person, for any cause whatsoever, or against any officer, civil or military, or other person, for any arrest or imprisonment, trespasses, or wrongs done or committed by virtue or under color of authority derived from this act or the act establishing a Bureau for the relief of Freedmen and Refugees, and all acts amendatory thereof, or for refusing to do any act upon the ground that it would be inconsistent with this act, such defendant shall have the right to remove such cause for trial to the proper district or circuit court in the manner prescribed by the "Act relating to habeas corpus and regulating judicial proceedings in certain cases," approved March three, eighteen hundred and sixty-three, and all acts amendatory thereof. The jurisdiction in civil and criminal matters hereby conferred on the district and circuit courts of the United States shall be exercised and enforced in conformity with the laws of the United States, so far as such laws are suitable to carry the same into effect; but in all cases where such laws are not adapted to the object, or are deficient in the provisions necessary to furnish suitable remedies and punish offences against law, the common law, as modified and changed by the constitution and statutes of the State wherein the court having jurisdiction of the cause, civil or criminal, is held, so far as the same is not inconsistent with the Constitution and laws of the United States, shall be extended to and govern said courts in the trial and disposition of such cause, and, if of a criminal nature, in the infliction of punishment on the party found guilty.

Sec. 4. *And be it further enacted*, That the district attorneys, marshals, and deputy marshals of the United States, the commissioners appointed by the circuit and territorial courts of the United States, with powers of arresting, imprisoning, or bailing offenders against the laws of the United States, the officers and agents of the Freedmen's Bureau, and every other officer who may be specially empowered by the President of the United States, shall be, and they are hereby, specially authorized and required, at the expense of the United States, to institute proceedings against all and every person who shall violate the provisions of this act, and cause him or them to be arrested and imprisoned, or bailed, as the case may be, for trial before such court of the United States or territorial court as by this act has cognizance of the offence. And with a view to affording reasonable protection to all persons in their constitutional rights of equality before the law, without distinction of race or color, or previous condition of slavery or involuntary servitude, except as a punishment for crime, whereof the party shall have been duly convicted, and to the prompt discharge of the duties of this act, it shall be the duty of the circuit courts of the United States and the superior courts of the Territories of the United States, from time to time, to increase the number of commissioners, so as to afford a speedy and convenient means for the arrest and examination of persons charged with a violation of this act; and such commissioners are hereby authorized and required to exercise and discharge all the powers and duties conferred on them by this act, and the same duties with regard to offences created by this act, as they are authorized by law to exercise with regard to other offences against the laws of the United States.

Sec. 5. *And be it further enacted*, That it shall be the duty of all marshals and deputy marshals to obey and execute all warrants and precepts issued under the provisions of this act, when to them directed; and should any marshal or deputy marshal refuse to receive such warrant or other process when tendered, or to use all proper means diligently to execute the same, he shall, on conviction thereof, be fined in the sum of one thousand dollars, to the use of the person upon whom the accused is alleged to have committed the offense. And the better to enable the said commissioners to execute their duties faithfully and efficiently, in conformity with the Constitution of the United States and the requirements of this act, they are hereby authorized and empowered, within their counties respectively, to appoint, in writing, under their hands, any one or more suitable persons, from time to time, to execute all such warrants and other process as may be issued by them in the lawful performance of their respective duties; and the persons so appointed to execute any warrant or process as aforesaid shall have authority to summon and call to their aid the bystanders or posse comitatus of the proper county, or such portion of the land or naval forces of the United States, or of the militia, as may be necessary to the performance of the duty with which they are charged, and to insure a faithful observance of the clause of the Constitution which prohibits slavery, in conformity with the provisions of this act; and said warrants shall run and be executed by said officers anywhere in the State or Territory within which they are issued.

Sec. 6. *And be it further enacted*, That any person who shall knowingly and willfully obstruct, hinder, or prevent any officer, or other person charged with the execution of any warrant or process issued under the provisions of this act, or any person or persons lawfully assisting him or them, from arresting any person for whose apprehension such warrant or process may have been issued, or shall rescue or attempt to rescue such person from the custody of the officer, other person or persons, or those lawfully assisting as aforesaid, when so arrested pursuant to the authority herein given and declared, or shall aid, abet, or assist any person so arrested as aforesaid, directly or indirectly, to escape from the custody of the officer or other person legally authorized as aforesaid, or shall harbor or conceal any person for whose arrest a warrant or process shall have been issued as aforesaid, so as to prevent his discovery and arrest after notice or knowledge of the fact that a warrant has been issued for the apprehension of such person, shall, for either of said offences, be subject to a fine not exceeding one thousand dollars, and imprisonment not exceeding six months, by indictment and conviction before the district court of the United States for the district in which said offense may have been committed, or before the proper court of criminal jurisdiction, if committed within any one of the organized Territories of the United States.

Sec. 7. *And be it further enacted*, That the district attorneys, the marshals, their deputies, and the clerks of the said district and territorial courts shall be paid for their services the like fees as may be allowed to them for similar services in other cases; and in all cases where the proceedings are before a commissioner, he shall be entitled to a fee of ten dollars in full for his services in each case, inclusive of all services incident to such arrest and examination. The person or persons authorized to execute the process to be issued by such commissioners for the arrest of offenders against the provisions of this act shall be entitled to a fee of five dollars for each person he or they may arrest and take before any such commissioner as aforesaid, with such other fees as may be deemed reasonable by such commissioner for such other additional services as may be necessarily performed by him or them, such as attending at the examination, keeping the prisoner in custody, and providing him with food and lodging during his detention, and until the final determination of such commissioner, and in general for performing such other duties as may be required in the premises; such fees to be made up in conformity with the fees usually charged by the officers of the courts of justice within the proper district or county, as near as may be practicable, and paid out of the Treasury of the United States on the certificate of the judge of the district within which the arrest is made, and to be recoverable from the defendant as part of the judgment in case of conviction.

Sec. 8. *And be it further enacted*, that whenever the President of the United States shall have reason to believe that offences have been or are likely to be committed against the provisions of this act within any judicial district, it shall be lawful for him, in his discretion, to direct the judge, marshal, and district attorney of such district to attend at such place within the district, and for such time as he may designate, for the purpose of the more speedy arrest and trial of persons charged with a violation of this act; and it shall be the duty of every judge or other officer, when any such requisition shall be received by him, to attend at the place and for the time therein designated.

Sec. 9. *And be it further enacted*, that it shall be lawful for the President of the United States, or such person as he may empower for that purpose, to employ such part of the land or naval forces of the United States, or of the militia, as shall be necessary to prevent the violation and enforce the due execution of this act.

Sec. 10. *And be it further enacted*, That upon all questions of law arising in any cause under the provisions of this act a final appeal may be taken to the Supreme Court of the United States.

SCHUYLER COLFAX,
Speaker of the House of Representatives

LAFAYETTE S. FOSTER,
President of the Senate, pro tempore.

In the Senate of the United States, April 6, 1866.

The President of the United States having returned to the Senate, in which it originated, the bill entitled "An act to protect all persons in the United States in their civil rights, and furnish the means of their vindication," with his objections thereto, the Senate proceeded, in pursuance of the Constitution, to reconsider the same; and,

Resolved, That the said bill do pass, two-thirds of the Senate agreeing to pass the same.

Attest: J.W. Forney, Secretary of the Senate.

In the House of Representatives U.S. April 9th, 1866.

The House of Representatives having proceeded, in pursuance of the Constitution, to reconsider the bill entitled, "An act to protect all persons in the United States in their civil rights, and furnish the means of their vindication," returned to the Senate by the President of the United States, with his objections, and sent by the Senate to the House of Representatives, with the message of the President returning the bill:

Resolved, That the bill do pass, two-thirds of the House of Representatives agreeing to pass the same.

Attest: Edward McPherson, Clerk,
by Clinton Lloyd, Chief Clerk.

GLOSSARY

cognizance: jurisdiction

not subject to any foreign power: not a foreign national serving a foreign government, e.g., embassy staff

posse comitatus: citizens of a jurisdiction who are given power, by legal authorities, to enforce the law in a particular situation

under color of any law/authority: under the presumed protections of a state or local law

Document Analysis

As with many laws, the essence of the Civil Rights Act of 1866 was contained in a very small section of the bill. Most of the bill was concerned with jurisdiction and the enforcement of the law. Accordingly, the first paragraph of the Act contains the heart of what was trying to be achieved through its passage. This was a partial definition of citizenship, economic rights of all citizens, and uniformity in legal punishments. Knowing the difficulties which former slaves were experiencing, especially in the Southern States, it was hoped that whites in all parts of the nation would accept this Act's statement of equality, and that it would push the process toward racial equality.

The Civil Rights Act stated that "all persons born in the United States" were citizens of the United States. This was to change the Supreme Court decision of 1857 that Dred Scott was a slave, not a citizen. Obviously, there were some exceptions, such as children of foreign embassy staff, or Native Americans living on treaty lands. However, having been a slave no longer meant that one was not a citizen. Declaring that everyone born in the United States was a citizen created a foundation for granting the rights, which whites had taken for granted, to people of all races.

The majority of the rights enumerated in the first paragraph were economic in nature. For an individual to be free, the individual has to have the means to survive. Thus the right to create contracts; lease, buy, sell, or hold property; to inherit; and to have "security of person and property" is necessary. Although some states later ignored these rights without interference from the federal government, the intent of the bill was that there would be equality of economic opportunity.

Within the legal realm, this Civil Rights Act clearly gave African Americans the right to "give evidence" and not to be punished any more severely than would "white citizens." As with other parts of the law, this was not followed in many Southern states after the end of Reconstruction. Whether through specific laws limiting African Americans' judicial rights or through widely accepted intimidation, African-Americans were placed in a second class status.

During Reconstruction, this Act and similar laws gave African Americans some hope that change might occur. However, this hope very quickly vanished as the post-Civil War society in which they lived remained as white-oriented as it always had been. While the federal courts were given jurisdiction and the executive branch granted the power to enforce this Act, in the later nineteenth century, there was little desire to do this, and most African Americans did not have the resources to press the issue.

Essential Themes

Although in the judicial arena much of this Act fell by the wayside, its importance as the first piece of national civil rights legislation cannot be overestimated. The fact that the national government was seeking a legal way to give full rights to citizens of whatever race was important. It recognized that it was not enough to grant freedom to the slaves and to pass constitutional amendments. True freedom should be granted to the former slaves and their descendants. During Reconstruction, additional civil rights acts were passed by Congress, with other laws referred to as enforcement acts, intended to support them and the Thirteenth through Fifteenth Amendments to the Constitution. Thus the Civil Rights Act of 1866 was the first step in the process to protect the rights of African Americans and, later, other minority groups. Although after Reconstruction, many of the provisions were overturned or ignored, and no further civil rights legislation was passed until 1957, this first Civil Rights Act was a landmark in moving the country toward social equality.

This Act was also important in the way it clearly outlined the fact that Federal officials had the jurisdiction and responsibility to enforce its provisions. Although the supremacy of the federal government had been accepted as a legal precedent for decades, there were (and are) areas, in which the states have specific rights and jurisdiction. As some of the areas outlined in this law normally fell into the states' jurisdiction, it was written with specific language, giving the national government jurisdiction even in these areas. (This was one reason some believed it was on shaky Constitutional ground.) Expanding on the power given to the national government to enforce these rights, the Act authorized the full force of the government to secure the rights, since in the next-to-last paragraph it stated that "it shall be lawful for the President . . . to employ such part of the land or naval forces . . . as shall be necessary." This was a very unsubtle reminder for the Southern states of what had recently occurred. Overall, the Civil Rights Act of 1866 was a major symbolic step toward racial equality, even if its implementation fell short of its sponsors' vision.

—*Donald A. Watt, PhD*

Bibliography and Additional Reading

"Civil Rights Act of 1866." *A Century of Lawmaking for a New Nation: U.S. Congressional Documents and Debates, 1774–1875*. Washington, DC: Library of Congress, 2003. Web. 20 March 2014.

Goldberg, Barry M. *The Unknown Architects of Civil Rights" Thaddeus Stevens, Ulysses S. Grant, and Charles Sumner*. Los Angeles: Critical Minds Press, 2011. Print.

Office of the Historian. "The Civil Rights Bill of 1866." *Historical Highlights*. Washington: United States House of Representatives, n.d. Web. 20 March 2014.

"Reconstruction: The Second Civil War." *The American Experience*. PBS Online, 2005. Web. 20 March 2014.

Rutherglen, George A. *Civil Rights in the Shadow of Slavery: The Constitution, Common Law, and the Civil Rights Act of 1866*. Oxford: Oxford UP, 2012. Print.

Smith, John David. *A Just and Lasting Peace: A Documentary History of Reconstruction*. New York: Signet Classics, 2013. Print.

■ First Reconstruction Act

Date: March 2, 1867
Authors: Thirty-ninth US Congress
Genre: law

Summary Overview

Following the Civil War, the United States of America and the former Confederate States of America began the process of reuniting. However, the states continued to disagree on many of the issues that led to the war in the first place; key among these was the abolition of slavery and the rights of former slaves. In 1866, Congress proposed the Fourteenth Amendment to the Constitution, which, among other provisions, guaranteed citizenship and equal protection under the law to anyone born in the United States—including, by implication, African Americans. However, most of the former Confederate states refused to ratify the amendment. In response, Congress passed the First Reconstruction Act of 1867. This act outlined clear rules for the readmission of former Confederate states into the United States—one of which was ratification of the Fourteenth Amendment—and established martial law in the Southern states to oversee the entire process. While this heavy-handed approach was not well-received, it nonetheless ultimately secured ratification of the amendment in all states of the Union.

Defining Moment

The Emancipation Proclamation of 1863 and the Thirteenth Amendment to the US Constitution (ratified in 1865) formally abolished slavery in the United States and its territories. However, in the years that followed the end of the Civil War, many former slave states enacted laws and codes designed to disenfranchise blacks—especially former slaves—and restrict other rights to which they were entitled under US law.

Finally, after much intense debate, Congress proposed the Fourteenth Amendment to the US Constitution in 1866. The amendment featured two critical components: All people born or naturalized in the Unit-

ed States were citizens entitled to equal protection under the law, and no one who had "engaged in insurrection or rebellion against" the United States could hold federal or state office. However, all of the Southern states, except for Tennessee, initially refused to ratify the amendment.

In response to this widespread refusal, Congress passed several Reconstruction acts to direct the reformation of Union-approved state governments in the South. The First Reconstruction Act, passed on March 2, 1867, required states to ratify the Fourteenth Amendment—in legislative bodies elected by all adult men irrespective of race—as a condition of full readmission to the United States and restoration of representation in Congress. It also established federal military rule within the former Confederate states, dividing them into five military districts. The Second Reconstruction Act, passed three weeks later on March 23, 1867, as a supplement to the first act, provided additional details regarding the readmission process; it also established a key requirement for constitutional approval: All eligible voters—including newly enfranchised black voters—must have the opportunity to participate in all relevant elections without any impedance, and states would not be readmitted until Congress was satisfied that the elections complied with all of the Acts' requirements.

Notably, Congress passed the Reconstruction Acts without the support of President Andrew Johnson, who rose to the presidency following Abraham Lincoln's assassination in 1865. Originally from the South, Johnson disapproved of the Confederate states' secession prior to the Civil War. However, after the war ended, he lobbied heavily for full pardoning of Confederate officials and immediate restoration of legislative representation for former Confederate states. He also vocally opposed the Fourteenth Amendment. Congress repeatedly overrode Johnson's presidential vetoes to pass the Reconstruction Acts, along with numerous other legislative acts to facilitate black suffrage and Southern reconstruction. This created significant tension between the legislative and executive branches during this period, but Congress argued that the dramatic social and economic changes wrought by the Civil War warranted a slow and deliberate approach to reuniting the country.

Author Biography

The Republican-dominated Thirty-ninth Congress held office from March 4, 1865, to March 4, 1867, during the last six weeks of President Abraham Lincoln's presidency before his assassination and the first two years of President Andrew Johnson's term. During this period, Congress and President Johnson disagreed vehemently on important matters related to Reconstruction in the South. In particular, President Johnson favored pardoning former Confederate officers and quickly restoring Southern states' representation in Congress, while Congress favored a slower, more deliberate approach to readmission.

The Thirty-ninth Congress had the difficult task of beginning to reunite a war-torn country and continuing to govern effectively while establishing the terms under which Confederate states were to rejoin the Union. During its term, Tennessee gained readmission to the United States, the first member of the former Confederacy to do so. In spite of these challenges, the Thirty-ninth Congress passed the Civil Rights Act of 1866, establishing the citizenship of former slaves, and the first of the four Reconstruction Acts, designed to reestablish Union-loyal governments in the South. It also oversaw the ratification in 1865 of the Thirteenth Amendment, which ended slavery in the United States, and in 1866, it passed the Fourteenth Amendment, which enshrined in the Constitution the citizenship provisions of the 1866 Civil Rights Act. The Fourteenth Amendment was ratified in 1868, during the term of the Fortieth Congress.

HISTORICAL DOCUMENT

An Act to provide for the more efficient Government of the Rebel States:

WHEREAS no legal State governments or adequate protection for life or property now exists in the rebel States of Virginia, North Carolina, South Carolina, Georgia, Mississippi, Alabama, Louisiana, Florida, Texas, and Arkansas; and whereas it is necessary that peace and good order should be enforced in said States until loyal and republican State governments can be legally established: Therefore,

Be it enacted . . ., That said rebel States shall be divided into military districts and made subject to the military authority of the United States as hereinafter prescribed, and for that purpose Virginia shall constitute the first district; North Carolina and South Carolina the second district; Georgia, Alabama, and Florida the third district; Mississippi and Arkansas the fourth district; and Louisiana and Texas the fifth district.

Section 2. *And be it further enacted*, That it shall be the duty of the President to assign to the command of each of said districts an officer of the army, not below the rank of brigadier-general, and to detail a sufficient military force to enable such officer to perform his duties and enforce his authority within the district to which he is assigned.

Section 3. *And be it further enacted*, That it shall be the duty of each officer assigned as aforesaid, to protect all persons in their rights of person and property, to suppress insurrection, disorder, and violence, and to punish, or cause to be punished, all disturbers of the public peace and criminals; and to this end he may allow local civil tribunals to take jurisdiction of and to try offenders, or, when in his judgment it may be necessary for the trial of offenders, he shall have power to organize military commissions or tribunals for that purpose, and all interference under color of State authority with the exercise of military authority under this act, shall be null and void.

Section 4. *And be it further enacted*, That all persons put under military arrest by virtue of this act shall be tried without unnecessary delay, and no cruel or unusual punishment shall be inflicted, and no sentence of any military commission or tribunal hereby authorized, affecting the life or liberty of any person, shall be executed until it is approved by the officer in command of the district, and the laws and regulations for the government of the army shall not be affected by this act, except in so far as they conflict with its provisions: Provided, That no sentence of death under the provisions of this act shall be carried into effect without the approval of the President.

Section 5. *And be it further enacted,* That when the people of any one of said rebel States shall have formed a constitution of government in conformity with the Constitution of the United States in all respects, framed by a convention of delegates elected by the male citizens of said State, twenty-one years old and upward, of whatever race, color, or previous condition, who have been resident in said State for one year previous to the day of such election, except such as may be disfranchised for participation in the rebellion or for felony at common law, and when such constitution shall provide that the elective franchise shall be enjoyed by all persons as have the qualifications herein stated for electors of delegates, and when such constitution shall be ratified by a majority of the persons voting on the question of ratification who are qualified as electors for delegates, and when such constitution shall have been submitted to Congress for examination and approval, and Congress shall have approved the same, and when said State, by a vote of its legislature elected under said constitution, shall have adopted the amendment to the Constitution of the United States, proposed by the Thirty-ninth Congress, and known as

article fourteen and when said article shall have become a part of the Constitution of the United States said State shall be declared entitled to representation in Congress, and senators and representatives shall be admitted therefrom on their taking the oath prescribed by law, and then and thereafter the preceding sections of this act shall be inoperative in said State: Provided, That no person excluded from the privilege of holding office by said proposed amendment to the Constitution of the United States, shall be eligible to election as a member of the convention to frame a constitution for any of said rebel States, nor shall any person vote for members of such convention.

Section 6. *And be it further enacted,* That, until the people of said rebel States shall be by law admitted to representation in the Congress of the United States, any civil governments which may exist there in shall be deemed provisional only, and in all respects subject to the paramount authority of the United States at any time to abolish, modify, control, or supersede the same; and in all elections to any office under such provisional governments all persons shall be entitled to vote, and none others, who are entitled to vote, under the provisions of the fifth section of this act; and no persons shall be eligible to any office under any such provisional government who would be disqualified from holding office under the provisions of the third article of said constitutional amendment.

Document Analysis

The First Reconstruction Act first establishes the United States' plan for enforcing laws and suppressing rebellion in the former Confederate states. Sections one and two divide the states into five military districts and allow the US president to assign an army officer to each district. These officers and the troops assigned to them have the authority to "suppress insurrection, disorder, and violence" within their district, as well as to punish "all disturbers of the public peace and criminals."

To further this goal, section three allows the district officer to engage local civil tribunals to handle offenders, or to establish military tribunals as necessary. This section specifies that any interference in this process "under color of State authority"—in other words, by the former Confederate state's government—shall be "null and void." This essentially prohibits the state from

trying to exercise any power over the US-appointed military leader. In an effort to keep some of this power in check, section four establishes that anyone placed under military arrest shall be tried "without unnecessary delay" and not subject to "cruel or unusual punishment."

Section five defines the steps each state must follow to be granted full readmission to the United States. First, all men aged twenty-one and older who have resided in the state for at least one year (except those disenfranchised due to rebellion or felony) are eligible to vote to establish a constitutional convention to draft a new state constitution. Significantly, men of any "race, color, or previous condition" are entitled to vote for delegates to this convention. Next, the delegates must frame a new constitution that specifically allows men of all races, colors, and previous conditions to vote. Once the delegates ratify the proposed constitution, it must be approved by the US Congress. Then the state can elect its legislature per the rules established by its constitution, and must adopt the Fourteenth Amendment to the US Constitution. Only then may the state send representatives to the US Congress and Senate; once they take their oath of office, readmission is complete, and the military-rule provisions of the act no longer apply in that state.

The final section reinforces that, until all of these conditions are met in full, any civil government that may exist within the state are considered "provisional only." The act reserves for the United States the power to "abolish, modify, control, or supersede" any such government, and affirms once again that all men must be allowed to vote, even in these provisional government elections.

Essential Themes

From the very beginning, the full title of the First Reconstruction Act—"An act to provide for the more efficient Government of the Rebel States"—set the tone for the rest of the act, and highlights the distrust the US government felt toward the "rebel states." Likewise, the opening paragraph of the act states that it is necessary to enforce "peace and good order" in the rebel states until "loyal and republican State governments can be legally established." This reinforces the United States' refusal to accept the former Confederate states back into the Union without significant reforms.

The Act defines a very strict procedure for readmission to the United States. Most significantly, it imposes martial law in ten Southern states and requires that any state seeking readmission (and the lifting of federal military control) ratify the Fourteenth Amendment to the US Constitution. This amendment indirectly establishes the citizenship of African Americans and their equal protection under the law. This amendment was bitterly opposed by the Southern states, so requiring them to ratify it as a condition of lifting US military rule was perceived as a heavy-handed decision by the Republican-led Congress.

Additionally, section three of the Fourteenth Amendment effectively prohibited any person who had held a government position within the Confederacy from becoming an elected representative—either state or federal—upon readmission to the United States (unless a supermajority in Congress lifts this prohibition). Section five of the First Reconstruction Act specifically mentions this provision when describing the election procedures states must follow to select their legislative representatives and further establishes that such persons are not to participate in any part of the readmission process, including framing the state constitution or voting for convention members.

In the wake of the Civil War, Radical Republicans pushed Congress to exert as much influence over the former Confederate states as possible, to ensure that readmission would take place only on terms that punished the rebels and secured the rights of former slaves. Congress also wanted to take all conceivable precautions against future rebellion by establishing strict rules for the reunited country. However, the resentment this fostered within the former Confederate states led to the eventual reassertion of racial injustices that would persist far into the twentieth century.

—*Tracey M. DiLascio, Esq.*

Bibliography and Additional Reading

"Black Americans in Congress." *History, Art & Archives.* US House of Representatives, n.d. Web. 8 Jan. 2014.

Donald, David Herbert, Jean Baker, and Michael Holt. *Civil War and Reconstruction.* New York: Norton, 2001. Print.

Foner, Eric. *Reconstruction: America's Unfinished Revolution, 1863–1877.* New York: Harper & Row, 1988. Print.

"Reconstruction: The Second Civil War." *The American Experience.* PBS Online, 2005. Web. 8 Jan. 2014.

Richter, William L. *The ABC-CLIO Companion to American Reconstruction, 1862–1877.* Santa Barbara, CA: ABC-CLIO, 1996. Print.

■ Second Reconstruction Act

Date: March 23, 1867
Authors: Thirty-ninth US Congress
Genre: law

Summary Overview

In the wake of the Civil War, Congress passed the Reconstruction Acts to establish a formal procedure for readmitting the former Confederate states into the Union. The First Reconstruction Act gave a rough outline for this process; the Second Reconstruction Act—passed twenty-one days later as a supplement to the previous act—provided more explicit details. Like its predecessor, the Second Reconstruction Act granted sweeping authority over elections and voter registration to US-appointed military officers. It also required oaths of loyalty from anyone participating in the state constitution-writing process, whether as a convention delegate or mere voter. Congress designed the Act's provisions to keep officers and representatives of the former Confederate government as far away from the readmission process as possible, but many states resented the distrust they felt from the federal government and the level of control they were subject to under the Acts' provisions.

Defining Moment

With the signing of the Emancipation Proclamation in 1863 and the ratification of the Thirteenth Amendment in 1865, the United States formally abolished slavery in its states and territories. However, many former slave states enacted laws designed to disenfranchise black voters—especially former slaves—and restrict other rights to which they had become entitled under US law.

In 1866, Congress proposed the Fourteenth Amendment to the US Constitution. This amendment contained two important components: All people born or naturalized in the United States were accorded US citizenship and equal protection under the law, and no one who had "engaged in insurrection or rebellion against" the United States could hold a government office.

However, all of the Southern states, except for Tennessee, refused to ratify the amendment. In response to this refusal, the Republican-led Congress passed the Reconstruction Acts in 1867 and 1868, giving itself significant control over every step of the process to re-establish loyal state governments in the former Confederacy.

The First Reconstruction Act, passed on March 2, 1867, required states seeking readmission to the Union to ratify the Fourteenth Amendment. after extending the vote to all adult men, including African Americans, but *not* including government officials involved in the rebellion. To oversee this process, the Act established martial law in the former Confederate states by granting Union-appointed military leaders the authority to enforce US laws in these territories.

The Second Reconstruction Act, passed three weeks later on March 23, 1867, more specifically defined these requirements, providing a detailed timeline of the procedures the former Confederate states had to follow before Congress would even consider readmission and restoration of the states' representation in Congress. Congress even included a provision that allowed it to deny readmission if it were not satisfied that a state had allowed all qualified individuals, including newly registered black voters, adequate opportunity to vote in every step of the process. These provisions highlight the distrust Congress felt toward the Southern states: It was not enough to simply pass laws allowing black men to vote; Congress also had to be convinced that the newly enfranchised voters were not threatened, intimidated, or otherwise kept away from the polls by either official or unofficial means.

Significantly, Congress did not have the support of President Andrew Johnson when passing these laws. Johnson rose to the presidency following President

Abraham Lincoln's assassination in 1865, and he lobbied heavily for the immediate restoration of congressional representation for the former Confederate states following the war, while vocally opposing the Fourteenth Amendment. However, Congress overrode Johnson's vetoes and enacted a number of laws to facilitate black suffrage and Southern Reconstruction. Many members of Congress believed that the significant social and economic changes brought about by the Civil War could not easily be overlooked and felt it was necessary to carefully control the process of reuniting the country.

Author Biography

The Republican-dominated Fortieth US Congress held office from March 4, 1867, to March 4, 1869, during the third and fourth years of President Andrew Johnson's term. This Congress oversaw both his impeachment and acquittal—the first of any sitting president in United States history—on charges of violating the Tenure of Office Act (1867). During this period, Congress and the president disagreed vehemently on important matters related to post–Civil War Reconstruction in the South. In particular, President Johnson favored pardoning former Confederate officers and quickly restoring Southern states' representation in Congress, while Congress favored a slower, more deliberate approach to readmission.

The Fortieth Congress had the difficult task of reuniting a war-torn country and continuing to govern effectively as former Confederate states rejoined the Union. During its term, Arkansas, Florida, Alabama, North Carolina, Louisiana, South Carolina, and Georgia were readmitted to representation; Tennessee had already been readmitted during the Thirty-Ninth Congressional term. In spite of these challenges, it passed three of the four Reconstruction Acts (the first having been passed at the end of the preceding term), designed to reestablish loyal governments in the South; oversaw ratification of the Fourteenth Amendment; and passed the Fifteenth Amendment, establishing voting rights for black men (ratified during the Forty-First Congress).

HISTORICAL DOCUMENT

An Act supplementary to an act entitled "An act to provide for the more efficient government of the rebel states," passed March second, eighteen hundred and sixty-seven, and to facilitate restoration.

Be it enacted, &c., That before the first day of September, eighteen hundred and sixty-seven, the commanding general in each district defined by an act entitled "An Act to provide for the more efficient government of the rebel States," passed March second, eighteen hundred and sixty-seven, shall cause a registration to be made of the male citizens of the United States, twenty-one years of age and upwards, resident in each county or parish in the State or States included in his district, which registration shall include only those persons who are qualified to vote for delegates by the act aforesaid, and who shall have taken and subscribed the following oath or affirmation: "I, _____, do solemnly swear, (or affirm,) in the presence of Almighty God, that I am a citizen of the State of _____; that I have resided in said State for _____ months next preceding this day, and now reside in the county of _____, or the parish of _____, in said State, (as the case may be;) that I am twenty-one years old; that I have not been disfranchised for participation in any rebellion or civil war against the United States, nor for felony committed against the laws of any State or of the United States; that I have never been a member of any State legislature, nor held any executive or judicial office in any State and afterwards engaged in insurrection or rebellion against the United States, or given aid or comfort to the enemies thereof; that I have never taken an oath as a member of Congress of the United States, or as an officer of the United States, or as a member of any State legislature, or as an executive or judicial officer of any State, to support the Constitution of the United States, and afterwards engaged in insurrection or rebellion against the United States or given aid or comfort to the enemies thereof; that I will faithfully support the Constitution and obey the laws of the United States, and will, to the best of my ability, encourage others so to do, so help me God;" which oath or affirmation may be administered by any registering officer.

Section 2. That after the completion of the registration hereby provided for in any State, at such time and places therein as the commanding general shall appoint and direct, of which at least thirty days' public notice shall be given, an election shall be held of delegates to a convention for the purpose of establishing a constitution and civil government for such state loyal to the Union, said convention in each State, except Virginia, to consist of the same number of members as the most numerous branch of the State legislature of such State in the year eighteen hundred and sixty, to be apportioned among the several districts, counties, or parishes of such State by the commanding general, giving to each representation in the ratio of voters registered as aforesaid, as nearly as may be. The convention in Virginia shall consist of the same number of members as represented the territory now constituting Virginia in the most numerous branch of the legislature of said State in the year eighteen hundred and sixty, to be apportioned as aforesaid.

Section 3. That at said election the registered voters of each State shall vote for or against a convention to form a constitution therefor under this act. Those voting in favor of such a convention shall have written or printed on the ballots by which they vote for delegates, as aforesaid, the words "For a convention," and those voting against such a convention shall have written or printed on such ballots the words "Against a convention." The person appointed to superintend said election, and to make return of the votes given thereat, as herein provided, shall count and make return of the votes given for and against a convention; and the commanding general to whom the same shall have been returned shall ascertain and declare the total vote in each State for and against a convention. If a majority of the votes given on that question shall be for a convention, then such convention shall be held as hereinafter provided; but if a majority of said votes shall be against a convention, then no such convention shall be held under this act: Provided, That such convention shall not be held unless a majority of all such registered voters shall have voted on the question of holding such convention.

Section 4. That the commanding general of each district shall appoint as many boards of registration as may be necessary, consisting of three loyal officers or persons, to make and complete the registration, superintend the election, and make return to him of the votes, lists of voters, and of the persons elected as delegates by a plurality of the votes cast at said election; and upon receiving said returns he shall open the same, ascertain the persons elected as delegates according to the returns of the officers who conducted said election, and make proclamation thereof; and if a majority of the votes given on that question shall be for a convention, the commanding general, within sixty days from the date of election, shall notify the delegates to assemble in convention, at a time and place to be mentioned in the notification, and said convention, when organized, shall proceed to frame a constitution and civil government according to the provisions of this act and the act to which is it supplementary; and when the same shall have been so framed, said constitution shall be submitted by the convention for ratification to the persons registered under the provisions of this act at an election to be conducted by the officers or persons appointed or to be appointed by the commanding general, as hereinbefore provided, and to be held after the expiration of thirty days from the date of notice thereof, to be given by said convention; and the returns thereof shall be made to the commanding general of the district.

Section 5. That if, according to said returns, the constitution shall be ratified by a majority of the votes of the registered electors qualified as herein specified, cast at said election, (at least one half of all the registered voters voting upon the question of such ratification,) the president of the convention shall transmit a copy of the same, duly certified, to the President of the United States, who shall forthwith transmit the same to Congress, if then in session, and if not in session, then immediately upon its next assembling; and if it shall, moreover, appear to Congress that the election was one at which all the registered and qualified electors in the State had an opportunity to vote freely and without restraint, fear, or the influence of fraud, and if the Congress shall be satisfied that such constitution meets the approval of a majority of all the qualified electors in the State, and if the said constitution shall be declared by Congress to be in conformity with the provisions of the act to which this is supplementary, and the other provisions of said act shall have been complied with, and the said constitution shall be approved by Congress, the State shall be declared entitled to representation, and Senators and Representatives shall be admitted therefrom as therein provided.

Section 6. That all elections in the States mentioned in the said "Act to provide for the more efficient government of the rebel States," shall, during the operation of said act, be by ballot; and all officers making the said registration of voters and conducting said elections shall, before entering upon the discharge of their duties, take and subscribe the oath prescribed by the act approved July second, eighteen hundred and sixty-two, entitled "An act to prescribe an oath of office:" Provided, That if any person shall knowingly and falsely take and subscribe any oath in this act prescribed, such person so offending and being thereof duly convicted, shall be subject to the pains, penalties, and disabilities which by law

are provided for the punishment of the crime of wilful and corrupt perjury.

Section 7. That all expenses incurred by the several commanding generals, or by virtue of any orders issued, or appointments made, by them, under or by virtue of this act, shall be paid out of any moneys in the treasury not otherwise appropriated.

Section 8. That the convention for each State shall prescribe the fees, salary, and compensation to be paid to all delegates and other officers and agents herein authorized or necessary to carry into effect the purposes of this act not herein otherwise provided for, and shall provide for the levy and collection of such taxes on the property in such State as may be necessary to pay the same.

Section 9. That the word article, in the sixth section of the act to which this is supplementary, shall be construed to mean section.

Document Analysis

The Second Reconstruction Act supplements the instructions defined in the First Reconstruction Act and provides additional details on voter registration and election procedures. Section one reiterates who is qualified to vote, and it establishes that the commanding general of each district has ultimate authority over the registration process and subsequent elections. Each potential voter must take an oath prior to registration. Aside from addressing the basic qualifications of gender (male), age (twenty-one or older), citizenship, and residence, the oath also requires the applicant to affirm that he has not "been disfranchised for participation in any rebellion or civil war against the United States." He must also affirm that he will "faithfully support the Constitution and obey the laws of the United States" as well as "encourage others so to do."

Sections three and four give each state's registered voters the power to decide whether to assemble a constitutional convention and begin the readmission process. The Act requires both a majority of registered voters to vote in the election and a majority of the ballots cast to be in favor of holding such a convention. If the voters decide in favor of a convention, delegates, in turn, are elected by the same process and draft a proposed state constitution, which itself must be ratified by the voters. The commanding general appointed

to each district retains control over the entire process and can appoint additional officers as necessary to carry out his responsibilities. Section six further requires that any such officers must take an official "oath of office," swearing allegiance to the United States, and section six also provides for "pains, penalties, and disabilities" for any officer who violates the oath.

Section five lists the conditions under which Congress will approve a state's proposed constitution. First, Congress must be satisfied that all registered and qualified voters within the state "had an opportunity to vote freely and without restraint, fear, or the influence of fraud." Then they must be satisfied that a majority of all qualified voters within the state approve of the proposed constitution. Finally, they must declare that the proposed constitution is "in conformity with" the provisions of both Reconstruction Acts. Once these conditions are met, Congress will approve the constitution, declare that the state is "entitled to representation," and allow that state's senators and representatives to rejoin the Congress.

Finally, sections seven and eight establish that the United States will pay any expenses the commanding generals incur while carrying out their responsibilities under the Act. The states must determine how to compensate their delegates and pay for any additional expenses not specifically provided for under the Act.

Essential Themes

In the wake of the Civil War, the United States wanted to keep anyone affiliated with the former Confederate government as far away from the Reconstruction process as possible. Because of the provisions of the Fourteenth Amendment, such individuals not only were prohibited from holding government offices in the newly reunited United States, they were also forbidden to vote in any elections related to the establishment of new state constitutions and representatives.

The Second Reconstruction Act gave full control over the entire process to the commanding generals of each military district, and decisions required the approval of a majority of qualified voters. Some perceived the latter provision as the United States trying to help each state's citizens regain control and choose their own destiny; others perceived it as a heavy-handed attempt by Congress to punish the states for their "insurrection and rebellion" by disqualifying their former leaders from future service.

The act also established strict conditions under which Congress would approve a state's proposed constitution and grant readmission to the Union. The first two requirements directly address the election process itself: Congress will not even evaluate the contents of the proposed document until it is satisfied that all qualified individuals were allowed to vote in the election—free from threats and undue influence—and that a majority of those individuals approve of the draft. Only then will Congress review the contents to ensure that they conform to the requirements of the two Reconstruction Acts and other US provisions. These strict rules, along with the requirement that all election of-ficers take an oath of office, demonstrate the distrust the United States still felt toward the former Confederate states. In particular, Congress did not trust that the Southern states would not try to disenfranchise black voters by using threats and intimidation to keep them away from the polls, even though they were officially granted the right to vote in the elections—and this is, indeed, what would later happen in those states for many decades.

Even the sections of the Second Reconstruction Act, addressing the expense of readmission, reflect the Union's attitude toward readmission. Congress sets the required procedure, but with only a few exceptions, the states had to foot their own bill for the process by collecting taxes from their citizens—a potentially challenging task, given that many states' economies had collapsed because of war expenses and the end of slavery.

—*Tracey M. DiLascio, Esq.*

Bibliography and Additional Reading

American Experience: Reconstruction: The Second Civil War. PBS Online, 2004. Web. 8 Jan. 2014.

"Black Americans in Congress." *History, Art & Archives.* US House of Representatives, n.d. Web. 8 Jan. 2014.

Donald, David Herbert, Jean Baker, and Michael Holt. *Civil War and Reconstruction.* New York: Norton, 2001. Print.

Foner, Eric. Reconstruction: *America's Unfinished Revolution, 1863–1877.* New York: Harper & Row, 1988. Print.

Richter, William L. *The ABC-CLIO Companion to American Reconstruction, 1862–1877.* Santa Barbara: ABC-CLIO, 1996. Print.

■ Fourteenth and Fifteenth Amendments to the Constitution

Date: July 9, 1868; February 3, 1870
Author: Fortieth and Forty-first US Congress
Genre: constitution, law

Summary Overview

At the conclusion of the Civil War, the United States government was saddled with the responsibility of rebuilding and restructuring a devastated South. Tasked with discerning how to deal with the political, economic, and population breakdown of half of the reunited nation, the government, dominated by Northern Republicans, began to propose and pass legislation to transform the Southern states. This period, known as Reconstruction, established profound legal change. In instituting unprecedented laws, acts, and constitutional amendments, the Fortieth and Forty-First Congresses not only redefined the citizenship status and legal rights of former slaves and other free blacks, but they also expanded the authority of the national government over the states. The redefinition of the federal and state relationship codified in the Fourteenth and Fifteenth Amendments was a highly controversial yet crucial aspect of Reconstruction that allowed the US government to institute and defend the newly established rights of black Americans.

Defining Moment

Signed in 1863, two years before the conclusion of the war, the Emancipation Proclamation declared the slave population of the Confederate states free from the bondage of slavery. In December 1865, the Thirty-Eighth Congress passed the Thirteenth Amendment, which abolished slavery throughout the rest of the Union, including the border slave states of Missouri, Kentucky, Delaware, and Maryland that had remained in the Union and were previously exempted from the dictates of the Proclamation. With almost four million newly freed African Americans, the majority of whom resided in Southern states that were hostile to their new status; the US government knew that a perma-

nent solution was needed to ensure the rights of former slaves. The government became determined to enact new legislation to ensure that the rights of freedmen would not be immediately abridged as soon as Southern states were reintegrated into the Union.

The government was also facing the question of what criteria Confederate states would have to meet in order to be allowed back into the Union. At the conclusion of the Civil War, Union troops remained an occupying force in the Southern states and the South had no federal representation in Congress. The federal government was in a position to wield unprecedented power over the rebuilding of Southern state governments. Congress also had the power to dictate the conditions under which these states could receive reinstatement to full federal representation. Seen as an affront by some to the critical issue of state rights, much debate ensued concerning what proof of loyalty or other qualifications rebel states would have to meet to be fully readmitted to the Union. Another crucial question for Reconstruction legislators was how to enforce these legal changes and requirements on the states without violating the constitutional limitations on the federal government. The writing and passing of the Fourteenth and Fifteenth Amendments reflects the struggles and attempted solutions by the Reconstruction-era Congress to establish legal equality between blacks and whites in the United States. Beyond these immediate goals, however, the Reconstruction amendments redefined the balance of power between the individual states and the federal government.

Author Biography

The Thirty-Ninth through the Forty-First Congresses of the United States were convened during one of the most unstable and demanding times in American political history. The Union victory in the Civil War provided a remarkable opportunity for Congress to institute sweeping legal, social, and constitutional changes, not only over the defeated Southern states, but over the nation as a whole. The efforts to bring these changes to fruition, however, were disrupted and marred by a presidential assassination, uncooperative Southern states, and repeated presidential vetoes to their legislative efforts.

In the aftermath of the Civil War, the Thirty-Ninth Congress was composed only of representatives from states loyal to the Union; Alabama, Arkansas, Florida, Georgia, North Carolina, South Carolina, Texas, Virginia, and Mississippi were all denied federal representation. Tennessee, though having seceded from the Union during the Civil War, became the only Southern state to regain congressional seats during the session. The Thirty-Ninth Congress was only assembled for one month before Abraham Lincoln's assassination, which shook the foundation of the newly victorious federal government. Andrew Johnson, Lincoln's successor to the presidency, vetoed nearly every bill, act, and amendment proposed by the Congress. Despite these hurdles, however, the Thirty-Ninth Congress used a two-thirds majority vote to override Johnson's presidential vetoes in order to pass landmark legislation. During its tenure, the Thirty-Ninth Congress debated and passed the Civil Rights Act of 1866, the Freedmen's Bureau Bill, and the Fourteenth Amendment to the Constitution. It would be an additional two years before the amendment was ratified.

The Fortieth Congress convened in March of 1867 and was populated largely by a political faction known as the Radical Republicans. The Radical Republicans pushed hard for the implementation of Reconstruction policies, which gave substantial civil rights to former slaves and doled out tough guidelines to govern Southern states. The Radical Republicans often clashed with President Andrew Johnson, who was much more conciliatory toward the ex-Confederate states. These tensions came to a head in 1868, when the Fortieth Congress impeached Johnson on charges of violating congressional policy (he was acquitted and finished his term). Despite these intragovernmental tensions, the Fortieth Congress was able to compose and pass three Reconstruction Acts and the Fifteenth Amendment to the Constitution, which would be ratified within the next year.

The Forty-First Congress convened in March of 1869 and contained the first African American member of Congress, Hiram Rhodes Revels from Mississippi, and the first African American member of the House of Representatives, Joseph H. Rainey from South Carolina. Ulysses S. Grant, the former Civil War general, was elected president of the United States during Congress's first session, and the following year, the four remaining Southern states were readmitted to the Union: Virginia (January), Mississippi (February), Texas (March), and Georgia (July) were once again granted federal representation.

Although the Fifteenth Amendment was passed by the Fortieth Congress one month before its final session, several states resisted ratification. The Forty-First Congress ruled, therefore, that in order for the remaining four Southern states to be readmitted to the Union, they had to accept both the Fourteenth and Fifteenth amendments, which, having no other choice, they eventually did. For many, this was the final step in Reconstruction.

HISTORICAL DOCUMENT

AMENDMENT XIV

Passed by Congress June 13, 1866. Ratified July 9, 1868.
Note: Article I, Section 2, of the Constitution was modified by Section 2 of the 14th amendment.

Section 1.

All persons born or naturalized in the United States, and subject to the jurisdiction thereof, are citizens of the United States and of the State wherein they reside. No State shall make or enforce any law which shall abridge the privileges or make or enforce any law which shall abridge the privileges or
immunities of citizens of the United States; nor shall any State deprive any person of life, liberty, or property, without due process of law; nor deny to any person within its jurisdiction the equal protection of the laws.

Section 2.

Representatives shall be apportioned among the several States according to their respective numbers, counting the whole number of persons in each State, excluding Indians not taxed. But when the right to vote at any election for the choice of electors for President and Vice-President of the United States, Representatives in Congress, the Executive and Judicial officers of a State, or the members of the Legislature thereof, is denied to any of the male inhabitants of such State, being twenty-one years of age,* and citizens of the United States, or in any way abridged, except for participation in rebellion, or other crime, the basis of representation therein shall be reduced in the proportion which the number of such male citizens shall bear to the whole number of male citizens twenty-one years of age in such State.

Section 3.

No person shall be a Senator or Representative in Congress, or elector of President and Vice-President, or hold any office, civil or military, under the United States, or under any State, who, having previously taken an oath, as a member of Congress, or as an officer of the United States, or as a member of any State legislature, or as an executive or judicial officer of any State, to support the Constitution of the United States, shall have engaged in insurrection or rebellion against the same, or given aid or comfort to the enemies thereof. But Congress may by a vote of two-thirds of each House, remove such disability.

Section 4.

The validity of the public debt of the United States, authorized by law, including debts incurred for payment of pensions and bounties for services in suppressing insurrection or rebellion, shall not be questioned. But neither the United States nor any State shall assume or pay any debt or obligation incurred in aid of insurrection or rebellion against the United States, or any claim for the loss or emancipation of any slave; but all such debts, obligations and claims shall be held illegal and void.

Section 5.

The Congress shall have the power to enforce, by appropriate legislation, the provisions of this article.
Changed by Section 1 of the 26th amendment.

AMENDMENT XV

Passed by Congress February 26, 1869. Ratified February 3, 1870.

Section 1.

The right of citizens of the United States to vote shall not be denied or abridged by the United States or by any State on account of race, color, or previous condition of servitude.

Section 2.

The Congress shall have the power to enforce this article by appropriate legislation.

Proposal and Ratification of 14th Amendment

Ratification was completed on July 9, 1868.
The amendment was subsequently ratified by Alabama, July 13, 1868; Georgia, July 21, 1868 (after having rejected it on November 9, 1866); Virginia, October 8, 1869 (after having rejected it on January 9, 1867); Mississippi, January 17, 1870; Texas, February 18,

1870 (after having rejected it on October 27, 1866); Delaware, February 12, 1901 (after having rejected it on February 8, 1867); Maryland, April 4, 1959 (after having rejected it on March 23, 1867); California, May 6, 1959; Kentucky, March 18, 1976 (after having rejected it on January 8, 1867).

Proposal and Ratification of 15th Amendment

The fifteenth amendment to the Constitution of the United States was proposed to the legislatures of the several States by the Fortieth Congress, on the 26th of February, 1869, and was declared, in a proclamation of the Secretary of State, dated March 30, 1870, to have been ratified by the legislatures of twenty-nine of the thirty-seven States. The dates of ratification were: Nevada, March 1, 1869; West Virginia, March 3, 1869; Illinois, March 5, 1869; Louisiana, March 5, 1869; North Carolina, March 5, 1869; Michigan, March 8, 1869; Wisconsin, March 9, 1869; Maine, March 11, 1869; Massachusetts, March 12, 1869; Arkansas, March 15, 1869; South Carolina, March 15, 1869; Pennsylvania, March 25, 1869; New York, April 14, 1869 (and the legislature of the same State passed a resolution January 5, 1870, to withdraw its consent to it, which action it rescinded on March 30, 1970); Indiana, May 14, 1869; Connecticut,

May 19, 1869; Florida, June 14, 1869; New Hampshire, July 1, 1869; Virginia, October 8, 1869; Vermont, October 20, 1869; Missouri, January 7, 1870; Minnesota, January 13, 1870; Mississippi, January 17, 1870; Rhode Island, January 18, 1870; Kansas, January 19, 1870; Ohio, January 27, 1870 (after having rejected it on April 30, 1869); Georgia, February 2, 1870; Iowa, February 3, 1870.

Ratification was completed on February 3, 1870, unless the withdrawal of ratification by New York was effective; in which event ratification was completed on February 17, 1870, when Nebraska ratified.

The amendment was subsequently ratified by Texas, February 18, 1870; New Jersey, February 15, 1871 (after having rejected it on February 7, 1870); Delaware, February 12, 1901 (after having rejected it on March 18, 1869); Oregon, February 24, 1959; California, April 3, 1962 (after having rejected it on January 28, 1870); Kentucky, March 18, 1976 (after having rejected it on March 12, 1869).

The amendment was approved by the Governor of Maryland, May 7, 1973; Maryland having previously rejected it on February 26, 1870.

The amendment was rejected (and not subsequently ratified) by Tennessee, November 16, 1869.

GLOSSARY

abridge: diminish the extent of

due process: an established system of legal procedures that ensure compliance with accepted rules and ideologies

equal protection: the concept that principles of law must be applied equally in all comparable situations

immunities: exemptions

insurrection: an uprising against an established regime

ratification: formal confirmation

Document Analysis

Throughout the South during the Civil War, both the rumored and real proximity of Union forces often resulted in slaves refusing to work, abandoning their plantations, or demanding to be paid wages by their masters. Even in yet unoccupied areas, slaves began fleeing to the Northern lines in substantial numbers. Eventually runaway slaves were permitted to join the Union Army to assist in combat. Military service had long been understood in the United States as linked to rights of citizenship. In enlisting with Union forces, escaped slaves were manifestly claiming access to rights

—an issue with which the federal government was soon forced to grapple. Simultaneously, the social philosophy and governmental theory of equal rights for slaves, long championed by abolitionist groups, was becoming increasingly influential in the halls of power. Many of the abolitionists' calls for equality under the law worked to inform the ideas ultimately contained in the Reconstruction amendments. Though a controversial and barely articulated goal at the start of the war, by the conclusion of the conflict, the freeing of slaves and the codification of their equal status became a defining objective of the Union forces as well as a political and legal goal of the US government. After the passage of the Thirteenth Amendment outlawing slavery, the Thirty-Ninth through the Forty-First Congresses set about writing and passing amendments to the Constitution that empowered the government to enact and enforce among all the states the equality of African Americans before the law. In doing so, the Reconstruction Congress expanded the definition of United States citizenship, the authority of the federal government over the states, and the legal status of African Americans.

The Fourteenth Amendment

The first section of the Fourteenth Amendment served to define the parameters of national citizenship. In 1857, the Supreme Court's decision in *Dred Scott v. Sandford* had classified people of African ancestry, slave or free, as noncitizens. Within the jurisdiction of the United States, blacks had no citizenship rights and enjoyed no constitutional protections. The Fourteenth Amendment directly refuted this decision by declaring all people born in the United States to be US citizens. Citizenship rights would henceforth be determined at the national level and the enumerated rights of citizens were to be considered unalterable by the states. This codification of citizenship was noted by Congressman Wendell Phillips, who participated in its passage, as being a profound step for the United States, a country that had previously left undefined the parameters of what constituted a citizen. The clause guaranteeing the "privileges and immunities" of citizenship, however, had a contested meaning almost from the moment of its writing. Crafted by the Joint Committee on Reconstruction and principally authored by John Bingham, a representative from Ohio, the clause likely sought to constitutionally protect the Civil Rights Act, which dictated that rights extended to whites must likewise be extended to all citizens. By constitutionalizing the equal

rights of citizens within states, Congress sought to prevent a repeal of the acts that enumerated the civil liberties states were required to provide for all of their citizens. The guarantees of "due process of law" and "equal protection under the law" were clauses that, at the time of their writing, were primarily concerned with guaranteeing that no citizen could be denied his or her liberty without just cause. Additionally, "just cause" could only derive from the applied rights and legal structures that operated equally for all citizens of the day.

The second section of the Fourteenth Amendment was written specifically to address the limitations on population representation in the Constitution's first article. When writing the original Constitution, Southern states were profoundly concerned that their seats in the House of Representatives could easily be overwhelmed by Northern states if they were prevented from including slave numbers into their overall population. As a result of vigorous negotiating over the manner in which populations should be calculated for the purpose of representation and taxation, Northern and Southern states came to a compromise regarding how to count Southern slaves. Article 1, section 2 of the Constitution states, "Representatives and direct Taxes shall be apportioned among the several States which may be included within this Union, according to their respective Numbers, which shall be determined by adding to the whole Number of free Persons, including those bound to Service for a Term of Years, and excluding Indians not taxed, three fifths of all other Persons." The section denoting "three fifths of all other persons" was a reference to slaves' inclusion in determining the amount of federal representation allowed to Southern states. Though every five slaves would count as three additional people in the South's representative populous, the slaves were barred from ever contributing to the selection of the representatives their numbers allowed. In the wake of the Civil War, the Fourteenth Amendment sought to reverse this constitutional edict. The second section of the amendment mandated that former slaves be counted as whole people. Additionally, the amendment dictated that if a state denied any men of voting age access to the vote, the number of representatives claimed by that state in Congress must likewise be reduced. This clause served the purpose of preserving federalism by keeping the right to create voting laws in the hands of the states while also attempting to prevent Southern states from instituting legislation specifically preventing former slaves from voting. According to the section, if states did institute such targeted discriminatory legislation, they would lose representation proportional to the population excluded from voting, thereby weakening their influence at the federal level.

The third section of the Fourteenth Amendment sought to deal with the reestablishment of Southern state governments as well as the reintegration of Southern delegates into the federal government. Of major concern to the Reconstruction Congress was the possibility of the immediate return of Confederate officials to positions of political and legal authority and thus a rapid return to the racial dynamics of Southern slavery and the immediate oppression of freedmen. Additionally, Congress feared that rebel leaders would escape punishment by simply retaking their positions of power without any apparent consequences for their betrayal of the Union. Congress' concern was well-founded: Andrew Johnson had already begun to assemble new state governments in the South that were replete with former Confederate leaders. To prevent a de-facto reenslavement of the African American population in the South, the Fourteenth Amendment precluded from holding office at the state or federal level those who had "engaged in insurrection or rebellion" against the government as well as those who had "given aid or comfort to [its] enemies."

The fourth section of the amendment expressed the commitment of the federal government to paying all Union debts and pensions, but it prohibited not only the federal government but also states from paying off debts to those who had supported the Confederacy. Most importantly, neither the government nor the states were permitted to reimburse former slaveholders for the value of their slaves. The majority of Southern wealth before the Civil War was located in the value of their slave population. When slaves were emancipated, the vast majority of the wealth held by slaveholders was instantly eliminated. Early in the war, President Lincoln had proposed that slave states still in the Union participate in "compensated emancipation," in which slaves residing within Union borders would be gradually freed in exchange for the government providing slave owners monetary compensation for the freed slaves' value. Though Lincoln's proposal was rejected by the slaveholding border states, the concept of "compensated emancipation" continued to be debated by those concerned about the postwar decimation of the South's economy. The Fourteenth Amendment prevented either the federal government or the states from compensating former slave owners for the slaves that had been emancipated.

Finally, and considered of paramount importance by the Reconstruction Congress, the Fourteenth Amendment granted Congress the right to make compulsory the provisions of the amendment. The Fourteenth Amendment clearly located the political authority to generate and enforce civil rights laws in the hands of the federal government. Prior to the passage of the Fourteenth Amendment, states retained authority over all aspects of the general welfare, heath, and safety of those citizens who resided within its borders. The federal government's powers over state action were restricted exclusively to issues of commerce, taxation, interstate disputes, and foreign relations. All other powers were reserved for the states. The Fourteenth Amendment was a defining moment in which the federal government was given license to override any state law or action that violated the rights of national citizenship.

The Fifteenth Amendment

The Fifteenth Amendment addressed the issue of political citizenship rights that had been largely ignored not only by the Thirteenth and Fourteenth Amendments, but also by the Reconstruction bills Congress had passed during its Thirty-Ninth session. Although no legislation had been put into place guaranteeing freedmen's voting rights, a precedent had already been set by the federal government in making black suffrage a requirement for Southern states seeking readmission to the Union. The Fortieth congressional session, which was comprised of a significant number of Radical Republicans, first attempted to remedy this oversight by implementing a voting rights bill. Constitutional debates soon began, however, over the right of the federal government to dictate voting parameters that were widely understood to be reserved to the states. Additionally, questions concerning the second section of the Fourteenth Amendment, which allowed states to restrict voting rights as long as they abdicated the right to added representation, was understood to indicate that states retained the right to create parameters around what part of their state population was allowed to vote. As a result, the Congress turned once again to the task of making constitutional the political rights of former slaves.

In debating the form the amendment would take, several congressmen proposed including additional disenfranchised groups into the amendment's guarantee of voting rights. It was proposed that the amendment protect from voting discrimination the Irish, women, religious dissenters, nonpropertied citizens, and immigrants. There was also concern that if race were the only protection mentioned by the amendment, states could find indirect means of excluding blacks from voting, such as requiring educational tests or proof of property ownership—problems that would indeed arise after the era of Reconstruction ended. Despite these more comprehensive proposals, the final result was direct and succinct. The amendment simply prohibited the federal and state government from denying any citizen the right to vote on "account of race, color, or previous condition of servitude." Additionally, just as in the Fourteenth Amendment, the Fifteenth conferred on Congress the ability to enforce African American voting rights through legislation. Though soon to face massive resistance by state law and even the federal judiciary, the protection of voting rights by the Fifteenth Amendment gave freedmen full political rights for the first time in United States history.

Essential Themes

The Due Process Clause of the Fourteenth Amendment had a profound and long-term legal effect in protecting the rights of the people outlined in the Bill of Rights against infringement by the states. Additionally, as a result of the federal enforcement of the amendments and acts implemented during the era of Reconstruction, African Americans experienced unprecedented access to political participation in the South. By the end of the nineteenth century, however, the gains of citizenship rights for African Americans began to experience a rapid and devastating decline. The Jim Crow era of social and legal subordination of the black population of the South began to emerge in full force. Jim Crow laws effectively functioned to dismantle the authority of the Fourteenth and Fifteenth Amendments over civil rights law in the South. The federal Congress and judiciary did little to prevent these racially discriminatory laws and, indeed, upheld many of their tenets. For example, the Supreme Court case of *Plessy v. Ferguson*, decided in 1896, made constitutional the doctrine of "separate but equal" and is an unambiguous example of just how quickly the Reconstruction amendments were taken apart through political and legal means. It would take nearly one hundred years for civil rights enforcement to receive federal support once more, and only as a result of mounting pressure from the activism of the civil rights movement.

Amanda Beyer-Purvis, MA

Bibliography and Additional Reading

Benedict, Michael Less. "Preserving the Constitution: The Conservative Basis of Radical Reconstruction." *Journal of American History* 61.1 (1974): 65–90. Print.

Bergesen, Albert, "Nation-Building and Constitutional Amendments: The Role of the Thirteenth, Fourteenth, and Fifteenth Amendments in the Legal Reconstitution of the American Polity Following the Civil War." *Pacific Sociological Review* 24.1 (1981): 3–15. Print.

Currie, David P. "The Reconstruction Congress." *University of Chicago Law Review* 75.1 (2008): 383–495. Print.

Epps, Garrett. *Democracy Reborn: The Fourteenth Amendment and the Fight for Equal Rights in Post–Civil War America*. New York: Holt, 2006. Print.

Foner, Eric. *Reconstruction: America's Unfinished Revolution, 1863–1877*. New York: Perennial, 2002. Print.

Foner, Eric. "The Strange Career of the Reconstruction Amendments." *Yale Law Journal* 108.8 Symposium: Moments of Change: Transformation in American Constitutionalism (1999): 2003–9. Print.

Goldstone, Lawrence. *Inherently Unequal: The Betrayal of Equal Rights by the Supreme Court, 1865–1903*. New York: Walker, 2011. Print.

Heiny, Louisa M. A. "Radical Abolitionist Influence on Federalism and the Fourteenth Amendment." *American Journal of Legal History* 49.2 (2007): 180–96. Print.

Mathews, John M. *Legislative and Judicial History of the Fifteenth Amendment*. New York: Da Capo, 1971. Print.

McKitrick, Eric L. *Andrew Johnson and Reconstruction*. Chicago: U of Chicago P, 1960. Print.

Meyer, Howard N. *The Amendment That Refused to Die: Equality and Justice Deferred: The History of the Fourteenth Amendment*. Lanham: Madison, 2000. Print.

Perry, Michael J. *We the People: The Fourteenth Amendment and the Supreme Court*. New York: Oxford UP, 1999. Print.

Reconstruction: The Second Civil War." *American Experience*. PBS Online/WGBH, 2004. Web. 29 Apr. 2013.

Richards, David A. J. *Conscience and the Constitution: History, Theory, and Law of the Reconstruction Amendments*. Princeton: Princeton UP, 1993. Print.

■ Articles of Impeachment against President Andrew Johnson

Date: February 1868
Author: House of Representatives, Fortieth US Congress
Genre: constitution, legislation, political tractSummary Overview

The articles of impeachment of President Andrew Johnson consist of eleven indictments, which were intended to remove him from the office of the president. The most important charges were based on the President having violated the Tenure of Office Act, a constitutionality questionable law. This was the first time the House of Representatives voted to impeach a president. The United States Senate conducted an impeachment trial, ending in a vote of 35-19, one vote short of the two thirds necessary for conviction; the Senate had rejected the House of Representatives' charges. Johnson went on to serve out the end of his term, which ended on March 4, 1869. By defying the Republican majority that had impeached him, Johnson had in effect repudiated the result of the 1864 election.

Defining Moment

The articles of impeachment's importance were greater than any individual words or thoughts contained within them. The impeachment process represented not only an effort to remove the president, but an attempt to effect a change in the results of the 1864 election.

Under normal circumstances Andrew Johnson would never have been on a national ticket with Abraham Lincoln, but 1864 was anything but an ordinary year. The Civil War was still in full swing at the time of the convention in June, and the end was still not in sight.

In June of 1864 Republicans and war Democrats met in convention as the "National Union" Party." The party easily nominated Abraham Lincoln for a second term as president, but the nomination for vice president was an open question. Johnson was an important leader among the war Democrats. The other major candidate was the incumbent vice president, Hannibal Hamlin. Johnson brought a couple of important advantages to the table. The fact that Johnson was a Democrat and from Tennessee created good balance both regionally and politically. At the time the election looked like it might be a close one, and the bipartisan nature of the ticket was a political bonus. Johnson was the biggest vote getter on the first ballot of the Convention, and with last-minute vote switching he ended up with 494 of the 521 votes cast. Still, there was little expectation that he would end up as president. Of the sixteen presidents up to that time, only two had acceded to the presidency on the death of their predecessor—and none through assassination. On Abraham Lincoln's assassination, however, Johnson rose to the presidency barely a month after becoming vice president.

Now President Johnson's relationship with Congress was rocky at best. Johnson was a Southerner and a Democrat, and while loyal to the Union he did not share the view of the Republicans in Congress on Reconstruction. He was seen as being too soft on the Southern states. His veto of the Civil rights Act of 1866, which was subsequently overridden, and his opposition to the Fourteenth Amendment, set him on course for a showdown with the Republicans in Congress. That contest came in the form of a debate over the Tenure of Office Act. Johnson intentionally violated the act and expected to test its constitutionality in the courts; instead, it became the centerpiece of an effort to have him removed from office.

Author Biography

The author of the articles of impeachment in this case was a select committee of the House of Representatives of the 40th Congress. The Committee was made up of George Boutwell, Thaddeus Stevens. John Bingham, James Wilson, John Logan, George Julian and Hamilton Ward. The most famous member of the committee was Thaddeus Stevens who also served on a committee of two that informed the Senate of the impeachment of the president, and he served as the chairman of the managers of the House's presentation of its case for conviction at the Senate trial.

The 40th Congress met from March 4, 1867, to March 4, 1869. At the time of the impeachment of

This Congress still excluded members from ten of the eleven states that seceded; only Tennessee had returned to full membership in the Union.

HISTORICAL DOCUMENT

Article I

That said Andrew Johnson, President of the United States, on the 21st day of February, in the year of our Lord 1868, at Washington, in the District Columbia, unmindful of the high duties of his office, of his oath of office, and of the requirement of the Constitution that he should take care that the laws be faithfully executed, did unlawfully, and in violation of the Constitution and laws of the United States, issue an order in writing for the removal of Edwin M. Stanton from the office of Secretary for the Department of War, said Edwin M. Stanton having been theretofore duly appointed and commissioned, by and with the advice and consent of the Senate of the United States, as such Secretary, and said Andrew Johnson, President of the United States, on the 12th day of August, in the year of our Lord 1867, and during the recess of said Senate, having suspended by his order Edwin M. Stanton from said office, and within twenty days after the first day of the next meeting of said Senate, that is to say, on the 12th day of December, in the year last aforesaid, having reported to said Senate such suspension with the evidence and reasons for his action in the case and the name of the person designated to perform the duties of such office temporarily until the next meeting of the Senate, and said Senate, thereafterward, on the 13th day of January, in the year of our Lord 1868, having duly considered the evidence and reasons reported by said Andrew Johnson for said suspension, and having refused to concur in said suspension, whereby and by force of the provisions of an act entitled "An act regulating the tenure of certain civil offices," passed March 2, 1867, said Edwin M. Stanton did forthwith resume the functions of his office, whereof the said Andrew Johnson had then and there due notice, and said Edwin M. Stanton, by reason of the premises, on said 21st day of February, being lawfully entitled to hold said

office of Secretary for the Department of War, which said order for the removal of said Edwin M. Stanton is, in substance, as follows, that is to say:
EXECUTIVE MANSION,
Washington, D.C., February 21, 1868.

SIR:

By virtue of the power and authority vested in me as President by the Constitution and laws of the United States you are hereby removed from office as Secretary for the Department of War, and your functions as such will terminate upon receipt of this communication.

You will transfer to Brevet Major General Lorenzo Thomas, Adjutant General of the army, who has this day been authorized and empowered to act as Secretary of War *ad interim,* all records, books, papers, and other public property now in your custody and charge.

Respectfully yours,

ANDREW JOHNSON

To the Hon. EDWIN M. STANTON,
Washington, D.C.

Which order was unlawfully issued with intent then and there to violate the act entitled "An act regulating the tenure of certain civil offices," passed March second, eighteen hundred and sixty-seven, and with the further intent, contrary to the provisions of said act, in violation thereof, and contrary to the provisions of the Constitution of the United States, and without the advice and consent of the Senate of the United States, the said Senate then and there being in session, to remove said Edwin M. Stanton from the office of Secretary for the Department of War, the said Edwin M. Stanton, being then and there Secretary for the Department of War, and being then and there in the due and lawful execution and discharge of the duties of said office, whereby said Andrew Johnson, President of the United States, did then and there commit, and was guilty of a high misdemeanor in office.

Article II

That on said twenty-first day of February, in the year of our Lord one thousand eight hundred and sixty-eight, at Washington, in the District of Columbia, said Andrew Johnson, President of the United States, unmindful of the high duties of his office, of his oath of office, and in violation of the Constitution of the United States, and contrary to the provisions of an act entitled "An act regulating the tenure of certain civil offices," passed March second, eighteen hundred and sixty-seven, without the advice and consent of the Senate of the United States, said Senate then and there being in session, and without authority of law, did, with intent to violate the Constitution of the United States, and the act aforesaid, issue and deliver to one Lorenzo Thomas a letter of authority in substance as follows, that is to say:

EXECUTIVE MANSION,
Washington, D.C., February 21, 1868.

SIR:

The Hon. Edwin M. Stanton having been this day removed from office as Secretary for the Department of War, you are hereby authorized and empowered to act as Secretary of War *ad interim*, and will immediately enter upon the discharge of the duties pertaining to that office.

Mr. Stanton has been instructed to transfer to you all the records, books, papers, and other public property now in his custody and charge.

Respectfully yours,

ANDREW JOHNSON

To Brevet Major General LORENZO THOMAS, Adjutant General U.S. Army, Washington, D.C.

Then and there being no vacancy in said office of Secretary for the Department of War, whereby said Andrew Johnson, President of the United States, did then and there commit, and was guilty of a high misdemeanor in office

Article III

That said Andrew Johnson, President of the United States, on the twenty-first day of February, in the year of our Lord one thousand eight hundred and sixty-eight, at Washington, in the district of Columbia, did commit and was guilty of a high misdemeanor in office in this, that, without authority of law, while the Senate of the United States was then and there in session, he did appoint one Lorenzo Thomas to be Secretary for the Department of War *ad interim*, without the advice and consent of the Senate, and with intent to violate the Constitution of the United States, no vacancy having happened in said office of Secretary for the Department of War during the recess of the Senate, and no vacancy existing in said office at the time, and which said appointment, so made by said Andrew Johnson, of said Lorenzo Thomas, is in substance as follows, that is to say:

EXECUTIVE MANSION,
Washington D.C., February 21, 1868.

SIR:

The Hon. Edwin M. Stanton having been this day removed from office as Secretary for the Department of War, you are hereby authorized and empowered to act as Secretary of War *ad interim*, and will immediately enter upon the discharge of the duties pertaining to that office.

Mr. Stanton has been instructed to transfer to you

all the records, books, papers, and other public property now in his custody and charge.

Respectfully yours,

ANDREW JOHNSON.

To Brevet Major General LORENZO THOMAS, Adjutant General U.S. Army, Washington, D.C

Article IV

That said Andrew Johnson, President of the United States, unmindful of the high duties of his office and of his oath of office, in violation of the Constitution and laws of the United States, on the twenty-first day of February, in the year of our Lord one thousand eight hundred and sixty-eight, at Washington, in the District of Columbia, did unlawfully conspire with one Lorenzo Thomas, and with other persons to the House of Representatives unknown, with intent, by intimidation and threats, unlawfully to hinder and prevent Edwin M. Stanton, then and there Secretary for the Department of War, duly appointed under the laws of the United States, from holding said office of Secretary for the Department of War, contrary to and in violation of the Constitution of the United States, and of the provisions of an act entitled "An act to define and punish certain conspiracies," approved July thirty-first, eighteen hundred and sixty-one, whereby said Andrew Johnson, President of the United States, did then and there commit and was guilty of a high crime in office.

Article V

That said Andrew Johnson, President of the United States, unmindful of the high duties of his office and of his oath of office, on the twenty-first day of February, in the year of our Lord one thousand eight hundred and sixty-eight, and on divers other days and times in said year, before the second day of March, in the year of our Lord one thousand eight hundred and sixty-eight, at Washington, in the District of Columbia, did unlawfully conspire with one Lorenzo Thomas, and with other persons to the House of Representatives unknown, to prevent and hinder the execution of an act entitled "An act regulating the tenure of certain civil offices," passed March second, eighteen hundred and sixty-seven, and in pursuance of said conspiracy, did unlawfully attempt to prevent Edwin M. Stanton, then and there being Secretary for the Department of War, duly appointed and commissioned under the laws of the United States, from holding said office, whereby the said Andrew Johnson, President of the United States, did then and there commit and was guilty of a high misdemeanor in office.

Article VI

That said Andrew Johnson, President of the United States, unmindful of the high duties of his office and of his oath of office, on the twenty-first day of February, in the year of our Lord one thousand eight hundred and sixty-eight, at Washington, in the District of Columbia, did unlawfully conspire with one Lorenzo Thomas, by force to seize, take, and possess the property of the United States in the Department of War, and then and there in the custody and charge of Edwin M. Stanton, Secretary for said Department, contrary to the provisions of an act entitled "An act to define and punish certain conspiracies," approved July thirty-one, eighteen hundred and sixty-one, and with intent to violate and disregard an Act entitled "An act regulating the tenure of certain civil offices," passed March second, eighteen hundred and sixty-seven, whereby said Andrew Johnson, President of the United States, did then and there commit a high crime in office.

Article VII

That said Andrew Johnson, President of the United States, unmindful of the high duties of his office and of his oath of office, on the twenty-first day of February, in the year of our Lord one thousand eight hundred and sixty-eight, at Washington, in the District of Columbia, did unlawfully conspire with one Lorenzo Thomas with intent unlawfully to seize, take, and possess the property of the United States in the Department of War, in the custody and charge of Edwin M. Stanton, Secretary for said Department, with intent to violate and disregard the act entitled "An act regulating the tenure of certain civil offices," passed March second, eighteen hundred and sixty-seven, whereby said Andrew Johnson, President of the United States, did then and there commit a high misdemeanor in office

Article VIII

That said Andrew Johnson, President of the United States, unmindful of the high duties of his office and of his oath of office, with intent unlawfully to control the disbursements of the moneys appropriated for the military service and for the Department of War, on the 21st day of February, in the year of our Lord 1868, at Washington, in the District of Columbia, did unlawfully and contrary to the provisions of an act entitled "An act regulating the tenure of certain civil offices," passed March 2, 1867, and in violation of the Constitution of the United States, and without the advice and consent of the Senate of the United States, and while the Senate was then and there in session, there being no vacancy in the office of Secretary for the Department of War, with intent to violate and disregard the act aforesaid, then and there issue and deliver to one Lorenzo Thomas a letter of authority in writing, in substance as follows, that is to say:

'EXECUTIVE MANSION.
Washington, D.C., February 21, 1868.

SIR:
Hon. Edwin M. Stanton having been this day removed from office as Secretary for the Department of War, you are hereby authorized and empowered to act as Secretary of War ad interim, and will immediately enter upon the discharge of the duties pertaining to that office.

'Mr. Stanton has been instructed to transfer to you all the records, books, papers, and other public property now in his custody and charge.

Respectfully, yours,

ANDREW JOHNSON.
To Brevet Maj. Gen. LORENZO THOMAS, Adjutant-

General United States Army, Washington, D.C.

whereby said Andrew Johnson, President of the United States, did then and there commit and was guilty of a high misdemeanor in office.

Article IX

That said Andrew Johnson, President of the United States, on the twenty-second day of February, in the year of our Lord one thousand eight hundred and sixty-eight, at Washington, in the District of Columbia, in disregard of the Constitution and the laws of the United States duly enacted, as commander-in-chief of the army of the United States, did bring before himself then and there William H. Emory, a major general by brevet in the army of the United States, actually in command of the Department of Washington and the military forces thereof, and did then and there, as such commander-in-chief, declare to and instruct said Emory that part of a law of the United States, passed March second, eighteen hundred and sixty-seven, entitled "An act making appropriations for the support of the army for the year ending June thirtieth, eighteen hundred and sixty-eight, and for other purposes," especially the second section thereof, which provides, among other things, that "all orders and instructions relating to the military operations issued by the President of Secretary of War shall be issued through the General of the army, and, in case of his inability through the next in rank" was unconstitutional, and in contravention of the commission of said Emory, and which said provision of law had been theretofore duly and legally promulgated by General Order for the government and direction of the army of the United States, as the said Andrew Johnson then and there well knew, with intent thereby to induce said Emory in his official capacity as commander of the Department of Washington, to violate the provisions of said act, and to take and receive, act upon, and obey such orders as he, the said Andrew Johnson, might make and give, and which should not be issued through the General of the Army of the United States, according to the provisions of said act, and with the further intent thereby to enable him, the said Andrew Johnson, to prevent the execution of the act entitled "An act regulating the tenure of certain civil offices," passed

March second, eighteen hundred and sixty-seven, and to unlawfully prevent Edwin M. Stanton, then being Secretary for the Department of War, from holding said office and discharging the duties thereof, whereby said Andrew Johnson, President of the United States, did then and there commit and was guilty of a high misdemeanor in office.

And the House of Representatives, by protestation, saving to themselves the liberty of exhibiting at any time hereafter any further articles or other accusation, or impeachment against the said Andrew Johnson, President of the United States, and also of replying to his answers which he shall make unto the articles herein preferred against him, and of offering proof to the same, and every part shall be exhibited by them, as the case shall require, DO DEMAND that the said Andrew Johnson may be put to answer the high crimes and misdemeanors in office herein charged against him, and that such proceedings, examinations, trials, and judgments may be thereupon had and given as may be agreeable to law and justice.

SCHULYER COLFAX, *Speaker of the House of Representatives.*
IN THE HOUSE OF REPRESENTATIVES UNITED STATES, March 3, 1868

Article X

The following additional articles of impeachment were agreed to, viz:

That said Andrew Johnson, President of the United States, unmindful of the high duties of his office and the dignity and proprieties thereof, and of the harmony and courtesies which ought to exist and be maintained between the executive and legislative branches of the government of the United States, designing and intending to set aside the rightful authority and powers of Congress, did attempt to bring into disgrace, ridicule, hatred, contempt and reproach the Congress of the United States, and the several branches thereof, to impair and destroy the regard and respect of all the good people of the United States for the Congress and legislative power thereof, (which all officers of the government ought inviolably to preserve and maintain,) and to excite the odium and resentment of all the good people of the United States against Congress and the laws by it duly and constitutionally enacted; and in pursuance of his said design and intent, openly and publicly, and before divers assemblages of the citizens of the United States convened in divers parts thereof to meet and receive said Andrew Johnson as the Chief Magistrate of the United States, did, on the eighteenth day of August, in the year of our Lord one thousand eight hundred and sixty-six, and on divers other days and times, as well before as afterward, make and deliver with a loud voice certain intemperate, inflammatory and scandalous harangues, and did therein utter loud threats and bitter menaces as well against Congress as the laws of the United States duly enacted thereby, amid the cries jeers and laughter of the multitudes then assembled and in hearing, which are set forth in the several specifications hereinafter written, in substance and effect, that is to say:

SPECIFICATION FIRST. In this, that at Washington, in the District of Columbia, in the Executive Mansion, to a committee of citizens who called upon the President of the United States, speaking of and concerning the Congress of the United States, said Andrew Johnson, President of the United States, heretofore, to wit, on the eighteenth day of August, in the year of our Lord one thousand eight hundred and sixty-six, did in a loud voice, declare in substance and effect, among other things, that is to say:

> So far as the Executive Department of the government is concerned, the effort has been made to restore the Union, to heal the breach, to pour oil into the wounds which were consequent upon the struggle, and (to speak in common phrase) to prepare as the learned and wise physician would, a plaster healing in character and coextensive with the wound. We thought, and we think, that we had partially succeeded; but as the work progresses, as

reconstruction seemed to be taking place, and the country was becoming reunited, we found a disturbing and marring element opposing us. In alluding to that element, I shall go no further than your convention and the distinguished gentleman who has delivered to me the report of its proceedings. I shall make no reference to it that I do not believe the time and the occasion justify.

We have witnessed in one department of the government every endeavor to prevent the restoration of peace, harmony, and Union. We have seen hanging upon the verge of the government, as it were, a body, called, or which assumes to be, the Congress of the United States, while in fact it is a Congress of only a part of the States. We have seen this Congress pretend to be for the Union, when its every step and act tended to perpetuate disunion and make a disruption of the States inevitable. . . . We have seen Congress in a minority assume to exercise power which, allowed to be consummated, would result in despotism or monarchy itself."

SPECIFICATION SECOND. In this, that at Cleveland, in the State of Ohio, heretofore, to wit, on the third day of September, in the year of our Lord one thousand eight hundred and sixty-six, before a public assemblage of citizens and others, said Andrew Johnson, President of the United States, speaking of and concerning the Congress of the United States did, in a loud voice, declare in substance and effect among other things, that is to say:

I will tell you what I did do. I called upon your Congress that is trying to break up the government."

In conclusion, beside that, Congress had taken much pains to poison their constituents against him. But what had Congress done? Have they done anything to restore the union of these States? No: on the contrary, they had done everything to prevent it; and because he stood now where he did when the rebellion commenced, he had been denounced as a traitor. Who had run greater risks or made greater sacrifices than himself? But Congress, factious and domineering, had undertaken to poison the minds of the American people."

SPECIFICATION THIRD - In this, that at St. Louis, in the State of Missouri, heretofore, to wit, on the eighth day of September, in the year of our Lord one thousand eight hundred and sixty-six, before a public assemblage of citizens and others, said Andrew Johnson, President of the United States, speaking of and concerning the Congress of the United States, did, in a loud voice, declare, in substance and effect, among other things, that is to say:

"Go on. Perhaps if you had a word or two on the subject of New Orleans you might understand more about it than you do. And if you will go back - if you will go back and ascertain the cause of the riot at New Orleans perhaps you will not be so prompt in calling out 'New Orleans.' If you will take up the riot at New Orleans, and trace it back to its source or its immediate cause, you will find out who was responsible for the blood that was shed there. If you will take up the riot of New Orleans and trace it back to the radical Congress, you will find that the riot at New Orleans was substantially planned. If you will take up the proceedings in their caucuses you will understand that they there knew that a convention was to be called which was extinct by its power having expired; that it was said that the intention was that a new government was to be organized, and on the organization of that government the intention was to enfranchise one portion of the population, called the colored population,

who had just been emancipated, and at the same time disfranchise white men. When you design to talk about New Orleans you ought to understand what you are talking about. When you read the speeches that were made, and take up the facts on the Friday and Saturday before that convention sat, you will there find that speeches were made incendiary in their character, exciting that portion of the population, the black population, to arm themselves and prepare for the shedding of blood. You will also find that that convention did assemble in violation of law, and the intention of that convention was to supersede the reorganized authorities in the State government of Louisiana, which had been recognized by the government of the United States; and every man engaged in that rebellion in that convention, with the intention of superseding and upturning the civil government which had been recognized by the government of the United States I say that he was a traitor to the Constitution of the United States, and hence you find that another rebellion was commenced, *having its origin in the radical Congress.*

"So much for the New Orleans riot. And there was the cause and the origin of the blood that was shed; and every drop of blood that was shed is upon their skins, and they are responsible for it. I could test this thing a little closer, but will not do it here to-night. But when you talk about the causes and consequences that resulted from proceedings of that kind perhaps, as I have been introduced here, and you have provoked questions of this kind, though it does not provoke me, I will tell you a few wholesome things that have been done by this radical Congress in connection with New Orleans and the extension of the elective franchise.

"I know that I have been traduced and abused. I know it has come in advance of me here as elsewhere - that I have attempted to exercise an arbitrary power in resisting laws that were intended to be forced upon the government; that I had exercised that power; that I had abandoned the party that elected me, and that I was a traitor, because I exercised the veto power in attempting, and did arrest for a time, a bill that was called a 'Freedman's Bureau' bill; yes, that I was a traitor. And I have been traduced, I have been slandered, I have been maligned, I have been called a Judas Iscariot and all that. Now, my countrymen, here to-night, it is very easy to indulge in epithets; it is easy to call a man Judas and cry out traitor, but when he is called upon to give arguments and facts he is very often found wanting. Judas Iscariot - Judas. There was a Judas, and he was one of the twelve apostles. Oh! yes, the twelve apostles had a Christ. The twelve apostles had a Christ, and he never could have had a Judas unless he had had twelve apostles. If I have played the Judas, who has been my Christ that I have played the Judas with? Was it Thad. Stevens? Was it Wendell Phillips? Was it Charles Sumner? These are the men that stop and compare themselves with the Saviour; and everybody that differs with them in opinion, and to try to stay and arrest their diabolical and nefarious policy, is to be denounced as a Judas."

Well, let me say to you, if you will stand by me in their action, if you will stand by me in trying to give the people a fair chance - soldiers and citizens - to participate in these offices, God being willing, I will kick them out. I will kick them out just as fast as I can.

"Let me say to you, in concluding, that what I have said I intended to say. I was

not provoked into this, and I care not for their menaces, the taunts, and the jeers. I care not for threats. I do not intend to be bullied by my enemies nor jeers. I care not for threats. I do not intend to be bullied by my enemies nor overawed by my friends. But, God willing, with your help, I will veto their measures whenever any of them come to me."

Which said utterances, declarations, threats, and harangues, highly censurable in any, are peculiarly indecent and unbecoming in the Chief Magistrate of the United States, by means whereof said Andrew Johnson has brought to high office of the President of the United States into contempt, ridicule, and disgrace, to the great scandal of all good citizens, whereby said Andrew Johnson, President of the United States, did commit, and was then and there guilty of a high misdemeanor in office

Article XI

That said Andrew Johnson, President of the United States, unmindful of the high duties of his office, and of his oath of office, and in disregard of the Constitution and laws of the United States, did, heretofore, to wit, on the eighteenth day of August, A.D. eighteen hundred and sixty-six, at the city of Washington, and the District of Columbia, by public speech, declare and affirm, in substance, that the thirty-ninth Congress of the United States was a Congress of the United States authorized by the Constitution to exercise a legislative power under the same, but, on the contrary, was a Congress of only part of the States, thereby denying, and intending to deny, that the legislation of said Congress was valid or obligatory upon him, the said Andrew Johnson, except in so far as he saw fit to approve the same, and also thereby denying, and intending to deny, the power of the said

thirty-ninth Congress to propose amendments to the Constitution of the United States; and, in pursuance of said declaration, the said Andrew Johnson, President of the United States, afterwards, to wit, on the twenty-first day of February, A.D. eighteen hundred and sixty-eight, at the city of Washington, in the District of Columbia, did, unlawfully, and in disregard of the requirement of the Constitution, that he should take care that the laws be faithfully executed, attempt to prevent the execution of an act entitled "An act regulating the tenure of certain civil offices," passed March second, eighteen hundred and sixty-seven, by unlawfully devising and contriving, and attempting to devise and contrive means by which he should prevent Edwin M. Stanton from forthwith resuming the functions of the office of Secretary for the Department of War, notwithstanding the refusal of the Senate to concur in the suspension theretofore made by said Andrew Johnson of said Edwin M. Stanton from said office of Secretary for the Department of War; and, also, by further unlawfully devising and contriving, and attempting to devise and contrive means, then and there, to prevent the execution of an act entitled "An act making appropriations for the support of the army for the fiscal year ending June thirtieth, eighteen hundred and sixty-eight, and for other purposes," approved March second, eighteen hundred and sixty-seven; and, also, to prevent the execution of an act entitled "An act to provide for the more efficient government of the rebel States," passed March second, eighteen hundred and sixty-eight, at the city of Washington, commit, and was guilty of, a high misdemeanor in office.

SCHULYER COLFAX, *Speaker of the House of Representatives*.
Attest: EDWARD McPHERSON, *Clerk of the House of Representatives*

GLOSSARY

40th Congress: U.S. Congress which meet from March 4, 1867, to March 3, 1869

Andrew Johnson: 17th President of the United States from 1865 to 1869

articles of impeachment: House of Representative resolution wherein wrongdoing by an executive or judicial branch official is described

high crimes and misdemeanors: Constitutional description of the types of wrongdoing for which executive or judicial branch official can removed from office; the exact meaning is up to Congress to decide

impeach: to accuse (via the House of Representatives) an executive or judicial branch official with misconduct important enough to require removal from office; the term is also used to describe the whole process by which an executive or judicial branch official is removed from office

pocket veto: a veto put into effect by a president not signing a bill for 10 days (Sundays not included) and Congress adjourning; this veto cannot be overridden

regular veto: a veto caused by the president sending back a bill to the originating house of Congress with a list of reasons for having rejected it; this type of veto can be overridden by a two-thirds vote in each house of Congress

Tenure of Office Act: an act passed by Congress over the president's veto that required Senate permission to fire any official who had been confirmed by the U.S. SenateDocument Analysis

Document Analysis

The true significance of these articles of impeachment is not in the words themselves, but rather in why they were written and what happened to them.

Johnson was a Democrat elected vice president under a Republican president who many in the Republican Party thought was too soft on the South; yet Lincoln was, particularly after the successful conclusion of the war, the undisputed leader of his party. Lincoln's violent and sudden death at the hands of a Southern sympathizer not only thrust Johnson into the presidency but also dealt him a hard hand to play as he tried to carry out Reconstruction.

Andrew Johnson's relationship with Congress was anything but good. Congress considered the conditions of "Presidential Reconstruction" too soft and they moved to impose what became known as "Congressional Reconstruction." Johnson's strained relationship with Congress can be seen in his problems with having his vetoes upheld. Throughout his presidency 15 of his 29 vetoes were overridden (counting eight pocket vetoes which cannot be overridden). Thus, 15 of the 21 times Congress could defeat the president

they did. As a point of comparison, both Presidents Harry Truman and Gerald Ford had 12 vetoes overridden, but that was out of 250 (70 pocket) and 66 (18 pocket) vetoes respectively.

During the period prior to his impeachment Congress overrode nine of Johnson's fourteen regular vetoes, including what is known as the Tenure of Office Act. The act required that any officer of the government requiring Senate approval for his appointment also required Senate approval for his removal, including the Cabinet. The act included fines and jail time for violating the law, which were important provisions when the efforts to impeach the president were brought forward.

The Tenure of Office Act left two important questions open. The first was, Was the act constitutional? This debate had been held in 1789, when the founders decided in favor of presidential discretion in this matter, a fact well known to the political leaders of the day. The other was, What constituted a presidential term? Cabinet members got to keep their office for 30 days after a president's term ended, but was that counted from the point when the president ceased to be president or from the end of the specific four-year cycle?

The Tenure of Office Act became law over the president's veto on March 2, 1867, by votes of 35-11 in the Senate and 138-40 in the House. It is worth noting that the final bill approved by the House differed markedly from the one initially passed by the Senate. The Senate bill specifically excluded the department heads, the cabinet, from its provisions. It was amended in the House of Representatives to include cabinet officers, and this amendment was central to the impeachment of the president.

This was not the first effort to impeach President Johnson. There had been an effort at impeachment that ended in December 1867. It failed primarily because it appeared to be based on policy disagreements between the Radical Republicans and the president. This failure was part of the development of an important aspect of the presidential impeachment philosophy. The president had to be guilty of an indictable offense; in other words, he had to commit a crime for which he could go to jail. This is where the provisions in the Tenure of Office Act that made its violation a crime punishable by jail time became important in the impeachment process.

The defining moment came when Johnson finally decided to fire Secretary of War Edwin Stanton. Johnson had suspended Stanton while the Congress was in recess, but this was not agreed to by the Senate. Finally on February 21, 1968, Johnson ordered General Lorenzo Thomas to take over the duties of the Secretary of War. Johnson's actions were meant as a test of the Tenure of Office Act but they gave his opponents an opportunity to move against him.

For a second time the idea of impeaching the president came to the fore, and the firing of Edwin Stanton played a central role. A formal resolution of impeachment was presented from the Committee on Reconstruction. During the debate on the resolution those in favor focused on the violation of the Tenure of Office Act. The president's defenders argued that the act itself was unconstitutional. In the end the resolution was passed by a vote of 128-47. The president had been impeached and a committee of seven was selected to write the formal articles of impeachment.

The first nine articles passed by the House on March 2, 1868, revolved around the idea that President Johnson had violated the Tenure of Office Act of 1867. Through a tortured use of language the House of Representatives found nine different ways to say the same thing: Johnson had fired Secretary Stanton and then moved to prevent him from carrying out the duties of his former office. The vote on each of the first nine articles was passed overwhelming by a Congress, dominated by Republicans. The smallest margin of victory was on article 9, which passed with a margin of 67 votes. On March 3rd the House added two further articles, article 10, charging the president with speaking against the Congress and bringing Congress into disrepute, and article 11 which was more of a summary of all of the charges against the president.

The debate on the articles led to a final solution of an important and not unrelated issue. Was Andrew Johnson the president of the United States, or was he the vice president acting as president? It was an important technicality. Did the House need to impeach the president or the vice president? Which office holder was being impeached? Using the precedents of both John Tyler in 1841 and Millard Fillmore in 1850 it was agreed in both houses of Congress that the vice president had become president on the death of his successor. Thus, the House had to impeach the president, not the vice president, as the latter position was now vacant.

The Senate prepared itself for the impeachment trial to be conducted by the House by adopting rules for the conduct of the trial on March 2 (rules, incidentally, that would lay the groundwork for the trial of Bill Clinton 130 years later). The Senate began the trial process on March 5, 1868, when the Chief Justice and senators took an oath to provide impartial justice in regards to the trial. The Senate of the 40th Congress in spring 1868 was made up of 54 Senators, 45 Republicans (including two Unconditional Unionists), nine more than the number required to convict and remove the president.

On March 13 the president's counsel asked for 40 days in which to prepare his defense, the request was denied and the Senate set March 23 as the day on which the resident needed to be prepared to respond to the charges. When the Senate reconvened, the question was raised whether it could act as a constitutional body while still excluding the members from ten of the eleven Southern states. The Senate determined it could by a vote of 40 to 2. The president's counsel then answered the House's charges.

The president's counsel gave Johnson's response to the charges to the Senate on March 23. He responded to article 1 by charging that the law itself was unconstitutional, thus Johnson could not have violated the law or the Constitution. To article 2 he responded that

Johnson's actions were lawful as there was a vacancy at the war department as he had fired the Secretary of War. For article 3 the defense was that the reasons expressed in his argument for articles 1 and 2 applied to this article as well. His argument for article 4 was that there was no effort to intimidate anyone; the president simply authorized General Thomas to take over as interim Secretary of War using the normal executive power. His defense for articles 5 through 8 can be summed up by saying that Johnson was simply trying to carry out his duties as president of the United States. He argued in response to article 9 that the president had been expressing to others the same sentiments he had expressed to the House of Representatives about the constitutionality of limits that had been placed on his role as commander in chief. For article 10 the president denied that the events accurately depicted not only what was said, but the tone and tenor of what was said, and that it was his duty as president to warn Congress when he saw them headed on the wrong course regarding Reconstruction. The response to article 11 contained the blanket denial that Johnson had done anything that constituted a high crime or a misdemeanor.

The trial itself began on March 30 and lasted until May 16, 1868. The Senate chose to vote on article 11 first. By this point, though, the outcome could little be in doubt. Earlier procedural votes had shown that nineteen members, including seven Republicans, would vote not guilty. The final vote on article 11 took place on May 16, 35 voted guilty and 19 voted not guilty, one short of the required number for conviction. The Senate reconvened on May 26 to try again to convict the president. The votes on articles 2 and 3 were identical to article 9, 35 to 19. After this additional failure the Senate agreed to go into "adjournment without day," meaning that they would not meet again as an impeachment trial court, effectively ending the efforts to impeach President Johnson without voting on eight of the articles. Of the nineteen votes, ten came from elected Republicans but three came from those often considered Democrats for practical purposes. The Republicans who voted against their party were Senators William Fressenden, James Grimes, John Brooks Henderson, Edmund Ross, Joseph Fowler, Lyman Trumbull, and Peter Van Winkle.

The Senate result kept Johnson in office for the remainder of his term and set the precedent that the Congress does not remove presidents for policy differences but only for actual crimes. After the trial Johnson remained in office for only ten more months, but his presidency was indeed weakened by the trial and he was left with little opportunity to accomplish his goals.

The Tenure of Office Act would be kept on the books until 1887 when it was finally repealed. The idea of a congressional veto over the presidential firing of executive branch officers was ended by the Supreme Court in 1926 when they decided *Myers v. United States*.

Essential Themes

The short-term impact of this process may be less than is often ascribed. When the process began in earnest there was slightly over one year left in the Johnson presidency, and when the trial ended there were only ten months left. Of that time Congress would be out of session for four months. So although Johnson was a weakened president, the same would have been true after he failed to get the Democratic nomination for president in 1868. The impeachment process did usher in a period of weakness in the presidency, but there is no way of knowing whether this might have occurred, or to what extent, under a Lincoln presidency in light of the diminishment of war powers.

The most important theme to come out of this document does not issue from the document itself but rather from events surrounding it and from its consequences. It is not uncommon in American history to hear the language of impeachment used against presidents who face a hostile majority in Congress. Johnson was not the first president to hear that impeachment was being discussed, but he was the first president to see the House of Representatives actually draft and pass articles of impeachment.

Two historical precedents were set by this action of the 40th Congress. The first is that the House of Representatives would impeach only for indictable offenses. The second is that the Senate would not convict on the grounds, merely, that they do not like a president or disagree with his policies.

Donald E. Heidenreich, Jr., PhD

Bibliography and Additional Reading

Cannon, Clarence. *Cannon's precedents of the House of Representatives of the United States. Washington, D.C.: GPO, 1945. Print.*

Graf, LeRoy, and Ralph W. Haskins, eds. *The Papers of Andrew Johnson.* Knoxville: U of Tennessee P, 1967-1999. Print.

Leibowitz, Arnold H. *An Historical-Legal Analysis of the Impeachments of Presidents Andrew Johnson, Richard Nixon, and William Clinton: Why the Process Went Wrong.* Lewiston, N.Y.: Edwin Mellen Press, 2012. Print.

Library of Congress. "A Century of Lawmaking for a New Nation: U.S. Congressional Documents and Debates." Web.

McKitrick, Eric L. *Andrew Johnson and Reconstruction.* New York: Oxford University Press, 1988. Print.

Nelson, Michael, editor. The Evolving Presidency: Landmark Documents, 1787-2010. Washington, D.C.: CQ Press, 2012. Print.

Republican National Convention. *Proceedings of the First Three Republican National Conventions of 1856, 1860 and 1864.* Minneapolis: C.W. Johnson, 1893. Print. *An Historical-Legal Analysis of the Impeachments of Presidents Andrew Johnson, Richard Nixon, and William Clinton: Why the Process Went Wrong.* Lewiston, N.Y.: Edwin Mellen Press, 2012. Print.

Republican National Convention. *Proceedings of the First Three Republican National Conventions of 1856, 1860 and 1864.* Minneapolis: C.W. Johnson, 1893. Print. *Andrew Johnson and Reconstruction.* New York: Oxford University Press, 1988. Print.

Republican National Convention. *Proceedings of the First Three Republican National Conventions of 1856, 1860 and 1864.* Minneapolis: C.W. Johnson, 1893. Print.

University of Missouri Kansas City Law School. "Famous American Trials: The Andrew Johnson Impeachment Trial, 1868." Web.

White, Horace. Life of Lyman Trumbull. New York: Houghton Mifflin, 1913. Print.

■ President Grant's First Inaugural Address

Date: March 4, 1869
Author: Ulysses S. Grant
Genre: speech

Summary Overview

Ulysses S. Grant was elected president of the United States in November 1868 and took office on March 4, 1869. In his inaugural address, he did not lay out any detailed plans for his administration, but promised to do his best in meeting the responsibilities of the office. Most of his address focused on three major problems. One was the need to pay off the enormous debt incurred by fighting the Civil War. Secondly, during the Civil War, the government had issued paper currency and suspended the practice of redeeming paper money in gold, and Grant believed the government must resume the redemption of paper money with gold coins as soon as possible. Grant expressed concern about "the original occupants of the land"—the Native Americans and promised to support policies aimed at their "civilization" and making them citizens of the United States. He also addressed the restoration of civil law in the former states of the Confederacy, including the issue of voting rights for the freed slaves.

Defining Moment

When Ulysses Grant became president in March 1869, it was less than four years since the Civil War had ended. The impact of the war was still being felt in the struggle over race relations and the civil rights of the freed slaves in the South, and in the enormous debt the federal government had incurred to conduct the war. Additionally, while the Republican Party had controlled the White House and both houses of Congress since Abraham Lincoln's election in 1860, the party was in serious disarray by 1869. When Lincoln had run for re-election in 1864, the Republicans had put Andrew Johnson, a former Democrat, on the ticket as a show of national support for the Union war effort. Johnson had been a US senator from Tennessee before the Civil War, but had opposed secession. But to the dismay of the Republican Party, when Johnson succeeded to the presidency upon Lincoln's death, he pursued a very lenient policy toward the former Confederate states and seemed determined to block any attempt to guarantee the rights of the freed slaves. An attempt to remove Johnson from office by impeachment had failed by a narrow vote, and Johnson had, in fact, tried unsuccessfully to secure the Democratic nomination for president in 1868.

Although speculation about Grant as a presidential candidate had started during the Civil War, Grant was not an automatic choice for the Republican Party in 1868. Before the Civil War, he had seemed to lean toward the Democrats in politics, and for a time, he had identified with Johnson's repudiated Reconstruction policies. His chief opponent for the Republican nomination was Salmon P. Chase, who had served as Secretary of the Treasury in Lincoln's cabinet and was the current Chief Justice of the US Supreme Court. But during Johnson's impeachment trial, Republicans came to believe that Chase favored acquittal of the president, and this cost him support in the 1868 convention. In a vote that followed sectional lines, except for Southern blacks voting Republican in areas where they were allowed to vote, Grant had defeated the Democratic candidate, Horatio Seymour, a former governor of New York. Grant won by a 400,000-vote margin in the popular vote, out of roughly 5.7 million votes cast; but in the Electoral College, his victory margin was more than 134 votes. As Grant took office, he knew two major problems facing the nation were the treatment of the freed slaves in the South—especially the right to vote for adult black males—and the tremendous federal debt caused by the Civil War. In his inaugural address, he promised to address both of these issues.

Author Biography

Ulysses S. Grant was the eighteenth president of the United States, but he had first risen to fame as the preeminent Union general in the American Civil War. He was born in Point Pleasant, Ohio on April 27, 1822. He graduated from West Point in 1843. Grant served with distinction in the US war with Mexico (1846 to 1848), but after the war, personal troubles led him to resign from the army in 1854. When the Civil War broke out, Grant became an officer in the Illinois volunteer troops. Due to his success as a commander, he rose steadily through the ranks. In the spring of 1864, Grant was promoted to the newly revived rank of lieutenant general and made the general-in-chief of the Union Army. He was elected president of the United States in November 1868, and re-elected in November 1872. Grant's presidency was marked by corruption and scandal, although it does not appear he was part of any of the scandals. After leaving the presidency, a bad business investment left Grant impoverished. He wrote his Personal Memoirs while dying of throat cancer, hoping to leave a legacy to provide financially for his family. He died at his family home near Saratoga, NY, on July 23, 1885.

HISTORICAL DOCUMENT

Your suffrages having elected me to the office of President of the United States, I have, in conformity to the Constitution of our country, taken the oath of office prescribed therein. I have taken this oath without mental reservation and with the determination to do to the best of my ability all that is required of me. The responsibilities of the position I feel, but accept them without fear. The office has come to me unsought; I commence its duties untrammeled. I bring to it a conscious desire and determination to fill it to the best of my ability to the satisfaction of the people.

On all leading questions agitating the public mind I will always express my views to Congress and urge them according to my judgment, and when I think it advisable will exercise the constitutional privilege of interposing a veto to defeat measures which I oppose; but all laws will be faithfully executed, whether they meet my approval or not.

I shall on all subjects have a policy to recommend, but none to enforce against the will of the people. Laws are to govern all alike—those opposed as well as those who favor them. I know no method to secure the repeal of bad or obnoxious laws so effective as their stringent execution.

The country having just emerged from a great rebellion, many questions will come before it for settlement in the next four years which preceding Administrations have never had to deal with. In meeting these it is desirable that they should be approached calmly, without prejudice, hate, or sectional pride, remembering that the greatest good to the greatest number is the object to be attained.

This requires security of person, property, and free religious and political opinion in every part of our common country, without regard to local prejudice. All laws to secure these ends will receive my best efforts for their enforcement.

A great debt has been contracted in securing to us and our posterity the Union. The payment of this, principal and interest, as well as the return to a specie basis as soon as it can be accomplished without material detriment to the debtor class or to the country at large, must be provided for. To protect the national honor, every dollar of Government indebtedness should be paid in gold, unless otherwise expressly stipulated in the contract. Let it be understood that no repudiator of one farthing of our public debt will be trusted in public place, and it will go far toward strengthening a credit which ought to be the best in the world, and will ultimately enable us to replace the debt with bonds bearing less interest than we now pay. To this should be added a faithful collection of the revenue, a strict accountability to the Treasury for every dollar collected, and the greatest practicable retrenchment in expenditure in every department of Government.

When we compare the paying capacity of the country now, with the ten States in poverty from the effects of war, but soon to emerge, I trust, into greater prosperity than ever before, with its paying capacity twenty-five years ago, and calculate what it probably will be twenty-five years hence, who can doubt the feasibility of paying every dollar then with more ease than we now pay for useless luxuries? Why, it looks as though Providence had bestowed upon us a strong box in the precious metals locked up in the sterile mountains of the far West, and which we are now forging the key to unlock, to meet the very contingency that is now upon us.

Ultimately it may be necessary to insure the facilities to reach these riches and it may be necessary also that the General Government should give its aid to secure this access; but that should only be when a dollar of obligation to pay secures precisely the same sort of dollar to use now, and not before. Whilst the question of specie payments is in abeyance the prudent business man is careful about contracting debts payable in the distant future. The nation should follow the same rule. A prostrate commerce is to be rebuilt and all industries encouraged.

The young men of the country—those who from their age must be its rulers twenty-five years hence—have a peculiar interest in maintaining the national honor. A moment's reflection as to what will be our commanding influence among the nations of the earth in their day, if they are only true to themselves, should inspire them with national pride. All divisions—geographical, political, and religious—can join in this common sentiment. How the public debt is to be paid or specie payments resumed is not so important as that a plan should be adopted and acquiesced in. A united determination to do is worth more than divided counsels upon the method of doing. Legislation upon this subject may not be necessary now, or even advisable, but it will be when the civil law is more fully restored in all parts of the country and trade resumes its wonted channels.

It will be my endeavor to execute all laws in good faith, to collect all revenues assessed, and to have them properly accounted for and economically disbursed. I will to the best of my ability appoint to office those only who will carry out this design.

In regard to foreign policy, I would deal with nations as equitable law requires individuals to deal with each other, and I would protect the law-abiding citizen, whether of native or foreign birth, wherever his rights are jeopardized or the flag of our country floats. I would respect the rights of all nations, demanding equal respect for our own. If others depart from this rule in their dealings with us, we may be compelled to follow their precedent.

The proper treatment of the original occupants of this land, the Indians, is one deserving of careful study. I will favor any course toward them which tends to their civilization and ultimate citizenship.

The question of suffrage is one which is likely to agitate the public so long as a portion of the citizens of the nation are excluded from its privileges in any State. It seems to me very desirable that this question should be settled now, and I entertain the hope and express the desire that it may be by the ratification of the fifteenth article of amendment to the Constitution.

In conclusion I ask patient forbearance one toward another throughout the land, and a determined effort on the part of every citizen to do his share toward cementing a happy union; and I ask the prayers of the nation to Almighty God in behalf of this consummation.

GLOSSARY

abeyance: lapse or temporary suspension; undetermined

civilization: in this case, assimilation or enculturation

sectional pride: geographical or regional bias—particularly, in this case, North versus South

specie: coin money, as against paper; gold as the basis for paper currency

suffrages: votes

wonted: likely, preferred, or most common

Document Analysis

Grant began his inaugural address noting that, although he had not sought the presidency, he was entering the office ready to fulfill the responsibilities it entailed. He did not lay out any detailed policy objectives, but promised to express his views on issues before Congress, to urge legislation in line with his views, and to use the presidential veto over laws that he opposed.

The bulk of Grant's address deals with the need to address financial and monetary issues resulting from the Civil War. The federal government had borrowed roughly three billion dollars to finance the war effort. Also, in December 1861, the US Treasury had suspended the policy of redeeming paper currency for gold, and early the following year, began printing paper money. Grant believed that the debt had to be repaid, but did not lay out any plan for how to do this, and even said the particular method was not as important as simply the determination to do so and getting the process started. Grant also called for the resumption of "specie redemption" as soon as possible—that is, the practice of the US Treasury redeeming paper money with gold coin. Grant believed that addressing these two problems would restore both the credit-worthiness of the nation and the confidence of the business community.

Grant commented briefly on foreign affairs, promising to treat foreign nations fairly, and also to protect the rights of American citizens overseas. He warned that the United States might respond in kind if any nation failed to respect our rights.

Grant also mentioned his concern for the American Indians, who he referred to as "the original occupants of this land." Since spending time on the West Coast in the Army, after the Mexican War, Grant had been impressed with the needs of the Indians. He favored policies that would tend to their "civilization," meaning their assimilation into the general American culture, and he also supported extending US citizenship to the Indians.

Problems involving Reconstruction issues in the former Confederate states received little notice in this address. Grant specifically addressed "suffrage"—the right to vote. Many Southern states were trying to restrict the rights of the freed slaves to vote. Grant believed this issue must be settled quickly, and he hoped it soon would be by the ratification of the Fifteenth Amendment, which forbade any state from using "race, color, or previous condition of servitude" as a basis for denying the right to vote.

Essential Themes

A major emphasis in Grant's inaugural address was the financial responsibility of the federal government, and related to this, the question of what kind of money the nation should use. Throughout early US history, it was generally assumed that the nation should incur debt only in emergency situations, and once the emergency was passed, the debt should be paid off as quickly as possible. Grant believed that the debt incurred fighting the Civil War must be addressed immediately. He also believed that the nation should, as soon as possible, resume the practice of redeeming paper money with gold coins—meaning that people could turn paper money in at the US Treasury and receive gold coinage in return. The government had issued the "greenbacks" during the Civil War as an emergency measure, and many who believed in a "sound money" policy would have agreed with Grant that a return to using only money made from (or clearly backed by) precious metal should be a first priority. Grant believed that the future credit-worthiness of the nation, and the confidence of the business community, required immediate steps to address the debt issue and the resumption of currency redemption. Monetary policy would be a political issue for the next thirty years, as the Greenbacker Party in the 1870s called for continued use of paper money, and the Populist Party in the 1890s demanded the coinage of silver dollars to expand the money supply.

Grant also addressed the issue of civil disorder in the former Confederate states, and the right to vote of the freed slaves. He hoped that the Fifteenth Amendment would soon be adopted. That amendment would prohibit any use of "race, color, or previous condition of servitude" as grounds for denying the right to vote. The Fifteenth Amendment was passed by Congress in March 1869 and ratified in February 1870. The record of Grant's two presidential administration on Reconstruction and the civil rights of African Americans was mixed. At times, strong action was taken to protect these rights, but in general, the commitment of the Republican Party and Northern voters generally to Reconstruction issues was waning during the 1870s.

—*Mark S. Joy, PhD*

Bibliography and Additional Reading

McFeely, William S. *Grant: A Biography.* New York: W. W. Norton, 1981. Print.

Scaturro, Frank J. *President Grant Reconsidered.* Latham, MD: Rowman & Littlefield, 1999. Print.

Smith, Jean Edward. *Grant.* New York: Simon and Schuster, 2001. Print.

BLACK CODES AND WHITE LIVES

Following the Civil War, many former Confederate states sought to limit the effects of Reconstruction by passing laws designed to discriminate against free blacks. These so-called black codes represented a form of repression less evil, perhaps, than slavery yet somewhat more overtly harsh and restrictive than the later Jim Crow laws. The codes imposed penalties for minor offenses, such as vagrancy, that allowed whites to selectively assert control over local populations of freedmen and return them to conditions of involuntary servitude. They also proclaimed white supremacy as the law of the land despite the dawning of Reconstruction and its stated aim of realizing for African Americans. Two examples of state black codes are given in the present section.

Not all Southern whites, of course, were enthusiastic supporters of such laws, but many of them accepted the black codes' underlying premise of white superiority and the supposed inherent inability of freedmen to develop as members of human society on par with whites. Such attitudes can be detected, among other places, in letters and diaries from the period. We present two examples of such writings in this section. Also included is a chapter from a published memoir, *Ten Years on a Georgia Plantation since the War*, by a former slave-holding plantation resident, Frances Butler Leigh. In all of these documents one can witness the complicated relationships between blacks and whites in an ostensibly free society as its members embarked on a new path.

■ Mississippi Black Code

Date: November 1865
Author: Mississippi Legislature
Genre: law

Summary Overview

After Union victories ended the Civil War in the spring of 1865, the United States faced the difficult task of creating a truly united nation. Among the challenges was the integration of a newly freed black population into a Southern society that had fought a devastating war to prevent just that result. Influenced by racist ideologies and a history of legalized oppression, Southern legislatures, led by Mississippi, began passing restrictive legislation that left former slaves in essentially the same conditions, practically speaking, as they had endured under slavery. These so-called Black Codes took hold across the South, effectively denying African Americans many civil rights and creating a racially discriminatory society. After Radical Republicans in Congress took control of Reconstruction, the Northern officials who managed Southern governments declared most of these codes invalid. However, they provided a model for the later "Jim Crow" laws that kept African Americans in a position of second-class citizenship for many decades.

Defining Moment

Slavery and racism had been a part of American life since the earliest days of white colonization. The agricultural fertility of lands in the Caribbean led to the creation of a society built on the backs of enslaved African workers. As British settlement spread north from the Caribbean to the southeastern reaches of what became the United States, it carried a slave-based agricultural economy with it. Fearing the possibility of slave uprisings that would topple this system, southern colonies enacted slave codes that kept enslaved workers in a state of oppression and white landowners in a state of essentially unchallenged authority. Slave codes established that bonded workers were chattel, or property, with few if any legal rights. As white settlers stretched westward during the 1700s and early 1800s, they instituted these practices across the American South.

The expansion of slavery became the key political question of the age. Increasingly, Northern states, lacking the kind of agricultural economy that necessitated large pools of very cheap labor, passed laws ending slavery and gradually emancipating enslaved residents. At the same time, Southern states saw an increase in enslaved populations as cotton plantations drove their economies. Southern leaders fought to ensure that Northern interests could not gain such control of the federal government that a ban on slavery in their states would become a possibility. Sectional disputes over slavery eventually tore the nation asunder. Convinced that the election of Republican Abraham Lincoln to the presidency in 1860 spelled the end of slavery, South Carolina's legislature voted for secession.

Between 1861 and 1865, federal Union and rebelling Confederate forces fought to determine the South's fate. At first, the war had the simple aim of denying Confederate secession and keeping the United States intact. Over time, however, political and moral imperatives made the war one also fought to abolish slavery. Lincoln issued the Emancipation Proclamation in 1863 and the US Congress passed the Thirteenth Amendment abolishing slavery in early 1865.

As the war ground to a close, Union officials looked for a way to rejoin the divided states. After Lincoln was assassinated, the new president, Andrew Johnson, devised a plan to restore the Union that allowed former Confederate states a great deal of leeway in developing their own postwar governments. The first state to hold a constitutional convention under Johnson's plan was Mississippi. In the summer of 1865, delegates gathered in the capital of Jackson to write a new constitution.

Their debates showed that Confederate ideals had outlived the failed secession attempt, as Mississippians at the convention hotly debated whether the abolition of slavery violated the state's sovereignty. In this atmosphere of commitment to traditional Southern practices, a new state legislature convened in the fall of 1865 to address the management of the new social order and prepare for readmission to the Union.

Author Biography

Mississippi was one of the first former Confederate states to begin the process of rejoining the Union, holding a constitutional convention in August of 1865 and electing a new government two months later. Unlike Southern state governments formed later in the Reconstruction era, under the watchful eye of the Republican-dominated federal government, this Mississippi government lay largely under the control of former Confederate supporters; the state's new governor, for example, had been a Confederate general. Equally, the state legislature filled its ranks with former Confederates, who wished to maintain the social structure of the antebellum South as much as the changes brought about by the Civil War would allow. Perhaps unsurprisingly, one of the first actions of the new state legislature was to enact legislation that sought to reinstitute the social and economic supremacy of white Mississippians over the black freedmen who had been their slaves just a short time before.

HISTORICAL DOCUMENT

Apprentice Law

Section 1. Be it enacted by the legislature of the state of Mississippi, that it shall be the duty of all sheriffs, justices of the peace, and other civil officers of the several counties in this state to report to the Probate courts of their respective counties semiannually, at the January and July terms of said courts, all freedmen, free Negroes, and mulattoes under the age of eighteen within their respective counties, beats, or districts who are orphans, or whose parent or parents have not the means, or who refuse to provide for and support said minors; and thereupon it shall be the duty of said Probate Court to order the clerk of said court to apprentice said minors to some competent and suitable person, on such terms as the court may direct, having a particular care to the interest of said minors:

Provided, that the former owner of said minors shall have the preference when, in the opinion of the court, he or she shall be a Suitable person for that purpose.

Section 2. Be it further enacted, that the said court shall be fully satisfied that the person or persons to whom said minor shall be apprenticed shall be a suitable person to have the charge and care of said minor and fully to protect the interest of said minor. The said court shall require the said master or mistress to execute bond and security, payable to the state of Mississippi, conditioned that he or she shall furnish said minor with sufficient food and clothing; to treat said minor humanely; furnish medical attention in case of sickness; teach or cause to be taught him or her to read and write, if under fifteen years old; and will conform to any law that may be hereafter passed for the regulation of the duties and relation of master and apprentice:

Provided, that said apprentice shall be bound by indenture, in case of males until they are twenty-one years old, and in case of females until they are eighteen years old.

Section 3. Be it further enacted, that in the management and control of said apprentices, said master or mistress shall have power to inflict such moderate corporeal chastisement as a father or guardian is allowed to inflict on his or her child or ward at common law:

Provided, that in no case shall cruel or inhuman punishment be inflicted.

Section 4. Be it further enacted, that if any apprentice shall leave the employment of his or her master or mistress without his or her consent, said master or mistress may pursue and recapture said apprentice and bring him or her before any justice of the peace of the county, whose duty it shall be to remand said apprentice to the service of his or her master or mistress; and in the event of a refusal on the part of said apprentice so to return, then said justice shall commit said apprentice to the jail of said county, on failure to give bond, until the next term of the county court; and it shall be the duty of said court, at the first term thereafter, to investigate said case; and if the court shall be of opinion that said apprentice left the employment of his or her master or mistress without good cause, to order him or her to be punished, as provided for the punishment of hired freedmen, as may be from time to time provided for by law, for desertion, until he or she shall agree to return to his or her master or mistress:

Provided, that the court may grant continuances, as in other cases; and provided, further, that if the court shall believe that said apprentice had good cause to quit his said master or mistress, the court shall discharge said apprentice from said indenture and also enter a judgment against the master or mistress for not more than $100, for the use and benefit of said apprentice, to be collected on execution, as in other cases.

Section 5. Be it further enacted, that if any person entice away any apprentice from his or her master or mistress, or shall knowingly employ an apprentice, or furnish him or her food or clothing, without the written consent of his or her master or mistress, of shall sell or give said apprentice ardent spirits, without such consent, said person so offending shall be deemed guilty of a high misdemeanor, and shall, on conviction thereof before the county court, be punished as provided for the punishment of persons enticing from their employer hired freedmen, free Negroes, or mulattoes.

Section 6. Be it further enacted, that it shall be the duty of all civil officers of their respective counties to report any minors within their respective counties to said Probate Court who are subject to be apprenticed under the provisions of this act, from time to time, as the facts may come to their knowledge; and it shall be the duty of said court, from time to time, as said minors shall be reported to them or otherwise come to their knowledge, to apprentice said minors as hereinbefore provided.

Section 7. Be it further enacted, that in case the master or mistress of any apprentice shall desire, he or she shall have the privilege to summon his or her said apprentice to the Probate Court, and thereupon, with the approval of the court, he or she shall be released from all liability as master of said apprentice, and his said bond shall be canceled, and it shall be the duty of the court forthwith to reapprentice said minor; and in the event any master of in apprentice shall die before the close of the term of service of said apprentice, it shall be the duty of the court to give the preference in reapprenticing said minor to the widow, or other member of said master's family:

Provided, that said widow or other member of said family shall be a suitable person for that purpose.

Section 8. Be it further enacted, that in case any master or mistress of any apprentice, bound to him or her under this act shall be about to remove or shall have removed to any other state of the United States by the laws of which such apprentice may be an inhabitant thereof, the Probate Court of the proper county may authorize the removal of such apprentice to such state, upon the said master or mistress entering into bond, with security, in a penalty to be fixed by the judge, conditioned that said master or mistress will, upon such removal, comply with the laws of such state in such cases:

Provided, that said master shall be cited to attend the court at which such order is proposed to be made and shall have a right to resist the same by next friend, or otherwise.

Section 9. Be it further enacted, that it shall be lawful for any freedman, free Negro, or Mulatto having a minor child or children to apprentice the said minor child or children as provided for by this act.

Section 10. Be it further enacted, that in all cases where the age of the freedman, free Negro, or mulatto cannot be ascertained by record testimony, the judge of the county court shall fix the age.

II.

Vagrancy Law

Section 1. Be it enacted by the legislature of the state of Mississippi, that all rogues and vagabonds, idle and dissipated persons, beggars, jugglers, or persons practising unlawful games or plays, runaways, common drunkards, common nightwalkers, pilferers, lewd, wanton, or lascivious persons, in speech or behavior, common railers and brawlers, persons who neglect their calling or employment, misspend what they earn, or do not provide for the support of themselves or their families or dependents, and all other idle and disorderly persons, including all who neglect all lawful business, or habitually misspend their time by frequenting houses of ill-fame, gaming houses, or tippling shops, shall be deemed and considered vagrants under the provisions of this act; and, on conviction thereof shall be fined not exceeding $100, with all accruing costs, and be imprisoned at the discretion of the court not exceeding ten days.

Section 2. Be it further enacted, that all freedmen, free Negroes, and mulattoes in this state over the age of eighteen years found on the second Monday in January 1966, or thereafter, with no lawful employment or business, or found unlawfully assembling themselves together either in the day or nighttime, and all white persons so assembling with freedmen, free Negroes, or mulattoes, or usually associating with freedmen, free Negroes, or mulattoes on terms of equality, or living in adultery or fornication with a freedwoman, free Negro, or mulatto, shall be deemed vagrants; and, on conviction thereof, shall be fined in the sum of not exceeding, in the case of a freedman, free Negro, or mulatto, 150, and a white man, $200, and imprisoned at the discretion of the court, the free Negro not exceeding ten days, and the white man not exceeding six months.

Section 3. Be it further enacted, that all justices of the peace, mayors, and aldermen of incorporated towns and cities of the several counties in this state shall have jurisdiction to try all questions of vagrancy in their respective towns, counties, and cities; and it is hereby made their duty, whenever they shall ascertain that any person or persons in their respective towns, counties, and cities are violating any of the provisions of this act, to have said party or parties arrested and brought before them and immediately investigate said charge; and, on conviction, punish said party or parties as provided for herein. And it is hereby made the duty of all sheriffs, constables, town constables, city marshals, and all like officers to report to some officer having jurisdiction all violations of any of the provisions of this act; and it shall be the duty of the county courts to inquire if any officers have neglected any of the duties required by this act; and in case any officer shall fail or neglect any duty herein, it shall be the duty of the county court to fine said officer, upon conviction, not exceeding $100, to be paid into the county treasury for county purposes.

Section 4. Be it further enacted, that keepers of gaming houses, houses of prostitution, all prostitutes, public or private, and all persons who derive their chief support in employments that militate against good morals or against laws shall be deemed and held to be vagrants.

Section 5. Be it further enacted, that all fines and forfeitures collected under the provisions of this act shall be paid into the county treasury for general county purposes; and in case any freedman, free Negro, or mulatto shall fail for five days after the imposition of any fine or forfeiture upon him or her for violation of any of the provisions of this act to pay the same, that it shall be, and is hereby made, the duty of the sheriff of the proper county to hire out said freedman, free Negro, or mulatto to any person who will, for the shortest period of service, pay said fine or forfeiture and all costs:

Provided, a preference shall be given to the employer, if there be one, in which case the employer shall be entitled to deduct and retain the amount so paid from the wages of such freedman, free Negro, or mulatto then due or to become due; and in case such freedman, free Negro, or mulatto cannot be hired out he or she may be dealt with as a pauper.

Section 6. Be it further enacted, that the same duties and liabilities existing among white persons of this state shall attach to freedmen, free Negroes, and mulattoes to support their indigent families and all colored paupers; and that, in order to secure a support for such indigent freedmen, free Negroes, and mulattoes, it shall be lawful, and it is hereby made the duty of the boards of county police of each county in this state, to levy a poll or capitation tax on each and every freedman, free Negro, or mulatto, between the ages of eighteen and sixty years, not to exceed the sum of s I annually, to each person so taxed, which tax, when collected, shall be paid into the county treasurer's hands and constitute a fund to be called the Freedman's Pauper Fund, which shall be applied by the commissioners of the poor for the maintenance of the poor of the freedmen, free Negroes and mulattoes of this state, under such regulations as may be established by the boards of county police, in the respective counties of this state.

Section 7. Be it further enacted, that if any freedman, free Negro, or mulatto shall fail or refuse to pay any tax levied according to the provisions of the 6th Section of this act, it shall be prima facie evidence of vagrancy, and it shall be the duty of the sheriff to arrest such freedman, free Negro, or mulatto, or such person refusing or neglecting to pay such tax, and proceed at once to hire, for the shortest time, such delinquent taxpayer to anyone who will pay the said tax, with accruing costs, giving preference to the employer, if there be one.

Section 8. Be it further enacted, that any person feeling himself or herself aggrieved by the judgment of any justice of the peace, mayor, or alderman in cases arising under this act may, within five days, appeal to the next term of the county court of the proper county, upon giving bond and security in a sum not less than $25 nor more than $150, conditioned to appear and prosecute said appeal, and abide by the judgment of the county court, and said appeal shall be tried de novo in the county court, and the decision of said court shall be final.

III.

Civil Rights of Freedmen

Section 1. Be it enacted by the legislature of the state of Mississippi, that all freedmen, free Negroes, and mulat-

toes may sue and be sued, implead and be impleaded in all the courts of law and equity of this state, and may acquire personal property and choses in action, by descent or purchase, and may dispose of the same in the same manner and to the same extent that white persons may:

Provided, that the provisions of this section shall not be construed as to allow any freedman, free Negro, or mulatto to rent or lease any lands or tenements, except in incorporated towns or cities, in which places the corporate authorities shall control the same.

Section 2. Be it further enacted, that all freedmen, free Negroes, and mulattoes may intermarry with each other, in the same manner and under the same regulations that are provided by law for white persons:

Provided, that the clerk of probate shall keep separate records of the same.

Section 3. Be it further enacted, that all freedmen, free Negroes, and mulattoes who do now and have heretofore lived and cohabited together as husband and wife shall be taken and held in law as legally married, and the issue shall be taken and held as legitimate for all purposes. That it shall not be lawful for any freedman, free Negro, or mulatto to intermarry with any white person; nor for any white person to intermarry with any freedman, free Negro, or mulatto; and any person who shall so intermarry shall be deemed guilty of felony and, on conviction thereof, shall be confined in the state penitentiary for life; and those shall be deemed freedmen, free Negroes, and mulattoes who are of pure Negro blood; and those descended from a Negro to the third generation inclusive, though one ancestor of each generation may have been a white person.

Section 4. Be it further enacted, that in addition to cases in which freedmen, free Negroes, and mulattoes are now by law competent witnesses, freedmen, free Negroes, or mulattoes shall be competent in civil cases when a party or parties to the suit, either plaintiff or plaintiffs, defendant or defendants, also in cases where freedmen, free Negroes, and mulattoes is or are either plaintiff or plaintiffs, defendant or defendants, and a white person or white persons is or are the opposing party or parties, plaintiff or plaintiffs, defendant or defendants. They shall also be competent witnesses in all criminal prosecutions where the crime charged is alleged to have been committed by a white person upon or against the person or property of a freedman, free Negro, or mulatto:

Provided, that in all cases said witnesses shall be examined in open court on the stand, except, however, they may be examined before the grand jury, and shall in all cases be subject to the rules and tests of the common law as to competency and credibility.

Section 5. Be it further enacted, that every freedman, free Negro, and mulatto shall, on the second Monday of January 1866, and annually thereafter, have a lawful home or employment, and shall have a written evidence thereof, as follows, to wit: if living in any incorporated city, town, or village, a license from the mayor thereof; and if living outside of any incorporated city, town, or village, from the member of the board of police of his beat, authorizing him or her to do irregular and job work, or a written contract, as provided in Section 6 of this act, which licenses may be revoked for cause, at any time, by the authority granting the same.

Section 6. Be it further enacted, that all contracts for labor made with freedmen, free Negroes, and mulattoes for a longer period than one month shall be in writing and in duplicate, attested and read to said freedman, free Negro, or mulatto by a beat, city, or county officer, or two disinterested white persons of the county in which the labor is to be performed, of which each party shall have one; and said contracts shall be taken and held as entire contracts; and if the laborer shall quit the service of the employer before expiration of his term of service without good cause, he shall forfeit his wages for that year, up to the time of quitting.

Section 7. Be it further enacted, that every civil officer shall, and every person may, arrest and carry back to his or her legal employer any freedman, free Negro, or mulatto who shall have quit the service of his or her employer before the expiration of his or her term of service without good cause, and said officer and person shall be entitled to receive for arresting and carrying back every deserting employee aforesaid the sum of $5, and 10 cents per mile from the place of arrest to the place of delivery, and the same shall be paid by the employer, and held as a setoff for so much against the wages of said deserting employee:

Provided, that said arrested party, after being so returned, may appeal to a justice of the peace or member of the board of police of the county, who, on notice to the alleged employer, shall try summarily whether said appellant is legally employed by the alleged employer and his good cause to quit said employer; either party shall have the right of appeal to the county court, pending which the alleged deserter shall be remanded to the alleged employer or otherwise disposed of as shall be right and just, and the decision of the county court shall be final.

Section 8. Be it further enacted, that upon affidavit made by the employer of any freedman, free Negro, or mulatto, or other credible person before any justice of the peace or member of the board of police, that any freedman, free Negro, or mulatto, legally employed by said employer, has illegally deserted said employment, such justice of the peace or member of the board of police shall issue his warrant or warrants, returnable before himself, or other such officer, directed to any sheriff, constable, or special deputy, commanding him to arrest said deserter and return him or her to said employer, and the like proceedings shall be had as provided in the preceding section; and it shall be lawful for any officer to whom such warrant shall be directed to execute said warrant in any county of this state, and that said warrant may be transmitted without endorsement to any like officer of another county, to be executed and returned as aforesaid, and the said employer shall pay the cost of said warrants and arrest and return, which shall be set off for so much against the wages of said deserter.

Section 9. Be it further enacted, that if any person shall persuade or attempt to persuade, entice, or cause any freedman, free Negro, or mulatto to desert from the legal employment of any person before the expiration of his or her term of service, or shall knowingly employ any such deserting freedman, free Negro, or mulatto, or shall knowingly give or sell to any such deserting freedman, free Negro, or mulatto any food, raiment, or other thing, he or she shall be guilty of a misdemeanor; and, upon conviction, shall be fined not less than $25 and not more than $200 and the costs; and, if said fine and costs shall not be immediately paid, the court shall sentence said convict to not exceeding two months' imprisonment in the county jail, and he or she shall moreover be liable to the party injured in damages:

Provided, if any person shall, or shall attempt to, persuade, entice, or cause any freedman, free Negro, or mulatto to desert from any legal employment of any person with the view to employ said freedman, free Negro, or mulatto without the limits of this state, such person, on conviction, shall be fined not less than $50 and not more than $1500 and costs; and, if said fine and costs shall not be immediately paid, the court shall sentence said convict to not exceeding six months' imprisonment in the county jail.

Section 10. Be it further enacted, that it shall be lawful for any freedman, free Negro, or mulatto to charge any white person, freedman, free Negro, or mulatto, by affidavit, with any criminal offense against his or her person or property; and, upon such affidavit, the proper process shall be issued and executed as if said affidavit was made by a white person; and it shall be lawful for any freedman, free Negro, or mulatto, in any action, suit, or controversy pending or about to be instituted, in any court of law or equity of this state, to make all needful and lawful affidavits, as shall be necessary for the institution, prosecution, or defense of such suit or controversy.

Section 11. Be it further enacted, that the penal laws of this state, in all cases not otherwise specially provided for, shall apply and extend to all freedmen, free Negroes, and mulattoes.

IV.

Penal Code

Section 1. Be it enacted by the legislature of the state of Mississippi, that no freedman, free Negro, or mulatto not in the military service of the United States government, and not licensed so to do by the board of police of his or her county, shall keep or carry firearms of any kind, or any ammunition, dirk, or Bowie knife; and, on conviction thereof in the county court, shall be punished by fine, not exceeding $10, and pay the costs of such proceedings, and all such arms or ammunition shall be forfeited to the informer; and it shall be the duty of every civil and military officer to arrest any freedman, free Negro, or mulatto found with any such arms or ammunition, and cause him or her to be committed for trial in default of bail.

Section 2. Be it further enacted, that any freedman, free Negro, or mulatto committing riots, routs, affrays, trespasses, malicious mischief, cruel treatment to animals, seditious speeches, insulting gestures, language, or acts, or assaults on any person, disturbance of the peace, exercising the function of a minister of the Gospel without a license from some regularly organized church, vending spirituous or intoxicating liquors, or committing any other misdemeanor the punishment of which is not specifically provided for by law shall, upon conviction thereof in the county court, be fined not less than $10 and not more than $100, and may be imprisoned, at the discretion of the court, not exceeding thirty days.

Section 3. Be it further enacted, that if any white person shall sell, lend, or give to any freedman, free Negro, or mulatto any firearms, dirk, or Bowie knife, or ammunition, or any spirituous or intoxicating liquors, such person or persons so offending, upon conviction thereof in the county court of his or her county, shall be fined not exceeding $50, and may be imprisoned, at the discretion of the court, not exceeding thirty days:

Provided, that any master, mistress, or employer of any freedman, free Negro, or mulatto may give to any freedman, free Negro, or mulatto apprenticed to or employed by such master, mistress, or employer spirituous or intoxicating liquors, but not in sufficient quantities to produce intoxication.

Section 4. Be it further enacted, that all the penal and criminal laws now in force in this state defining offenses and prescribing the mode of punishment for crimes and misdemeanors committed by slaves, free Negroes, or mulattoes be and the same are hereby reenacted and declared to be in full force and effect against freedmen, free Negroes, and mulattoes, except so far m the mode

and manner of trial and punishment have been changed or altered by law.

Section 5. Be it further enacted, that if any freedman, free Negro, or mulatto convicted of any of the misdemeanors provided against in this act shall fail or refuse, for the space of five days after conviction, to pay the fine and costs imposed, such person shall be hired out by the sheriff or other officer, at public outcry, to any white person who will pay said fine and all costs and take such convict for the shortest time.

GLOSSARY

ardent spirits: liquor, alcoholic beverages

dirk: a dagger

houses of ill-fame: bordellos, houses of prostitution

implead: plead, in a court of law

mulatto: a person of mixed black and white ancestry

tippling shops: drinking establishments

Document Analysis

The Civil War had unquestionably ended slavery. But former Confederates were unwilling to transform their society from one based on chattel slavery to one of complete equality simply because of a change in the legal standing of the region's former slaves. The Mississippi Black Code, passed shortly after the final shots of the Civil War, reveals the extent to which Southern leaders wished to maintain the status quo by supporting white dominance over black freedman through social, economic, and civil controls. To do this, the Black Codes drew on a blend of former slave codes, contemporary laws regulating African American life in the North, and laws addressing vagrancy and other issues to create a system that aimed to keep freedmen from exercising power in society.

Much of the dominance that white Southerners wished to maintain was economic. Mississippi's Black Code established systems of labor that largely prevented freedmen from competing in the labor market and ensured that white land and business owners had a

continuing source of cheap labor. The Code's Apprentice Law granted the state the power to assign underage orphans to the care of a guardian who in turn had the right to indenture the young person to another until he or she reached the age of majority. The law required indentured apprentices to be fed, clothed, and given a basic education; however, masters had the right to "inflict moderate corporeal chastisement" and to recapture any apprentice who attempted to desert his or her employment before the indenture period had ended.

Equally, the Code's stated Civil Rights of Freedmen required African American workers with jobs lasting longer than one month to sign binding employment contracts that they could not end without forfeiture of all payment for the time that they had already worked. Unemployed freedmen ran the risk of being declared vagrants and hired out to pay off the resulting fines. Other laws barred freedmen from owning property in incorporated areas and denied others the right to recruit their labor. Under the Black Code, former slaves still lacked true economic freedom.

The Black Code also prevented genuine social and civil equality between the races. Although the laws clearly acknowledged that slavery was over, they kept freedmen from personal liberties large and small. Along with economic restrictions, the Code barred freedman from owning weapons, acting as an unlicensed religious minister, or selling alcohol. African Americans had the right to marry one another, but not to intermarry with whites. Yet the law did guarantee at least some basic rights. African Americans were permitted to sue in the courts and act as reliable witnesses.

Essential Themes

Mississippi was among the first of the former Confederate states to begin the work of rebuilding a government and society. Because of this, its passage of the Black Code set an example that other Southern states quickly followed. The Black Codes allowed white Southern leaders to show their commitment to maintaining the social and economic order of the antebellum period. Contracts rather than bondage tied worker to employer, and laws granted African Americans some basic rights. But the supremacy of white landowners over the black workers whom they oversaw was clear.

In practice, however, the Black Codes had a limited short-term impact. Northern newspapers seized upon the laws as an example of Southern racial tyranny, inflaming Northern sentiment and ultimately paving the way for the Radical Republican faction to create a form of congressional Reconstruction in which the Freedmen's Bureau and Northern military governors enforced desegregation and racial equality in the South. During this era, the most egregious laws of the Black Codes were declared null and void.

However, the influence of the Mississippi Black Code was again felt in the post-Reconstruction era that began in 1877. After Republican-controlled military governments ended their control of Southern states, Democratic "Redeemer" governments steadily gained ground across the former Confederacy. These governments, which shut out African American involvement in politics and government, instituted laws—popularly known as "Jim Crow laws"—that created legal segregation and institutionalized discrimination across the South. Some of these laws directly echoed the post–Civil War Black Codes, just as those laws had recalled the slave codes of earlier eras. Mississippi's Black Code had, for example, barred interracial marriage, and with the passage of Jim Crow laws, these unions remained legally forbidden until the 1960s.

Although federal legislation eventually ended government-sanctioned social oppression of African Americans, the legacy of the Black Codes and the social structures they strove to maintain remained a reality for Southern African Americans for years to come. In the early twenty-first century, poverty rates among black Mississippians were significantly higher than those among their white counterparts, a reflection of African Americans' ongoing struggles for true economic equality.

—*Vanessa E. Vaughn, MA*

Bibliography and Additional Reading

Foner, Eric. *Forever Free: The Story of Emancipation and Reconstruction*. New York: Knopf, 2005. Print.

Foner, Eric. *Reconstruction: America's Unfinished Revolution, 1863–1877*. New York: Harper, 2011. Print.

Garner, James Wilford. *Reconstruction in Mississippi*. New York: Macmillan, 1902. Print.

Wynne, Ben. *Mississippi's Civil War: A Narrative History*. Macon, GA: Mercer UP, 2006. Print.

■ Louisiana Black Code

Date: December 21, 1865
Author: Duncan F. Kenner
Genre: law

Summary Overview

The Louisiana Black Code consisted of a series of laws passed in December 1865 to regulate the transition of former slaves into a society where they would be allowed to earn a living without disrupting the economic and social order of the state. The newly elected, all-white legislature feared that without strict controls on the newly emancipated black population, the state's agrarian economy might not recover from the setbacks of the Civil War. The code set out certain limited rights for blacks, especially the right to enter into contracts, but at the same time placed heavy restrictions on their right to seek employment by creating penalties for vagrancy and establishing requirements for apprenticeship that effectively forced former slaves and their descendants to continue working for those who had once been their masters. Local authorities were given wide authority to enforce these restrictive practices.

Defining Moment

At the end of the Civil War, the agrarian economy of the South was in ruins. Nowhere was the devastation worse than in Louisiana, which during the antebellum period, depended heavily on slave labor to produce profitable crops. Whites wondered if newly emancipated African Americans would migrate to the North or West, creating a labor shortage. Some also feared that, unless strictly controlled, former slaves might take up arms against their former masters or other whites. At the same time, in the North, several influential politicians, civic leaders, and former abolitionists were campaigning for programs to grant former slaves equal rights immediately. Several radical groups and individuals urged that large plantations be broken up and their land given to former slaves.

In the fall of 1865, the newly reconstituted Louisiana Legislature decided that dealing with the potential labor crisis and thwarting more radical calls for equal rights for blacks was one of its most pressing issues. Legislators thought the most efficient and effective solution to avoiding potential chaos and thwarting Northern attempts to dictate economic policy was to adopt laws similar to those already passed in Mississippi, where legislators had enacted statutes to limit the ability of newly freed slaves to relocate out of areas where they were once held in bondage. Mississippi's Black Code actually granted new (though limited) rights to blacks, such as the right to acquire and dispose of property, to bring suit and sit on juries when issues involved other blacks, and to marry other blacks legally. At the same time, however, local authorities were given power to arrest any black person they determined to be a vagrant—that is, one not able to prove employment. Blacks were permitted to enter into contracts with employers, almost all of whom were white. However, to keep wages down and assure owners of large farms and other businesses a ready supply of labor, owners were prohibited from attempting to lure away workers by offering more lucrative wages to those already employed at another business or plantation.

Despite cries of alarm from newspapers such as the *New Orleans Tribune*, which championed the rights of African Americans, Louisiana's legislators moved quickly to enact a series of laws that would achieve two important goals: First, these laws would provide assurances for upper-class whites that they might continue to enjoy cheap, if not free, labor to restore the lifestyles they enjoyed before the war. Second, the laws would send a signal to the entire population that, despite the outcome of hostilities, the caste system that existed before the Civil War would remain intact, preserving the privileged status of all whites over blacks within the state.

Author Biography

Although Louisiana's new Black Code was officially the work of a joint committee of the legislature (signed by Duncan S. Cage and Albert Voorhies), the driving force behind the legislation was Duncan Farrar Kenner, a wealthy sugar planter and entrepreneur from Ascension Parish in the southern part of the state. Born in New Orleans in 1813, Kenner built a thriving business before the Civil War, becoming one of Louisiana's wealthiest citizens and largest slave owners. He also served several terms in the state legislature. When Louisiana seceded, Kenner helped draft the Confederate Constitution and served in the Confederate Legislature. After the war, he regained his property, which had been confiscated by federal troops. In October 1865, he was elected to the new Louisiana Legislature and immediately began lobbying for laws that would secure a workforce for himself and his fellow plantation owners. Until his death in 1887, he led efforts to improve Louisiana's sugar harvest, and was the first president of the Louisiana Sugar Planters' Association.

HISTORICAL DOCUMENT

AN ACT Relative to apprentices and indentured servants.

Section 1. Be it enacted by the Senate and House of Representatives of the State of Louisiana, in General Assembly convened, That it shall be the duty of Sheriffs, Justices of the Peace and other civil officers of this State, to report to the Clerks of the District Courts of their respective Parishes, and in the Parish of Orleans (left bank) to the Mayor of the City of New Orleans, and on the right bank to the President of the Police Jury, on the first Monday of each month, for each and every year, all persons under the age of eighteen years, if females, and twenty-one, if males, who are orphans, or whose parent, parents, or tutor, have not the means, or who refuse to provide for and maintain said minors; and, thereupon, it shall be the duty of the Clerks of the District Courts, Mayor and President of the Police Jury aforesaid, to examine whether the party or parties, so reported from time to time, come within the purview and meaning of this Act, and if so, to apprentice said minor or minors, in manner and form as prescribed by the Civil Code of the State of Louisiana; provided, that orphans coming under the provisions of this Act shall be authorized to select said employers when they have arrived at the age of puberty, unless they shall have been previously apprenticed; provided, that any indenture of apprentice or indented servant, made before a Justice of the Peace and two disinterested witnesses, and the original deposited with and recorded by the Recorder of Mortgages for the Parish, in a book provided for that purpose, shall be valid and binding on the parties, and when made by the clerk, shall be also deposited with the Recorder of Mortgages, and all expenses for passing said acts of indenture shall be paid by the employer.

Sec. 2. Be it further enacted, &c., That persons who have attained the age of majority, whether in this State or any other State of the United States, or in a foreign country, may bind themselves to services to be performed in this country, for the term of five years, on such terms as they may stipulate, as domestic servants and to work on farms, plantations or in manufacturing establishments, which contracts shall be valid and binding on the parties to the same.

Sec. 3. Be it further enacted, &c., That in all cases, when the age of the minor cannot be ascertained by record testimony, the Clerks of the District Courts, Mayor and President of the Police Jury, or Justices of the Peace aforesaid, shall fix the age, according to the best evidence before them.

Sec. 4. Be it further enacted, &c., That all laws or parts of laws conflicting with the provisions of this Act, be, and the same are hereby repealed, and that this Act take effect from and after its passage.

DUNCAN S. CAGE, Speaker of the House of Representatives.

ALBERT VOORHIES, Lieutenant Governor and President of the Senate.

Approved December 21, 1865.

J. MADISON WELLS

Governor of the State of Louisiana

GLOSSARY

age of majority: legal adulthood; when a person is no longer a minor

Civil Code: the written laws of Louisiana

parish: in Louisiana, the equivalent of a county

Police Jury: the governing body of a parish

Document Analysis

The idea of instituting a Black Code in Louisiana was hardly radical. The first Black Code —or slave code, as such laws were known in the antebellum period— had been passed in the eighteenth century, and subsequent legislation over the next 150 years tightened restrictions on activities of Louisiana's slave population. Duncan Kenner, author of Louisiana's statutes, saw the new Black Code as a way to achieve a goal he had first proposed in the Confederate Congress. Near the end of the Civil War, he had argued that the South might justify secession and ward off defeat by freeing its slaves, but could maintain the master-slave relationship by passing legislation that would in effect keep blacks subservient to whites.

On first reading, the language of the Louisiana Black Code appears moderate. The principal stated argument of section one is that, because the state requires a system to regulate labor, local officials are empowered to identify minors and apprentice them to someone who will be responsible for their welfare. Section two grants those who have reached the age of "majority" the right to enter into contracts for certain kinds of employment, and that contracts are binding on both parties. Sections three and four of the legislation clarify the role of local officials in determining who is a minor and make clear that these new laws supersede any earlier ones passed by the state.

Unlike Black Codes in other states, the Louisiana law does not mention African Americans specifically, but embedded in the language of these statutes are words and phrases that point indirectly at the population the legislators wished to control. Under the law, local governments can identify minors for apprenticeships if their parents or guardians "have not the means" or "refuse to provide for and maintain said minors." Children among Louisiana's indigent black population were most likely to fall into the former category, and determining who was refusing to provide for children is left to white authorities. The term "apprentice" can be seen as a code word for a form of indenture that binds youngsters for years of service to someone free to exploit their labor until they reach the age of majority (under this law, eighteen for women and twenty-one for men). Similarly, the right to enter into contracts is circumscribed by noting that these valid, binding, and oppressive agreements were only for those becoming domestic servants, farmworkers, or laborers in manufacturing establishments—positions that, in Louisiana, were dominated by slaves before the war. Hence, the new employment regulations gave owners the security of hiring workers who could not move easily to better paying jobs, in essence replacing the former system of bondage with one eerily similar to the previous arrangement between slaves and masters.

Essential Themes

Assessing the true impact of Louisiana's 1865 Black Code is difficult because the code remained in effect for only a brief period; within three years all Black

Codes in the South were nullified, either by state legislatures or by the actions of the federal government. Although intended to help white planters resurrect the agrarian economy that had allowed them to live luxuriously at the expense of black laborers, the codes alone could not restore real estate confiscated during the war or rebuild homes, mills, and factories destroyed during the conflict. While a few formerly wealthy plantation owners were able to regain prosperity in the postwar South, many were forced to sell their estates at a fraction of their prewar value; others simply abandoned their property, unable to pay taxes. Much of the migration that the Code was intended to stop had already occurred, and Southerners had no mechanism—nor could they create one legally—to force blacks who had fled from plantations during the war to return to the places where they once were enslaved.

Like all other Southern legislators who moved swiftly to enact black codes at the end of the Civil War, Louisiana lawmakers witnessed an almost immediate backlash. Many in the North viewed Black Codes as subterfuges to reinstitute slavery under the guise of labor regulation. Northern newspapers mounted a campaign against these laws, and many Republican legislators (later to become known as Radical Republicans) worked to enact laws that would overturn this new form of racial discrimination. Congress quickly passed the Civil Rights Act of 1866, guaranteeing equal protection to all citizens regardless of race, and the Reconstruction Acts of 1867, effectively abolishing white legislatures like Louisiana's and placing most Southern states under military rule. Most significantly, although Black Codes enacted by Louisiana and other Southern states were not the sole cause, they contributed to sentiment that led to the drafting and eventual passage of the Fourteenth Amendment to the US Constitution, which grants citizenship to everyone born or naturalized in the United States and prohibits individual states from abridging a citizen's rights in any way.

—*Laurence W. Mazzeno, PhD*

Bibliography and Additional Reading

Bauer, Craig A. *A Leader among Peers: The Life and Times of Duncan Farrar Kenner.* Lafayette: U of Southwestern Louisiana, 1993. Print.

Cohen, William. *At Freedom's Edge: Black Mobility and the Southern White Quest for Racial Control, 1861–1915.* Baton Rouge: Louisiana State UP, 1991. Print.

Dubois, W. E. B. *Black Reconstruction.* New York: Harcourt, 1935. Print.

Taylor, Joe Gray. *Louisiana Reconstructed, 1863–1877.* Baton Rouge: Louisiana State UP, 1974. Print.

Wilson, Theodore B. *The Black Codes of the South.* Tuscaloosa: U of Alabama P, 1965. Print.

■ Letter to T.P. Chandler

Date: June 1865
Author: Edwin McCaleb
Genre: letter

Summary Overview

A letter written by Edwin McCaleb to T.P. Chandler illustrates the experience of a white resident of the South in the aftermath of the Civil War and the assassination of President Abraham Lincoln. McCaleb describes the overall sense of chaos and confusion, which was furthered by the abrupt end of Lincoln's presidency and the installation of President Johnson. Although McCaleb was a Confederate soldier, he wrote in a way that demonstrated his high regard for President Lincoln and his disdain and distrust for Lincoln's successor, President Andrew Johnson.

Defining Moment

The Confederate states of the South suffered much destruction during the four years of the American Civil War. The population was drastically reduced, the economy was crippled, and the Thirteenth Amendment threatened the plantation lifestyle which had defined the South. In addition to the financial drain of the war efforts, the abolition of slavery forced the South to restructure its economy which had previously been dependent upon free slave labor. Reconstruction, an effort initiated by President Abraham Lincoln before the end of the war, sought to amend physical damages endured by the South and restore relations between the Union and the Confederacy. Upon Lincoln's assassination, Vice President Andrew Johnson became the new president, and continued restoration efforts. Johnson, however, essentially ignored the chaos created in the South by the sudden freedom of African American slaves, leaving the problem to be handled by individual states. His leniency toward participants in the rebellion was viewed as a violation of the Constitution.

In his letter, McCaleb expressed his beliefs regarding how the transition of African Americans from slavery to freedom should be handled. He outlines a gradual plan for emancipation, which contrasts with the reality of sudden emancipation that was granted to African American slaves. The reigning attitude of white supremacy is evident in McCaleb's letter, as he describes the recently freed population in a derogatory manner. While writing in favor of abolition, McCaleb demonstrates that his sympathy for African Americans stops there. An attitude of fear, bigotry, and intolerance, an attitude that was common even among citizens in the North, comes out in McCaleb's description of the dangers of equal regard for emancipated African Americans. McCaleb's expression of distrust of the president, and early recognition of his penchant for sidestepping the law for his own benefit were reflected in statements made in favor of impeachment of Johnson years later.

Author Biography

Edwin McCaleb was a Confederate officer during the Civil War. He was held captive as a prisoner of war in the North. McCaleb was seventeen years of age at the beginning of the war, when he left college for the army. Little information exists about McCaleb, but based on his statement that he was seventeen at the beginning of the Civil War, his birth year can be calculated to have been 1844. Although from the South, McCaleb spoke against secession. He fought as a soldier for the Mississippi Twelfth Infantry Regiment, Company K. McCaleb believed whites were intellectually and socially superior to African Americans, but opposed slavery.

HISTORICAL DOCUMENT

...As mail communication has been partially reopened with the North I avail myself of this my first opportunity to write to you. I have not been with the army since my release from prison. I can never forget the kindness shown me by yourself & family and I shall cherish to the day of my death sentiments of profound gratitude & esteem for your noble generosity & christianlike charity....

Our country is now in a disturbed condition caused by the fiery ordeal through which we just passed & the total absence of both military or civil law in all parts of this state except the few garrisoned towns. Were it not for the national quiet and law abiding disposition of our people we would be subjected to the augur of lawlessness and outrage. All good citizens deeply deplore the assassination of Pres. Lincoln.... Mr. L— was a great man and more than that was a good man and the country could ill afford to lose his services at this important crisis.... Mr. Johnson has disregarded the requirements of the Constitution & undertakes to enact military governments over the states that have hitherto only been at war with the Federal Government. And more than this, men are now being tried for their lives before military courts... instead of the civil tribunals of the land. This is in direct violation of the Constitution as these...were in no way connected with the Army.

This looks very much as that he has assumed arbitrary power & was overstepping his oath of office. I hoped he would convene Congress in Extra Session or take the counsel & advice of the able & learned statesmen of the Country. But even this he has failed to do. All the good men of the land desire to return to their peaceful avocations & be permitted to enjoy the blessings of liberty transmitted by our ancestors who fought side by side through the Revolution & on the plains of Mexico. But this they are not permitted to do & they are told that those who have taken up arms of defense of what they believed to be their rights under the old Federal Compact have no claims but mercy upon the General Government and those who now hold...power.... By this sudden system of Emancipation, this spasmodic transformation of the ignorant Negro from a peaceful laborer who has been accustomed to have all needs...provided...both in sickness & health to a self reliant citizen will paralyze the productive resources of the South. It... can cause a famine in this our fertile land. If we could have a system of gradual emancipation & colonization our people would universally rejoice & be glad to get rid of slavery which has ever been a cancer upon the body politic of our social organization.... We would gladly substitute white for slave labor but we can never regard the Negro our equal either intellectually or socially. The doctrine of "Miscegenation" or as the word which is a Latin compound ("Misco" to mix & "genus" race) signifies an amalgamation of the races, is odious, destructive & contrary to the laws of God & Man. If such a detestable dogma becomes a law we shall soon have a race of mulattoes as fickle & foolish as the Mongrel population of Mexico never content with their present condition but always desiring a change of government & rulers. The government ought to pursue a magnanimous merciful & conciliatory course toward those who have striven to be honorable...& who have acknowledged ourselves fairly beaten. Let the northern people arise in the majesty of their power & stay the uplifted hand of official oppression & hatred.... Let not the pages of American history be stained with a second recital of the reign of terror like the frightful record of the French Revolution in the memorable days of Danton & Robespierre. The only way to avoid these disasters is by a strict compliance with the Constitution & the laws.

I was only 17 years of age when this war commenced & the last speech I made before leaving college for the army was against secession and advocating the sovereignty of the Federal Government and yet I am now among the proscribed because I held a petty office in the army.

GLOSSARY

amalgamation: the process of uniting two or more things into one thing

miscegenation: the mixing of members of different racial groups through cohabitation, marriage, or sexual relations

mongrel: a term relating to an animal such as a dog that is of mixed breed used in a derogatory way to describe an individual of more than one racial origin

mulatto: a term that is considered offensive in modern times to describe a person from both African and European descent

Document Analysis

This letter illustrates the postwar conditions of the South, and the dissatisfaction with restoration efforts following the assassination of President Lincoln. The South is described as chaotic and lawless, while rebels are threatened with retaliation from the government, which is believed by the writer to be unconstitutional. Emancipation was sudden, and dramatically impacted the status quo of the South. The views of African Americans held by the writer represent typical attitudes of whites in both the North and the South at the time during which the letter was written.

While this letter was written to and intended for a single acquaintance rather than a large audience, it has historical significance. It provides an intimate synopsis of the experience in the South after the Civil War and the assassination of President Lincoln. Confederate soldiers, like McCaleb, returned to find their home states ravaged by war. The population was reduced by about one-fourth, property values had plummeted, and land and structures had been destroyed. The economy of the South was weakened and further threatened by the sudden emancipation of African American slaves, upon whom plantation owners had relied for free labor.

In addition to the economic hardships with which Southerners were faced following the war, Confederate states also had to accept the reality of living among free African Americans. A tremendous social adjustment was in order. In his letter, McCaleb accurately represents the attitude of white Americans toward African Americans, stating "we can never regard the Negro our equal either intellectually or socially." McCaleb goes on to warn against the destruction that would be faced by the nation if African Americans were ever to be regarded as equals and interactions between races were to be permitted. McCaleb asserts that the laws of God prohibit such interactions and to ignore such laws would result in "a race of mulattoes as fickle and foolish as the Mongrel population of Mexico."

Despite his belief in superiority of whites over African Americans, McCaleb demonstrates opposition to slavery, referring to it as "a cancer upon the body politic of our social organization." In his letter, McCaleb suggests an alternative procedure of emancipation, which is more gradual and allows both plantation owners and African American slaves time to adjust to the economic and social shift. Not only is the economy of the South threatened by the removal of slavery as a resource, McCaleb argues, but by the responsibility to care for this population that is presumed to be ignorant, incompetent, and unable to care for itself without the intervention of whites.

McCaleb's letter represents his high regard for the recently assassinated President Abraham Lincoln, as well as his distrust of President Johnson. His affinity for President Lincoln likely was not representative of the popular opinion in the South of the president during the Civil War, but accurately reflected the growing sentiment for Johnson. Johnson, despite being advised to advocate for African American rights, deferred the responsibility to the states. Johnson was far more lenient than his predecessor in his punishment of rebels, granting amnesty for those who owned property valued above $20,000. In contrast to his lenient policy, McCaleb described Johnson's trial of rebels as unconstitutional because of his use of military, rather than civil courts to try rebels with no affiliation with the army.

Essential Themes

McCaleb's letter contains themes with lasting significance, including his positions on slavery, race equality, and reconstruction in the South. Although slavery never again became permitted in the United States following the Emancipation Proclamation, African Americans continued to be treated poorly by whites and were often employed under unfair, binding contracts that offered little more freedom than they had as slaves. Race inequality remained a topic of contention, which erupted during the Civil Rights Movement of the 1960s. Efforts to grant rights and freedoms to African Americans were made during the Reconstruction Era, but were largely unsuccessful. The South maintained an impoverished identity despite charities and programs designed to support the Reconstruction efforts. The Panic of 1873, which led to a national economic depression, further crippled the South.

Opposing viewpoints were held regarding how restoration should be implemented. While economic and structural restoration of the South were common goals, McCaleb's letter demonstrates the viewpoint of the side advocating for the limitation of rights of African Americans. Opponents pressed for freedom and rights of former slaves. Historically, a social compromise can be seen. The Black Codes sought to further white supremacy and restrict the freedoms of African Americans. The Fourteenth Amendment was passed, granting legal citizenship to anyone born in the United States, including African Americans. While this gave citizenship rights and protection by laws to African Americans, it provided little in terms of equal treatment. African Americans continued to be viewed as inferior to whites, and it was out of this belief that Jim Crow laws were born. These laws required racial segregation and remained in effect for nearly a century, until the Civil Rights Movement of the 1960s.

—*Jennifer D. Henry, MEd*

Bibliography and Additional Reading

"Constitution of the United States: Amendments 11–27." *National Archives*. National Archives and Records Administration. Web. 29 March, 2014.

Kennedy, Stetson. *Jim Crow Guide to the U.S.A.: The Laws, Customs and Etiquette Governing the Conduct of Nonwhites and Other Minorities as Second-Class Citizens*. 2nd ed. Tuscaloosa, AL: University of Alabama Press, 2011. Print.

McCaleb, Edwin H. "Letter to T.P. Chandler." 1865. *Digital History*. Eds. S. Mintz & S. McNeil. University of Houston, 2012. Web. 29 Mar. 2014.

"Reconstruction." The Columbia Encyclopedia. New York: Columbia University Press, 2013. Credo Reference. Web. 29 March 2014.

Schultz, Kevin. *HIST2*. 2nd ed. Vol. 1. Boston, MA: Wadsworth-Cengage Learning, 2012. Print.

■ "A Long Silence"

Date: September 22, 1867
Author: Kate Stone
Genre: diary

Summary Overview

This diary entry by Kate Stone represents the perspective of a young Southern woman who believed in the Confederate cause, opposed abolition, and was forced to adjust to the realities of the post-Civil War South. The entry illustrates the common experience of many landowners of the South who had returned home after the war to find their property destroyed. Like Stone's family, many were faced with the burden of having to reconstruct their land with fewer financial and physical resources than they had before the war. Her family, like many landowners during the Reconstruction period, produced cotton for investors instead of focusing on producing food for their own household. Stone describes the common practice of receiving credit from a merchant. The financial drain of paying wages to laborers prevented Stone and her family from affording the luxuries they had enjoyed before the war.

Defining Moment

The years following the Civil War, known as Reconstruction, were a time of political, economic, and social transition for United States citizens living in the South. Landowners and their families struggled to recover from the physical destruction that took place as a result of the war. Many men were killed in the war, leaving their families to fend for themselves. The lucrative plantation lifestyle that was dependent upon slave labor was no longer feasible for most landowners when slavery was abolished by the Thirteenth Amendment. Plantation ownership became much more costly, and luxuries had to be sacrificed in order to compensate laborers. In addition to higher expenses, landowners had less control over their laborers as African Americans began taking advantage of their freedoms. Former slaves now had the option to send their children to school rather than into the fields. African American women could devote their time to their families, focusing on responsibilities in the home. The harsh Black Codes imposed by many Southern states promoted racism, and fostered an environment of racial inequality.

Kate Stone's diary entry was one of many written by her between the years of 1861 and 1868. She documented her experiences, presumably with only herself as her intended audience. This particular entry describes the difficulties of adjusting to the unfamiliar life of poverty. Stone also discusses natural threats to what remains of her family's livelihood, such as cotton worms and flooding. She describes the African American workers as out of control and expresses an intense fear of them. What may have been more frightening for Stone than the behavior of the African Americans was her understanding of the justification they would have in seeking retaliation for the many years of mistreatment they endured. Stone's diary entry highlights the many challenges, feelings, and attitudes that were shared by Confederates like her during the Reconstruction era. She mentions, at the end of her entry, that attending social events and being among others who are similarly affected makes her struggles more bearable. This demonstrates the commonality of her circumstances in the South at this time in history. The hardships described by Stone were the same that caused many landowners to go into debt, and prompted alternative labor systems, such as sharecropping.

Author Biography

Sarah Katherine Stone, who was known as "Kate," was born in Mississippi in 1841. She began keeping a diary when the Civil War began in 1861. Stone was educated, and enjoyed a privileged childhood growing up on a large 1,260 acre plantation in Louisiana called

"Brokenburn." At the time of the diary entry, Stone was living with her mother, Amanda Susan Ragan Stone. Stone had five brothers and one sister, with whom she also lived at Brokenburn. Her family owned about 150 slaves. In 1863, Stone and her family relocated to Texas after a Union Army presence became apparent in their neighborhood. From late 1863 until the end of the war, Kate Stone and her family resided in Tyler, Texas. It was in Tyler that she met the man who would later become her husband. They returned to Brokenburn after the war ended. Stone firmly believed in the Confederate cause, and demonstrated her ongoing loyalty through activism long after the Civil War. She married Henry Bry Holmes in 1869, with whom she had four children. Kate Stone died in 1907.

HISTORICAL DOCUMENT

September 22, 1867

A long silence and a year of hard endeavor to raise a crop, reconstruct the place with the problem of hired labor, high water, and cotton worms. Mamma had little trouble in getting advances in New Orleans to plant. Cotton is so high that merchants are anxious to advance to put in a crop, and there is much Northern capital seeking investment in that field. Mr. Given became Mamma's merchant. Col. Cornelius Fellowes, her old friend, has not resumed business, or only in a small way. The Negroes demanded high wages, from $20 to $25 for men, in addition to the old rations of sugar, rice, tobacco, molasses, and sometimes hams. Many of the old hands left, and My Brother went to New Orleans and brought back a number of ex-Negro soldiers, who strutted around in their uniforms and were hard to control. I was deadly afraid of them. During the spring while Mamma and I were in New Orleans (Mamma on business and she took me for my pleasure), and Uncle Bo and My Brother and Jimmy were away for a few hours, Johnny had a fight with a young Negro in the field, shot and came near killing him, and was mobbed in return. Johnny would have been killed but for the stand one of the Negroes made for him and Uncle Bo's opportune arrival just as the Negroes brought him to the house—a howling, cursing mob with the women shrieking, "Kill him!" and all brandishing pistols and guns. It came near breaking up the planting, and it is a pity it did not as it turned out. Johnny had to be sent away. He was at school near Clinton [Miss.] and the Negroes quieted down and after some weeks the wounded boy recovered, greatly to Johnny's relief. He never speaks now of killing people as he formerly had a habit of doing. He came home when school closed and there was no further trouble.

Then the water came up and we were nearly overflowed. The cotton planted was very late, and when it was looking as luxuriant and promising as possible and we saw ease of mind before us, the worms came. In a few days the fields were blackened like fire had swept over them. We made about twenty bales and spent $25,000 doing it. What most distresses me is that none of that money went for our personal comfort. All of it went to the Negroes. Mamma would buy only bare necessities for the table and plainest clothes for the family. Not a luxury, no furniture, carpets, or anything. We are worse off for those things than even in Texas and such a sum spent! But Mamma said it was not honest to spend the money on anything but making the crop. All in this section have suffered in the same way, and for awhile they seemed stunned by their misfortunes. But now the reaction has come, and all are taking what pleasure offers.

Old neighbors and new ones have come in and all seemed to be anxious to be together and talk over their trials and tribulations. There has been much visiting and various picnics and fish frys. I would not go at first. I felt like I did not want to see anybody or ever dance again. I felt fully forty years old, but Mamma made me go after a good cry. Once there, I was compelled to exert myself, and soon I was enjoying it all. The burden of some of the years slipped from my shoulders, and I was young again. It was pleasant to talk nonsense, to be flattered though one knew it was flattery, and to be complimented and fussed over. So since then, Mamma, the boys, and all of us have been going to everything and have found even poverty in company more bearable than when suffered alone.

GLOSSARY

advance: cash advance, to be paid back (in this case) after a crop is harvested and sold

cotton worm: a.k.a, cotton leafworm: the larva of a moth, *Alabama argillacea*, that feeds on the cotton plant

Document Analysis

Kate Stone's diary entry provides an intimate portrait of the life of the daughter of a plantation owner in Louisiana following the events of the Civil War and the passage of the Thirteenth Amendment, which abolished slavery. Growing up on the Brokenburn plantation, Stone enjoyed luxuries such as carpets, furniture, and curtains. She was educated and literate. Her family depended upon slave labor to operate their plantation. When Union soldiers began to occupy her neighborhood, she and her family fled to Texas, where they stayed until the war ended. Natural factors including flooding and cotton worms threatened the family's crops. Abolition had eliminated free slave labor, and provision of wages to laborers caused Stone and her family to face financial hardships they had previously never experienced. Stone's diary entry describes the dramatic shift to an impoverished lifestyle from one of luxury, means, and financial stability.

As with Stone and her family, many landowners faced this new financial burden. Stone states, "All in this section have suffered in the same way, and for awhile they seemed stunned by their misfortunes." The sudden necessity of paid labor was incompatible with the slave-dependent plantation model that had been so common and successful in the South before the war. Stone laments the loss of the many luxuries, and expresses resentment toward the African Americans for their role in her family's poverty. She complains of the high wages and accommodations expected by the African American laborers. Stone further expresses her dissatisfaction with having to pay for labor, writing, "What most distresses me is that none of that money went for our personal comfort. All of it went to the Negroes." Although the African American laborers clearly worked for their earnings, Stone perceives it as an injustice. Her attitude represents the reigning white supremacist view among whites in the South in the years following the Civil War.

Kate Stone was certainly not alone in her feelings of fear and disgust for African Americans. Beliefs such as those held by Stone played an important role in the South's threat to secede, which sparked the Civil War. Although legislation interrupted their way of life, the values and beliefs of the Confederacy remained strong. These values and beliefs became evident through the assembly and actions of the extreme white supremacist group, the Ku Klux Klan. The Black Codes were passed in Southern states, including Mississippi and Louisiana (incidentally, the state in which Stone was born and the location of Brokenburn, respectively). These Codes limited the rights and employment options of African Americans; resulted in labor contracts that were unfair to African Americans; and, in some cases, permitted slavery through vagrancy laws. Vagrancy laws allowed homeless African Americans to be arrested and punished with unpaid labor. Stone also describes examples of power struggles that took place between African American laborers and her brother. Such disagreements were common as African Americans sought to assert themselves as employees rather than property, and landowners intended to maintain the same dynamic they had maintained as slave owners.

Essential Themes

One of the most significant themes of Kate Stone's diary entry is the fall of the plantation lifestyle as it existed before the Civil War. Dramatic economic and social changes took place as a result of the war and the ratification of the Thirteenth Amendment. Like many wealthy plantation owners in the South, Kate Stone and her family were forced to suddenly adjust to paying wages to laborers. The success of plantations had hinged on free slave labor, and abolition represented the loss of the most crucial resource of plantation owners. Plantations could no longer yield nearly the profits they had, and many landowners resorted to alternative labor systems, such as sharecropping.

Kate Stone's diary entry illustrates her fear of African Americans, as well as her resentment toward them. She embraces Confederate values and perspectives, including racial inequality. Another important theme of Stone's diary entry is the attitude she expresses toward African Americans. Common viewpoints of Confederates included the belief that African Americans were inferior to whites, as well as widespread opposition to abolition. Such viewpoints were essential in the establishment of the Ku Klux Klan, the Black Codes, and Jim Crow laws that enforced racial segregation for nearly a century. Attitudes, such as those of Confederates, created a lengthy and difficult struggle for African Americans. The Fourteenth and Fifteenth Amendments, which granted to African Americans citizenship and voting rights, respectively, were met with much opposition from Southern whites. As African Americans were granted more rights and had reason to view themselves as equal to whites, such views were challenged by the enforcement of Jim Crow laws and the violence of the Ku Klux Klan. While the frustrations of a young woman, whose lifestyle had recently been dramatically altered for the worse, seems to barely represent such extremes as racial segregation and violence, the attitudes and beliefs are not far removed from one another.

—*Jennifer D. Henry, MEd*

Bibliography and Additional Reading

"America's Reconstruction: People and Politics After the Civil War." *Digital History*. Eds. S. Mintz & S. McNeil. University of Houston, 2013. Web. 6 Apr. 2014.

"Constitution of the United States: Amendments 11–27." *National Archives*. National Archives and Records Administration. n.d. Web. 29 Mar. 2014.

Kennedy, Stetson. *Jim Crow Guide to the U.S.A.: The Laws, Customs and Etiquette Governing the Conduct of Nonwhites and Other Minorities as Second-Class Citizens*. 2nd ed. Tuscaloosa, AL: University of Alabama Press, 2011. Print.

Rubin, Anne Sarah. "Stone, Sarah Katherine 'Kate' (1841–1907)." *Encyclopedia of the American Civil War: A Political, Social, and Military History*. Santa Barbara: ABC-CLIO, 2000. Credo Reference. Web. 6 Apr. 2014.

Stone, Kate. "All Have Suffered" *Reconstruction: America's Second Civil War*. PBS.org. 19 Dec. 2003. Web. 6 Apr. 2014.

■ From *Ten Years on a Georgia Plantation since the War*

Date: 1868 (published 1883)
Author: Frances Butler Leigh
Genre: memoir

Summary Overview

In her memoir, Frances Butler Leigh provides an account of the changes in plantation life during the chaos and uncertainty of the Reconstruction period. Leigh's family had significant holdings on the Georgia Sea Islands that had relied upon slave labor. In this excerpt, she describes her attempts to reinvigorate the plantations owned by her family and to navigate a strange new racially-charged and ethnically-divided postwar reality. Leigh strongly defended slavery and bemoaned the difficulty of managing a paid labor force, one that was not as deferential as she felt was appropriate. Describing her efforts to set up a sharecropping system on her family's plantations, Leigh also comments at length on her views of various ethnic groups, such as the Irish and Chinese, whom she describes in terms of their fitness and willingness to perform certain types of labor.

Defining Moment

At the end of the Civil War, most of the land seized in the South was returned to its former owners. Many landowners in the former Confederacy, who had previously owned plantations worked by slaves, returned to try to reestablish their livelihoods. Many plantation owners attempted to set up sharecropping systems with their former slaves. This was not necessarily a smooth transition, as Frances Butler Leigh records in her memoir. Former slaves were reluctant to work as they had before and harbored a deep distrust of these landowners. Former owners and plantation managers were often unable to accept the new status of the people they had considered their property and ingrained hostility and racism tainted these relationships. Some white Southerners attempted to return black laborers to a condition of servitude by force or by refusing to pay wages that had been earned. Some found it difficult to accept any change in race relations, let alone having black men in public office or positions of authority. When combined with the loss of a generation of young white men in the former Confederacy and the influx of relief workers, teachers, politicians, and profiteers from the North, there was a nostalgic feeling on the part of many white Southerners that life had been much better before the war and that the proper relationship between black and white was as it had been then—that of slave and master. Leigh herself believed that black men and women were only fit for this. "I confess I am utterly unable to understand them, and what God's will is concerning them, unless He intended they should be slaves." This belief, and the unwillingness of many white Southerners to accept the rights of newly enfranchised black citizens, undermined social interactions in the Reconstruction period.

In addition to the perceived threat that a free black population posed to the rebuilding of the South, there was the very real problem of establishing a profitable management model when plantations had previously relied on unpaid slave labor. Former slaves now had options other than manual labor and could leverage their labor for greater pay and better working conditions. Leigh bemoaned the fact that "we have a gang of Irishmen doing the banking and ditching, which the negroes utterly refuse to do any more at all." Throughout former Confederate states, former slaves and their former masters negotiated the terms of labor, with both sides wary and resentful of one another.

Author Biography

Frances Butler Leigh was born in 1838 to Pierce Mease Butler, a slave-holding Georgia plantation owner, and Frances Anne "Fanny" Kemble, a famous British actress and an antislavery activist and writer. Leigh's parents' incompatible stances on slavery led to their divorce in 1849, when Leigh was eleven. Pierce Butler gained custody of their two daughters, and Leigh spent the Civil War years in the North, traveling to the Georgia Sea Islands with her father in 1866 to try to save their interests in cotton and rice plantations there. After her father died of malaria the following year, she became the sole proprietor of the plantations on St. Simons Island and Butler Island. She married Reverend John Wentworth Leigh, an English clergyman, in 1871, and they lived on St. Simons Island until moving to England in 1877, after more than a decade of struggle trying to return the plantation to profitability. In 1883, Leigh published *Ten Years on a Georgia Plantation since the War*, a book that many believe was written as a direct response to her mother's antislavery treatise, *Journal of a Residence on a Georgian Plantation* in 1838–1839, which had been published in 1863. Leigh died in England in 1910.

HISTORICAL DOCUMENT

Christmas 1868.

Dearest M____, You have heard of our safe arrival, and how much more comfortable the travelling was than last year. We arrived about a month ago, and I have been hard at work ever since. The negroes do not seem to be in a very satisfactory condition, but it is owing in a great measure, I think, to its being Christmas time. They are all prepared again to make their own, and different, terms for next year, but except for the bother and trouble I don't feel very anxious about it, for we have a gang of Irishmen doing the banking and ditching, which the negroes utterly refuse to do any more at all, and therefore, until the planting begins, we can do without the negro labour.

Last year they humbugged me completely by their expressions of affection and desire to work for me, but now that the novelty of their getting back once more to home has entirely worn off and they have lost their old habits of work, the effects of freedom are beginning to tell, and everywhere sullen unwillingness to work is visible, and all round us people are discussing how to get other labourers in the place of negroes. But alas! on the rice lands white labour is impossible, so that I really don't know what we shall do, and I think things look very gloomy for the planters. Our Northern neighbours on St. Simon's, the D___s, who were most hopeful last year, are now perfectly discouraged with the difficulties they have to encounter with their labour, and of course having to lose two or three months every year while the negroes are making up their minds whether they will work or not, obliges us to plant much less ground than we should otherwise do. However, there is no use taking evil on account, and when we are ruined will be time enough to say free labour here is a failure, and I still hope that when their Christmas excitement is over, the people will settle down to work…

We had a small excitement about this time, owing to a report which went the round of the plantations, that there was to be a general negro insurrection on the 1st of the year. I did not much believe it, but as I had promised my friends at the North, who were very anxious about me, to run no risks and to take every precaution against danger, I thought it best to seek some means of protection. I first asked my friend whether she felt nervous and would rather leave the Island, but she, being a true soldier's daughter, said no, she would stay and take her chance with me. We then agreed to say nothing about it to my maid, who was a new English maid, thinking that if we did not mind having our throats cut, neither need she—particularly as she now spent most of her time weeping at the horrors which surrounded her.

I wrote therefore to our nearest military station and asked that a guard of soldiers might be sent over for a day or two, which was done. But as they came without any officer, and conducted themselves generally disagreeably, stealing the oranges, worrying the negroes, and making themselves entirely at home even to the point of demanding to be fed by me, I packed them off, preferring to take my chance with my negroes than with my protectors. I don't believe that there was the least foundation for the report of the insurrection, but we had trouble enough the whole winter in one form or other.

The negroes this year and the following seemed to reach the climax of lawless independence, and I never slept without a loaded pistol by my bed. Their whole manner was changed; they took to calling their former owners by their last name without any title before it, constantly spoke of my agent as old R___, dropped the pleasant term of "Mistress," took to calling me "Miss Fanny," walked about with guns upon their shoulders, worked just as much and when they pleased, and tried speaking to me with their hats on, or not touching them to me when they passed me on the banks. This last rudeness I never permitted for a moment, and always said sharply, "Take your hat off instantly," and was obliged to take a tone to them generally which I had never done before. One or two, who seemed rather more inclined to be insolent than the rest, I dismissed, always saying, "You are free to leave the place, but not to stay here and behave as you please, for I am free too, and moreover own the place, and so have a right to give my orders on it, and have them obeyed."

I felt sure that if I relaxed my discipline for one moment all was up, and I never could control the negroes or plant the place again; and to this unerring rule I am sure I owe my success, although for that year, and the two following, I felt the whole time that it was touch-and-go whether I or the negroes got the upper hand.

A new trouble came upon us too, or rather an old trouble in a new shape. Negro adventurers from the North, finding that politics was such a paying trade at the South, began pouring in, and were really worse than the whites, for their Southern brethren looked upon their advent quite as a proof of a new order of things, in which the negroes were to rule and possess the land.

We had a fine specimen in one Mr. Tunis Campbell, whose history is rather peculiar. Massachusetts had the honour of giving him birth, and on his first arrival in Georgia he established himself, whether with or without permission I know not, on St. Catherine's Island, a large island midway between Savannah and Darien, which was at that time deserted. The owner, without returning, rented it to a Northern party, who on coming to take possession found Mr. Campbell established there, who declined to move, on some pretended permission he had from the Government to occupy it, and it was necessary to apply to the authorities at Darien to remove

him, which was done by sending a small armed force. He then came to Darien, and very soon became a leader of the negroes, over whom he acquired the most absolute control, and managed exactly as he pleased, so that when the first vote for State and county authorities was cast, he had no difficulty in having himself elected a magistrate, and for several years administered justice with a high hand and happy disregard of law, there being no one to oppose him.

Happily, he at last went a little too far, and arrested the captain of a British vessel, which had come to Darien for timber, for assault and battery, because he pushed Campbell's son out of the way on the deck of his own ship. The captain was brought before Campbell, tried, and sentenced to pay a heavy fine, from which he very naturally appealed to the English Consul in Savannah, who of course ordered his release at once. This and some other equally lawless acts by which Mr. Campbell was in the habit of filling his own pockets, drew the attention of the authorities to him, and a very good young judge having just been put on our circuit, he was tried for false imprisonment, and sentenced to one year's imprisonment himself, which not only freed us from his iniquitous rule, against which we had had no appeal, but broke the spell which he held over the negroes, who up till the time of his downfall, had believed his powers omnipotent, and at his instigation had defied all other authority; which state of things had driven the planters to despair, for there seemed to be no remedy for this evil, the negroes throwing all our authority to the wind, and following Campbell wherever he chose to lead them.

So desperate were some of the gentlemen, that at one time they entertained the idea of seeing if they could not buy Campbell over, and induce him by heavy bribes to work for us, or rather to use his influence over our negroes to make them work for us. And this proposition was made to me, but I could not consent to such a plan. In the first place it was utterly opposed to my notions of what was right, and my pride revolted from the idea of making any such bargain with a creature like Campbell; besides which I felt sure it was bad policy, that if we bought him one day he would sell us the next. So I refused to have anything to do with the project, and it was fortunately never carried out, for although during the next three or four years Campbell gave us infinite trouble, he would have given us far more had we put ourselves in his power by offering him a bribe.

Among other subjects connected with our rice plantations was one which interested us all very much at that time—the question of introducing Chinese labour on our plantations in the place of negro labour, which just then seemed to have become hopelessly unmanageable. There seemed to be a general move in this direction all through the Southern States, and I have no doubt was only prevented by the want of means of the planters, which, as far as I personally am concerned, I am glad was the case. Just then, however, we were all very keen about it, and it sounded very easy, the Pacific Railway having opened a way for them to reach us. One agent actually came for orders, and I, with the others, engaged some seventy to try the experiment with, first on General's Island. I confess I felt a little nervous about the result, but agreed with my neighbours in not being willing to see half my property uncultivated and going to ruin for want of labour. It was not only that negro labour could no longer be depended upon, but they seemed to be dying out so fast, that soon there would be but few left to work. This new labour would of course have sealed their doom,

and in a few years none would have been left. I wrote about it at the time—

Poor people! it seems impossible to arouse them to any good ambition, their one idea and desire being—not to work. Their newspaper in Charlestown, edited by a negro, published an article the other day on the prospect, and said it would be the best thing that could happen to the negroes if the Chinese did come, as then they too could get them as servants, and no longer have to work even for themselves. I confess I am utterly unable to understand them, and what God's will is concerning them, unless He intended they should be slaves. This may shock you; but why in their own country have they no past history, no monuments, no literature, never advance or improve, and here, now that they are free, are going steadily backwards, morally, intellectually, and physically. I see it on my own place, where, in spite of school and ministers, and every inducement offered them to improve their condition, they are steadily going downwards, working less and worse every year, until, from having come to them with my heart full of affection and pity for them, I am fast growing weary and disgusted.

GLOSSARY

banking and ditching: the making of earthen slopes and ditches; working the land; landscaping

guard of soldiers: military guard unit

humbug: to deceive or hoax

Document Analysis

Leigh's memoir examines a political and social world in flux and portrays the struggle of white Southerners to accept the changed status of their former slaves. Many Southerners staunchly believed in the inherent inferiority of black people, and it was this deeply ingrained belief that had been used to justify the institution of slavery, enabling slavery to spread to the western territories. Part of this ideology was the belief that slavery was a positive influence on people of African descent, and without the structure that slavery provided, they would slip into moral degeneracy. Leigh assumed that her former slaves would welcome the chance to do

the same work they had done before—work that she deemed white laborers would not perform. She was quite appalled when her former slaves sought to negotiate the terms of their relationship with their employers, and she quickly decided that slavery had been a better, more "natural" state of being for them. The "effects of freedom," she writes, was "sullen unwillingness to work."

Leigh expresses her relief that she did not need to rely on black laborers for her winter projects, as she had managed to find Irish men willing to perform the work. She is very concerned with her rice plantations, as rice farming was particularly onerous work, and for the most part, "on the rice lands white labour is impossible." Leigh also feels deceived by her former slaves, whose initial relief and pleasure at the "novelty of their getting back once more to home" to their plantations as wage-earners after the war failed to produce the placid, reliable work force that Leigh and others had envisioned. They often failed to agree to the plantation owners' proposed terms, and Leigh worries that the owners would "lose two or three months every year while the negroes are making up their minds whether they will work or not." Leigh and other plantation owners contemplated bringing in Chinese laborers to work on the rice plantations, an idea that many former slaves welcomed. "Their newspaper in Charlestown, edited by a negro, published an article the other day on the prospect, and said it would be the best thing that could happen to the negroes if the Chinese did come, as then they too could get them as servants, and no longer have to work even for themselves," Leigh writes, shocked to see her former slaves adapting to the lifestyle to which she was accustomed.

Leigh and other plantation owners also worried about violence in uncertain times, and when rumors circulated about a potential insurrection, she asked for soldiers to be sent over to protect her. The soldiers proved to be more trouble than they were worth, and Leigh wound up "preferring to take my chance with my negroes than with my protectors." Note Leigh's continued use of the possessive when referring to the freedmen working on her land. This attitude permeates her writing, and indeed, the biggest strain on Leigh's well-being seems to have been the insolence and disrespect of her former slaves, who dropped titles of respect and no longer removed their hats as she walked by. When she felt disrespected by her workers, she dismissed them, using their freedom as the reason for doing so: "You are free to leave the place, but not to stay here and behave as you please, for I am free too, and moreover own the place, and so have a right to give my orders on it, and have them obeyed."

In the book's addenda, Leigh writes of her impressions of the freedmen upon visiting the South after an absence of six years, noting, "I cannot help thinking things are worse than when they were disciplined and controlled by a superior race, notwithstanding the drawbacks to the system, and, in some cases, grave abuses attending it." Throughout her memoir, Leigh maintains a strong apologist stance for slavery, arguing that the abuses that took place under the slave system were balanced out by the resultant subservience and efficiency of her slaves.

Essential Themes

Leigh's memoir offers a fascinating perspective into the minds of former slaveholders in the years following the Civil War, as they attempted to adapt not only to the drastic economic changes that occurred with the abolition of slavery but to the dramatic social changes as well. Leigh's memoir provides insight into the challenges plantation owners faced in managing their holdings after the war, with Leigh seemingly less upset about the expense of having to pay her laborers than with the inconvenience of having to negotiate with them. Despite Leigh's decade-long struggle to return the plantation to profitability, her account seems less preoccupied with the economic changes that occurred with the abolition of slavery than with the changes to the power dynamic between former slaves and slaveholders.

—*Bethany Groff, MA*

Bibliography and Additional Reading

Bell, Malcolm, Jr. *Major Butler's Legacy: Five Generations of a Slaveholding Family*. Athens: U of Georgia P, 1987. Print.

Berry, Stephen W. "Butler Family." *New Georgia Encyclopedia*. Georgia Humanities Council and the University of Georgia Press, 16 Dec. 2013. Web. 29 Jan. 2014.

"Frances Butler Leigh, 1838–1910." *Documenting the American South*. University Library, University of North Carolina at Chapel Hill, 2004. Web. 29 Jan. 2014.

Leigh, Frances Butler. *Ten Years on a Georgia Plantation since the War, 1866–1876*. Savannah: Beehive Press, 1992. Print.

Morsman, Amy Feely. *The Big House after Slavery: Virginia Plantation Families and Their Postbellum Domestic Experiment*. Charlottesville: U of Virginia P, 2010.

EXTREME REACTIONS

The rise of the Ku Klux Klan (KKK), a hate group responsible for violence against blacks (and their white supporters), was an unforeseen consequence of Reconstruction. Although some government officials and members of the public did warn against the prospect of white vigilante groups forming after the war, the scope and range of the Klan and its activities took many observers by surprise. In truth, most of these Klan organizations were independent outfits only loosely affiliated with each another; some of them even actively competed against one another. Still, there is no doubt that they managed to disrupt postwar efforts to bring civil rights to African Americans living in the South.

Several descriptions of Klan activities are presented in this section. These range from an unofficial "notice" by a KKK group to a black Republican elected official in Georgia to various accounts of violence and faulty elections in Georgia, North Carolina, and Tennessee to a book chapter recalling Klan outrages in South Carolina written by a black "'Carpet-Bagger' [i.e., Northerner] Who Was Born and Lived There."

■ Notice from the Ku Klux Klan to Davie Jeems

Date: 1868
Author: anonymous
Genre: letter

Summary Overview

The first years after the Civil War proved to be a time of racial and political violence in the former Confederacy. Federal troops enforced the rights of former slaves to vote and own property, and many of the former Confederate states achieved biracial Republican legislatures and set up schools, transportation networks, and civil assistance organizations for former slaves. Former Confederate soldiers—disenfranchised, armed, and eager to restore white supremacy—took advantage of the postwar chaos to threaten and intimidate African American citizens. Republicans, white and black, were targets of gangs, especially the newly formed Ku Klux Klan (KKK), which used violence to deprive newly enfranchised Southern black citizens of their rights. In 1868 alone, the Freedmen's Bureau catalogued 336 cases of murder or attempted murder. The KKK attacked black men and women and white "carpetbaggers," outsiders who were assumed to be (and usually were) aiding the cause of the former slaves. In this letter, an anonymous writer assumes the character of the ghost of a Confederate soldier to threaten a black elected official in Lincoln County, Georgia.

Defining Moment

In the Georgia state elections of 1867 and 1868, many seats were won by black candidates or white Republicans seen to be closely allied with their interests. This outraged many former Confederates, and the Ku Klux Klan, formed in 1866 in Tennessee, gained significant support in Georgia. For many white people in Georgia, the KKK and its public wing, the Young Men's Democratic Club, offered the chance to take action and return the states to what they considered the proper racial hierarchy. In early 1868, Confederate General Nathan Bedford Forrest visited Atlanta several times,

and though his meetings were secret, it is widely believed that he used these visits to set up a formal Ku Klux Klan organization in the state. On March 31, 1868, Republican organizer George Ashburn was murdered in Columbus, and by the summer of 1868, attacks against African Americans and their allies were widespread across Georgia.

Many of the members of the Ku Klux Klan were former Confederate soldiers who were armed, experienced fighters with a personal reason to hate carpetbaggers, or Northerners who moved to the South after the Civil War, and the changes to the political and social structure that came with the enfranchisement of African American voters. Many believed that black voters were being tricked into supporting Republican candidates, since they were too ignorant to know for whom to vote. Like the Confederate "rebel yell," early Klan activity was designed to terrorize and intimidate. They paraded at night dressed in ominous white costumes and left letters and posters signed by the ghosts of dead Confederate soldiers. They threatened Republican leaders with violence unless they left their post. Homes and barns were burned to the ground, and livestock was stolen or slaughtered. The Ku Klux Klan became increasingly violent through 1868, and to add to threats and intimidation, there were hundreds of cases of whippings, particularly of women, as well as arson and murder.

The political terrorism of the Ku Klux Klan was very effective in Georgia. At some polling places, the Klan was able to overpower federal troops protecting voters. In elections from April to November of 1868, the Democrats won dozens of seats, as voters were too intimidated to vote for Republican candidates. Some elected officials were too frightened to take their seats and resigned. Georgia was almost completely under conservative Democratic control by the end of 1871.

In addition to political terrorism, the Ku Klux Klan attempted to return free Southern blacks to a state of servitude. They whipped women seen as insolent, burned churches and schools, disrupted social gatherings, and attacked teachers and relief workers. Anyone who was accused of not showing the proper deference to a white man could be beaten or killed. African American communities became increasingly isolated, but also developed strong internal support networks. After the Klan's political goals were realized and its leaders aggressively pursued by the federal government, the popularity of the organization waned, though local groups remained active. The note left for Davie Jeems in 1868 was typical of the kind of intimidation technique employed by the Ku Klux Klan that resulted in Republican losses throughout the state.

Author Biography

The writer of the note to Davie Jeems is an anonymous Ku Klux Klan member, so nothing is known about him. He adopted the character of the ghost of a Confederate soldier—"I was Killed at Manassus in 1861"—and notes that there are 200,000 dead Confederates all around. "I am here now as Locust in the day Time and at night I am a Ku Klux sent here to look after you and all the rest of the radicals and make you know your place."

Davie Jeems, the man to whom the note is addressed, was a black Republican who had recently won the election for Lincoln County sheriff. It is not clear how Jeems responded to this note.

HISTORICAL DOCUMENT

Notice

To Jeems, Davie, you, must, be, a good boy. and. Quit. hunting on Sunday and shooting your gun in the night, you keep people from sleeping. I live in a big rock above the Ford of the Creek. I went from Lincoln County … during the War I was Killed at Manassus in 1861. I am here now as Locust in the day Time and. at night I am a Ku Klux sent here to look after you and all the rest of the radicals and make you know your place. I have got my eye on you every day, I am at the Ford of the creek every evening From Sundown till dark I want to meet you

there next Saturday tell platt Madison we have, a Box. For him and you. We nail all, radicals up in Boxes and send them away to K K K — there is 200 000 ded men retured to this country to make you and all the rest of the radicals good Democrats and vote right with the white people you have got it to do or leave this country no nigger is safe unless he Joins the Democratic Club then you will be safe and have friends, Take heed and govern yourself accordingly and give all your Friends timely warning

Ku, Ku, Klux, Klan

GLOSSARY

Ford: ford, a place to cross a stream or river

Manassus: Manassas, location in Virginia where two major battles were fought during the Civil War

radicals: most likely, a reference to the Radical Republicans

Document Analysis

This letter is typical of the kind of terrorism used by the Ku Klux Klan in 1868 to turn the political tide in their favor. The Klan was murdering elected officials during this time, so a note like this was a very real threat.

The writer of the note begins with sinister humor, telling Jeems to be "be a good boy" and not shoot his gun in the night, as it "keep[s] people from sleeping." This may be a reference to an earlier altercation, or is offered as evidence that the writer is familiar with Jeems' habits. The writer then identifies himself as a ghost living "above the Ford of the Creek" and says that he is a Confederate soldier killed at the First Battle of Manassas (or Bull Run), in Virginia, in 1861.

The threatening tone continues with a promise of constant surveillance: "I have got my eye on you every day." The writer identifies the members of the Ku Klux Klan as the ghosts of Confederate soldiers who come out at night, saying, "at night I am a Ku Klux sent here to look after you and all the rest of the radicals and make you know your place." Jeems and another man, identified as Platt Madison, are issued a thinly veiled death threat: "We have, a Box. For him and you. We nail all, radicals up in Boxes."

The writer returns a number of times to the theme of the dead Confederate soldier as the new Ku Klux Klan member, such as when he states, "There is. 200 000 ded men returned to this country." Their mission is clearly political: "to make you and all the rest of the radicals good Democrats and vote right with the white people." According to the writer, the only way that Jeems and other black Georgians would be safe would be to join the local Democrats, or get out of town. If they chose not to, "no nigger is safe." Jeems is encouraged to pass the threat on to his friends.

This note makes the political objectives of the Ku Klux Klan plain. Davie Jeems was instructed to switch political allegiances, "leave this country," or be killed. The haunting image of Confederate ghosts coming back to restore racial and political order is employed throughout the note, and it connects the KKK once again to white Southerners who were angry and armed following the recent war.

Essential Themes

The most prominent theme in this note is the author's desire to control the political behavior of the recipient through threats of violence. The note makes it clear that black voters and officeholders will not be safe from the Ku Klux Klan unless they step down or declare their allegiance to the Democratic Party.

Another theme of this note is the role that Confederate soldiers played in the Ku Klux Klan. The writer of the note claims to be a dead soldier and also states that there were 200,000 more ghosts like him all around. They were watching black men and women by day and became Klan members at night. Thus the Klan was tied directly to the soldiers who had fought the Union, and the Klan paid homage to their deaths.

—*Bethany Groff, MA*

Bibliography and Additional Reading

Bryant, Jonathan M. "Ku Klux Klan in the Reconstruction Era." *New Georgia Encyclopedia*. Georgia Humanities Council, 9 May 2013. Web. 22 Jan. 2014.

Martinez, J. Michael. *Carpetbaggers, Cavalry, and the Ku Klux Klan: Exposing the Invisible Empire during Reconstruction*. Lanham: Rowman, 2007. Print.

Onion, Rebecca. "Threats from a Ghost: An 1868 Intimidation Letter Sent by the KKK." *Slate*. TheSlateGroup, 8 Apr. 2013. Web. 22 Jan. 2014.

Trelease, Allen W. *White Terror: The Ku Klux Klan Conspiracy and Southern Reconstruction*. 1971. Baton Rouge: Louisiana State UP, 1995. Print.

■ "The First-Class Men in Our Town"

Date: 1872
Author: Abram Colby
Genre: memoir, report

Summary Overview

Abram Colby was one of the hundreds of African Americans who held political office as a Republican in the South during Reconstruction. While in the middle of serving three terms in the Georgia state legislature, he was kidnapped, beaten, and left for dead by the Ku Klux Klan. After President Ulysses Grant and the US Congress broke the power of the KKK in 1871, Colby was one of the many who testified to Congress about his experience. Colby's life and office-holding reveal much about African American agency in the post-Civil War South, the violence that black Southerners endured to pursue a better world during Reconstruction, the eventual plight of the Republican Party in the South in the late 1860s and 1870s, and, correspondingly, the end of Northern support for black civil and economic rights and, therefore, for Reconstruction itself.

Defining Moment

Between 1865 and the early 1870s, an increasing number of Southern blacks were able to win election to public office in the South because Southern black and white Republicans were united and many former white Confederates were still not able to vote. However, as early as 1868, just three years after the Civil War ended and the Reconstruction era began, the Ku Klux Klan was growing rapidly in numbers and influence. When Congress turned against President Andrew Johnson after he vetoed the Freedmen's Bureau Bill and the Civil Rights Bill in 1866, thus ending the more moderate period of Presidential Reconstruction and starting Radical Reconstruction, which was aimed at a deeper alteration of the South's society, white southerners became more and more opposed to Northern-led changes. Historian Eric Foner has noted in his excellent work, *Reconstruction: America's Unfinished Revolution: 1863–1877*, that

the violence against southern black and white Republicans in the late 1860s and early 1870s was "a measure of how far change had progressed that the reaction against Reconstruction proved so extreme" (425). Colby's experience was thus part of this larger pattern.

In Georgia specifically, events were turning against Colby and the Republicans already at the time of his beating in 1869. In fact, by the next year, even though he won a second term in the state legislature, Democrats had regained control of that body. They rapidly set about instituting legislation that would trap African Americans into sharecropping arrangements and other inferior positions for almost the next century (Foner 423–4). The Ku Klux Klan were obviously in league with the "redeeming" Democrats and, therefore, assisted with this Southern white resurgence by employing a wave of violence aimed at forcing black and white Republicans out of office. Even though Reconstruction would officially last until late 1876, Colby's beating and the Democratic "redemption" of Georgia occurred less than halfway through the period. In actuality, therefore, these events occurred when Republican strength, and federal commitment to black Southerners, was already beginning to ebb away.

For Colby personally, this attack occurred almost halfway through his time in the Georgia state legislature, since he was elected in 1866, 1868, and 1870 for two year terms each. His actual speech to the US Congress occurred three years after the incident, in 1872, after the power of the Ku Klux Klan had been broken. Congress passed the Ku Klux Klan Act in 1871, which made many of the types of things the KKK did, like intimidating voters and blocking their civil rights, eligible to be punished under federal law (Foner 454–5). Grant's administration then successfully prosecuted hundreds of Klan members and most of the rest ended their illegal activities. Colby's testimony was therefore aimed at helping to continue to bolster northern support for blacks in the South and also as part of the inquiry into the violence in the South in the late 1860s and very early 1870s.

Author Biography

Abram Colby was born in 1820 the son of a white owner and his black female slave. When his owner died in 1850, an acquaintance technically owned Colby until the Civil War, although he had a large degree of freedom and became a barber (Inscoe 15–16). Immedi-ately after the Civil War, he was the head of the Equal Rights Association in Greene County, Georgia, which advocated for African American rights and opportunities (Foner 205). He also actively protested the Presidential Reconstruction of President Andrew Johnson, which was much more lenient on former white Southern rebels and not as concerned with protecting black political and economic rights as was the later period of Radical Reconstruction. He was elected to the lower house of the Georgia state legislature in 1868, 1870, and 1872, although by the time he left, Reconstruction was clearly coming to an end.

HISTORICAL DOCUMENT

Colby: On the 29th of October 1869, [the Klansmen] broke my door open, took me out of bed, took me to the woods and whipped me three hours or more and left me for dead. They said to me, "Do you think you will ever vote another damned Radical ticket?" I said, "If there was an election tomorrow, I would vote the Radical ticket." They set in and whipped me a thousand licks more, with sticks and straps that had buckles on the ends of them.

Question: What is the character of those men who were engaged in whipping you?

Colby: Some are first-class men in our town. One is a lawyer, one a doctor, and some are farmers. They had their pistols and they took me in my night-clothes and carried me from home. They hit me five thousand blows. I told President Grant the same that I tell you now. They told me to take off my shirt. I said, "I never do that for any man." My drawers fell down about my feet and they took hold of them and tripped me up. Then they pulled my shirt up over my head. They said I had voted for Grant and had carried the Negroes against them. About two days before they whipped me they offered me $5,000 to go with them and said they would pay me $2,500 in cash if I would let another man go to the legislature in my place. I told them that I would not do it if they would give me all the county was worth.

The worst thing was my mother, wife and daughter were in the room when they came. My little daughter begged them not to carry me away. They drew up a gun and actually frightened her to death. She never got over it until she died. That was the part that grieves me the most.

Question: How long before you recovered from the effects of this treatment?

Colby: I have never got over it yet. They broke something inside of me. I cannot do any work now, though I always made my living before in the barber-shop, hauling wood, etc.

Question: You spoke about being elected to the next legislature?

Colby: Yes, sir, but they run me off during the election. They swore they would kill me if I stayed. The Saturday night before the election I went to church. When I got home they just peppered the house with shot and bullets.

Question: Did you make a general canvas there last fall?

Colby: No, sir. I was not allowed to. No man can make a free speech in my county. I do not believe it can be done anywhere in Georgia.

Question: You say no man can do it?

Colby: I mean no Republican, either white or colored.

GLOSSARY

canvas: to contact voters in a district; campaign for political office

radical ticket: Radical Republican candidates for office

shot: buckshot, from a shotgun

Document Analysis

Abram Colby's testimony about his treatment at the hands of the Ku Klux Klan in 1869 revealed two key facets of the black experience in the Reconstruction South. First, he was physically harmed through a severe beating that was made even more humiliating by the fact that he had first been stripped naked. The white men were trying to convince him to abandon the Republican Party, since they asked if he would vote for the candidates they considered to be the radicals (i.e., the Republicans) and he said that he still would. He received even more blows for not changing his stance. Additionally, the physical threat extended to his family, as when his daughter had a gun pointed at her simply because she did not want her father taken from their home in the middle of the night. A father's helplessness and heartache is apparent in Colby's words about his daughter, "She never got over it until she died. That was the part that grieves me the most." Finally, even during the next election cycle, whites "peppered the house with shot and bullets" while he was at church. The physical threats that many African Americans, especially those in public office, experienced during Reconstruction, and for nearly a century afterwards, were very severe and very real.

Second, his testimony provided a window onto how white southerners attempted to "redeem" control of the South from what they perceived as unjust northern and black southern "oppression." At least, that was the viewpoint of white southerners, and unfortunately also many historians, until the Civil Rights Movement of the mid-twentieth century. The key to reasserting white Democratic control of the South was the destruction of any viable organized political opposition to their power, meaning the Republican Party. That is why the KKK members who assaulted Colby spoke in such political terms. They derided Colby for voting for Republican Ulysses Grant and for the fact that Colby "had carried the Negroes against them," which meant the white

Southerners held Colby at least partly responsible for helping to deliver the black vote in Georgia to Grant in the election of 1868. They had also attempted to bribe Colby to abandon his seat in the Georgia legislature and presumably then allow a Democrat to go in his place. In general, Colby told Congress later, the Republicans could no longer try to get their voters to the polls due to such intimidation and, therefore, Republicans could not "make a free speech in my county. I do not believe it can be done anywhere in Georgia." As this type of violent intimidation went unpunished, and as it was participated in by whites at all levels of Southern society as the title of Colby's speech indicated, the Republican Party slowly deteriorated in power and numbers in Georgia and the South.

Essential Themes

Colby's experience and testimony shed light on two major themes—the personal agency of African Americans during Reconstruction and the unique events that occurred in the American South when compared to other countries. First, although several generations of historians often focused on the roles of either Southern or Northern whites, and respectively portrayed black Southerners as oppressors or victims, more recent scholarship has highlighted the very real extent to which African Americans were able to control their own circumstances in the post-Civil War South, at least for a while. Colby epitomized this trend as he held public office for several years and testified to Congress about the violence in the South as part of an effort to bolster Northern support for blacks. He was, therefore, actively involved in attempting to shape the context in which he, and millions of other African Americans, lived.

Second, as historian Eric Foner writes in *Reconstruction*, "The wave of counterrevolutionary terror that swept over large parts of the South between 1868 and 1871 lacks a counterpart either in the American experience or in that of the other Western Hemisphere societies that abolished slavery in the nineteenth century" (425). While the KKK was not exactly a guerilla movement, apart from the open armed rebellion of the Civil War, they were the most effective and influential violent opposition to the federal government in American history. Additionally, while in Latin American nations there have, of course, been militant opposition movements to a national government, none were nearly as racially-oriented as the KKK in its targeting of black Southerners and those who supported them. Seen through these lenses, Colby's experience and testimony tell us much about the role of African Americans in Reconstruction and the extent of the violent opposition to the wide-ranging northern attempt to change Southern society after the Civil War.

—*Kevin Grimm, PhD*

Bibliography and Additional Reading

Bryant, Jonathan M. "The Freedman's Struggle for Power in Greene County, Georgia, 1865–1874" *Georgia in Black and White: Explorations in Race Relations of a Southern State, 1865–1950.* Ed. John. C. Inscoe. Athens, GA: University of Georgia Press, 2009. Print.

Foner, Eric. *Reconstruction: America's Unfinished Revolution, 1863–1877.* New York: Harper & Row Publishers, 1988. Print.

"White Men Unite: Primary Sources." *American Experience: Reconstruction.* WGBH: PBS Online, 19 Dec. 2003. Web. 5 Apr. 2014.

■ Letter to Senator Joseph C. Abbott on the Ku Klux Klan

Date: May 24, 1870
Author: Albion W. Tourgée
Genre: letter

> *"The habit of regarding the South as simply a laboratory, where every demagogue may carry on his reconstructionary experiments at will, and not as an integral party of the Nation itself, has led our Government to shut its eyes to the atrocities of these times."*

Summary Overview

After the murder of North Carolina state senator John Walter Stephens, radical Republican and district judge Albion W. Tourgée sent Joseph Carter Abbott a detailed letter outlining atrocities committed by the Ku Klux Klan in central North Carolina. A former general in the Union Army, Abbott had moved to North Carolina after the war and was then serving as a US senator. Concentrating on acts of violence committed against African Americans, poor whites, and Republican politicians, Tourgée presents grim statistics of murder and mayhem as evidence for his compelling argument that swift action by the federal government was necessary to stop the violence. Copies of the letter were sent to several prominent politicians, including North Carolina governor William Woods Holden. That summer, it was published in the *New York Tribune*, bringing national attention to the Klan's activities and rousing the public and Congress to take action against the secret society.

Defining Moment

Albion Tourgée's letter outlining the atrocities committed by the Ku Klux Klan in North Carolina was prompted by the murder of his friend and protégée John W. Stephens. A native North Carolinian, Stephens had worked as a tobacco trader and agent for the American Bible and Tract Society. During the Civil War, he had served the Confederacy, but after the South surren-

dered, he became a Republican and worked to advance the enfranchisement of African Americans and assure them equal treatment. Tourgée, a district judge, mentored Stephens in his law studies, enabling Stephens to become a justice of the peace in Caswell County, a hotbed of Ku Klux Klan activity in 1869 and 1870. Conservatives were outraged at Stephens's activities in support of African Americans, and he quickly became a target for the Klan.

On May 21, 1870, Stephens attended a Democratic political meeting at the Caswell County Courthouse in Yanceyville. There, he met former Democratic sheriff Frank Wiley, whom he hoped to convince to run again for the office as a Republican. Wiley, a member of the Klan, lured Stephens into the basement of the courthouse. There, a group of Klansmen stabbed him, leaving his body in a locked storage room, where it was discovered the next day.

Tourgée must have learned of the murder almost immediately, as his letter to Senator Abbott was written only a few days after the event. Stephens's murder was far from anomalous, however; it was simply the latest is a long list of outrageous violations committed by the Klan against African Americans and their white supporters. In his letter, Tourgée provides a catalog of some of these crimes, which include murders, beatings, rapes, and property damage. Tourgée calls for the federal government to take swift, specific action to curb the violence occurring in North Carolina and elsewhere throughout the South.

It is worth noting that others besides Tourgée were moved to act against the Klan after Stephens was killed. Most notable among them was Governor William Holden, who, in June 1870, cited a list of criminal activities similar to those described in Tourgée's letter as justification for calling out the state militia to quell Klan violence. Holden was given a copy of Tourgée's letter, and he likely arranged its publication in the *New York Tribune*, then one of the most widely read papers in America.

Author Biography

Albion Winegar Tourgée was born May 2, 1838, in Williamsfield, Ashtabula County, Ohio, and raised on his father's farm. He enrolled at the University of Rochester in 1859 but was forced to leave for financial reasons in 1861. He worked briefly as an educator in New York before enlisting in the Twenty-Seventh New York Volunteers in April 1861. Injured during the Battle of Bull Run in July, he left active service to recuperate but returned to duty with the 105th Ohio Volunteers. Because of his exemplary service, the University of Rochester awarded him a bachelor's degree in 1862 and a master's degree in 1865. Tourgée married Emma Kilbourne, his longtime sweetheart, in May 1863. Harsh conditions in the western theater and several months in a prisoner of war camp exacerbated his prior injury, forcing him to resign his commission in late 1863.

After leaving the military, Tourgée completed studies in law and worked as an attorney, journalist, and teacher. In October 1865, he moved to Greensboro, North Carolina, where he set up a law practice. One of thousands of Northerners intent on reforming political, social, and economic conditions in the South, Tourgée proved a staunch radical Republican. In 1868, he was elected a district judge, a position he held for six years. That same year, he played a major role in drafting the state's civil code. Tourgée's six years on the bench were filled with controversy, as his consistent support of African Americans and fellow Republican reformers angered Southern conservatives, who referred to him and other transplanted Northerners as "carpetbaggers." He received numerous death threats from the secretive Ku Klux Klan and, for some time, found it necessary to carry arms when going out in public.

Tourgée moved back north in 1879 and became a writer and advocate for civil rights. His most widely read work, *A Fool's Errand by One of the Fools* (1879), is a fictionalized account of his experiences in North Carolina. Tourgée's 1880 nonfiction work *The Invisible Empire* exposes the reign of terror caused by the Ku Klux Klan.

In 1896, Tourgée filed a brief in the United States Supreme Court on behalf of the plaintiff in *Plessy v. Ferguson*, a landmark civil rights case that set the course for race relations in America for more than half a century. Tourgée argued for what he called "color-blind justice" that would guarantee equal rights to every American. The Supreme Court decided instead that "separate but equal" accommodations were sufficient.

In 1897, Tourgée was appointed US consul to Bordeaux, France, where he spent the last years of his life. He died on May 21, 1905, of complications from the wounds he had received during the Civil War.

HISTORICAL DOCUMENT

My Dear General:

It is my mournful duty to inform you that our friend John W. Stephens, State Senator from Caswell, is dead. He was foully murdered by the Ku-Klux in the Grand Jury room of the Court House on Saturday or Saturday night last. The circumstances attending his murder have not yet fully come to light there. So far as I can learn, I judge these to have been the circumstances: He was one of the Justices of the Peace in that township, and was accustomed to hold court in that room on Saturdays. It is evident that he was set upon by some one while holding this court, or immediately after its close, and disabled by a sudden attack, otherwise there would have been a very sharp resistance, as he was a man, and always went armed to the teeth. He was stabbed five or six times, and then hanged on a hook in the Grand Jury room, where he was found on Sunday morning. Another brave, honest Republican citizen has met his fate at the hands of these fiends. Warned of his danger, and fully cognizant of the terrible risk which surrounded him, he still manfully refused to quit the field. Against the advice of his friends, against the entreaties of his family, he constantly refused to leave those who had stood by him in the day of his disgrace and peril. He was accustomed to say that 3,000 poor, ignorant, colored Republican voters in that county had stood by him and elected him, at the risk of persecution and starvation, and that he had no idea of abandoning them to the Ku-Klux. He was determined to stay with them, and either put an end to these outrages, or die with the other victims of Rebel hate and national apathy: Nearly six months ago I declared my belief that before the election in August next the Ku-Klux would have killed more men in the State than there would be members to be elected to the Legislature. A good beginning has been made toward the fulfillment of this prophecy. The following counties have already filled, or nearly so, their respective "quotas:" Jones County, quota full, excess 1; Orange County quota full; excess, 1. Caswell County quota full; excess, 2; Alamance County quota full; excess, 1. Chatham County quota nearly full. Or, to state the matter differently, there have been twelve murders in five counties of the district during the past eighteen months, by bands of disguised villains. In addition to this, from the best information I can derive, I am of the opinion that in this district alone there have been 1,000 outrages of a less serious nature perpetrated by the same masked fiends. Of course this estimate is not made from any absolute record, nor is it possible to ascertain with accuracy the entire number of beatings and other outrages which have been perpetrated. The uselessness, the utter futility of complaint from the lack of ability in the laws to punish is fully known to all. The danger of making such complaint is also well understood. It is therefore not unfrequently by accident that the outrage is found out, and unquestionably it is frequently absolutely concealed. Thus, a respectable, hard working white carpenter was working for a neighbor, when accidentally his shirt was torn, and disclosed his back scarred and beaten. The poor fellow begged for the sake of his wife and children that nothing might be said about it, as the Ku-Klux had threatened to kill him if he disclosed how he had been outraged. Hundreds of cases have come to my notice and that of my solicitor. . . .

Men and women come scarred, mangled, and bruised, and say: "The Ku-Klux came to my house last night and beat me almost to death, and my old woman right smart, and shot into the house, 'bust' the door down, and told me they would kill me if I made complaint;" and the bloody mangled forms attest the truth of their declarations. On being asked if any one knew any of the party it will be ascertained that there was no recognition, or only the most uncertain and doubtful one. In such cases as these nothing can be done by the court. We have not been accustomed to enter them on record. A man of the best standing in Chatham told me that he could count up 200 and upward in that county. In Alamance County, a citizen in conversation one evening enumerated upward of 50 cases which had occurred within his own knowledge, and in one section of the county. He gave it as his opinion that there had been 200 cases in that county. I have no idea that he exceeded the proper estimate. That was six months ago, and I am satisfied that another hundred would not cover the work done in that time.

These crimes have been of every character imaginable. Perhaps the most usual has been the dragging of men and women from their beds, and beating their naked bodies with hickory switches, or as witnesses in an examination the other day said, "sticks" between a "switch" and a "club." From 50 to 100 blows is the usual allowance, sometimes 200 and 300 blows are administered. Occasionally an instrument of torture is owned. Thus in one case two women, one 74 years old, were taken out, stripped naked, and beaten with a paddle, with several holes bored through it. The paddle was about 30 inches long, 3 or 4 inches wide, and 1/4 of an inch thick, of oak. Their bodies were so bruised and beaten that they were sickening to behold. They were white women and of good character until the younger was seduced, and swore her child to its father. Previous to that and so far as others were concerned her character was good.

Again, there is sometimes a fiendish malignity and cunning displayed in the form and character of the outrages. For instance, a colored man was placed astride of a log, and an iron staple driven through his person into the log. In another case, after a band of them had in turn violated a young negro girl, she was forced into bed with a colored man, their bodies were bound together face to face, and the fire from the hearth piled upon them. The K. K. K. rode off and left them, with shouts of laughter. Of course the bed was soon in flames, and somehow they managed to crawl out, though terribly burned and scarred. The house was burned.

I could give other incidents of cruelty, such as hanging up a boy of nine years old until he was nearly dead, to make him tell where his father was hidden, and beating an old negress of 103 years old with garden pallings because she would not own that she was afraid of the Ku-Klux. But it is unnecessary to go into further detail. In this district I estimate their offenses as follows, in the past ten months: Twelve murders, 9 rapes, 11 arsons, 7 mutilations, ascertained and most of them on record. In some no identification could be made.

Four thousand or 5,000 houses have been broken open, and property or persons taken out. In all cases all arms are taken and destroyed. Seven hundred or 800 persons have been beaten or otherwise maltreated. These of course are partly persons living in the houses which were broken into.

And yet the Government sleeps. The poor disarmed nurses of the Republican party—those men by whose ballots the Republican party holds power—who took their lives in their hands when they cast their ballots for U.S. Grant and other officials—all of us who happen to be beyond the pale of the Governmental regard—must be sacrificed, murdered, scourged, mangled, because some contemptible party scheme might be foiled by doing us justice. I could stand it very well to fight for Uncle Sam, and was never known to refuse an invitation on such an occasion; but this lying down, tied hand and foot with the shackles of the law, to be killed by the very dregs of the rebellion, the scum of the earth, and not allowed either the consolation of fighting or the satisfaction that our "fall" will be noted by the Government, and protection given to others thereby, is somewhat too hard. I am ashamed of the nation that will let its citizens be slain by scores, and scourged by thousands, and offer no remedy or protection. I am ashamed of a State which has not sufficient strength to protect its own officers in the discharge of their duties, nor guarantee the safety of any man's domicile throughout its length and breadth. I am ashamed of a party which, with the reins of power in its hands, has not nerve or decision enough to arm its own adherents, or to protect them from assassinations at the hands of their opponents. A General who in time of war would permit 2,000 or 3,000 of his men to be bushwhacked and destroyed by private treachery even in an enemy's country without any one being punished for it would be worthy of universal execration, and would get it, too. How much more worthy of detestation is a Government which in time of peace will permit such wholesale slaughter of its citizens? It is simple cowardice, inertness, and wholesale demoralization. The wholesale slaughter of the war has dulled our Nation's sense of horror at the shedding of blood, and the habit of regarding the South as simply a laboratory, where every demagogue may carry on his reconstructionary experiments at will, and not as an integral party of the Nation itself, has led our Government to shut its eyes to the atrocities of these times. Unless these evils are speedily remedied, I tell you, General, the Republican party has signed its death warrant. It is a party of cowards or idiots—I don't care which alternative is chosen. The remedy is in our hands, and we are afraid or too dull to bestir ourselves and use it.

But you will tell me that Congress is ready and willing to act if it only knew what to do. Like the old Irish woman it wrings its hands and cries, "O Lawk, O Lawk; if I only knew which way." And yet this same Congress has the control of the militia and can organize its own force in every county in the United States, and arm more or less of it. This same Congress has the undoubted right to guarantee and provide a republican government, and protect every citizen in "life, liberty, and the pursuit of happiness," as well as the power conferred by the XVth Amendment. And yet we suffer and die in peace and murderers walk abroad with the blood yet fresh upon their garments, unharmed, unquestioned and unchecked. Fifty thousand dollars given to good detectives would secure, if well used, a complete knowledge of all this gigantic organization of murderers. In connection with an organized and armed militia, it would result in the apprehension of any number of these Thugs *en masque* and with blood on their hands. What then is the remedy? *First:* Let Congress give to the U. S. Courts, or to Courts of the States under its own laws, cognizance of this class of crimes, as crimes against the nation, and let it provide that this legislation be enforced. Why not, for instance, make going armed and masked or disguised, or masked or disguised in the night time, an act of insurrection or sedition? *Second:* Organize militia, National—State militia is a nuisance—and arm as many as may be necessary in each county to enforce its laws. *Third:* Put detectives at work to get hold of this whole organization. Its ultimate aim is unquestionably to revolutionize the Government. If we have not pluck enough for this, why then let us just offer our throats to the knife, emasculate ourselves, and be a nation of self-subjugated slaves at once.

And now, Abbott, I have but one thing to say to you. I have very little doubt that I shall be one of the next victims. My steps have been dogged for months, and only a good opportunity has been wanting to secure to me the fate which Stephens has just met, and I speak earnestly upon this matter. I feel that I have a right to do so, and a right to be heard as well, and with this conviction I say to you plainly that any member of Congress who, especially if from the South, does not support, advocate, and urge immediate, active, and thorough measures to put an end to these outrages, and make citizenship a privilege, is a coward, a traitor, or a fool. The time for action has come, and the man who has now only speeches to make over some Constitutional scarecrow, deserves to be damned.

GLOSSARY

bushwhacked: attacked by a person or group waiting in hiding; "bushwhackers" was a term commonly used to describe Confederate irregulars

Chatham: Chatham County, North Carolina

Court House: the Caswell County Court House in Yanceyville, North Carolina

palings: boards sharpened at one end, used for fencing

XVth Amendment: Fifteenth Amendment to the US Constitution, guaranteeing voting rights to former slaves and people of color

Document Analysis

The murder of John W. Stephens, Albion Tourgée's close friend, served as the impetus for the long letter Tourgée wrote on May 24, 1870, to Joseph C. Abbott, then representing North Carolina in the United States Senate. The two men had similar backgrounds. Like Tourgée, Abbott was from the North, having been born and raised in New Hampshire, but remained in the South after the war. He served in the Union Army, rising to the rank of brevet brigadier general in 1865. Both men were delegates at North Carolina's 1868 constitutional convention. Tourgée no doubt felt confident that, in writing to Abbott, he was addressing a friend to whom he could lay out a series of complaints about activities of the Ku Klux Klan in North Carolina and ask for assistance in putting an end to them, lest the Klan's reign of terror undo the activities of Republicans to reform the Southern political system and guarantee civil rights for African Americans in the South.

Although cast in the form of personal correspondence, Tourgée's letter is actually a carefully crafted argument that lays out the case for federal intervention in North Carolina and other Southern states to end the atrocities being perpetrated by the Ku Klux Klan. As such, it is similar to the Declaration of Independence, in which Thomas Jefferson, writing for the committee appointed by the Second Continental Congress to draft the document, carefully delineates the specific offenses that justified the colonists' decision to break away from Britain. One important formal difference between the two documents may help highlight the difficulty Tourgée faced in making his case. The Declaration of Independence employs deductive logic and is organized as a formal syllogism. Jefferson first states as a major premise what he believes is a universal truth: when a ruler denies people their inalienable rights, those people are justified in rebelling. Jefferson follows this assertion with a list of facts (his minor premise) that explain how King George III has violated the colonists' rights. The conclusion that Americans are justified in their cause follows logically. Tourgée has no major premise from which to argue, or if he does, he leaves it unstated. Instead, he employs inductive logic to build his case, relying on the accumulation of specific evidence to convince Abbott that the federal government, especially the Republicans in Congress, should take immediate action to relieve the suffering of African Americans and their white Republican allies in the South. It should be noted, though, that while Tourgée relies on logic to lead Abbott (and others) to conclude that immediate relief is necessary, he peppers his letter with words that evoke strong emotions to supplement the logic of his appeal.

Tourgée's argument may be outlined as follows. The murder of state senator John W. Stephens, a hero in the cause of enfranchisement and equal rights for African Americans, is a high-profile example of what has been happening in North Carolina for some time. Statistics prove that Klan violence is widespread, and reports of specific incidents reveal that it is grotesque and sadistic. Government officials have so far been powerless or unwilling to stop the violence. Therefore, action is needed at the federal level to protect citizens and bring Klan members and their supporters to justice.

Tourgée begins by paying tribute to Stephens, whom he calls a "brave, honest Republican citizen" who "manfully refused to quit the field," even in the face of repeated threats from the Klan. Calling Stephens a Republican is a way for Tourgée to remind Abbott that Stephens had the same objectives as Abbott in his own political activities. In fact, Tourgée continues, Stephens was determined to remain with the African Americans who had elected him to office in order to end the "outrages" to which they were being subjected, or "die with the other victims of Rebel hate and national apathy." The last phrase is one to which Tourgée returns at the end of his letter, but first he describes the level and types of violence that prompt him to appeal to Abbott (and the United States Congress) for assistance.

Tourgée relies on two types of evidence to make his case: statistics that demonstrate the magnitude of the problem of unchecked Klan violence and graphic anecdotes of individual atrocities. For example, he notes "twelve murders in five counties of the district during the past eighteen months" and "1,000 outrages of a less serious nature." He reports that a source in Chatham County has evidence of more than two hundred similar events, while one in Alamance County has firsthand knowledge of fifty and strong evidence of nearly two hundred as well. He closes the first major section of his argument, the presentation of evidence of Klan atrocities, with a list of powerful statistics: in the district where Tourgée lives, there have been "twelve murders, 9 rapes, 11 arsons, 7 mutilations" confirmed, four to five thousand instances of property damage, and seven to eight hundred cases of beatings and other instances of maltreatment.

At the same time, Tourgée seldom misses an opportunity to present his statistics in a context aimed at generating strong emotional reaction from his reader. For example, pointing out that "3,000 poor, ignorant, colored Republican voters" had elected Stephens to the North Carolina Senate not only highlights the wide support Stephens had among the formerly disenfranchised portion of the local populace, but also reminds Abbott that the African Americans for whom people like himself and Tourgée had fought were the ones who were now being victimized again by Stephens's murder. Numbers provide specificity, and Tourgée makes good use of them in dramatizing the impact of the Klan's reign of terror. He details the way men and women, dragged from their beds, are beaten with sticks or switches, fifty to one hundred blows being the "usual allowance," although occasionally "200 and 300" are "administered." The use of neutral terms, such as "allowance" and "administered," creates a macabre counterpoint to the high number of blows given to these defenseless victims.

Perhaps the best example of Tourgée's ability to employ specific data for emotional effect is in his description of the beating of two women (one of them in her seventies) with a paddle. With the precision of a carpenter outlining measurements for the construction of a household item such as a cabinet or storage chest, Tourgée gives exact dimensions of this cruel "instrument of torture" that Klan members used to punish two white women "of good character." The point that Klan violence extends beyond the African American community would not have been lost on Abbott or on anyone else who might read Tourgée's impassioned plea for outside help.

While statistics may provide an indication of the scope of the problem on which Tourgée wishes to report, he relies on other rhetorical methods to engage Abbott emotionally so that he may be prompted to act against the Klan. One of Tourgée's most effective techniques is to relate specific anecdotes about the Klan's treatment of victims. The story of the two white women beaten with a paddle is one such example. Equally effective in rousing emotions of revulsion are examples used to support Tourgée's claim that there is "a fiendish malignity and cunning" in some of the Klan's activities. The simple sentence noting an attack on a black man in which "an iron staple [was] driven through his person into the log" is an example of understatement and circumlocution. The word "person" is used euphemistically: Abbott and other nineteenth-century readers would have understood that Tourgée was referring to the man's genitalia.

A longer anecdote recounts what might be the most horrific act Tourgée ascribes to the Klan, an attempt to murder a young African American couple by burning them alive in bed. The hideous unstated link between the heat of sexual passion and the literal heat of the fire may well have motivated this particular form of torture, as many Southern whites at this time believed African Americans were incapable of controlling sexual urges. Tourgée renders a graphic account of the young couple's plight as their attackers meticulously prepare them for what should have been certain death. That they escaped may be little short of miraculous, but their bodies forever bear the scars of the incident. To emphasize his point, Tourgée ends the paragraph with a monumental understatement: "The house was burned." The juxtaposition of this bald report of property damage stands in sharp contrast to the agony which the young man and woman have suffered and will continue to suffer at the hands of these night riders who depart the scene with "shouts of laughter."

Tourgée concludes this section of his argument with a typical rhetorical device, noting that he "could give other incidents of cruelty" and then citing two more specific examples. He says at this point "it is unnecessary to go into further detail" but follows his disclaimer with the list of statistics that provide a frightening summation of Klan violence. Having demonstrated to his satisfaction that a serious problem exists, Tourgée then moves the next section of his argument, a damning account of government inaction in the face of these atrocities.

"And yet the Government sleeps," Tourgée states. This jarring indictment is the lead-in for an emotional diatribe against all levels of government, which, to date, had been ineffective in quelling the Klan's activities. Chief among the targets of Tourgée's wrath is his own Republican Party, which he feels has abandoned brave souls like Stephens (and himself). Instead of receiving support from the national party, these "poor disarmed nurses" who "took their lives in their hands" to foster Republicanism are now being "sacrificed, murdered, scourged, mangled," Tourgée claims, because the party "scheme" to bring about Reconstruction gradually while placating Democrats (especially conservative Southerners) might be derailed should stronger actions be undertaken in their defense.

The language Tourgée employs in this section of his argument is particularly emotional. He claims to be "ashamed" of his state, which cannot protect its duly elected officials. Behind that statement is his knowledge that many in North Carolina, including some public officials, supported the Klan's objectives. He is especially "ashamed" of the Republican Party, which, despite holding the reins of political power, lacks "nerve or decision enough to arm its own adherents." That statement reveals Tourgée's radical stance, since arming "adherents" would have meant giving weapons to African Americans. Following through on such a plan would have infuriated Southern conservatives, who believed arming a large population of former slaves would lead to a much-feared black uprising that could wipe out all whites in the South.

To impress upon Abbott the seriousness of his complaint, Tourgée employs a military analogy that was sure to hit home with the former Union officer. "A General" who would permit thousands of his troops to be "destroyed by private treachery even in an enemy's country without any one being punished" would deserve "universal execration." Therefore, in times of peace, a government that permits similar "wholesale slaughter of its citizens" is even more detestable. Not to act on behalf of those being oppressed can only be attributed to "cowardice, inertness, and wholesale demoralization," Tourgée concludes. Certainly neither Abbott nor any Republican could have failed to be startled or even angered by such strong words.

Sadly, Tourgée continues, the sense of outrage that ought to be felt by every person of good moral character is absent, perhaps because four years of war had "dulled our Nation's sense of horror." Tourgée believes too many Southern demagogues have been allowed to get away with outrageous behavior because Republicans have been unwilling to face up to their responsibilities to oppressed people in the region. At this pivotal point in the nation's history, Tourgée suggests, the Republican Party lacks leadership. Someone must step forward—a strong politician with the qualities of generalship that helped the North win the war, perhaps—to remedy these evils.

Abbott, the former commander-turned-politician, could see himself in both roles presented in Tourgée's comparison. In fact, the letter contains strong evidence that Tourgée wants Abbott to see himself as a military commander who must take decisive action against an enemy that is slaughtering his forces. A look back at the letter's salutation makes this point clear. Rather than addressing Abbott as "Senator," Tourgée addresses him as "My Dear General." Already reminded subtly of his role as a defender of the rights of African Americans and of Republican values, Abbott would have quickly grasped the point Tourgée was making. It was time for men of action like Abbott to take steps to bring the Klan to justice.

Tourgée is ready with specific suggestions for solving the problems he outlines in his missive. Rather than moaning and wringing their hands in uncertainty and indecision, the members of Congress should exercise their power to bring about change, using military force if necessary. Tourgée claims an effective remedy can be provided by implementing three specific strategies: making the activities of the Klan acts of "insurrection or sedition," punishable by federal, rather than state, law; organizing and employing the national military, not state militia, to enforce the new law; and employing detectives to identify those who are perpetrating atrocities.

Tourgée believes the Klan's activities are no different from those of the Southerners who attempted to secede nearly a decade earlier. The group's "ultimate aim is unquestionably to revolutionize the Government." In the most impassioned sentence in his letter, Tourgée concludes with a graphic description of the only plausible possibilities for his Republican colleagues should Congress not move to curb the Klan's activities. Failing the courage to act, Republicans should simply "offer our throats to the knife"—in other words, become sacrificial lambs, although there is no hope that the cause in which they will be sacrificed will be won. Republicans, including Tourgée, would thereby "emasculate" themselves, because failure to act would be unmanly. Worst of all, failure to act would make Republicans (and their followers) "a nation of self-subjugated slaves," revert-

ing to the intolerable conditions that existed in America before the Civil War. The many hard-fought battles in which the party and its agents have engaged in the five years since the war's end will have been for naught, Tourgée warns, and as noted earlier in the letter, the Republican Party will have "signed its death warrant."

The care with which Tourgée took to craft his argument suggests that he knew the letter would become a public document at some time. Certainly he would have expected Senator Abbott to share it with others in Congress, whether by reading it or by using it as the basis for making a case for the government to intervene in affairs in North Carolina and elsewhere. In fact, the letter circulated on Capitol Hill during the summer of 1870, helping shape the opinion of members of Congress who initiated a series of laws to curb the Klan's activities. Additionally, although Tourgée was not pleased that the letter was published in *New York Tribune* on August 3, the document once again proved effective as a weapon against the Klan. In what was then among the most widely read papers in the country, Tourgée's missive was used to point out the nature and extent of the Klan's activities (although the published version may have exaggerated the statistical data Tourgée originally shared) and to highlight the difficulties state and local politicians were experiencing in trying to eliminate its pernicious influence.

Essential Themes

Written while Congress was deliberating legislation to restrict activities of the Ku Klux Klan, Tourgée's letter to Abbott may have influenced legislation that made much of what the Klan did a violation of civil and criminal law. Certainly his pleas and those of other Republicans living in the South prompted Congress to investigate the Klan's activities and enact a series of laws to protect civil rights for all citizens. The Enforcement Act of 1870 banned the use of force, intimidation, or other means of coercion to keep people from voting; the Enforcement Act of 1871 gave the federal government the right to oversee elections, and the Civil Rights Act of 1871 granted federal officials wide powers to enforce provisions of the Fourteenth Amendment. At the legislative level, these strong actions provided a framework to curtail the Klan's activities and guarantee the safety of African Americans and those who sympathized with their cause when these groups chose to exercise rights guaranteed to them under the Constitution. In the short term, these laws effectively negated the Klan's influence, and by 1872, the organization had disbanded.

Sadly, Tourgée's prophesy regarding the effects of Republican inactivity in vigorously promoting civil rights for African Americans proved devastatingly accurate. In 1877, Reconstruction came to an end, and the president withdrew federal troops that had been dispatched to the South specifically to assist in bringing former Confederate states into compliance with new laws designed to guarantee equal rights for former slaves. At the same time, federal oversight of state governments ended. With little interference from the federal government, Southern states were allowed to enact a series of repressive segregationist laws, known as Jim Crow laws, which affected African Americans' ability to receive the same education, hold the same jobs, or live in the same neighborhoods as whites.

Ironically, Tourgée was a principal participant in the Supreme Court case that effectively gave federal government sanction to segregation. In 1896, as lead member of the plaintiff's counsel, Tourgée filed a brief with the court on behalf Homer A. Plessy in his suit to overturn Louisiana's Separate Car Act (1890), which required passengers of different races to ride in separate rail cars. Tourgée's plea for what he called "color-blind justice" was passed over in favor of a decision that segregation was permissible as long as "separate but equal" facilities and services were provided to all citizens of a state. Worse, after World War I, the Klan reorganized and African Americans were once again subjected to intimidation and physical violence throughout the South. The Supreme Court decision permitting state-sponsored segregation stood for half a century until the civil rights movement of the 1950s and 1960s resulted in the passage of the Civil Rights Act of 1964, which eliminated legal segregation and paved the way for greater racial equality in the United States.

Laurence W. Mazzeno, PhD

Bibliography and Additional Reading

Beckel, Deborah. *Radical Reform: Interracial Politics in Post-Emancipation North Carolina.* Charlottesville: U of Virginia P, 2011. Print.

Blight, David W. *Race and Reunion: The Civil War in American Memory.* Cambridge: Harvard UP, 2001. Print.

Bradley, Mark L. *Bluecoats and Tar Heels: Soldiers and Civilians in Reconstruction North Carolina.* Lexington: UP of Kentucky, 2009. Print.

Elliott, Mark. *Color-Blind Justice: Albion Tourgée and the Quest for Racial Equality: From the Civil War to* Plessy v. Ferguson. New York: Oxford UP, 2006. Print.

Escott, Paul D., ed. *North Carolinians in the Era of the Civil War and Reconstruction.* Chapel Hill: U of North Carolina P, 2008. Print.

Gross, Theodore L. *Albion W. Tourgée.* New York: Twayne, 1963. Print.

Hume, Richard L. "Carpetbaggers in the Reconstruction South: A Group Portrait of Outside Whites and the 'Black and Tan' Constitutional Conventions." *Journal of American History* 64.2 (1977): 313–30. Print.

Katz, William L. *The Invisible Empire: The Ku Klux Klan Impact on History.* Seattle: Open Hand, 1987. Print.

McIver, Stuart. "The Murder of a Scalawag." *American History Illustrated* 8 (1973): 12–18. Print.

Newkirk, Vann R. *Lynchings in North Carolina: A History, 1865–1941.* Jefferson: McFarland, 2009. Print.

Newton, Michael. *The Ku Klux Klan: History, Organization, Language, Influence and Activities of America's Most Notorious Secret Society.* Jefferson: McFarland, 2007. Print.

Nye, Russel B. "Judge Tourgée and Reconstruction." *Ohio Archaeological and Historical Quarterly* 50 (1941): 101–14. Print.

Olsen, Otto H. *Carpetbagger's Crusade: The Life of Albion Winegar Tourgée.* Baltimore: Johns Hopkins UP, 1965. Print.

Parsons, Elaine Frantz. "Midnight Rangers: Costume and Performance in the Reconstruction-Era Ku Klux Klan." *Journal of American History* 92.3 (2005): 811–36. Print.

Randel, William P. *The Ku Klux Klan: A Century of Infamy.* Philadelphia: Chilton, 1965. Print.

Tourgée, Albion W. "Letter to Senator Joseph C. Abbott (1870)." *Undaunted Radical: The Selected Writings and Speeches of Albion W. Tourgée.* Ed. Mark Elliott and John David Smith. Baton Rouge: Louisiana State UP, 2010. 47–51. Print.

Trelease, Allen W. *White Terror: The Ku Klux Klan Conspiracy and Southern Reconstruction.* New York: Harper, 1971. Print.

Zuczek, Richard. "The Federal Government's Attack on the Ku Klux Klan: A Reassessment." *South Carolina Historical Magazine* 97.1 (1996): 47–64. Print.

■ A Contested Election: Report to Congress on the Activities of the Ku Klux Klan

Date: February 11, 1870
Author: United States House of Representatives
Genre: report

"The object of the Klan is to whip unarmed negroes,
scare timid white men, break up elections, and
interfere with the State government, and steal
and plunder the goods of the people."

Summary Overview

The activities of the newly organized Ku Klux Klan in Tennessee so disrupted the 1868 election in the Fourth Congressional District that Governor William Brownlow invalidated the election results and declared Republican candidate Lewis Tillman the winner. Conservative candidate C. A. Sheafe, who received the majority of votes, contested the decision and petitioned the US House of Representatives to reverse Brownlow's ruling. The House committee tasked with investigating the matter took extensive testimony, which revealed the nature and extent of the Klan's efforts to intimidate African Americans and their white supporters. As a result, the House of Representatives decided that Tillman should be awarded the seat in Congress. The committee's inquiry prompted widespread interest in Klan activities and was instrumental in the establishment of a joint committee of Congress to investigate the Klan's influence across the South.

Defining Moment

In August 1868 the Tennessee state legislature had initiated its own investigation into the activities of the Ku Klux Klan as part of an ongoing campaign by Radical Republican Governor William Brownlow to reactivate the Tennessee State Guard, a militia under his control.

The Guard was established in 1867 and used effectively to keep peace during elections that year; however, early in 1868 it was deactivated. Reports during the spring of 1868 of growing violence against African Americans and white Americans who supported Republicans made Brownlow fearful that congressional elections in November would be disrupted. Convinced that federal troops would be unavailable to stop Klan violence, Brownlow called a special session of the Tennessee legislature in July 1868 to push through legislation reactivating the Guard.

During the session, a joint military committee conducted an inquiry into Klan activities. Led by Tennessee state senator William J. Smith and state representative William F. Prosser, former Union officers and staunch supporters of Reconstruction, the committee took testimony from dozens of witnesses who told horrifying stories of intimidation, physical abuse, rape, and murder. The committee's report was printed in September 1868. To Brownlow's dismay, however, the bill authorizing reestablishment of the Guard did not pass in time for him to deploy troops to areas where Klan violence was likely to be highest during the November election.

Initial results in Tennessee's Fourth Congressional District indicated that conservative C. A. Sheafe defeated Republican Lewis Tillman by a comfortable majority. Governor Brownlow was convinced that Klan intimidation kept many of the district's nearly eight thousand African Americans from voting; he declared the results invalid and certified Tillman as the winner. Sheafe contested the decision, and in 1869 the matter was taken up in the US House of Representatives, which has the power to seat its members.

The House committee adjudicating Sheafe's claim heard testimony from individuals who had been subject to Klan intimidation. Also testifying was Tennessee state senator William J. Wisener, another member of the state legislature's joint military committee. Through him, extracts from the joint military committee's report were made part of the House investigation. The House committee also incorporated into its report information from an 1868 account of Klan activities in Tennessee submitted by Major General William P. Carlin, assistant commissioner of the Tennessee Freedmen's Bureau, to Major General Oliver O. Howard, commissioner of the Freedmen's Bureau in Washington, DC, as well as accounts from other bureau agents. Their reports confirmed the testimony of witnesses to both the Tennessee legislature in 1868 and the House committee in 1869 that the Ku Klux Klan was a growing menace, posing a serious threat to the restoration of democracy and the guarantee of equal rights in former Confederate states.

Author Biography

The principals in the 1868 election in Tennessee's Fourth Congressional District were little more than pawns in the chess game between Southerners intent on restoring the social and political order as it had existed before the war and Radicals bent on reconstructing the state in the image of its Northern neighbors. Ironically, Republican candidate Lewis Tillman was a Tennessee native who had spent his career in the state's court system and as a newspaper editor, while his conservative opponent, C. A. Sheafe, was an Ohioan who had served in the federal army before moving to Tennessee.

That the Ku Klux Klan played a role in keeping Tillman's supporters from the polls seems indisputable, yet it is in some ways remarkable. Founded in 1866, the Klan had no strong formal organization; many bands of miscreants rode through the countryside calling themselves Klansmen. While the perpetrators of violence were most often members of the working classes, a number of prominent Southerners had ties to the Klan, helping to protect other Klansmen accused of crimes. The Klan remained active throughout the South until the mid-1870s.

In Tennessee the fight against the Klan was led by William G. Brownlow. Born in 1805 in Virginia, Brownlow became a minister and was a traveling preacher throughout Appalachia before settling in Elizabethton, Tennessee, in 1836. Before the Civil War he was editor of a pro-Union newspaper. He left the state after Tennessee seceded but returned in 1863 when Union troops established an occupation force there. He was elected governor in 1865 and was reelected in 1867, largely on votes of his new constituency, freed slaves. Shortly after the 1868 elections, he began lobbying the legislature to appoint him US senator for Tennessee, a position he assumed in March 1869. After serving one term, he returned to Tennessee and resumed his newspaper career until his death in 1877.

Among the groups that gathered information on atrocities committed by the Ku Klux Klan and other reactionary groups in the South, none was more important than the Bureau of Refugees, Freedmen, and Abandoned Lands. Established by Congress in 1865, the Freedmen's Bureau, as it was popularly known, assisted freed slaves with a variety of economic and political issues. Led by Union General Oliver O. Howard, a native of Maine, the Bureau placed agents throughout the South to carry out its mission. These agents were often targets of Klan violence themselves, and their reports to the Bureau's headquarters in Washington, DC, provided further evidence of the difficulties African Americans faced in becoming fully integrated into postwar society.

HISTORICAL DOCUMENT

This pertains to the deposition of William H. Wisener in case of C. A. Sheafe vs. Lewis Tillman, contested election.

WM. GALBREATH, Mayor.

Report of the joint military committee of the two houses in relation to the organization of the militia of the State of Tennessee, submitted to the extra session of the thirty-fifth general assembly, September 2, 1868.

Mr. Speaker: Your committee to whom was referred that part of the governor's message relating to outrages perpetrated by an organization known as the Ku-Klux Klan, and the necessity of organizing the militia for the protection of the loyal people of the State of Tennessee, have had the same under consideration; and after summoning a great many witnesses before them, are satisfied that there exists an organization of armed men going abroad disguised, robbing poor negroes of their fire-arms, taking them out of their houses at night, hanging, shooting, and whipping them in a most cruel manner, and driving them from their homes. Nor is this confined to the colored men alone. Women and children have been subjected to the torture of the lash, and brutal assaults have been committed upon them by these night-prowlers, and in many instances, the persons of females have been violated, and when the husband or father complained, he has been obliged to flee to save his own life.

Nor has this been confined to one county or one section of the State alone. Your committee find, that, after a careful investigation of all the facts, that these depredations have been committed all over Middle and West Tennessee, and in some parts of East Tennessee; particularly has this been the case in Maury, Lincoln, Giles, Marshall, Obion, Hardeman, Fayette and Gibson Counties. In Lincoln County, they took Senator Wm. Wyatt from his house in the night, and inflicted all sorts of indignities upon him. They beat him over the head with their pistols, cutting a frightful gash, and saturating his shirt with blood, leaving him insensible. Senator Wyatt is a Christian gentleman, and sixty-five years of age; his

only offense being that he is a Union man and a member of the State legislature.

We also find that the same spirit exists in Obion County; that it was rife there, indeed, one year and a half ago, when the disloyalists so inhumanly and brutally murdered Senator Case and his son. Since then, depredations have been committed all over the country that calls loudly for redress. No loyal man is safe in that country at the present time.

Your committee's attention has also been directed to Maury County. We find that a perfect reign of terror exists there; that some two hundred colored men have had to flee from their homes, and take refuge in the city of Nashville; afraid to return, although here they are destitute of food, or any means of subsistence. In this county, school-houses have been burned down, teachers driven away, and colored men shot, whipped, and murdered at will. Hon. S. M. Arnell, congressman from that district, was sought for, when he was at home on a visit, by members of the Ku-Klux Klan, who were thirsting for his blood.

In Fayette County, the teacher of colored children has been assaulted and driven away by the Ku-Klux Klan.

Your committee find, that to enumerate all the outrages committed by this organization of outlaws, would take more time than can be spared. They would most respectfully direct your attention to a synopsis of the evidence taken before your committee; remarking at the same time, that much valuable information is necessarily left out on account of the witnesses fearing to have their names mentioned in this report, lest they should hereafter, on account of their testimony, lose their lives.

One of the most brutal assaults perhaps, that had been committed, was on the person of a school teacher, in Shelbyville, Bedford County, Tennessee. Mr. Dunlap, a white instructor, was taken from his house in the night by the Ku-Klux Klan, and most inhumanly whipped; and for no other reason than he was a white man, teaching a colored school. One witness testified that he was a confederate soldier, a native Tennessean; has been with negroes all his life, and seen them whipped by different persons; but never saw any one beaten as this man, Dunlap, was. It is in evidence that Mr. Dunlap is a member of the Methodist Church, and a very quiet, inoffensive man. Attention is especially directed to the evidence in this case.

Your committee also find that there has been a determined effort and is still a determined purpose all over Middle and West Tennessee, to keep colored men from the polls, and thus secure the election to office of candidates of the democratic party. Very many of the outrages committed have been against men who were formerly soldiers in the national army. The proof shows that there is an eternal hatred existing against all men that voted the republican ticket, or who belong to the Loyal League, or are engaged in teaching schools, and giving instruction to the humbler classes of their fellow-men.

The committee are compelled to conclude, from the evidence before them, that the ultimate object of the Ku-Klux Klan is, to intimidate Union men, both black and white, keep them from the polls on election day, and, by a system of anti-lawry and terrorism, carry the State in November next for Seymour and Blair.

Your committee would again call the attention of the general assembly to the following synopsis of testimony, as better calculated to show the true condition of the country than anything your committee could say:

We are permitted to make the following extracts from the report of Major General Carlin to General Howard, for the month of June, 1868:

"General: I have the honor to submit the following report on the condition of affairs pertaining to this department, during the month of June last. It is with deep regret that I am compelled to begin this report with the statement, that, since my connection with the bureau, no such discouraging state of affairs has prevailed in Tennessee, during any one month, as that for the month of June last. I say discouraging, because it is totally beyond the powers of myself and subordinates to remedy evils that cry aloud for redress."

"In the counties of Marshall, Rutherford, Maury, and Giles, it may be said that a reign of terror has been established, and will doubtless remain, unless the State, or United States, should provide a military force to be stationed in those counties."

"The hostility of the implacable pro-slavery people to colored education has manifested itself in numerous instances of violence toward teachers of colored schools."

"Your attention is called especially to the case of Mr. Newton, who was assaulted and badly wounded at Somerville. He would doubtless have been slain if he had not escaped in time. The case was reported by the undersigned to Major General Thomas, commanding the department, and troops were asked for to protect the school and teachers. Mr. Newton was escorted back by them to his school-house, where he has continued to conduct his school."

"This affair is more particularly described in the extracts from the report of Lieutenant Colonel Palmer, sub-assistant commissioner of the sub-district of Memphis."

"There will doubtless be great excitement and frequent disturbances in the State during the present political canvass for President and State officers. Nearly every day furnishes additional evidence of the determination of the Ku-Klux Klan and their friends to bring about a state of affairs that will preclude the possibility of personal liberty for the colored people, and the active, out-spoken Union men. I doubt if any measure, short of martial law, will preserve peace and insure safety till after the next election."

A. H. Eastman, agent at Columbia, Tennessee, reports the following extracts:

"The Ku-Klux Klan appear to be on the 'war path.' Complaints of visitations by night, all over my district, of the breaking into of houses and assaults upon the inmates, are very frequent. The Klan went to the house of Joshua Ferrell, an old and quiet colored man, on the night of the 12th instant, called him from his bed, and, while he was unfastening the door, they jumped in upon him and beat his head with a pistol, cutting a gash half an inch wide, four inches long, and to the skull. Then they asked him for fire-arms, which he said he had not. They then took him into a field and whipped him so badly that it nearly killed him. They also tore up everything in the house, and then went to his son's house, took him from his bed, smashed a large looking-glass over the head of his sick wife, who was in bed. They then whipped the man with stirrup-straps and buckles, which cut long and deep gashes into the flesh, and all because, they said, he was a 'big-feeling nigger, voted for Brownlow, and belonged to the Union League.'

J. K. Nelson, agent at Murfreesboro, Tennessee, says the Ku-Klux Klan took from his house, about midnight, Bill Carlton, (colored) living in Middleton district, and beat him very severely, giving him, as he says, one hundred and fifty lashes with a heavy leather strap.

"On Thursday night last, the Klan went to the house of Minor Fletcher, living eight miles from here, on the Shelbyville pike, rode into his front and back porches on their horses, and called him out. They then proceeded to the house of D. Webb, about ten or twelve in number, and, as he reports, called to him to come out. This he refused to do, until they assured him that he should not be hurt, and threatened him with violence in case of his refusal. He went out; they then accused him of being a radical, and a Loyal Leaguer. He denied being a member of the league, but told them that he was a Union man and always had been. They called him a liar, and threatened to hang him, calling at the same time for a halter. His wife, who was in a critical condition, screamed and plead for him, and begged them to spare him on her account. They then told him to go back to his wife. He turned to go, when one of them caught him by the hair, jerked him to the ground, sprang upon him, and beat him in the face in a shocking manner, at the same time holding a pistol to his head, and threatening to shoot him. They then left him in an almost insensible condition, scarcely able to crawl to his house."

"More than half the outrages perpetrated by this Klan are not reported to me. The parties are afraid, or have a want of confidence in the bureau. There is a feeling of insecurity among the people (Unionists) that has not been equaled since 1861. I am so impressed with my own inability to fully understand the exact condition of affairs that I will be excused for not making the same comprehensible to you."

"This I do know, that I have been sleeping for months with a revolver under my pillow, and a double-barreled shot-gun, heavily charged with buck shot, at one hand, and a hatchet at the other, with an inclination to sell the little piece of mortality with which I am entrusted as dearly as possible. I have had to submit to insults, which make a man despise himself for bearing, and which I cannot submit to any longer. Many freedmen are afraid to sleep in their own houses. Many have already been driven from the country." . . .

Rev. H. O. Hoffman, Shelbyville, Tenn.:

"Have never seen any of the Klan, but that it exists in our county no one doubts. Several have been harmed by this secret organization. Mr. Dunlap and a colored man by the name of Jeff were badly whipped on the night of the 4th of July. His person was cut in great gashes, from the middle of his back to his knees. Mr. Dunlap's offense was teaching a colored school. I have been repeatedly threatened, and was told that the Ku-Klux Klan had a list made of men they designed driving from the country. Found the following note in my yard:

"In Ku-klux Council, July 24, 1868.

Rev. Mr. Hoffman: Your name is before the council. Beware! We will attend to you. You shall not call us villains—damn you. Ku-Klux."

"I believe the object of the Klan is to whip unarmed negroes, scare timid white men, break up elections, and interfere with the State government, and steal and plunder the goods of the people." . . .

GLOSSARY

Blair: Francis Blair; politician, Union Army general, and unsuccessful candidate for vice president of the United States on the Democratic ticket in 1868

Galbreath, William: mayor of Shelbyville, Tennessee, in 1869

Mr. Speaker: DeWitt C. Senter, speaker of the Tennessee State Legislature in 1868

Radical: term generally used by Southerners after the Civil War to describe those who supported Reconstruction policies and equal rights for former slaves

Seymour: Horatio Seymour, two-term governor of New York (1853–1854 and 1863–1864) and unsuccessful Democratic candidate for president of the United States in 1868

stirrup-straps: leather loops attached to a saddle to assist riders in mounting

Thomas, George Henry: US Army major general, a career soldier and in 1868 commander of the Department of the Cumberland (Tennessee and Kentucky)

Document Analysis

The excerpt above is part of an official report of a committee of the US House of Representatives appointed in 1869 to investigate a contested election that took place the previous November in Tennessee's Fourth Congressional District. The committee was charged with making recommendations to the full House regarding a challenge filed by C. A. Sheafe, who had won the popular vote. Governor William Brownlow, determining that voter intimidation had been rampant in the district, certified Sheafe's opponent, Republican candidate Lewis Tillman, as the winner. The committee's report is contained in the Miscellaneous Documents of the Forty-First Congress (1869–71) under the title *Papers in the Contested Election Case of Sheafe vs. Tillman in the Fourth Congressional District of Tennessee*, which has an official printing date of February 11, 1870. The excerpted passages are taken from official reports and witness testimony that describe conditions in Tennessee during the spring and summer of 1868. The initial selection provides a summary and findings from a joint military committee appointed in August 1868 by the Tennessee legislature to investigate activities of the Ku Klux Klan. The Klan was thought to be responsible for an ongoing campaign of intimidation directed at recently freed slaves and their white supporters in order to keep those in the state supportive of Radical Republicans from voting or exercising other civil rights. Reports written by agents or managers of the Freedmen's Bureau provide information to superiors about the conditions of freed slaves in regions for which the agents were responsible. The brief excerpt from testimony by Reverend H. O. Hoffman describes his experience with the Klan.

Like most reports, the document prepared by the House of Representatives has a formal organization that reflects the conduct of the investigation. In the full report, transcripts of questions posed to each witness and witnesses' responses are recorded verbatim. Among those testifying before the House committee was Tennessee state senator William Wisener, who provided information about his own experiences with the Klan as well as information from reports he had received while serving as a member of the joint military committee. As a supplement to Wisener's testimony, the congressional committee authorized the printing of an appendix that offers further evidence of the scope and characteristics of activities being conducted by the Klan. The excerpts above are taken from this appendix, which provides graphic details of the Klan's activities throughout Tennessee.

Founded as a social club in Pulaski, Tennessee, the Ku Klux Klan quickly transformed into an agency of white supremacists and former secessionists disgruntled with Radical Republican efforts to give African Americans equal rights. At a meeting held in Nashville in 1867, former Confederate General Nathan Bedford Forrest was selected as national head of the organization. Despite some attempt to create a structure and hierarchy (complete with mysterious titles for leaders such as "Grand Wizard," "Grand Dragon," and "Grand Cyclops," to name a few), the Klan remained only loosely organized and its leaders had little control over individual groups operating locally under its aegis. In keeping with the secretive nature of the organization, Klan members tended to act at night and nearly always wore disguises. Many Southerners insisted that the Ku Klux Klan did not exist at all. Supporters claimed that much of the violence attributed to the Klan was imagined by its supposed victims, and that night riders who might have caused injury on occasion were simply vigilantes or misguided fun-seeking youth who meant no real harm.

The Testimony

The excerpts from the House of Representatives report represent a sampling of firsthand testimony describing encounters between the Ku Klux Klan and its many victims, and secondhand accounts from officials who routinely received reports of acts of violence. In the first passage, the authors of the joint military committee's report to the Tennessee legislature make clear that, despite protests from many white citizens that the Klan was not really dangerous, this "organization of armed men" posed a serious threat to the safety and well-being of the state's African American population. The summary statement that "poor negroes" were being robbed of their firearms, whipped, hanged, shot, and driven from their homes is based on testimony from numerous African American victims and from white Americans who either witnessed the atrocities or learned of them shortly after they occurred.

The committee seems to go out of its way to stress the widespread nature of the Klan's reign of terror. Traditionally, Tennesseans viewed their state as being divided into three broad regions. When talk of secession grew in 1861, West and Middle Tennessee, areas with many slaveholders, sided with the newly forming Confederacy. East Tennessee, populated by small farmers, was inclined to remain in the Union. While one might have expected trouble in the western and middle regions of the state, the authors of the report make it explicit that all three sections were experiencing an upsurge of Klan violence. After claiming that the "depredations" caused by the Klan extended across the entire state, the committee lists specific counties in which

violence was especially prevalent. This list actually served a second purpose: it provided Governor Brownlow a reason for declaring martial law in particularly troubled areas and for deploying troops from the Tennessee State Guard there. Although the governor was unable to send troops in before the November election, after the State Guard was finally reactivated early in 1869, Brownlow declared martial law in nine counties in February.

Particularly noteworthy, too, is the report's stress on the violence committed against white Americans in Tennessee who were working to advance the improvement of the African American population. Virtually every person identified in the excerpt from the joint military committee report is white, including numerous individuals teaching in African American schools who had been intimidated, beaten, or otherwise threatened simply for wanting to educate former slaves. The report's authors also play upon a fear common among Southerners, the desecration of the family ("women and children have been subjected to the torture of the lash") and especially of women ("the persons of females have been violated"). Though perhaps not intentional, there is a note of irony in this behavior. One of the principal arguments of white supremacists was that, if not checked, African Americans would take advantage of white women and adulterate the purity of the race.

Because the joint military committee report was being submitted to colleagues in the legislature, the authors include incidents in which elected officials have suffered at the hands of Klansmen who have no respect for the law or those sworn to uphold it. The extensive description of the treatment of the aging Senator William Wyatt is intended to make fellow legislators realize that the danger posed by the Klan could easily be visited upon them. The allusion to State Senator Almon Case and his son would have also caused consternation among Radical legislators. Case was murdered in January 1867, his son four months earlier. Case's assailant was known but escaped prosecution because he enjoyed the protection of white Americans sympathetic to the Klan's activities. The committee may have been looking toward the upcoming congressional elections when they cited the case of Samuel M. Arnell, who had been elected to the US House of Representatives in a contested election a year earlier. Arnell's experience makes it clear that even members of Congress had much to fear from Klansmen "thirsting" for their blood.

Reports from various officials of the Freedmen's

Bureau corroborate the testimony of witnesses before the joint military committee and the congressional committee investigating the contested election. The Freedmen's Bureau was established as the Civil War was coming to a close by President Abraham Lincoln, who foresaw that former slaves would need assistance in becoming independent citizens. Designed to provide legal, medical, educational, and economic aid, the Bureau established offices and deployed agents throughout the South. Their efforts met with stiff resistance from the white population, and many agents found themselves subjected to harassment and intimidation similar to that suffered by the clients they were supposed to be serving. Major General William Carlin's report on conditions in West Tennessee highlights several cases of brutality that had occurred recently in this region, among them the ongoing hostility toward education for African Americans exhibited by "pro-slavery people," by which he means former secessionists who had adopted the mantle of white supremacists. Throughout the South, many white Americans were fearful that, once educated, African Americans would become a powerful political force in communities where they outnumbered white people, and therefore posed a threat to their former masters. Few in the South believed that the races could coexist harmoniously; white Americans especially feared that educating and arming the African American population would inevitably lead to a revolution aimed at wiping out all white people.

Undoubtedly many of the attacks on African Americans perpetrated by the Klan were launched randomly against any African American unfortunate enough to be spotted by night riders out to cause mayhem and create terror. As the reports by agents A. H. Eastman and J. K. Nelson indicate, however, some African Americans were targeted for their political activity. Both Joshua Ferrell and D. Webb were told they were chosen by the Klan because they supported the Union League or the Loyal League, held Radical sympathies, or voted for the Radical Republican candidate for governor in the most recent election. The activities of the Union League (sometimes called the Loyal League) were particularly vexing to former secessionists and white supremacists. Founded in 1862 in Northern cities to support the Union cause, the Union League organized chapters in the South after the war to promote the Republican political agenda and to encourage African Americans to vote and become involved in politics. Many former slaves joined the Union League even if they were not political activists.

As every witness testifies, the Klan's actions ranged from simple intimidation to significant physical violence, sometimes resulting in murder. In many cases threats alone were enough to cause white and African Americans alike to submit to the Klan's will. One intimidation technique typical of many groups of Klansmen is described by the Reverend H. O. Hoffman, who reports having received threats himself, including one delivered in a fashion typical of Klansmen at the time: a note left in his yard warning him that his "name is before the Council" and that the Klan "will attend to you." Such notes alone were often sufficient to deter whites from continuing to support African Americans, and in some cases caused them to leave the region rather than face the prospect of reprisal for their actions.

A number of whites were forced to submit to public insult, which, coupled with secondhand reports of violence, caused them to behave like agent J. K. Nelson, who slept with firearms nearby. Many African Americans, fearing for their lives and wishing to keep themselves and their families safe from Klan attacks, simply fled to what they perceived to be safer regions. As the joint military committee report indicates, this posed new problems: the "two hundred colored men" who fled to Nashville ended up "destitute of food, or any means of subsistence." This early instance of African American flight to urban centers is a harbinger of what would come for many who left the harsh life of the segregated rural South only to end up no better off in crowded cities, where they remained victims of inequality and prejudice.

Language and Rhetoric

Some of the hyperbolic language in these excerpts can be attributed to a general tendency during the nineteenth century for Americans to assume an oratorical posture in their writing. A comparison of these reports with contemporary sermons might reveal striking similarities. Words such as "outrage," "depredation," and "reign of terror" appear regularly in written communications from this period, particularly in newspapers. While some accounts are emotionally charged and may be exaggerated, the sheer volume of reporting makes it evident that the Klan's campaign of terror was effective in keeping freed slaves and their white supporters from exercising their civil rights.

The inclusion of lengthy descriptions of specific acts of mayhem and torture, however, would have had immediate impact on readers of these reports, and would have convinced even the most skeptical to agree that strong countermeasures were required to curb the Klan's activities. Reverend Hoffman's description of the injuries suffered by the "colored man by the name of Jeff," agent Eastman's testimony about the treatment Joshua Ferrell received simply because he supported Governor Brownlow and the Union League, and the manhandling of Minor Fletcher and D. Webb described by agent J. K. Nelson contain little overblown rhetoric. Instead, the graphic language used in a series of declarative sentences filled with strong action verbs conveys without exaggeration the horror of the circumstances in which these men found themselves. The detail with which incidents of brutality are described is clearly intended to provoke both fear and outrage. The elderly Senator Wyatt was pistol-whipped so badly that he suffered a "frightful gash, saturating his shirt with blood, leaving him insensible." Joshua Ferrell, also old and apparently harmless, was similarly beaten, the pistol "cutting a gash half an inch wide, four inches long" into his skull. Little is left to the imagination except the unstated conclusion that incidents like these will continue to occur unless the Klan is neutralized.

Also common among these reports is the tendency to establish clear political and moral differences between perpetrators and victims in the attacks. For example, Senator Wyatt is described as "a Christian gentleman" and "a Union Man." The schoolteacher Dunlap is "a member of the Methodist Church," quiet and inoffensive. Many of the victims are former members of the Union Army. Those who threaten these honest, law-abiding, loyal citizens of the United States are violent, lawless bands intent on sedition. The attack on Senator Case indicates to the writers of the joint committee report that "no loyal man" is safe at present. Additionally, there is a sense running through these reports that these individual groups of "night-prowlers" are part of a larger, sinister organization that was creating a "system of anti-lawry and terrorism" for political motives: to deliver votes in the upcoming presidential election to the Democratic ticket.

The testimony recorded in these reports displays the power of anecdotal evidence in supporting an argument for government support of victims. The specific action sought by both state and federal officials was armed intervention. In his June 1868 report, Carlin makes it clear that Freedmen's Bureau agents were powerless to "remedy" the "evils that cry out for redress," and he pre-dicts exactly what Governor Brownlow feared. The level of Klan activity in the early months of 1868 strongly suggested that "frequent disturbances" would continue to occur during the fall campaigns for president and seats in Congress. The Klan's activities were certain to "bring about a state of affairs that will preclude the possibility for the colored people, and the active, outspoken Union men" to vote in the November election. Carlin is clear in his belief that nothing short of martial law "will preserve the peace and insure safety." No doubt in the summer of 1868 Governor Brownlow was pleased to see this kind of support for his own position against the Klan. For members of Congress receiving this report in 1870, the message was equally clear: some definite action was needed to ameliorate or eliminate Klan violence, or the country as a whole might slip back into anarchy and civil strife.

Essential Themes

The importance of congressional investigations into the activities of the Ku Klux Klan during the first decade following the end of the Civil War can hardly be overstated. Between 1866 and 1870 the Klan had spread to virtually every state in the former Confederacy. Its brutal campaign to intimidate the African American population in those states not only affected the political climate, but also caused many former slaves to fear for their lives and their property. The ability of Klansmen to act with impunity, knowing that sympathetic white officials in law enforcement and government would do little to prosecute them for any crimes they committed, created a virtual state of anarchy that many then and later would equate with terrorism. Although it is impossible to speculate on what might have happened, many scholars agree with those who witnessed Klan violence that the United States may well have slipped back into civil war had the Klan's activities not been checked. Hence, reports that document the Klan's systematic assault on equal rights were instrumental in bringing about action at the federal level to suppress the organization and restore order and the rule of law in the South.

Various investigations led to decisions that influenced the future of the nation. Undoubtedly the 1868 report prompted Tennessee legislators to reestablish the State Guard. In 1870 the House of Representatives was convinced by its committee's report that the African American population in Tennessee had been denied their civil rights; it voted to allow Tillman to retain the disputed Fourth District seat in Congress. Widespread accounts of Klan violence such as the ones documented in the House committee's report were instrumental in generating further action at the federal level. In 1871, Senator John Scott of Pennsylvania convened a congressional committee to investigate Klan activities in the South. The extensive testimony presented before Smith's committee was published in thirteen volumes in 1872 as *Report of the Joint Select Committee Appointed to Inquire in to the Condition of Affairs in the Late Insurrectionary States*. It became the most important contemporary document outlining the nature and extent of Klan violence during the early years of Reconstruction. The report also prompted passage of a stronger law allowing the federal government to counter Klan activities, which were identified as supporting a specific political agenda, that of the Democratic Party.

As a result of strong enforcement by President Ulysses S. Grant, the Ku Klux Klan's influence was almost completely nullified by 1877, when Reconstruction ended and former Confederate states were once again allowed to participate as full partners in the national government. Unfortunately, once free to act without federal supervision, many Southern states enacted laws that brought about the same result that the Klan had sought through violence: a segregated society in which African Americans remained separate and decidedly unequal.

Laurence W. Mazzeno, PhD

Bibliography and Additional Reading

Alexander, Thomas B. *Political Reconstruction in Tennessee*. Nashville: Vanderbilt UP, 1950. Print.

Bergeron, Paul H., Stephen V. Ash, and Jeanette Keith. *Tennesseans and Their History*. Knoxville: U of Tennessee P, 1999. Print.

Budiansky, Stephen. *The Bloody Shirt: Terror after Appomattox*. New York: Viking, 2008. Print.

Coulter, E. Merton. *William G. Brownlow: Fighting Parson of the Southern Highlands*. Chapel Hill: U of North Carolina P, 1937. Print.

Foner, Eric. *Reconstruction: America's Unfinished Revolution, 1863–1877*. New York: Harper, 1988. Print.

Horn, Stanley F. *Invisible Empire: The Story of the Ku Klux Klan, 1866–1871*. Cos Cob: Edwards, 1969. Print.

Katz, William L. *The Invisible Empire: The Ku Klux Klan Impact on History*. Washington: Open Hand, 1986. Print.

Martinez, J. Michael. *Carpetbaggers, Cavalry, and the Ku Klux Klan: Exposing the Invisible Empire during Reconstruction*. Lanham: Rowman, 2007. Print.

Newton, Michael. *The Ku Klux Klan: History, Organization, Language, Influence, and Activities of America's Most Notorious Secret Society*. Jefferson: McFarland, 2007. Print.

Patton, James Welch. *Unionism and Reconstruction in Tennessee 1860–1869*. Chapel Hill: U of North Carolina P, 1980. Print.

Queener, Verton M. "A Decade of East Tennessee Republicanism, 1867–1876." *East Tennessee Historical Society's Publications* 14 (1942): 59–85. Print.

Rable, George C. *But There Was No Peace: The Role of Violence in the Politics of Reconstruction*. Athens: U of Georgia P, 2007. Print.

Randel, William P. *The Ku Klux Klan: A Century of Infamy*. Philadelphia: Chilton, 1965. Print.

Severance, Ben H. *Tennessee's Radical Army: The State Guard and Its Role in Reconstruction, 1867–1869*. Knoxville: U of Tennessee P, 2005. Print.

Summers, Mark W. *A Dangerous Stir: Fear, Paranoia, and the Making of Reconstruction*. Chapel Hill: U of North Carolina P, 2009. Print.

Trelease, Allen W. *White Terror: The Ku Klux Klan Conspiracy and Southern Reconstruction*. New York: Harper, 1971. Print.

■ From *Recollections of the Inhabitants, Localities, Superstitions, and Ku Klux Outrages of the Carolinas, by a "Carpet-Bagger" Who Was Born and Lived There*

Date: 1870s
Author: John Patterson Green
Genre: memoir

Summary Overview

The period following the American Civil War was a time of racial and political violence in the states of the former Confederacy. During the Reconstruction era, the United States was divided largely along party lines as to how to address the significant social changes that were occurring in the South following the abolition of slavery. Radical Republicans called for punitive measures against former Confederate rebels and demanded voting rights for black men, whereas Democrats strongly opposed civil rights for former slaves and federal intervention in the Southern states. Federal troops were stationed throughout the South to enforce the rights of newly emancipated slaves to vote and own property, and many of the former Confederate states elected biracial Republican legislatures and established schools, transportation networks, and civil assistance organizations for freed slaves. Confederate soldiers, disenfranchised, armed, and eager to restore white supremacy, took advantage of the postwar chaos to threaten and intimidate black citizens. Republicans, white and black, were the particular targets of gangs that used violence to deprive newly enfranchised Southern black citizens of their rights. These gangs attacked black men and women as well as white "carpet-baggers," who were assumed to be outsiders aiding the former slaves' cause and undermining traditional Southern society. In his memoir, John Patterson Green, a black man born in South Carolina but raised in Ohio, recalls witnessing the activities of the most notorious of these gangs, the Ku Klux Klan, upon his return to South Carolina in 1870.

Defining Moment

President Abraham Lincoln, a moderate Republican, and his successor, Andrew Johnson, a Democrat, encouraged a conciliatory approach to the former Confederate states following the end of the Civil War. They returned seized property to its former owners and allowed Southern states to elect their own representatives. After the Radical Republicans gained control of Congress in a landslide victory in 1866, however, federal troops were stationed the former Confederacy to enforce the rights of black citizens, and many former Confederate officers were no longer allowed to hold office, prompting widespread outrage across the South. The army supervised elections at which free black men could now vote, and Republican governments overtook the South. Coalitions of blacks, Northern Republicans, and their Southern sympathizers canvassed the South, registering black men to vote and setting up polling stations and schools.

In retaliation for what many former Confederates saw as an unjust, corrupt, outside influence in their political process and an unnatural commingling of the races, armed groups began terrorizing anyone thought to support the Republicans. The most notorious of these groups, the Ku Klux Klan (KKK), was founded in 1865 by Confederate veterans and quickly spread throughout the South. The KKK used violence and threats to discourage black men from voting and to attempt to return them to their former subservient position. They drove out white politicians, teachers, and clergy who worked with the black population. Though the KKK was highly unorganized during this time, its membership grew rapidly until reports of its violent and disruptive activities resulted in the passage of the Enforcement Acts in 1870 and 1871, a series of laws that allowed federal intervention in states that did not ensure the equal treatment of all people under the law, which effectively drove the KKK underground. Other paramilitary groups were active in the South during this time, but none had the local and regional support enjoyed by the Klan.

When John Patterson Green graduated from law school and moved to South Carolina in 1870, he witnessed the activities of the Ku Klux Klan firsthand. Green was a skilled orator, and he commented at length on the rationale of many Southerners, who resented the cultural and ideological changes that had transpired with the abolition of slavery. It was this resentment and their refusal to let go of their "preconceived prejudices" that brought about the violence that Green saw perpetrated by the KKK and other white supremacist groups throughout South Carolina.

Author Biography

John Patterson Green was born in 1845 to free black parents in New Bern, North Carolina. His family moved to Cleveland, Ohio, in 1857 after the death of his father. Though never enslaved, Green's family was poor, and he struggled to complete his education, finally graduating at the age of twenty-four. In 1869, he began to study law, and in 1870 he passed the bar in South Carolina, where he lived for two years before deciding to return to Ohio. He enjoyed a successful political career in Cleveland, serving as a justice of the peace and later becoming the first black man to win election to the Ohio state senate, where he served one term.

Green published several books and articles throughout his career, beginning with a self-published collection of essays when he was still in secondary school. He died in Cleveland in 1940.

HISTORICAL DOCUMENT

CHAPTER X.

The Ku Klux-Klan.—Its Origin. —Its Name. —Objects and Deeds of Violence. —Recollections of its Early Days.— Proofs of its Existence.—What Hon. Reverdy Johnson thought of its Members. —The Origin of the Exodus, and Probable Result.

We had only proceeded a short distance further on our way, when we were confronted by the charred remains of what had been a dwelling house.

"What's that?" I asked for the hundredth time, addressing Jones.

"That" said he, "is the work of the Ku-Klux-Klan. The man who lived there was nominated for an office of inconsiderable importance; but being a 'Yankee' and for that reason displeasing to his Democratic neighbors, he was warned to leave the country; and failing to heed the notice, he was taken from his house one night by a body of masked men, given a coat of tar and feathers, and twenty-four hours in which to make his escape. After that treatment he hesitated no longer, but left for parts unknown, glad enough to be spared his life. On the fol-

lowing night his house, with all its contents, were burned to the ground, and left in the condition you now see it."

Further inquiry only tended to strengthen the truth of Jones' statement; not only this but the additional fact that throughout the region we were then traversing, there was a thoroughly organized association of men under the name given above. The Ku-Klux-Klan was an organization conceived in sin, and born in iniquity; based not so much upon any wrongs or oppression that its members were actually suffering at the hands of the members of the newly organized government of the State, as upon an imagined violence done to "all their preconceived opinions and prejudices," in the language of our Southern correspondent, whose letter we have given in a previous chapter. One of those opinions was that the South ought to have been left alone to secede from the Union of these States, and not restrained by the vigorous North; hence a violence had been done the South in restraining her. Another opinion was that, after having been scourged back into the line of States, South Carolina ought to have been given loose reins to reconstruct herself, and make her own laws; even though their tendency were such as to crush out every spark of civil life from the freedmen, deprive them of their newly acquired political privileges, and relegate them to the condition of "corn-field darkies," with overseers to crack their whips over their heads, and not even a master to say them nay. Violence had been done to their "preconceived opinions" by denying them this privilege, and to cap the climax, their "preconceived prejudices" had been violated by permitting "corn-field darkies and army sutlers" to hold offices of emolument and trust, notwithstanding the fact they utterly refused to fraternize with them even politically, and reap a portion of the benefits accruing there-from. There was no reasonable cause of complaint existing on the part of the people of that State that could not have been adjusted by lawful means entirely within their power and under their control; and that, in any one of our more considerate States of the North would have been modified without resort to violence and incendiarism. Not so with these impulsive people, however. "Their preconceived opinions and prejudices" had been violated, and now, just as when the Republican party of the North had violated them by electing Abraham Lincoln to the Presidential chair, nothing short of blood would wipe out the stain.

They regarded the "carpet-bagger" as the common foe, and, as a consequence, all arguments that could be lavished upon him, having in view his conversion to their doctrines, would be worse than wasted. Hence they let him severely alone, and in his state of ostracism he was left to fraternize with "corn-field darkies" or else live the life of a hermit. He chose the former.

But to the colored men they poured forth their souls in all the eloquence at their command, in the vain effort to lure them back again to all their former felicities (?). In this attempt as well they were doomed to disappointment, for their colored brethren had lived among them long enough to understand the difference between freedom and slavery, and took no heed of their prayers and entreaties. The colored men were then, as now, true to the cause of the Union. They had prayed for it; they had fought for it; and now they would vote for it, and not all the fair promises of their former masters, nor even the reputed wealth of the Indies could swerve them one inch from their recognized path of duty. I have known freedmen to walk twenty miles, in a thinly populated region, to the nearest voting precinct to cast their ballots, even when they knew that such action on their part widened

the breach between them and their employers and jeopardized their dearest interests, so true were they to the principles which they had espoused. Being foiled in their efforts to coax or scare their former slaves into a support of their "preconceived opinions and prejudices," and being fully determined to yield no jot or tittle to the policy pursued by the Republican party, as a last resort, and one more in consonance with their tastes, inclinations and early training, they adopted the policy now known as ku-klux-ism—a policy of cowardice, perjury, rapine and murder; one ill-suited to any people other than such as are found in the South among her half civilized white population.

The "klan" was thoroughly organized, having a ritual, signs, grips and passwords. They wore masks to conceal their cowardly faces, and bound each other with a solemn oath not to reveal the name of any member, nor divulge any secret of the order.

Their name, "Ku-Klux-Klan," is said to have been suggested to them by the sound made in the act of cocking and discharging the rifles and shot-guns carried by them—the first two syllables being repeated in a subdued tone of voice, as Ku Klux, represented the cocking of the piece; while the last syllable, *Klan,* being repeated with emphasis, betokened its discharge.

The objects of the Klan, as have been already hinted at, were to banish the so-called "carpet baggers" from the State, restore the freedmen to positions of serfdom under their former masters, and regain control of the government of the State. They carried a knife in one hand and a torch in the other, while in their belt they wore a revolver. The bull-whip and raw-hide were also instruments of their torture, and made to produce arguments which none dared refute. In their expeditions they spared neither age, sex nor color, and the reputation of being a "black republican" was all that was needed to place one under the ban of their condemnation.

To note the progress of the sentiment which culminated in the organization of this "Klan," was a matter of much curiosity; and since the writer was located in one portion of the State of South Carolina, from its inception until its discovery and prosecution under the administration of President Grant, he enjoyed many facilities in this connection not within reach of persons at a distance from the scene of their diabolism.

As early as the gubernatorial contest in 1870, while the writer, with others, were assisting in the canvass of the State in behalf of the Republican party, frequent paroxysms of rage were noted on the part of the "respectable people" of the State, which on more occasions than one, well nigh resulted in blood shed. In one instance this was so manifestly true that ever afterward our party went out "upon the stump" prepared for the worst. On the occasion referred to, while one of us, mounted upon a rustic rostrum, was descanting on the evils of Democratic rule, and lauding to the skies the magnanimous policy of the Republican party, a coarse looking man with his pants tucked into the legs of a pair of cow-hide boots, and wearing a broad-brimmed straw hat, who had been standing under a tree near by with a few others of similar stamp, paring a sweet potato with a dangerous looking knife which he held in his hand, becoming incensed at something which the speaker said, dropped his potato, and brandishing his knife, rushed toward him. In an instant a dozen sable sons of our party stood between the speaker and his assailant, and with drawn blades defied the assassin to touch a hair of his head. His violence soon subsided without harm being done.

On another occasion, when the orator of the day, during the delivery of a Fourth of July oration, was drawing a very striking contrast between the times that had been and those that were, a former nominee of the Democratic party for Congressman who was present, took umbrage at something that was said, and catching the speaker by one leg attempted to pull him from the stand. He came well high being paid for his temerity by a thrust from a sword in the hands of one of the audience, who was a captain of militia. And thus on nearly every occasion that offered these offended people would betoken their active hostility to every thing of a political nature not in full harmony with "all their preconceived opinions and prejudices."

As time wore on apace their opposition increased in virulence, and assumed a more open form. About six months later direct opposition in the nature of Ku-Klux outrages began to be felt and heard from. In the adjoining county a white Republican was summoned to his door one night by the usual alarm; he went accompanied by his wife and daughter, and instead of welcoming a neighbor or friend who had come to perform a friendly errand, they were confronted by a band of Ku-Klux, who, without any word of warning or even opportunity of making his peace with his God, shot him down like a dog.

In another section of the State a loving husband and kind father was bound and flogged in the presence of his family, because he heeded not their warning to desist from taking an active part in the campaign then inaugurated; houses and well-filled barns were burned and a perfect reign of terror inaugurated. Their deeds of violence being heralded abroad, alarm seized upon all Republicans who inhabited sparsely-settled counties, having their places of abode, in some instances, separated by miles of intervening forest, and their cries for help were such as to attract the attention of the General Government, who sent its ministers of justice to the scene, where a full investigation of the transactions of the infamous "Klan" was had, of which more anon.

It was at about this time that numerous suspicious looking "dodgers," written in an unknown hand, were scattered promiscuously through the streets and stores of Hudsonville, some of them even having been posted to the trees of the Public Square during the night time. These dodgers and placards bore threats of vengeance swift and dire to all who belonged to the "black Republican party," unless they severed their connection with it, and prophesied that the day of retribution was near at hand. To the State senator representing our own county they said, "Beware, oh, beware! Your doom is sealed!" Under the circumstances, we were alarmed. It is true that a matter of a similar nature in the well-regulated North would have excited only derision at the expense of the originators of the scheme; but in that disturbed locality, with many recent murders staring us in the face, and a knowledge of the fact that in other sections of the State much violence had been committed by this same organization. I think our perturbation was excusable. Accordingly, during the following night and several others thereafter, every able-bodied man in the village, of both colors, who had at heart the welfare of the party and its threatened representatives, was summoned to do guard duty at the house of our senator, as well as to patrol the streets, in anticipation of any outburst of violence.

The first night was dark and dismal; the rain fell in torrents, drenching everything exposed to its action; and the darkness was so intense as to be almost felt, save when an occasional flash of lightning exposed all nature to view, and filled the imagination with weird forms. On such a night as the foregoing the writer was summoned to do guard duty. He had just retired for the night, and his wife and little infant, snugly ensconced, were protected from the fury of the elements. It was a sore affliction to arise and go forth into that pelting storm, but when duty called we had to obey. My wife suggested that, owing to the inclemency of the weather, the danger might not be great on that occasion, for surely, she said, the Ku Klux would not venture forth in such weather; however, remembering the old maxim, "The darker the night, the darker the deed," we trusted them as to nothing, and obeyed the summons. Why were we thus deprived of our needed and dearly-bought rest? What had we done contrary to our country's weal? What law had been broken or set at defiance that we, like fugitives from justice, were driven from pillar to post without finding rest for our feet or place to lay our heads? Not one of these trespasses had we been guilty of, and yet we were the objects of their relentless persecutions.

Whether it was owing to our continued vigilance, or to some stroke of policy on their part, I cannot say; but, nevertheless, the Ku Klux did not visit us on that occasion, and before another season we had changed our place of abode.

Many persons in both sections of the United States have affected a certain incredulity with reference to recitals of the outrages perpetrated on the Republicans of the South by this infamous band, and have gone so far as to ridicule the very idea as being preposterous, and stamp it as a trick of political demagogues to create sympathy on the part of the people of the North in behalf of a government of "corn-field darkies and army sutlers." We not only hurl the insinuation back at them, but challenge all such to a careful perusal of some of the admissions of their most able men and public journals, as well as other convincing proofs that are at our command. It is a well-known fact that, upon the arrest and prosecution of some of the leaders of the "klan" in the State of South Carolina, during the winter of 1871, with a great show of indignation and not a little expense, Hon. Reverdy Johnson was procured to go from his pleasant home in the North to that forsaken country, for the purpose of making a defense of their interests. It was a matter for congratulation on the part of many well-disposed persons in the North, whose minds had become somewhat biased, because of the unfortunate reports of misrule and political corruption which were constantly coming up from the South, as well as the loud protestations of innocence that were constantly being made on the part of the accused, that such a man as Mr. Johnson had been selected to defend these cases; for, knowing his political predilections, but withal having the utmost confidence in his integrity as a lawyer and citizen, they felt assured that the truth, pure and simple, would be disclosed. Imagine their feelings of surprise then, when, after a protracted trial, guarded by all the ingenuity of so distinguished an attorney as he, with full and free access to every means of defense, Mr. Johnson, in the course of his speech in one of these cases, on the 31st day of December, 1871, in the presence of the accused and their friends, delivered himself of the following sentiments:

I have listened with unmixed horror to some of the testimony which has been brought before you. The outrages proved are shocking to humanity; they admit of neither excuse nor justification; they violate every obligation which law and nature impose upon men: they show that the parties engaged were brutes, insensible to the obligations of humanity and religion. The day will come, however, if it has not already arrived, when they will deeply lament it. Even if justice shall not overtake them, there is one tribunal from which there is no hope. It is their own judgment—that tribunal which sits in the breast of every living man—that small, still voice that thrills through the heart—the soul of the mind, and as it speaks, gives happiness or torture—the voice of conscience, the voice of God. If it has not already spoken to them in tones which have startled them to the enormity of their conduct, I trust in the mercy of heaven, that, that voice will speak before they shall be called above to account for the transactions of this world. That it will so speak as to make them penitent, and that trusting in the dispensation of Heaven, whose justice is dispensed with mercy, when they shall be brought before the bar of their great tribunal, so to speak, that incomprehensible tribunal, there will be found in the fact of their penitence, or in their previous lives, some grounds upon which God may say, 'PARDON.'

Such sentiments, coming from the lips of their own paid counsel, together with the fact that the accused were convicted by a jury of their peers, ought most assuredly to carry conviction with them to the mind of every fair thinking man. But if anything further were needed, let the following from a Georgia newspaper—the *Oglethorpe Echo,* a "Conservative" paper of that section—speak:

> Anthony Thurster, the negro preacher who was so severely whipped by a party of disguised men near Maxley's lately, asks that we announce to his white friends that from this time forward he will prove himself a better man; will never again make a political speech, deliver a sermon, or vote a Republican ticket: from henceforth he is an unswerving Democrat. We are glad that Anthony's eyes are at last opened to a proper course for him to pursue, but sorry that such stringent measures had to be adopted ere he would, as it were, be 'born again.'

Again, we have the statement of H. M. Dixon, who was not long since murdered in Mississippi because he dared to run on an independent ticket, supported by men of all political tendencies, as follows:

> Owing to certain reports that Patterson, a member of the Republican Legislature *who was hanged* in the eventful campaign of 1875, had a considerable sum of money on his person, and that said money was used for my own benefit, I feel in honor bound to vindicate myself, although I deplore to refer to the past as it will bring before the public *many of our best citizens.* I will briefly state that *said money,* and larger sums, was raised to defray the current expenses of the campaign and to stuff the ballot-boxes if necessary; to purchase certificates of election for two officers now holding offices of trust and emolument in our county. I have in my possession the necessary proof, and if called upon will furnish it.

Signed: H. M. Dixon

These proofs, together with the voluminous reports of committees appointed by Congress to investigate this subject, ought to leave no candid man in doubt. But in addition to all that has been said and written on this subject, if more were needed, we have a condition of well-established circumstances more patent than all. Witnesses will sometimes falsify; even men who are disposed to deal fairly in their testimony, at times become biased by reason of their interest in the issue at stake, or, perhaps, their peculiar surroundings; but circumstances, when admitted, never lie. What shall we say then of the sudden and precipitate flight of the men of the North who went to the South and invested their capital and labor, intending, in good faith, to become residents of that section? Surely it was no trivial cause that produced that result. The Goldsboro, North Carolina, *State,* commenting on this action on the part of this class of citizens in the South, uses the following suggestive language:

> It is a sad fact for this worn-out and famished State, that of the thousands of men who came hither, invested their means, and attempted to make homes under Republican rule, to-day but few remain. At the loss of their all they have wandered away to seek a home where they can speak their sentiments and vote as they deem best, without subjection to insult, abuse and vilification from such men as Governor Vance. Immigrants from all countries and all states pass us by, the "carpet-baggers" lose their all rather than remain, and many of her own sons seek in states where schools, polls and speech are free—a new home.

These citations are in part from sources outside of the State of South Carolina, but notwithstanding, they show a common purpose and unity of action on the part of the Democratic party of the South, to usurp by unfair means that power they cannot justly obtain at the ballot box, and trample the rights of others under their feet.

The question is sometimes asked: "Why don't the freedmen fight?" If our readers will for a moment consider that these men were, from their infancy, taught to fear and obey white men; that they are uneducated and unsophisticated, while their former masters are educated and shrewd; that while the white men of the South were educated to the use of the rifle and the shot-gun, the freedmen were kept in ignorance of their use; and further, that in many instances the freedmen are without leaders, they will appreciate the condition of these poor men with their unfortunate surroundings.

In our humble opinion the solution of the problem of the future of the South is involved in the outcome of the present movement of the colored farm hands of the South to Northern and Western States. If it shall continue until the laboring element of that section is materially weakened, a change of policy on the part of the intolerant faction there will, of necessity, be adopted; and this change will be of such a character as shall admit to equal terms of civil and political fraternity the sable freedmen then remaining among them; or else invite as participants in the profits of their estates, a foreign element who will be willing to cultivate them and preserve them from ruin. Time alone can unfold the result.

Of one thing there can be no reasonable doubt—the colored men of the South, having been robbed and murdered, their wives and daughters having been subjected to the insults and outrages of a brutalized populace, have long since become disgusted, and now having their eyes opened to a proper sense of their degradation and abuse, are rapidly seeking homes in the free Northwest, where they can serve God and their country according to the dictates of their own conscience, and reap a rich reward as the result of honest labor.

GLOSSARY

black Republican: a Republican or Radical Republican who supports the cause of African Americans

carpet bagger: or carpetbagger, a Northerner in the South; an outsider

incendiarism: use of fire; arson

say them nay: "tell them no"

sutler: an army provisioner; a seller of goods

tar and feathers: a method of physical abuse and humiliation

Document Analysis

This passage, taken from Green's memoir *Recollections of the Inhabitants, Localities, Superstitions, and Ku Klux Outrages of the Carolinas* (1880), provides examples of the violence inflicted on black Southerners and their white sympathizers by armed paramilitary groups eager to restore white supremacy in the former Confederacy, and of the determination of black men to retain and enforce their rights in the face of this intimidation. Green emphasized his unique perspective as a Southern-born black man who had returned to the South as an adult, making him both an insider and a self-proclaimed "carpet-bagger."

Green first witnessed Klan violence when passing the charred remains of a house. When he asked his companions what had happened, they replied "that is the work of the Ku-Klux-Klan." The man who had lived in the house, a "Yankee" Republican who had been nominated for an important office, had been warned to leave and, when he failed to do so, was tarred and feathered and run out of town. His house and all his belongings were then burned. Green identifies the KKK as a "thoroughly organized association," whose grievances were based not upon their perceived suffering at the hands of the Republican government but "upon an imagined violence done to 'all their preconceived opinions and prejudices.'" Having had their sense of white racial superiority and authority challenged, "nothing short of blood" could atone for the insult of allowing black men to vote and hold political office.

Green also notes that, while white outsiders were treated with silent contempt, black Southerners were cajoled, threatened, and entreated to give up their newly won rights. They refused, choosing the "cause of the Union" over the "fair promises of their former masters." Green recounts how some black men walked for more than twenty miles in order to exercise their right to vote. When black men refused to voluntarily give up their voting rights, some white Southerners adopted a plan of "ku-klux-ism—a policy of cowardice, perjury, rapine and murder" as a "last resort" to assert their authority, Green wrote.

The KKK operated as a terrorist organization—with "a knife in one hand and a torch in the other, while in their belt they wore a revolver." They also employed whips, the symbol of the slave driver. Green outlines the atrocities committed by the Klan, from floggings to murder, writing that a "perfect reign of terror" had been inaugurated across much of the South by Klan members. Republicans living and working in far-flung rural areas had no choice but to appeal to the federal government for protection.

Green also offers examples of how this violence was met with resistance. After placards were posted and distributed through Hudsonville, where Green was living, that threatened the life of the state senator from that county, Green and others took the threat seriously and organized a nightly guard around the senator's house. Green also notes how, when a knife-wielding man rushed the stage at a Republican rally, "a dozen sable sons of our party stood between the speaker and his assailant." When a Democrat took issue with an oration given by a Republican and tried to pull him off stage, "he came well nigh being paid for his temerity by a thrust from a sword."

Essential Themes

The primary purpose of this account was to document the danger faced by black and white Republicans in the South after the Civil War at the hands of violent paramilitary groups such as the Ku Klux Klan. John Patterson Green describes what he thinks gave rise to these groups—namely, former Confederates' inability to convince black Southerners to voluntarily give up their newly won civil rights, and their unwillingness to adapt to the changed racial relationship. The Ku Klux Klan and other groups like it used violence and threats to bring about what they were unable to accomplish through the political process: the return of black Southerners to a subordinate position. Green also describes the resistance to the threat of violence, particularly the gritty determination on the part of black Southerners to vote and to provide physical protection to politicians who represented their interests. Their support of Republican politicians was crucial. However, so was that of the federal government, and after Reconstruction ended and federal troops withdrew from the last of the Southern states in 1877, Democratic politicians were to return to power and strip away many of the political and social gains African Americans had made in those states.

—*Bethany Groff, MA*

Bibliography and Additional Reading

Alexander, Danielle. "Forty Acres and a Mule: The Ruined Hope of Reconstruction." *Humanities* 25.1 (2004): 26–29. Print.

Bullard, Sara. *The Ku Klux Klan: A History of Racism and Violence*. 4th ed. Montgomery: Klanwatch Project of the Southern Poverty Law Center, 1991. Print.

Du Bois, W. E. B. *Black Reconstruction in America 1860–1880*. New York: Simon, 1935. Print.

Foner, Eric. *Reconstruction: America's Unfinished Revolution, 1863–1877*. New York: HarperCollins, 2011. Print.

"Green, John Patterson." *The Encyclopedia of Cleveland History*. Case Western Reserve, 16 Jul. 1997. Web. 27 Jan. 2014.

Martinez, James Michael. *Carpetbaggers, Cavalry, and the Ku Klux Klan: Exposing the Invisible Empire during Reconstruction*. Lanham: Rowman, 2007. Print.

RECONSTRUCTION MOVES AHEAD

Despite all of its troubles and set-backs, Reconstruction lurched forward through the mid-1870s. By then, state governments in the South had experienced an evolution. In the years immediately following the war many of them had become redoubts of radical Republicanism and included many black Republicans in their numbers. At the same time, they also included former Confederate lawmakers who formally were to have been barred from office but under the presidency of Andrew Johnson found a place in government. Finally, in the years leading up to the contentious 1876 presidential election some of those state governments started to reject Republicans, particularly those of the radical variety, in favor of greater numbers of Democrats. That by the 1870s clear evidence existed of corruption in Republican-controlled governments did not help the cause of Reconstruction and its proponents.

In this section we sample some of the conflicting points of view that this evolution produced. We start with a strong and eloquent African American supporter of Reconstruction, Hiram Revels, who in a speech in Congress points to the positive contributions "the colored race" has made to the war effort and the nation at large. Next we hear from a Republican governor of Georgia, Rufus Bullock, who is accused of corruption and forced to leave office under pressure from the Ku Klux Klan and others. Then we hear from the prominent German-American thinker, general, and moderate Republican government official Carl Schurz, who writes of the need to authorize a broad amnesty for former Confederates who were officially barred from holding office or participating in the military. Next, in the person of James Rapier, an African American Republican representative from Alabama, we hear of the urgent need to push ahead with Reconstruction, including the enactment of additional civil rights laws to help those who were still "half free, half slave." Finally, we look at the fruits of Rapier's and others' urging, the Civil Rights Act of 1875, the last best hope of the radical reformers.

■ "The North Owes the Colored Race a Deep Obligation"

Date: March 16, 1870
Author: Hiram Revels
Genre: speech

"I rose to plead for protection for the defenseless race... the people of the North owe to the colored race a deep obligation which is no easy matter to fulfill... the colored race saved to the noble women of New England and the middle states men on whom they lean today for security and safety"

Summary Overview

Using vivid language and rhetoric in this speech to the president, Hiram Revels, the first African American to be elected to the U.S. Senate and the embodiment of the Fifteenth Amendment, presented himself as a representative of all free black men and women throughout the country. He passionately spoke about reinstating black lawmakers in Georgia who were forced out of office in 1868 by moderate white Republicans and Democrats. Revels argued that the North was obligated to support these black legislators because of all of the sacrifice blacks gave during the war in order to save the Union. Rather than engaging in bloody revolt against their former oppressors, African Americans exhibited responsible, loyal behavior. Thus, they deserved the right to vote and hold political office, which the federal and state law sanctioned.

Revels' entrance into the U.S. Senate marked him as the voice and leader of African Americans during this time period. He personified African American freedom and enfranchisement. Although he was a moderate politician who was embraced by both Republicans and Democrats, this portion of Revels' speech reveals that Revels unapologetically refused to be diplomatic on the issue of denying African Americans their basic rights as American citizens. It also reveals the historical trend within the counter-narrative of African American history that African Americans as well as other subaltern groups participated in war efforts in order to prove their loyalty and gain equal rights in an American society that privileged the white male.

Defining Moment

The conclusion of the Civil War ushered in a period known as Reconstruction in which the Union sought to reconcile with the Confederate states and reconstruct the South. Because President Abraham Lincoln was assassinated shortly after the Civil war ended, his vice president Andrew Johnson was put in charge of reintegrating the South back into the Union. Republicans dominated in the former Confederate states and would only allow Southern states to be readmitted into the Union if the Thirteenth and Fourteenth Amendments were ratified into the Constitution. Passed in 1865, the Thirteenth Amendment made it illegal to have people perform coerced work unless incarcerated while the Fourteenth Amendment, passed in 1868 under the first Reconstruction Act, recognized African Americans as citizens. This right had been denied to slaves in the Dred Scott U.S. Supreme Court decision, which stated that African Americans could not testify in court because they were not citizens. Under the Reconstruction

Act, new constitutions were drawn up in the Southern states, and the South was redrawn into five military districts and subject to martial law. Finally, in 1870, the Fifteenth Amendment was ratified and guaranteed the right to vote for African American men. It enabled African Americans to be elected into the U.S. House of Representatives and U.S. Senate and thus set the stage for Hiram Revels to be elected into the U.S. Senate early that year.

Congress took over Reconstruction from President Johnson in 1867 and implemented its own vision for rebuilding the South. This period differed from Presidential Reconstruction because Congress supported the political rights of former slaves while President Johnson neglected their well-being. During this period African Americans were elected into office, although several white Southern men refused to vote because they disliked that suffrage was extended to African American men. Over 600 African Americans were elected to state legislatures in the South; whites turned to both violent and nonviolent tactics to try and keep African Americans out of the government. Black Codes were enacted in the Southern states that limited the rights of African Americans such as the right to enter into contracts, live in cities or towns, and bear arms. Vigilante groups such as the Ku Klux Klan sprung up in order to terrorize blacks and prevent them from exercising their right to vote.

Despite the attempts of Southern Democrats to prevent the U.S. Senate from allowing Revels to be a senator, the majority Republicans in the Senate prevailed in seating him. In his first speech to the Congress, he spoke before a packed gallery and chamber filled with white lawmakers as well as black men and women and addressed a bill regarding readmitting the former Confederate state of Georgia back into the Union. The bill addressed the representation in the Union for Georgia that included an amendment that made it illegal for African Americans to hold state office. Revels contended that the Republican Party and the North owed the black legislators in Georgia their support. In 1868, voters in Georgia ratified a new state constitution that extended suffrage to African American men, a necessary step under the stipulations of Congressional Reconstruction to allow Georgia to be readmitted to the Union. In that same year, twenty-nine black legislators were elected into the state house of representatives and three to the Georgia senate. When the state legislature convened later that year, however, white legislators from both parties unseated the black lawmakers because they claimed that the state constitution did not allow African Americans to hold office. African in Americans in Georgia turned to the federal government to intervene and force Georgia to comply with the Fourteenth and Fifteenth Amendments. Revels spoke vehemently in favor of getting the black lawmakers reinstated as a prerequisite for Georgia to be readmitted. Eventually, a congressional mandate was agreed upon that reinstated the black lawmakers in order for Georgia to rejoin the Union in July 1870.

As the 1870s wore on, the North felt less inclined to support Reconstruction in the South because of the turmoil it was causing in the South. African American politicians and members of the Republican Party were being driven from their offices and murdered in their homes by disgruntled white Southerners. Northerners felt that peace could only be achieved if Southern whites won back control of both state governments and African Americans despite the fact that whites would dominate once again and undermine the notion of equal rights. White Democrats regained control of the South and enacted various measures to prevent African Americans from voting through poll taxes, property qualifications, and other means. Although Revels embodied the achievements of Reconstruction, those achievements were short-lived, as the Reconstruction acts were struck down and the status of African Americans soon resonated with their status in the antebellum period.

Author Biography

Hiram Revels was born on September 27, 1827 in Fayetteville, North Carolina a freeman to parents of European and African ancestry. Early on he received an education by an African American woman at an all-black school. In 1838 he moved to Lincolnton, North Carolina to live with his older brother where he worked as an apprentice in his brother's barbershop. He attended the Union Quaker Seminary in Indiana and then furthered his studies at a black seminary in Ohio. In 1845, Revels became a minister at African Methodist Episcopal Church and worked as a preacher and teacher throughout the Midwest states. Throughout his career as a religious teacher and preacher, Revels faced some opposition and was even imprisoned in 1854 for preaching the gospel to African Americans. In 1862, he served as a chaplain in the U.S. Army where he partook in the recruitment and organization of black regiments for the

Union during the Civil War in both Missouri and Maryland. When African Americans were allowed to fight for the Union in 1862, Revels served as a chaplain in various campaigns, most notably one in Vicksburg.

Revels' political career as a Republican took off during Reconstruction. In 1869, he was elected to Congress to represent Adams County in the state senate in Mississippi. Because less than one thousand free blacks in Mississippi received an education, Revels' entrance into politics because essential to the Republican Party to rally a new electorate after the war when blacks were enfranchised. Although reluctant to enter into politics out of fear of violent opposition, Revels was quickly embraced by both whites and blacks because he was moderate and held empathetic political beliefs. In 1870, Revels was overwhelmingly elected by the Mississippi state senate to finish out the last year of the term of a vacated U.S. Senate seat as a result of the Civil War, which made him the first African American to serve in the U.S. Congress when he was sworn in on February 25, 1870. Democrats opposed Revels filling the seat and pointed to the Dred Scott decision, which stated that African Americans could not testify in court because they were not citizens . Furthermore, they contended, no African American man was a citizen prior to the ratification of the Fourteenth Amendment in 1868, which meant that Revels did not meet the requirement for holding political office that mandated that he had to be a U.S. citizen for at least nine years. Nonetheless, Revels was elected because Republicans dominated the U.S. Senate, and the vote split along party lines.

Once sworn into the Senate, Revels was assigned to the Committee on Education and Labor and the Committee on the District of Columbia. He became the voice and representative for all black men and women throughout the country, and he advocated for reinstating black legislators who were forced from office in Georgia by white Democrats in 1868. As a moderate, he also favored granting amnesty to former Confederates as long as they swore an oath of loyalty. Revels promoted civil rights for African Americans throughout the year he held a Senate seat. At the conclusion of his term, he declined various positions offered to him by President Ulysses Grant and opted to return to Mississippi and serve as the first president of Alcorn University, an all-black college. Revels retired in 1882 and died suddenly at a religious conference on January 16, 1901. Despite his limited success while he served the U.S. Congress, Revels was a symbol of Union victory in the Civil War as well as the idealism evident during Radical Reconstruction.

HISTORICAL DOCUMENT

I remarked, Mr. President, that I rose to plead for protection for the defenseless race who now send their delegation to the seat of government to sue for that which this Congress alone can secure to them. And let me say further. That the people of the North owe to the colored race a deep obligation which is no easy matter to fulfill. When the federal armies were thinned by death and disaster, and somber clouds overhung the length and breadth of the Republic, and the very air was pregnant with the rumors of foreign interference—in those dark days of defeat whose memories even yet haunt us as an ugly dream, from what source did our nation in its seeming death throes gain additional and new-found prayer? It was the sable sons of the South that valiantly rushed to the rescue, and but for their intrepidity and ardent daring many a northern fireside would miss today paternal counsels of brotherly love.

Sir, I repeat the fact that the colored race saved to the noble women of New England and the middle states men on whom they lean today for security and safety. Many of my race, the representatives of these men on the field of battle, sleep in the countless graves of the South. If those quiet resting-places of our honored dead could speak today what a mighty voice, like to the rushing of a mighty wind, would come up from those sepulchral homes! Could we resist the eloquent pleadings of their appeal? Ah, sir, I think that this question of immediate and ample protection for the loyal people of Georgia would lose its legal technicalities, and we would cease to hesitate in our provisions for their instant relief. Again, I regret the delay on other grounds. The taunt is frequently flung at us that Nemesis more terrible than the Greek impersonation of the anger of the gods awaits her hour of direful retribution. We are told that at no distant day a great uprising of the American people will demand that the Reconstruction acts of Congress be undone and blotted forever from the annals of legislative enactment. I inquire, sir, if this delay in affording protection to the loyalists of the state of Georgia does not lend an uncomfortable significancy to this boasting sneer with which we so often meet? Delay is perilous at best; for us it is as true in legislation as in psychic, that the longer we procrastinate to apply the proper remedies the more chronic becomes the malady that we seek to heal.

The land wants such
As dare with rigor execute the laws.
Her festered members must be lanced and tented
He's a bad surgeon that for pity spares
The part corrupted till the gangrene spread
And all the body perish. He that's merciful
Unto the bad is cruel to the good.

GLOSSARY

annals: a record of events in a specific year or a record in a historical chronicle

ardent: passionate or intensely devoted

festered: full of pus; putrefied or rotten

gangrene: death of soft tissue that results in putrefaction

intrepidity: state of being fearless or undaunted

malady: a disease or disorder of the body

sable: the color black

sepulchral: pertaining to burial; funereal

Document Analysis

The Reconstruction era in the South offered a glimmer of hope for African Americans in the South to obtain equal rights as citizens and to be integrated into the political process. The Fourteenth and Fifteenth Amendments recognized African Americans as citizens under the law and enfranchised African American men, which opened up the doors for African American men to be elected into office. Although African American members symbolized a new democratic order in the United States, they did not achieve as much success as their white counterparts who held higher political positions during Reconstruction. Nonetheless, they had a significant role as advocates for America's newest citizens. On February 25, 1870, Hiram Revels, a highly educated and religious man, became the first black man to be elected into the U.S. Congress to finish out the term of former Mississippi senator. Revels embraced his role as an advocate for all African Americans and articulated his beliefs unapologetically in his maiden speech. In a poignant part of his speech, Revels argues that the North owed the "colored race" protection as free citizens because of their service to the Union during the Civil War. Fervent in his conviction, Revels uses vivid and descriptive language to paint African Americans as loyal saviors for this country during the most desperate and desolate times. He alludes to the fact that despite being free African Americans remain a "defenseless race" in need of protection by the federal government. Addressing a packed gallery and chambers composed of both white and black spectators for the first time, Revels delivered a passionate and eloquent plea to legislators to address and rectify the injustice that occurred in Georgia. Revels depicts himself as a staunch advocate for and representative of all African Americans throughout the country and conveys a sense of hope that the government would recognize and appreciate the sacrifices African Americans made in order to save the Union.

Despite the fact that African Americans were free and equal citizens by law, Revels characterizes them as a "defenseless race," which the expulsion of black lawmakers in Georgia clearly demonstrated. In November 1867, an election in Georgia was held under Congressional Reconstruction policy in order to create a new state congress who would draft a new state constitution. Both black and white voters participated, although many white voters abstained from voting because they were upset that African Americans had the right to partake in the elections. As a result, several black candidates were voted into office. However, by 1868 white legislators in Georgia concluded that the Reconstruction acts were unconstitutional and asserted that anyone with 1/8 African blood or more could not serve in the state legislature. As a result, twenty nine black lawmakers were forcibly removed from office. Congress did not intervene in Georgia, thereby allowing white lawmakers to infringe on the rights of black people preserved in Georgia's new state constitution. Although a moderate politician throughout his career, Revels felt obligated to address this injustice in his inaugural speech as a member of the Senate because he wanted to show that he would become the defender of justice for all African Americans in the federal government since they have never had one before.

Using vivid and emotion language, Revels imparts his belief that the North was in debt to African Americans because they helped secure a Union victory during the bleakest moments of the Civil War. During the war, many male slaves sought liberty by running away to the Union lines despite receiving harsh treatment by Union soldiers. At the outset of the war, the Union army put escaped slaves to work as cooks, construction workers, drivers and blacksmiths. In 1862, African American men were allowed to serve in the army because less white men wanted to serve in the Union army "thinned by death and disaster." Most African American soldiers were former slaves in the South, and they served in all-black regiments that faced unfair government policies such as lower pay and inferior weaponry. Many whites in the North did not think that African Americans were

fit or competent to fight because slavery rendered them servile and docile. However, once they began to fight, their white critics had a quick change of mind and were surprised how valiantly and courageously they fought. Revels stresses these qualities in his speech when he characterizes them as valiant and intrepid.

Revels cites how slaves quelled the looming threat of foreign interference to help the South win the war. President Lincoln issued the Emancipation Proclamation in 1863, which freed the slaves in Southern states but not in the border states. Lincoln believed that freeing the slaves would hasten the end of the war by breaking the South's resistance. Furthermore, it was a preemptive measure to safeguard against the possibility of Great Britain entering the war on the South's side because England depended on cotton produced in the South. Britain espoused an anti-slavery sentiment, so by freeing the slaves Lincoln was confident that England would stay out of the war and northern victory would ensue. As a result of their contributions once freed, the Union army ultimately prevailed against the Confederate army, which is why Revels believes the North owes the black legislators in Georgia protection.

Revels uses hyperbolic language in order to emphasize how indispensable African Americans were to the Union's victory and to convince his black spectators that he would fight to protect their rights while in office. The "sable son of the South" bravely came to rescue the Union, and without them many northern families would not have survived the war. He reiterates the fact that without the help of African Americans during the war, the white elite would have perished. It is ironically those "noble women of New England" and "men in the middle states" that African Americans saved are the very people that African Americans rely on for safety and security. However, they remain a defenseless race despite their contributions. Revels' assertion alludes not only to the injustice in Georgia but also to the reality that since emancipation former slaves faced unchecked violence by vigilante groups, white mobs and disgruntled Democrats. Violence or the threat of violence against African Americans was widespread and random. An age of lynchings commenced during Reconstruction whereby white Southerners would murder African Americans as a spectacle for the public to see. These heinous attacks occurred often with the participation of law enforcement officials, and the perpetrators were seldom punished or punished very lightly. The murder of African Americans was thus viewed not as murder in the eyes of the law but pushed into a separate legal category by a government undergirded by white hegemony. Furthermore, white vigilante groups formed in the South to terrorize African Americans and prevent them from exercising their rights as free people. Revels recognized the fabric of American society for African Americans changed very little years after emancipation, so he invoked hyperbolic language to depict the African American contributions during the Civil War as indispensable to saving both the lives of northerners as well as the Union itself.

Framing his plea for federal intervention in Georgia around the concepts of justice and injustice, Revels stresses that the loyalty shown and sacrifices made by African Americans during the Civil War must be rewarded. Countless black men lost their lives fighting to save the Union, and Revels declares that if they were alive they would plead to the federal government to help protect their civil rights that the U.S. Constitution promised to protect. Revels makes an emotional appeal to the U.S. Congress to not let those black men and women who protected them and preserved the Union die in vain. He represented their intermediary, and he felt an obligation to listen to their pleas for protection. Using the metaphor of illness to represent injustice, Revels suggests that if the federal government does not protect its loyal citizens in the state of Georgia then other states will follow in Georgia's footsteps and the disease of injustice would become more "chronic." It is this "malady" that the government sought to eradicate with the passage of the Fourteenth and Fifteenth Amendment. Revels' speech thus criticizes the apathy of the federal government to protect its loyal citizens in the face of racial injustice. This emotional plea to the government to stand up for African Americans suggests that because many African Americans died both during slavery times and during the war that Revels saw himself in his political role as the voice and representative of the black community. Many black members were in the audience and were hopeful that he would stand up and vouch for them, which Revels did so through this subtle critique and emotional appeal to lawmakers to recognize the African American man as their brother.

Essential Themes

As the first African American man to take a seat in the U.S. Senate, Hiram Revels emerged as a representative for all African Americans throughout the country. His speech illustrates the important theme that during the Reconstruction period as well as afterwards, Southern whites, former slave owners and white lawmakers resisted treating African Americans as free. Even if they reconciled themselves to the notion that African Americans were no longer slaves, Southern whites believed that African Americans were not equal citizens and thus should not be granted the same rights as privileges as whites. Certain racial stereotypes were perpetuated throughout the Reconstruction era in order to espouse this view. Black legislators in Georgia voted into office had their rights violated in 1868 because of these prevailing attitudes towards the African American community despite the fact that the Fourteenth and Fifteenth Amendments were ratified into both the U.S. Constitution as well as in Georgia's new state constitution. Although a moderate politician, Revels could not stay silent regarding the federal government's apathy toward the violation of civil rights that occurred there

Many times throughout U.S. history African Americans as well as other subaltern groups fought in wars in order to prove their loyalty and worthiness of citizenship and equal rights. Despite facing hardships, African Americans felt proud of their wartime contributions and felt that they earned freedom for their families and for themselves. Revels vividly reminds the audience that when it appeared that the Union was going to lose, African American men from the South courageously came to its rescue. He further emphasizes the loyalty and sacrifices African Americans made for the Union during the war in order to argue that they merited protection when their civil rights were so viciously trampled on thereafter. African Americans saw World War I as a good opportunity to prove themselves as Americans and believed that if they fought in the war they would be entitled to rights. The war thus ushered in the "New Negro" movement which revived a sense of expectation in the African American community not seen since emancipation during the Civil War. Revels convey a sense of hope and expectation that the U.S. government would reward its loyal citizens by protecting the oppressed for their oppressors.

Maddie Weissman, M.A.

Bibliography and Additional Reading

Du Bois, W.E.B. *Black Reconstruction in America*. New York: Harcourt, Brace, 1935. Print.

Foner, Eric. *Reconstruction: America's Unfinished Revolution, 1863-1877*. New York: Harper & Row, 1988. Print.

Goldman, Robert M. *Reconstruction and Black Suffrage: Losing the Vote in Reese and Cruikshank.* Kansas: UP of Kansas, 2001. Print.

Kelley, Robin D. G., and Earl Lewis. *To Make Our World Anew: A History of African Americans.* Oxford: Oxford UP, 2000. Print. Potts, Kenneth. "Hiram Rhoades Revels," in Jessie Carney Smith, ed., *Notable Black American Men.* Farmington Hills: Gale, 1999. Print.

Lawson, Elizabeth. *The Gentleman From Mississippi: Our First Negro Representative, Hiram R. Revels.* New York: The Author, 1960. Print.

Matthews, John M. "Negro Republicans in the Reconstruction of Georgia," in Donald G. Nieman, ed., *The Politics of Freedom: African Americans and the Political Process During Reconstruction.* New York: Garland, 1994. 253–268. Print.

U.S. House of Representatives, Office of the Historian. "Revels, Hiram Rhodes." U.S. House of Representatives, n.d. Web. 10 Oct. 2013.

Letter to Republican Senators and Representatives

Date: May 21, 1870
Author: Rufus B. Bullock
Genre: letter

Summary Overview

In this letter to Republicans in Congress, Rufus B. Bullock, the governor of Georgia, responded to accusations of corruption. Bullock was accused of trying to buy votes to defeat the Bingham amendment, which would have pushed forward elections in 1870, cutting his term as governor short by two years. Bullock was widely reviled as a carpetbagger, since he was born in New York (though he moved to Georgia long before the Civil War), and his unwavering support of citizenship and voting rights for former slaves added to his unpopularity among many white Georgians. His letter illustrates the difficulties faced by Republicans in Georgia after the Civil War as they tried to shape the governments of the former Confederate states. It also illustrates the complexity of the issues involved in returning Georgia to full participation in national government.

Defining Moment

The state of Georgia took a circuitous route to full readmission into the Union. In May 1865, with federal soldiers occupying the state, the government of Confederate Georgia was abolished. In December 1865, Georgia repealed secession, abolished slavery, repudiated its debt, and recognized the authority of the federal government. In 1866, however, when Alexander H. Stephens, the former vice president of the Confederacy, and Confederate senator Herschel Johnson were elected to the US Senate representing Georgia, they were barred from taking their seats, and their election was widely regarded as proof that Georgia was not fit for statehood. Georgia also refused to ratify the Fourteenth Amendment, which granted citizenship rights to former slaves.

In 1867, Republicans in Congress were able to use their power to enact strict Reconstruction Acts. This included the demand that Georgia ratify the Fourteenth Amendment, give black men full voting rights, and elect a new state government. By late 1867, a constitutional convention in Atlanta gathered to draft a new state constitution that codified the reforms required by the national government. Bullock was a key participant in this convention, and in 1868, he was elected as a Republican to the governorship of Georgia.

From the beginning of his time in office, Bullock faced stiff opposition, not only from Democrats, but also from members of his own party who were unwilling to accept the full political participation of black men. In September 1868, Democrats and their white Republican allies succeeded in expelling black legislators from the state government. Bullock began a series of increasingly desperate letters and visits to Washington, DC, to ask the federal government to enforce the Reconstruction Acts. The threats to Bullock himself and other Republicans, black and white, were very real. The newly formed Ku Klux Klan routinely made good on threats of violence, and legislation that would have opened up political participation to thousands of former Confederates, whose allegiance was certainly not with the Republicans, seemed always about to pass.

With Bullock's support, the military continued to oversee political activities in Georgia, and it was widely believed that Bullock engineered the defeat of the Fifteenth Amendment in Georgia in order to keep Reconstruction—and the military support of his government—in place. In February 1870, however, the Georgia legislature ratified the Fifteenth Amendment. Bullock wrote this letter in May 1870, attempting to refute charges that he was attempting to maintain his political position to further his personal financial interests. In July, Georgia was readmitted to the Union, and the Republicans quickly lost control of the legislature, and Bullock lost the governorship.

Author Biography

Rufus B. Bullock was born in Bethlehem, New York, in 1834, but he moved to Georgia in 1859 to manage railroad systems. During the Civil War, Bullock worked for the Confederate government on transportation and communication systems. Bullock first entered political life as a delegate to the 1867 Constitutional Convention, and he was elected to the governorship the following year. Bullock's tenure was marked by threats and accusations. Georgia Democrats and some members of his own party found Bullock's support of full citizenship rights for black men unacceptable, and he was often threatened by the Ku Klux Klan and others. Rumors of corruption circulated widely during his administration, and in late 1870, Bullock resigned his governorship and fled to New York. He was reviled in the Georgia press, and in 1876, Bullock was returned to Georgia to face charges of fraud and corruption. After his acquittal, Bullock stayed in Georgia until 1903 and died in New York in 1907.

HISTORICAL DOCUMENT

Gentlemen: I regret that duty to myself personally, and to my official position, requires that I should address myself in this manner to those with whom I am politically associated. My reasons for so doing are found in the following extract from a speech made by the honorable Senator from Connecticut, Mr. Ferry, on the 17th instant:

"But I do say that had Georgia for the last two years been in the hands of men of high patriotism; if it had been in the hands of men who were looking to the welfare of the nation instead of their own pecuniary advancement, we might have had a different state of things there from what exists to-day." And also in the conclusion arrived at by four Republicans and one Democratic member of the Judiciary Committee of the Senate that in paying D. C. Forney, the publisher of the Chronicle, bills as rendered for printing pamphlets, extracts, and speeches on the Georgia question, I did "use improper means to influence the vote of Senators upon the Georgia question."

Were these the production of Democrats, neither my voice nor my pen would be raised to notice them; coming from Republican sources, they are worthy of notice.

In noticing first the allegation of Senator Ferry, "that had Georgia for the last two years been in the hands of men of high patriotism, if it had been in hands of men who were looking to the welfare of the nation, instead of their own pecuniary advancement, we might have had a different state of things there from what exists to-day,"

I would say that from my stand-point I can fully concur with the Senator in this statement, from the fact that for the last two years, or at least until the 20th of January last, Georgia has been in the hands of a rebel Democratic legislative organization. But as the remark is evidently intended to apply to the Republicans of that State and to myself, as the head of the State government, I shall refer to a few historical facts for the purpose of establishing the injustice, to use the mildest form of expression, which is done by the Senator to the Republicans of our State and to myself by his remark.

On the 4th day of July, 1867, a convention met in Atlanta to organize a Republican party in our State, in opposition to that kind of Republicanism which claimed Andrew Johnson as its chief. That convention resolved to sustain the Reconstruction Acts of Congress, and to endeavor to establish a government for the State under and by virtue of those acts. It was a small beginning, and the men who participated in that organization were surrounded by all the malignity of rebel hate, inflamed and embittered by the endorsement of the colored men so lately their slaves. And the little band who thus bravely met were threatened on all sides and their lives were by no means secure.

In November of the same year an election was had to decide by a vote whether a convention under the Reconstruction Acts should be called, and at the same time for the election of delegates to the convention should its call be ratified. In this election the Republicans of the State were successful. The convention was called, and during the winter of 1867–'8 a constitution was framed in which there is no sign of proscription, no test oaths, no disfranchisement. All men of sound mind, who have not been convicted of a felony, and who are twenty-one years of age and residents of the State, are under it entitled and to hold office....

Under and by virtue of the act of June 25, 1868, the General Assembly convened on the 4th of July of the same year. Among those elected by the opposite party were at least thirty who were especially prohibited by the act of June 25, and by previous acts, from holding office, they being disqualified by the 3rd section of the fourteenth amendment.... Notwithstanding this presentation of facts, however, the commanding general deemed it wise to make no objection to those members retaining their seats, and the Legislature this organized in violation of the law, having gone through the form of adopting the conditions then required in the Reconstruction Acts, the State, by military order, was remanded to the civil government thus established.

In September of the same year this legislative organization excluded from their seats some twenty-eight of its members, who were of African descent.

At this point the contest originating from the enfranchisement of the colored men was renewed with all its bitterness. While the question of this expulsion was being considered by the Legislature, I, in an official communication, impressed upon them, in the strongest terms which I was capable of using, the great wrong which was about to be perpetrated, and, of course, thereby stimulated a renewal of our political animosities. Earnest appeals were made to me by frightened and discouraged Republicans to acquiesce in this outrage, and offers of high political preferment and advancement were indirectly tendered to me by the opposite party to effect the same object, accompanied by threats of the vengeance that would be visited upon me if I did not accept their terms....

If away out on the confines of civilization a settler is threatened in his cabin by a prowling band of Indians, troops are at once moved, money is lavishly spent, and the whole country is aroused for his protection; but, on the other hand, if white and African American friends of the Union are whipped and murdered in the South by prowling bands of disguised Kuklux, the President is prevented from granting protection because the laws do not authorize him; and when men or delegations come to the capital from the South to plead with Congress for help and for their rights, haste is made to put them under "investigation" with the vain hope that the lies of the interested rebels may have some foundation in fact.... While we risk our lives and our property, will you aid in taking from us that which is dearer than all these—our good name and our reputation?

... The most atrocious lies and insinuations have been telegraphed from Washington to different parts of the country, and circulated among members of both houses, to the effect that I have attempted to influence the votes of Senators by offers of Georgia bonds or money, and every possible means had been employed to create prejudice against myself and the Republican party of Georgia....

These infamous lies have a common origin, and have been coined and well put into circulation by men who hypocritically pretend to belong to the Republican party, but who are, and have been, acting in concert with the rebel Democracy in Georgia.

For two years in Georgia I have been pursued by threats of personal violence and assassination, and, during that period, my friends have believed my life was in danger. For two years I have been pursued by the most villainous slanders that rebel ingenuity could invent, charging corruption in office, personal immorality, and in every way impeaching my character as a man and an officer. One after another these slanders have been worn out and abandoned only to be renewed in some other form. Every attempt to sustain any one of them, and in every instance, has proved an utter and shameless failure....

Whatever else may happen to me, I shall leave the office of Governor of Georgia with clean hands, and without having performed any act for which my children or my friends shall have occasion to blush, but with my private fortune greatly diminished by the heavy expenses which I have been subjected to sustain myself and the loyal men of Georgia....

Rufus B. Bullock

Willard's Hotel, Washington

May 21, 1870

GLOSSARY

especially prohibited: specifically barred—here, referring to former Confederates

instant: of the present month

malignity: intense ill will; great malice

opposing party: the Democratic Party

proscription: legal disqualification; prohibition

Document Analysis

Bullock's letter to Republicans in Congress was primarily a defense of his political decisions and a refutation of corruption charges. The letter was initiated as a response to a fellow Republican, Senator Orris S. Ferry from Connecticut, who implicated Bullock in his remarks about politicians in Georgia. "Had Georgia for the last two years been in the hands of men of high patriotism . . . looking to the welfare of the nation instead of their own pecuniary advancement, we might have had a different state of things there from what exists today." Bullock points out that he had been accused of attempting to influence the senators on "the Georgia question," or the readmission of Georgia to the Union, but was cleared of the charge that he improperly used funds.

Bullock spends significant energy refuting charges that he offered bribes to try to persuade senators to admit Georgia into the Union without the amendment that called for new elections, and which would have cut Bullock's four-year term in half. "Every possible means had been employed to create prejudice against myself and the Republican party of Georgia who were asking for the admission of the State without the Bingham amendment." Bullock outlines all of the attempts that had been made to drive him out of office, from "threats of personal violence and assassination" to "the most villainous slanders that rebel ingenuity could invent, charging corruption in office, personal immorality, and in every way impeaching my character as a man and an officer." He points out that, in every case in which he was investigated for corruption, the charges were not substantiated.

Bullock lays the blame for these false charges at the feet of Joshua Hill, a Republican US senator from Georgia. Bullock accuses Hill of being friendly to the Confederacy, of not supporting citizenship rights for former slaves, and of assisting in the return of enemies of Bullock to full political power, including a Ku Klux Klan member who had threatened to "cut Bullock's heart out before he should ever be allowed to take his seat as Governor." Bullock alleges that Hill gave the press a false story that he had been offered "railroad bonds, endorsed by the State of Georgia, to the amount of $10,000" to vote down the amendment that would have cut Bullock's term and opened up new elections. Bullock spends a significant portion of his letter disputing the claim.

Bullock's primary charge is that factions in opposition to the enforcement of the Reconstruction Acts, the new Georgia Constitution, and full citizenship rights for black men were trying to tarnish the reputation of "loyal men," such as himself, in order to "break down or greatly injure the Republican party." He does not hesitate to implicate other Republicans in that charge, calling them "agents" of the Democratic opposition. Bullock then catalogs the ways that he had been harassed. His private accounts had been investigated. He had been accused of paying off newspapers, and money had gone unaccounted for and was presumed to be used for bribes. These activities seemed to be the result of his opposition to what he calls the Bingham amendment. In Bullock's opinion, it "seeks to deny to the Republican party in Georgia the fruits of the political victory that they have achieved after the terrible trials of the past two years," and would "promote the interests and the wishes of the very men and the very party who have persistently, and by every conceivable means and meanness, sought to defeat those [Reconstruction] acts."

Bullock blames the abandonment of loyal Republicans in Georgia on those congressional Republicans who did not support the progress made during Reconstruction. "There is no 'amnesty' with rebels for men in Georgia who have dared to be Republicans and to sustain measures which enfranchised the black man." Whether Bullock was a corrupt and self-serving politician is still debated, but his prediction of the end of Georgia Republican power was correct. Within a year of statehood, Georgia's political offices were held overwhelmingly by Democrats.

Essential Themes

Bullock's letter primarily addressed the charges of fraud and corruption leveled against him, but it also illustrates the complex issues facing the readmission of former Confederate states to the Union. Bullock responded to the accusations by accusing, in turn, certain Republican members of Congress of abandoning their colleagues who had worked to implement the Reconstruction Acts to protect the citizenship rights of black men. At worst, Bullock accused fellow Republicans of working secretly with the Democrats to undo Reconstruction reforms. Bullock was repeatedly threatened with violence while in office, and he saw the accusations of corruption as one more way to intimidate and silence him.

—*Bethany Groff, MA*

Bibliography and Additional Reading

Duncan, Russell. *Entrepreneur for Equality: Governor Rufus Bullock, Commerce, and Race in Post–Civil War Georgia*. Athens: U of Georgia P, 1994. Print.

Duncan, Russell. "Rufus Bullock (1834–1907)." *New Georgia Encyclopedia*. Georgia Humanities Council and the U of Georgia P, 2004. Web. 28 Dec. 2013.

Foner, Eric. *Reconstruction: America's Unfinished Revolution, 1863–1877*. New York: HarperCollins, 2011. Print.

"Georgia Governor Rufus Brown Bullock." *National Governors Association*. National Governors Association. n.d. Web. 28 Dec. 2013.

■ "A Plea for General Amnesty"

Date: January 30, 1872
Author: Carl Schurz
Genre: speech

Summary Overview

By 1872, all states in the former Confederacy had been readmitted to the Union, and the tide of public opinion was turning away from the strict measures imposed on Southern states after the Civil War. The right of African Americans to citizenship and of black men to vote had been secured, at least on paper, by the Fourteenth and Fifteenth Amendments to the Constitution, but it was still necessary, in some cases, for federal troops to enforce these rights. There was widespread violence against Republican politicians, black and white, and despite significant suppression of the Ku Klux Klan, white-supremacist organizations continued to grow. While some believed that continued penalties were needed to force the South to protect the rights of black citizens, others believed that the practices of Northern Republicans had been counterproductive, creating an environment in which Southern citizens were angry and resentful; also, some felt that it had been a mistake to give black men the vote when there were so many white men who could not vote because of their association with the Confederacy. Carl Schurz, a Republican senator from Missouri, represented those who believed that the South should be governed by its educated, propertied class, despite their support of the Confederacy or their racial bias.

Defining Moment

After the Civil War, the United States was deeply divided over how best to readmit states that had left the Union. Andrew Johnson, who became president after Abraham Lincoln's assassination, took a conciliatory approach to the Southern states. His strategy brought him into sharp conflict with Republicans in Congress, who pursued a punitive approach and demanded that the states of the former Confederacy be made, by force

if necessary, to accept full citizenship rights for black men. The Reconstruction Acts provided that states should be readmitted to the Union with full representation only after they had proven their commitment to the rights of free black citizens, and that former Confederate leaders, with some exceptions, were not allowed to serve in political or military positions. These contingencies remained on the books when Schurz gave his speech in 1872.

Ulysses S. Grant became president in 1869 and worked with Congress to admit states to the Union only when they had implemented laws protecting the rights of black Southerners. He also successfully suppressed the Ku Klux Klan and was willing to employ federal troops to protect black voters. By 1872, however, Grant's presidency was marred by scandal and allegations of corruption, and congressional factions that believed former Confederates were the natural ruling class of the South and should be relieved of their disabilities were gaining ground.

Schurz delivered his speech in response to a bill that was brought to the floor of the Senate that would exclude any former Confederate from political or military office. Though this bill made the exception that this provision could be removed by the House of Representatives, many senators felt that it was time for a general amnesty, or lifting of all restrictions for former Confederates. Debate on the Senate floor was wide-ranging—from those who felt that anyone who had openly served the Confederacy should be barred from public office for life, to those, such as Schurz, who felt that it was time to lift all such restrictions.

Passed on May 22, 1872, the Amnesty Act allowed most former Confederates to vote and hold office. About five hundred leaders of the Confederacy were still barred from political and military life, but more than 150,000 white Southerners who had fought for the Confederacy were once again able to vote. Most Southern states then quickly undid many of the reforms made during Reconstruction.

Author Biography

Carl Schurz was born in Germany in 1829 and immigrated to the United States in 1852. He settled first in Wisconsin and later lived in Missouri and New York. In 1861, he was appointed ambassador to Spain and then served with distinction as a brigadier general during the Civil War. After the war, Schurz was the first German-born American to be elected to the US Senate. By all accounts, he was a moderate Republican. President Johnson sent Schurz to the South in 1866, and he returned with the opinion that Southern states should be readmitted with full rights. During Reconstruction, Schurz was opposed to the use of the military to enforce the voting rights of former slaves in the South, breaking with President Grant over these issues. Schurz served as secretary of the interior from 1877 to 1881; he then moved to New York to pursue a career in business management. He died in New York in 1906.

HISTORICAL DOCUMENT

In the course of this debate we have listened to some senators, as they conjured up before our eyes once more all the horrors of the Rebellion, the wickedness of its conception, how terrible its incidents were, and how harrowing its consequences. Sir, I admit it all; I will not combat the correctness of the picture; and yet if I differ from the gentlemen who drew it, it is because, had the conception of the Rebellion been still more wicked, had its incidents been still more terrible, its consequences still more harrowing, I could not permit myself to forget that in dealing with the question now before us we have to deal not alone with the past, but with the present and future interests of this republic.

What do we want to accomplish as good citizens and patriots? Do we mean only to inflict upon the late rebels pain, degradation, mortification, annoyance, for its own sake; to torture their feelings without any ulterior purpose? Certainly such a purpose could not by any possibility animate high-minded men. I presume, therefore, that those who still favor the continuance of some of the disabilities imposed by the Fourteenth Amendment do so because they have some higher object of public usefulness in view, an object of public usefulness sufficient to justify, in their minds at least, the denial of rights to others which we ourselves enjoy.

What can those objects of public usefulness be? Let me assume that, if we differ as to the means to be employed, we are agreed as to the supreme end and aim to be reached. That end and aim of our endeavors can be no other than to secure to all the States the blessings of good and free government and the highest degree of prosperity and well-being they can attain, and to revive in all citizens of this republic that love for the Union and its institutions, and that inspiring consciousness of a common nationality, which, after all, must bind all Americans together.

What are the best means for the attainment of that end? This, sir, as I conceive it, is the only legitimate question we have to decide. Certainly all will agree that this end is far from having been attained so far. Look at the Southern States as they stand before us to-day. Some are in a condition bordering upon anarchy, not only on account of the social disorders which are occuring there, or the inefficiency of their local governments in securing the enforcement of the laws; but you will fiind in many of them fearful corruption pervading the whle political organization; a combination of rascality and ignorance wielding official power; their finances deranged by profligate practises; their credit ruined; bankruptcy staring them in the face; their industries staggering under a fearful load of taxation; their property-holders and capitalists paralyzed by a feeling of insecurity and distrust almost amounting to despair. Sir, let us not try to disguise these facts, for the world knows them to be so, and knows it but too well.

What are the causes that have contributed to bring about this distressing condition? I admit that great civil wars, resulting in such vast social transformations as the sudden abolition of slavery, are calculated to produce similar results; but it might be presumed that a recuperative power such as this country possesses might, during the time which has elapsed since the close of the war, at least have very materially alleviated many of the consequences of that revulsion, had a wise policy been followed.

Was the policy we followed wise? Was it calculated to promote the great purposes we are endeavoring to serve? Let us see. At the close of the war we had to establish and secure fre labor and the rights of the emancipated class. To that end we had to disarm those who could have prevented this, and we had to give the power of self-protection to those who needed it. For this reason temporary restrictions were imposed upon the late rebels, and we gave the right of suffrage to the colored people. Until the latter were enabled to protect themselves, political disabilities even more extensive than those which now exist rested upon the plea of eminent political necessit. I would be the last man to conceal that I thought so then, and I think there was a very good reason for it.

But, sir, when the enfranchisement of the colored people was secured; when they had obtained the political means to protect themselves, then another problem began to loom up. It was not only to find new guarantees for the rights of the colored people, but it was to secure good and honest government to all. Let us not underestimate the importance of that problem, for in a great measure it includes the solution of the other. Certainly nothing could have been more calculated to remove the prevailing discontent concerning the changes that had taken place, and to reconcile men's minds to the new order of things, than the tangible proof that that new order of things was practically working well; that it could produce a wise and economical administration of public affairs, and that it would promote general prosperity, thus healing the wounds of the past and opening to all the prospect of a future of material well-being and contentment.

And, on the other hand, nothing could have been more calculated to impede a general, hearty, and honest acceptance of the new order of things by the late rebel population than just those failures of public administration which involve the people in material embarrassments and so seriously disturb their comfort. In fact, good, honest, and successful government in the Southern States would in its moral effects, in the long run,

have exerted a far more beneficial influence than all your penal legislation, while your penal legislation will fail in its desired effects if we fail in establishing in the Southern States an honest and successful administration of the public business.

Now, what happened in the South? It is a well-known fact that the more intelligent classes of Southern society almost uniformly identified themselves with the Rebellion; and by our system of political disabilities just those classes were excluded from the management of political affairs. That they could not be trusted with the business of introducing into living practise the results of the war, to establish true free labor, and to protect the rights of the emancipated slaves, is true; I willingly admit it. But when those results and rights were constitutionally secured there were other things to be done. Just at that period when the Southern States lay prostrated and exhausted at our feet, when the destructive besom of war had swept over them and left nothing but desolation and ruin in its track, when their material interests were to be built up again with care and foresight—just then the public business demanded, more than ordinarily, the cooperation of all the intelligence and all the political experience that could be mustered in the Southern States. But just then a large portion of that intelligence and experience was excluded from the management of public affairs by political disabilities, and the controlling power in those States rested in a great measure in the hands of those who had but recently been slaves and just emerged from that condition, and in the hands of others who had sometimes honestly, sometimes by crooked means and for sinister purposes, found a way to their confidence.

But while the colored people of the South earned our admiration and gratitude, I ask you in all candor could they be reasonably expected, when, just after having emerged from a condition of slavery, they were invested with political rights and privileges, to step into the political arena as men armed with the intelligence and experience necessary for the management of public affairs and for the solution of problems made doubly intricate by the disasters which had desolated the Southern country? Could they reasonably be expected to manage the business of public administration, involving to so great an extent the financial interests and the material well-being of the people, and surrounded by difficulties of such fearful perplexity, with the wisdom and skill required by the exigencies of the situation?

That as a class they were ignorant and inexperienced and lacked a just conception of public interests, was certainly not their fault; for those who have studied the history of the world know but too well that slavery and oppression are very bad political schools. But the stubborn fact remains that they *were* ignorant and inexperienced; that the public business *was* an unknown world to them; and that in spite of the best intentions they *were* easily misled, not infrequently by the most reckless rascality which had found a way to their confidence. Thus their political rights and privileges were undoubtedly well calculated, and even necessary to protect their rights as free laborers and citizens; but, they were not well calculated to secure a successful administration of other public interests.

But what did we do? To the uneducated and inexperienced classes—uneducated and inexperienced, I repeat, entirely without their fault—we opened the road to power; and, at the same time, we condemned a large proportion of the intelligence of those States, of the property-holding, the industrial, the professional, the tax-paying interest, to a worse than passive attitude. We made it, as it were, easy for rascals who had gone South in quest of profitable adventure to gain the control of masses so easily misled, by permitting them to appear as the exponents and representatives of the national power and of our policy; and at the same time we branded a large number of men of intelligence, and many of them of personal integrity, whose material interests were so largely involved in honest government, and many of whom would have cooperated in managing the public business with care and foresight—we branded them, I say, as outcasts; telling them that they ought not to be suffered to exercise any influence upon the management of the public business, and it would be unwarrantable presumption in them to attempt it.

The introduction of the colored people, the late slaves, into the body-politic as voters, pointedly affronted the traditional prejudices prevailing among the Southern whites. What should we care about those prejudices? In war, nothing. After the close of the war, in the settlement of peace, not enough to deter us from doing what was right and necessary, and yet, still enough to take them

into account when considering the manner in which right and necessity were to be served. Statesmen will care about popular prejudices as physicians will care about the diseased condition of their patients, which they want to ameliorate. Would it not have been wise for us, looking at those prejudices as a morbid condition of the Southern mind, to mitigate, to assuage, to disarm them by prudent measures, and thus to weaken their evil influence?

We desired the Southern whites to accept in good faith universal suffrage, to recognize the political rights of the colored man, and to protect him in their exercise. Was not that our sincere desire? But if it was, would it not have been wise to remove as much as possible the obstacles that stood in the way of that consummation? But what did we do? When we raised the colored people to the rights of active citizenship and opened to them all the privileges of eligibility, we excluded from those privileges a large and influential class of whites; in other words, we lifted the late slave, uneducated and inexperienced as he was—I repeat, without his fault—not merely to the level of the late master class, but even above it. We asked certain white men to recognize the colored man in a political status not only as high but even higher than their own. We might say that under the circumstances we had a perfect right to do that, and I will not dispute it; but I ask you most earnestly, sir, was it wise to do it? If you desired the white man to accept and recognize the political equality of the black, was it wise to imbitter and exasperate his spirit with the stinging stigma of his own inferiority?

You tell me that the late rebels had deserved all this in the way of punishment. Granting that, I beg leave to suggest that this is not the question. The question is: What were the means best calculated to overcome the difficulties standing in the way of a willing and universal recognition of the new rights and privileges of the emancipated class? What were the means to overcome the hostile influences impending the development of the harmony of society in its new order? I am far from asserting that, had no disabilities existed, universal suffrage would have been received by the Southern whites with universal favor. No, sir, most probably it would not; but I do assert that the existence of disabilities, which put so large and influential a class of whites in point of political privileges below the colored people, could not fail to inflame those prejudices which stood in the way of a general and honest acceptance of the new order of things; they increased instead of diminishing the dangers and difficulties surrounding the emancipated class; and nobody felt that more keenly than the colored people of the South themselves. To their honor be it said, following a just instinct, they were among the very first, not only in the South but all over the country, in entreating Congress to remove those odious discriminations which put in jeopardy their own rights by making them greater than those of others. From the colored people themselves, it seems, we have in this respect received a lesson in statesmanship.

Well, then, what policy does common sense suggest to us now? If we sincerely desire to give to the Southern States good and honest government, material prosperity, and measurable contentment, as far at least as we can contribute to that end; if we really desire to weaken and disarm those prejudices and resentments which still disturb the harmony of society, will it not be wise, will it not be necessary, will it not be our duty to show that we are in no sense the allies and abettors of those who use their political power to plunder their fellow citizens, and that we do not mean to keep one class of people in unnecessary degradation by withholding from them rights and privileges which all others enjoy? Seeing the mischief which the system of disabilities is accomplishing, is it not time that there should be at least an end of it; or is there any good it can possibly do to make up for the harm it has already wrought and is still working?

Look at it. Do these disabilities serve in any way to protect anybody in his rights or in his liberty or in his property or in his life? Does the fact that some men are excluded from office, in any sense or measure, make others more secure in their lives or in their property or in their rights? Can anybody tell me how? Or do they, perhaps, prevent even those who are excluded from official position from doing mischief if they are mischievously inclined? Does the exclusion from office, does any feature of your system of political disabilities, take the revolver or the bowie-knife or the scourge from the hands of anyone who wishes to use it? Does it destroy the influence of the more intelligent upon society, if they mean to use that influence for mischievous purposes?

We accuse the Southern whites of having missed their chance of gaining the confidence of the emancipated class when, by a fairly demonstrated purpose of recognizing and protecting them in their rights, they might have acquired upon them a salutary influence. That accusation is by no means unjust; but must we not admit, also, that by excluding them from their political rights and privileges we put the damper of most serious discouragement upon the good intentions which might have grown up among them? Let us place ourselves in their situation, and then I ask you how many of us would, under the same circumstances have risen above the ordinary impulses of human nature to exert a salutary influence in defiance of our own prejudices, being so pointedly told every day that it was not the business of those laboring under political disabilities to meddle with public affairs at all? And thus, in whatever direction you may turn your eyes, you look in vain for any practical good your political disabilities might possibly accomplish. You find nothing, absolutely nothing, in their practical effects but the aggravation of evils already existing, and the prevention of a salutary development.

Is it not the part of wise men, sir, to acknowledge the failure of a policy like this in order to remedy it, especially since every candid mind must recognize that, by continuing the mistake, absolutely no practical good can be subserved?

You tell me that many of the late rebels do not deserve a full restoration of their rights. That may be so—I do not deny it; but yet, sir, if many of them do not deserve it, is it not a far more important consideration how much the welfare of the country will be promoted by it?

I am told that many of the late rebels, if we volunteer a pardon to them, would not appreciate it. I do not deny this—it may be so, for the race of fools, unfortunately, is not all dead yet; but if they do not appreciate it, shall we have no reason to appreciate the great good which by this measure of generosity will be conferred upon the whole land?

Look at the nations around us. In the Parliament of Germany how many men are there sitting who were once what you would call fugitives from justice, exiles on account of their revolutionary acts, now admitted to the great council of the nation in the fulness of their rights and privileges?—and mark you, without having been asked to abjure the opinions they formerly held, for at the present moment most of them still belong to the Liberal Opposition. Look at Austria, where Count Andrassy, a man who, in 1849, was condemned to the gallows as a rebel, at this moment stands at the head of the imperial ministry; and those who know the history of that country are fully aware that the policy of which that amnesty was a part, which opened to Count Andrassy the road to power, has attached Hungary more closely than ever to the Austrian Crown, from which a narrow-minded policy of severity would have driven her.

Now, sir, ought not we to profit by the wisdom of such examples? It may be said that other governments were far more rigorous in their first repressive measures, and that they put off the grant of a general amnesty much longer after suppressing an insurrection than we are required to do. So they did; but is not this the great republic of the New World which marches in the very vanguard of modern civilization, and which, when an example of wisdom is set by other nations, should not only rise to its level, but far above it?

It seems now to be generally admitted that the time has come for a more comprehensive removal of political disabilities than has so far been granted. If that sentiment be sincere, if you really do desire to accomplish the greatest possible good by this measure that can be done, I would ask you what practical advantage do you expect to derive from the exclusions for which this bill provides? Look at them, one after another.

First, all those are excluded who, when the Rebellion broke out, were members of Congress, and left their seats in these halls to join it. Why are these men to be excluded as a class? Because this class contains a number of prominent individuals, who, in the Rebellion, became practically conspicuous and obnoxious, and among them we find those whom we might designate as the original conspirators. But these are few, and they might have been mentioned by name. Most of those, however, who left their seats in Congress to make common cause with the rebels were in no way more responsible for the Rebellion than other prominent men in the South who do not fall under this exception. If we accept at all the argument that it will be well for the cause of good government and the material welfare of the South to readmit to the management of public affairs all the intelligence and political experience in those States, why, then, exclude as a class men who, having been mem-

bers of Congress, may be presumed to possess a higher degree of that intelligence and experience than the rest? If you want that article at all for good purposes, I ask you, do you not want as large a supply of that article as you can obtain?

Leaving aside the original conspirators, is there any reason in the world why those members of Congress should be singled out from the numerous class of intelligent and prominent men who were or had been in office and had taken the same oath which is administered in these halls? Look at it! You do not propose to continue the disqualification of men who served this country as foreign ministers, who left their important posts, betrayed the interests of this country in foreign lands to come back and join the Rebellion; you do not propose to exclude from the benefit of this act those who sat upon the bench and doffed the judicial ermine to take part in the Rebellion; and if such men are not to be disfranchised, why disfranchise the common run of the congressmen, whose guilt is certainly not greater, if it be as great? Can you tell me? Is it wise even to incur the suspicion of making an exception merely for the sake of excluding somebody, when no possible good can be accomplished by it, and when you can thus only increase the number of men incited to discontent and mischief by small and unnecessary degradations?

And now as to the original conspirators, what has become of them? Some of them are dead; and as to those who are still living, I ask you, sir, are they not dead also? Look at Jefferson Davis himself. What if you exclude even him—and certainly our feelings would naturally impel us to do so; but let our reason speak—what if you exclude even him? Would you not give him an importance which otherwise he never would possess, by making people believe that you are even occupying your minds enough with him to make him an exception to an act of generous wisdom? Truly to refrain from making an act of amnesty general on account of the original conspirators, candidly speaking, I would not consider worth while. I would not leave them the pitiable distinction of not being pardoned. Your very generosity will be to them the source of the bitterest disappointment. As long as they are excluded, they may still find some satisfaction in the delusion of being considered men of dangerous importance. Their very disabilities they look upon today as a recognition of their power. They may still make themselves and others believe that, were the Southern people only left free in their choice, they would eagerly raise them again to the highest honors.

So much for the first exception. Now to the second. It excludes from the benefit of this act all those who were officers of the army or of the navy and then joined the Rebellion. Why exclude that class of persons? I have heard the reason very frequently stated upon the floor of the Senate; it is because those men had been educated at the public expense, and their turning against the government was therefore an act of peculiar faithlessness and black ingratitude. That might appear a very argument at first sight. But I ask you was it not one of the very first acts of this administration to appoint one of the most prominent and conspicuous of that class to a very lucrative and respectable public office? I mean General Longstreet. He had obtained his military education at the expense of the American people. He was one of the wards, one of the pets of the American Republic, and then he turned against it as a rebel. Whatever of faithlessness, whatever of black ingratitude there is in such conduct, it was in his; and yet, in spite of all this, the president nominated him for an office, and your consent, senators, made him a public dignitary.

Why did you break the rule in his case? I will not say that you did it because he had become a Republican, for I am far from attributing any mere partizan motive to your action. No; you did it because his conduct after the close of hostilities had been that of a well-disposed and law-abiding citizen. Thus, then, the rule which you, senators, have established for your own conduct is simply this: you will, in the case of officers of the army or the navy, waive the charge of peculiar faithlessness and ingratitude if the persons in question after the war had become law-abiding and well-disposed citizens. Well, is it not a fact universally recognized, and I believe entirely uncontradicted, that of all classes of men connected with the Rebellion there is not one whose conduct since the close of the war has been so unexceptionable, and in a great many instances so beneficial in its influence upon Southern society, as the officers of the army and the navy, especially those who before the war had been members of our regular establishments? Why, then, except them from this act of amnesty? If you take subsequent good conduct into account at all, these men are the very last who as a class ought to be excluded. And would it not be well to encourage them in well-doing by a sign on your part that they are not to be looked upon as outcasts whose influence is not desired, even when they are inclined to use it for the promotion of the common welfare?

The third class excluded consists of those who were members of State conventions, and in those State conventions voted for ordinances of secession. If we may judge from the words which fell from the lips of the senator from Indiana, they were the objects of his particular displeasure. Why this? Here we have a large number of men of local standing who in some cases may have been leaders on a small scale, but most of whom were drawn into the whirl of the revolutionary movement just like the rest of the Southern population. If you accept the proposition that it will be well and wise to permit the intelligence of the country to participate in the management of the public business, the exclusion of just these people will appear especially inappropriate, because their local influence might be made peculiarly beneficial; and if you exclude these persons, whose number is considerable, you tell just that class of people whose cooperation might be made most valuable that their cooperation is not wanted, for the reason that, according to the meaning and intent of your system of disabilities, public affairs are no business of theirs.

You object that they are more guilty than the rest. Suppose they are—and in many cases I am sure they are only apparently so—but if they were not guilty of any wrong, they would need no amnesty. Amnesty is made for those who bear a certain degree of guilt. Or would you indulge here in the solemn farce of giving pardon only to those who are presumably innocent? You grant your amnesty that it may bear good fruit; and if you do it for that purpose, then do not diminish the good fruit it may bear by leaving unplanted the most promising soil upon which it may grow.

Let me tell you it is the experience of all civilized nations the world over, when an amnesty is to be granted at all, the completest amnesty is always the best. Any limitation you may impose, however plausible it may seem at first sight, will be calculated to take away much of the virtue of that which is granted. I entreat you, then, in the name of the accumulated experience of history, let there be an end of these bitter and useless and disturbing questions; let the books be finally closed, and when the subject is for ever dismissed from our discussions and our minds, we shall feel as much relieved as those who are relieved of their political disabilities.

Sir, I have to say a few words about an accusation which has been brought against those who speak in favor of universal amnesty. It is the accusation resorted to, in default of more solid argument, that those who advise amnesty, especially universal amnesty, do so because they have fallen in love with the rebels. No, sir, it is not merely for the rebels I plead. We are asked, Shall the Rebellion go entirely unpunished? No, sir, it shall not. Neither do I think that the Rebellion has gone entirely unpunished. I ask you, had the rebels nothing to lose but their lives and their offices? Look at it. There was a proud and arrogant aristocracy, planting their feet on the necks of the laboring people, and pretending to be the born rulers of this great Republic. They looked down, not only upon their slaves, but also upon the people of the North, with the haughty contempt of self-asserting superiority. When their pretensions to rule us all were first successfully disputed, they resolved to destroy this Republic, and to build up on the corner-stone of slavery an empire of their own in which they could hold absolute sway. They made the attempt with the most overweeningly confident expectation of certain victory.

Then came the Civil War, and after four years of struggle their whole power and pride lay shivered to atoms at our feet, their sons dead by tens of thousands on the battle-fields of this country, their fields and their homes devastated, their fortunes destroyed; and more than that, the whole social system in which they had their being, with all their hopes and pride, utterly wiped out; slavery for ever abolished, and the slaves themselves created a political power before which they had to bow their heads, and they, broken, ruined, helpless, and hopeless in the dust before those upon whom they had so haughtily looked down as their vassals and inferiors. Sir, can it be said that the Rebellion has gone entirely unpunished?

You may object that the loyal people, too, were subjected to terrible sufferings; that their sons, too, were slaughtered by tens of thousands; that the mourning of countless widows and orphans is still darkening our land; that we are groaning under terrible burdens which the

Rebellion has loaded upon us, and that therefore part of the punishment has fallen upon the innocent. And it is certainly true.

But look at the difference. We issued from this great conflict as conquerors; upon the graves of our slain we could lay the wreath of victory; our widows and orphans, while mourning the loss of their dearest, still remember with proud exultation that the blood of their husbands and fathers was not spilled in vain; that it flowed for the greatest and holiest and at the same time the most victorious of causes; and when our people labor in the sweat of their brow to pay the debt which the Rebellion has loaded upon us, they do it with the proud consciousness that the heavy price they have paid is infinitely overbalanced by the value of the results they have gained: slavery abolished; the great American Republic purified of her foulest stain; the American people no longer a people of masters and slaves, but a people of equal citizens; the most dangerous element of disturbance and disintegration wiped out from among us; this country put upon the course of harmonious development, greater, more beautiful, mightier than ever in its self-conscious power. And thus, whatever losses, whatever sacrifices, whatever sufferings we may have endured, they appear before us in a blaze of glory.

But how do the Southern people stand there? All *they* have sacrificed, all *they* have lost, all the blood *they* have spilled, all the desolation of *their* homes, all the distress that stares *them* in the face, all the wreck and ruin *they* see around them—all for nothing; all for a wicked folly; all for a disastrous infatuation; the very graves of their slain nothing but monuments of a shadowy delusion; all their former hopes vanished for ever; and the very magniloquence which some of their leaders are still indulging in, nothing but a mocking illustration of their utter discomfiture! Ah, sir, if ever human efforts broke down in irretrievable disaster, if ever human pride was humiliated to the dust, if ever human hopes were turned into despair, there you behold them.

You may say that they deserved it all. Yes, but surely, sir, you cannot say that the Rebellion has gone entirely unpunished. Nor will the senator from Indiana, with all his declamation (and I am sorry not now to see him before me), make any sane man believe that had no political disabilities ever been imposed, the history of the Rebellion, as long as the memory of men retains the recollection of the great story, will ever encourage a future generation to rebel again, or that if even this great example of disaster should fail to extinguish the spirit of rebellion, his little scarecrow of exclusion from office will be more than a thing to be laughed at by little boys.

Sir, such appeals as these, which we have heard so frequently, may be well apt to tickle the ear of an unthinking multitude. But unless I am grievously in error, the people of the United States are a multitude not unthinking. The American people are fast becoming aware that, great as the crime of rebellion is, there are other villainies beside it; that, much as it may deserve punishment, there are other evils flagrant enough to demand energetic correction; that the remedy for such evils does, after all, not consist in the maintenance of political disabilities, and that it would be well to look behind those vociferous demonstrations of exclusive and austere patriotism to see what abuses and faults of policy they are to cover, and what rotten sores they are to disguise. The American people are fast beginning to perceive that good and honest government in the South, as well as throughout the whole country, restoring a measurable degree of confidence and contentment, will do infinitely more to revive true loyalty and a healthy national spirit, than keeping alive the resentments of the past by a useless degradation of certain classes of persons; and that we shall fail to do our duty unless we use every means to contribute our share to that end. And those, I apprehend, expose themselves to grievous disappointment who still think that, by dinning again and again in the ears of the people the old battle-cries of the Civil War, they can befog the popular mind as to the true requirements of the times, and overawe and terrorize the public sentiment of the country.

But, sir, as the people of the North and of the South must live together as one people, and as they must be bound together by the bonds of a common national feeling, I ask you, will it not be well for us so to act that the history of our great civil conflict, which cannot be forgotten, can never be remembered by Southern men without finding in its closing chapter this irresistible assurance: that we, their conquerors, meant to be, and were after all, not their enemies, but their friends? When the Southern people con over the distressing catalog of the misfortunes they have brought upon themselves, will it

not be well, will it not be "devoutly to be wished" for our common future, if at the end of that catalog they find an act which will force every fair-minded man in the South to say of the Northern people, "When we were at war they inflicted upon us the severities of war; but when the contest had closed and they found us prostrate before them, grievously suffering, surrounded by the most perplexing difficulties and on the brink of new disasters, they promptly swept all the resentments of the past out of their way and stretched out their hands to us with the very fullest measure of generosity—anxious, eager to lift us up from our prostration?"

Sir, will not this do something to dispel those mists of error and prejudice which are still clouding the Southern mind? I ask again, will it not be well to add to the sad memories of the past which for ever will live in their minds, this cheering experience, so apt to prepare them for the harmony of a better and common future?

No, sir, I would not have the past forgotten, but I would have its history completed and crowned by an act most worthy of a great, noble, and wise people. By all the means which we have in our hands, I would make even those who have sinned against this republic see in its flag, not the symbol of their lasting degradation, but of rights equal to all; I would make them feel in their hearts that in its good and evil fortunes their rights and interest are bound up just as ours are, and that therefore its peace, its welfare, its honor, and its greatness may and ought to be as dear to them as they are to us.

I do not, indeed, indulge in the delusion that this act alone will remedy all the evils which we now deplore. No, it will not; but it will be a powerful appeal to the very best instincts and impulses of human nature; it will, like a warm ray of sunshine in springtime, quicken and call to light the germs of good intention wherever they exist; it will give new courage, confidence, and inspiration to the well-disposed; it will weaken the power of the mischievous, by stripping off their pretexts and exposing in their nakedness the wicked designs they still may cherish; it will light anew the beneficent glow of fraternal feeling and of national spirit; for, sir, your good sense as well as your heart must tell you that, when this is truly a people of citizens equal in their political rights, it will then be easier to make it also a people of brothers.

GLOSSARY

ameliorate: lessen or eliminate

disabilities: in this context, disqualifications or encumbrances

partizan: or partisan: motivated by party politics; divisive

Document Analysis

Carl Schurz made the speech for general amnesty on the floor of the Senate in response to a bill that would continue limiting the political power and voting rights of former supporters of the Confederacy. Though Schurz had been an abolitionist and a friend and a supporter of President Lincoln, he felt that the government had gone too far in allowing black Southerners, whom he assumed to be unprepared or unfit for full participation in political life, to vote and to hold office while so many educated, propertied white Southerners were unable to do so. This inequality, he felt, had contributed to the breakdown of order in the South, and to widespread corruption.

Schurz argued that the use of force to secure the rights of freed slaves had been necessary at the end of the war—"we had to establish and secure free labor and the rights of the emancipated class"—but, once that had been done, and black Southerners had the vote (secured through the Fifteenth Amendment), Schurz argued that it was counterproductive to continue to restrict the rights of other Southerners. According to Schurz, once the Constitution had been amended, and freedmen's rights ostensibly protected, the states should have begun setting up the best governments possible, using the best-educated citizens with the most invested in their states; such people, in Schurz's opinion, were likely to be former Confederates. By barring the best minds of the South from political office, the government had set up corrupt and ignorant political systems that were guaranteed to promote resentment and racial disharmony.

Though, he says, "the colored people of the South earned our admiration and gratitude," Schurz argues that they were not suited to play a major role in political life, especially given the ruined state of the South after the war. Schurz did not believe that African Americans were ready to enter "the political arena as men armed with the intelligence and experience necessary for the management of public affairs," and that promoting them to such a level had brought disaster. The lack of experience and education was not the fault of African Americans, he argues, but as "a class they were ignorant and inexperienced," and therefore easily misled by opportunistic outsiders who did not have the best interests of the South in mind. At the same time, those Southerners with education and political and business experience, as well as the most to gain by wise government, were shut out of the process because of their former association with the Confederacy.

Schurz did not deny that strong racial prejudices existed in the South. He believed that barring white Southerners from government while black Southerners were given a political voice had made these prejudices worse and that the continued disabilities leveled against Southern whites had led to an unnatural imbalance of power between ignorant, easily misguided former slaves and their educated, experienced former masters. This could not help but make a bad situation worse, in his opinion. He thought Southerners would have more quickly accepted black political participation if they had been fully part of the process.

Essential Themes

Schurz's Senate speech emphasized beliefs that were shared by many politicians and citizens in the 1870s: Black Southerners, while not deserving of enslavement, were not worthy of full political participation either, and the South was best ruled by white Southern landowners. Many felt that removing former Confederates from political life had given black men, and their corrupt allies, an unnatural superiority over white people, and this had enflamed existing racial prejudice and violence. Schurz and others called for a general amnesty to allow former Confederates full military and political participation. Whether Schurz intended it or not, the result of this amnesty, which later that year became reality, was the removal of many of the rights and protections given to black Southerners during Reconstruction.

—*Bethany Groff, MA*

Bibliography and Additional Reading

"Carl Schurz, German American." *Watertown History.* Watertown Historical Society. 2013. Web. 28 Dec. 2013.

Foner, Eric. *Reconstruction: America's Unfinished Revolution, 1863–1877.* New York: HarperCollins, 2011. Print.

Schurz, Carl. *The Reminiscences of Carl Schurz.* 3 vols. New York: McClure, 1907–1908. Print.

_____. *Report on the Condition of the South.* New York: Arno, 1969 Print.

Trefousse, Hans Louis. *Carl Schurz: A Biography.* New York: Fordham UP, 1998. Print.

■ "Half Free, Half Slave"

Date: February 4, 1875
Author: James Rapier
Genre: speech

Summary Overview

Representative James Rapier, an Alabama Republican, was one of three African Americans who held congressional office during Reconstruction. Strong Republican support for African American rights and political involvement during this period meant that a number of black leaders were able to turn temporary Republican majorities in Southern states into political success. While in office, these black leaders encouraged the enshrinement of black civil rights into law, and a speech Rapier gave in 1875 is a prime example of such efforts. He delivered this speech, his most famous, to support what would become the Civil Rights Act of 1875, the second civil rights bill in American history, and the last until the mid-twentieth century. Rapier's speech is remarkable not only for his passion, but also because it revealed the intersection of black political involvement with black military service in the Civil War, Social Darwinism, nineteenth-century American gender norms, US international relationships, and the rise of socialist and communist movements in Europe.

Defining Moment

Rapier gave his speech in support of one of the most important pieces of legislation in the Reconstruction era, Republican Charles Sumner's Civil Rights Act, first introduced in 1870. The bill explicitly forbade racial discrimination in public transportation, such as trains, and in other public places, such as restaurants, schools, and cemeteries. In addition to his arguments that black civil rights should be granted on moral, religious, and practical grounds, Rapier tackled two emerging issues of the late nineteenth century that challenged black attainment of civil rights. Thus, his speech revealed the deep connections between black civil rights and other significant global developments during the 1800s.

By the 1870s, Charles Darwin's ideas concerning evolution and natural selection had inspired theorists such as Herbert Spencer and William Graham Sumner to develop the racist tenets of Social Darwinism, which posited that the "survival of the fittest" principle that governed the natural world also applied to human society; thus, the fact that white Europeans had colonized and enslaved Africans and other peoples implied that whites were the "fittest" humans, with greater capacities for intelligence, government, and industry than other races. Many white leaders in both the United States and European nations used these ideas to justify white rule and expansion around the world from the mid-nineteenth century to the mid-twentieth century. Rapier condemned such beliefs "that the Negro is not a man and is not entitled to all the public rights common to other men." He also famously asserted, "Either I am a man or I am not a man." Of course, Rapier believed he was a man, and thus, he—and all African Americans—should have guaranteed civil rights.

The second issue that Rapier exposed was the faulty equation of socialist or communist movements with black civil rights, a comparison that many segregationists would employ much more widely throughout the twentieth century. Even in the mid-1870s, however, Friedrich Engels and Karl Marx's 1848 *The Communist Manifesto* was over twenty-five years old and the Paris Commune had just occurred. While Rapier did not use the terms "socialist" or "communist" openly, he argued that African Americans were not trying to "break down all Social barriers" and that the bill "does not and cannot contemplate any such ideas as social equality." By this, Rapier meant that, while African Americans wanted their political and civil rights enshrined in law, they were arguing for equality of opportunity only, not the sort of equality of outcome that communism envisions.

Author Biography

Rapier was born in 1837 in Alabama to a father who was a former slave and had become a successful barber. Rapier worked variously as a teacher and farmer until joining the Republican Party during Reconstruction and becoming active in various local, state, national, and international endeavors. Rising through the ranks, he won election to Congress in 1872 and worked in Washington, DC, from 1873 to 1875. He ran for a second term, but a Republican rival caused the Republican vote to split and a Democratic win to result. In addition, with Northern support ebbing near the end of Reconstruction, which officially ended in 1877, he was part of a wave of African American politicians who began losing their positions in the mid-1870s and onward. He remained involved in local politics and issues affecting the black population in the South, such as immigration to Kansas, until his death from tuberculosis in 1883.

HISTORICAL DOCUMENT

MR. SPEAKER, I had hoped there would be no protracted discussion on the civil rights bill. It has been debated all over the country for the last seven years; twice it has done duty in our national political campaigns; and in every minor election during that time it has been pressed into service for the purpose of intimidating the weak white men who are inclined to support the Republican ticket. I was certain until now that most persons were acquainted with its provisions, that they understood its meaning; therefore it was no loner to them the monster it had been depicted, that was to break down all social barriers, and compel one man to recognize another socially, whether agreeable to him or not.

I must confess it is somewhat embarrassing for a colored man to urge the passage of this bill, because if he exhibits an earnestness in the matter and expresses a desire for its immediate passage, straightway he is charged with a desire for social equality, as explained by the demagogue and understood by the ignorant white man. But then it is just as embarrassing for him not to do so, for, if he remains silent while the struggle is being carried on around, and for him, he is liable to be charged with a want of interest in a matter that concerns him more than anyone else, which is enough to make his friends desert his cause. So in steering away from Scylla I may run upon Charybdis. But the anomalous and, I may add, the supremely ridiculous position of the Negro at this time, in this country, compels me to say something. Here his condition is without comparison, parallel alone to itself Just that the law recognizes my right upon this floor as a lawmaker, but that there is no law to secure to me any accommodations whatever while traveling here to discharge my duties as a Representative of a large and wealthy constituency. Here I am the peer of the proudest, but on a steamboat or car I am not equal to the most degraded. Is not this most anomalous and ridiculous?

I wish to say in justice to myself that no one regrets more than I do the necessity that compels one to the manor born to come in these halls with hat in hand (so to speak) to ask at the hands of his political peers the same public rights they enjoy. And I shall feel ashamed for my country if there be any foreigners present who have been lured to our shores by the popular but untruthful declaration that this land is the asylum of the oppressed, to hear a member of the highest legislative body in the world declare from his place, upon his responsibility as a Representative, that, notwithstanding his political position, he has no civil rights that another class is bound to respect.

Here a foreigner can learn what he cannot learn in any other country, that it is possible for a man to be half free and half slave, or, in other words, he will see that it is possible for a man to enjoy political rights while he is denied civil ones; here he will see a man legislating for a free people, while his own chains of slavery hang about him and are far more galling than any the foreigner left behind him; here he will see and what is not to be seen elsewhere, that position is no mantle of protection in our "land of the free and home of the brave"; for I am subjected to far more outrages and indignities in coming to and going from this capital in discharge of my public duties than any criminal in the country provided he be white. Instead of my position shielding me for insult, it too often invites it.

I affirm, without the fear of contradiction, that any white ex-convict (I care not what may have been his crime, nor whether the hair on the shaven side of his head has had time to grow out or not) may start with me today to Montgomery, that all the way down he will be treated as a gentleman, while I will be treated as the convict. He will be allowed a berth in a sleeping car with all its comforts, while I will be forced into a dirty, rough box with the drunkards, apple sellers, railroad hands, and next to any dead that be in transit, regardless of how far decomposition may have progressed. Sentinels are placed at the doors of the better coaches, with positive instructions to keep persons of color out; and I must do them the justice to say that they guard these sacred portals with a vigilance that would have done credit to the flaming swords at the gates of Eden. Tender, pure, intelligent young ladies are forced to travel in this way if they are guilty of the crime of color, the only unpardonable sin known in our Christian and Bible lands, where sinning against the Holy Ghost (whatever that may be) sinks into significance when compared with the sin of color. If from any cause we are compelled to lay over, the best bed in the hotel is his if he can pay for it, while I am invariably turned away, hungry and cold, to stand around the railroad station until the departure of the next train, it matters not how long, thereby endangering my health, while my life and property are at the mercy of any highwayman who may wish to murder and rob me.

And I state without the fear of being gainsaid, the statement of the gentleman from Tennessee to the contrary notwithstanding, that there is not an inn between Washington and Montgomery, a distance of more than a thousand miles that will accommodate me to bed or meal. Now, then, is there a man upon this floor who is so heartless, whose breast is so void of the better feelings, as to say that this brutal custom needs no regulation? I hold that it does and that Congress is the body to regulate it. Authority for its action is found not only in the Fourteenth Amendment to the Constitution, but by virtue of that amendment (which makes all persons born here citizens) authority is found in Article 4, Section 2, of the federal Constitution, which declares in positive language that "the citizens of each state shall have the same

rights as the citizens of the several states." Let me read Mr. Brightly's comment upon this clause; he is considered good authority, I believe. In describing the several rights he says they may all be comprehended under the following general heads: "Protection by the government; the enjoyment of life and liberty, with the right to acquire and possess property of every kind, and to pursue and obtain happiness and safety; the right of a citizen of one state to pass through or to reside in any other state for purposes of trade, agriculture, professional pursuits, or otherwise."

Sir, I submit that I am degraded as long as I am denied the public privileges common to other men, and that the members of this House are correspondingly degraded by recognizing my political equality while I occupy such humiliating position. What a singular attitude for lawmakers of this great nation to assume, rather come down to me than allow me to go up to them. Sir, did you ever reflect that this is the only Christian country where poor, finite man IS held responsible for the crimes of the infinite God whom you profess to worship? But it is; I am held to answer for the crime of color, when I was not consulted in the matter. Had I been consulted, and my future fully described, I think I should have objected to being born in this Gospel land. The excuse offered for all this inhuman treatment is that they consider the Negro inferior to the white man, intellectually and morally. This reason might have been offered and probably accepted as truth some years ago, but not one now believes him incapable of a high order of culture, except someone who is himself below the average of mankind in natural endowments.

Mr. Speaker, time will not allow me to review the history of the American Negro, but I must pause here long enough to say that he has not been properly treated by this nation; he has purchased and paid for all, and for more than, he has yet received. Whatever liberty he enjoys has been paid for over and over again by more than two hundred years of forced toil; and for such citizenship as is allowed him he paid the full measure of his blood, the dearest price required at the hands of any citizen. In every contest, from the beginning of the Revolutionary struggle down to the War Between the States, has he been prominent. But we all remember in our late war when the government was so hard pressed for troops to sustain the cause of the Union, when it was so difficult to fill up the ranks that had been so fearfully decimated by disease and the bullet; when every train that carried to the front a number of fresh soldiers brought back a corresponding number of wounded and sick ones; when grave doubts as to the success of the Union arms had seized upon the minds of some of the most sanguine friends of the government; when strong men took counsel of their fears; when those who had all their lives received the fostering care of the nation were hesitating as to their duty in that trying hour, and others questioning if it were not better to allow the star of this Republic to go down and thus be blotted out from the great map of nations than to continue the bloodshed; when gloom and despair were widespread; when the last ray of hope had nearly sunk below our political horizon, how the Negro then came forward and offered himself as a sacrifice in the place of the nation, made bare his breast to the steel, and in it received the thrusts of the bayonet that were aimed at the life of the nation by the soldiers of that government in which the gentleman from Georgia figured as second officer.

Sir, the valor of the colored soldier was tested on many a battlefield, and today his bones lie bleaching beside every hill and in every valley from the Potomac to the Gulf; whose mute eloquence in behalf of equal rights for all before the law, is and ought to be far more persuasive than any poor language I can command.

...Either I am a man or I am not a man. if one, I am entitled to all the rights, privileges and immunities common to any other class in this country; if not a man, I have no right to vote, no right to a seat here; if no right to vote, then 20 percent of the members on this floor have no right here, but, on the contrary, hold their seats in violation of the law. If the Negro has no right to vote, then one eighth of your Senate consists of members who have no shadow of a claim to the places they occupy; and if no right to vote, a half-dozen governors in the South figure as usurpers.

This is the legitimate conclusion of the argument, that the Negro is not a man and is not entitled to all the public rights common to other men, and you cannot escape it. But when I press my claims I am asked, "Is it good policy?" My answer is, "Policy is out of the question; it has nothing to do with it; that you can have no policy in dealing with your citizens; that there must be one law for all; that in this case justice is the only standard to be used, and you can no more divide justice than you can divide Deity." On the other hand, I am told that I must respect the prejudices of others. Now, sir, no one respects reasonable and intelligent prejudice more than I. I respect religious prejudices, for example, these I can comprehend. But how can I have respect for the prejudices that prompt a man to turn up his nose at the males of a certain race, while at the same time he has a fondness for the females of the same race to the extent of cohabitation? Out of four poor unfortunate colored women, who from poverty were forced to go to the lying-in branch of the Freedman's Hospital here in the District last year, three gave birth to children whose fathers were white men, and I venture to say that if they were members of this body, would vote against the civil-rights bill. Do you, can you wonder at my want of respect for this kind of prejudice? To make me feel uncomfortable appears to be the highest ambition of many white men. It is to them a positive luxury, which they seek to indulge at every opportunity.

Mr. Speaker, I trust this bill will become law, because it is a necessity, and because it will put an end to all legislation on this subject. It does not and cannot contemplate any such ideas as social equality; nor is there any man upon this floor so silly as to believe that there can be any law enacted or enforced that would compel one man to recognize another as his equal socially; if there be, he ought not to be here, and I have only to say that they have sent him to the wrong public building. I would oppose such a bill as earnestly as the gentleman from North Carolina, whose associations and cultivations have been of such a nature as to lead him to select the crow as his standard of grandeur and excellence in the place of the eagle, the hero of all birds and our national emblem of pride and power. I will tell him that I have seen many of his race to whose level I should object to being dragged.

Sir, it matters not how much men may differ upon the question of state and national rights; here is one class of rights, however, that we all agree upon, namely, individual rights, which include the right of every man to select associates for himself and family, and to say who shall and who shall not visit at his house. This right is God-given and custom-sanctioned, and there is, and there can be, no power overruling your decision in this matter. Let this bill become law, and not only will it do much toward giving rest to this weary country on this subject, completing the manhood of my race and perfecting his citizenship, but it will take him from the political arena as a topic of discussion where he has done duty for the last fifty years, and thus freed from anxiety respecting his political standing, hundreds of us will abandon the political fields who are there from necessity, and not from choice, and seek other and more pleasant ones; and thus relieved, it will be the aim of the colored man as well as his duty and interest, to become a good citizen, and to do all in his power to advance the interests of a common country.

GLOSSARY

demagogue: a political agitator; a leader who plays on prejudice and emotion

Scylla and Charybdis: from Greek mythology, a pair of monsters

Document Analysis

Rapier employs several different types of arguments to support Sumner's 1875 civil rights bill. Throughout the speech, Rapier notes a disconnect between the espousals of democracy and freedom by white Americans and the actual condition of African Americans. He argues that having political rights means nothing if they are not accompanied by civil rights. In addition, the diverse types of arguments he employs on behalf of the bill are what make his speech so interesting, because he also uses nineteenth-century gender roles, international affairs, and black military service to support black civil rights.

In the 1870s, women were generally seen as holding more and stronger virtues than men, and Rapier attempts to appeal to this ideal by claiming that, simply because they were black, "tender, pure, intelligent young ladies are forced to travel" with "drunkards" and corpses. He is suggesting that to protect all female virtue, Congress must pass the bill. Rapier also uses gender in a more graphic, although certainly historically accurate, way when he later notes that a number of white men had fathered children with black women; thus, he wonders why black men are so ridiculed "while at the same time [the white man] has a fondness for the females of the same race to the extent of cohabitation." Rapier is highlighting the hypocrisy that white men considered their sexual relationships with black women to be acceptable but did not think black men should have civil rights.

Rapier also attempts to use the United States' international image in support of the bill. While the immense wave of eastern and southern European immigration would not begin until the 1880s, the United States had certainly experienced previous waves of immigrant settlement, most notably in the 1840s, when large numbers of Irish and Germans arrived in the United States, and many whites considered the United States a bastion of freedom and refuge amid a world still populated by kings and despots. By noting "the popular but untruthful declaration that this land is the asylum of the oppressed," Rapier hints that the lack of black civil rights undermines the image of a nation of democracy and freedom that many white American leaders wanted to project internationally.

Thirdly, Rapier invokes African American military service during the Civil War as a key reason to grant black civil rights. He points out that black servicemen began to join the Union Army at exactly the time when immense Union losses, especially in the spring and summer of 1864, could have undermined the war effort. Exposing the fact that many of his fellow representatives had fought for or served a government in rebellion to the United States, he states that the black soldier "made bare his breast to the steel, and in it received the thrusts of the bayonet that were aimed at the life of the nation by the soldiers of that government in which the gentleman from Georgia figured as second officer." As African Americans would also do after World War I and World War II, Rapier uses black military service as an example of African Americans' patriotism and a reason that they deserved their full civil rights.

Essential Themes

Rapier's presence in Congress in the 1870s and the passage of the 1875 Civil Rights Act that he supported are relevant to the way historians have argued about this period ever since. For decades, members of a group of historians known as the Dunning School presented racist images of African Americans and argued that Reconstruction was oppressive and unfair to white Southerners. Some black writers, including W. E. B. Du Bois, tried to combat these claims, but it was not until the 1950s and 1960s that these dominant interpretations were consistently challenged. Then, in 1988, historian Eric Foner's impressive *Reconstruction: America's Unfinished Revolution, 1863–1877* appeared. Rather than a period of Northern aggression against the South or even the comparably better image of a period that tried hard to achieve changes in the South and failed, Foner argued that Reconstruction was "a massive experiment in interracial democracy without precedent in the history of this or any other country that abolished slavery in the nineteenth century." In addition, rather than viewing African Americans as upstarts, like the Dunning School, or as victims, as other historians tended to do, Foner claimed, "Blacks were active agents in the making of Reconstruction. . . . Their quest for individual and community autonomy did much to establish Reconstruction's political and economic agenda." Thus Rapier, the other African American members of Congress, and the hundreds of black state and local officeholders in the South in the 1860s and 1870s clearly illustrated Foner's point that Reconstruction was a tremendous period of opportunity for African Americans. Likewise, Rapier's speech in support of Sumner's bill revealed that African Americans were actively engaged in advancing their collective position in the South and across the entire nation.

—*Kevin Grimm, PhD*

Bibliography and Additional Reading

"Black Legislators: Primary Sources." American Experience: Reconstruction, The Second Civil War. PBS Online/WGBH, 12 Dec. 2003. Web. 19 Jan. 2014.

Foner, Eric. Reconstruction: America's Unfinished Revolution, 1863–1877. New York: Harper & Row, 1988. Print.

Lynch, Matthew, ed. Legacies Lost. Santa Barbara: Praeger, 2012. Print.

■ Civil Rights Act of 1875

Date: March 1, 1875
Author: Charles Sumner
Genre: law

Summary Overview

The Civil Rights Act of 1875 was the last, and arguably the most progressive, major piece of civil rights legislation in the Reconstruction era. It was drafted in 1870 by Charles Sumner, a Republican senator from Massachusetts. Sumner, who had been an outspoken abolitionist since before the Civil War, was considered by many to represent the most radical element of the Republican Party of his day.

The bill that Sumner initially proposed forbade racial discrimination in all forms of public accommodation licensed by state or federal governments, including transportation, hotels, theaters, schools, and cemeteries. It also criminalized the exclusion of African American citizens from jury duty. After intense debates and delays because of the 1874 elections, a modified version of the bill was signed into law by second-term president Ulysses S. Grant on March 1, 1875. The Civil Rights Act of 1875 was poorly enforced, challenged by state and local governments, and ultimately ruled unconstitutional by the Supreme Court in 1883.

Defining Moment

When the American Civil War officially ended on May 10, 1865, the United States was in chaos. More than six hundred thousand Americans had died in what remains the most destructive military conflict in US history. President Abraham Lincoln had just been assassinated by a pro-Southern activist, and the freshly defeated South was in a state of political turmoil.

Many politicians wanted to reinstate the Southern states' rights to govern themselves. Others argued that these states had given up their right to exist when they seceded from the Union and should be treated as conquered territories. This ideological debate was between Democrats, who championed a rapid return to the pre-war order, and Republicans, who insisted that the rebellious states should not immediately be given back their prewar political rights.

Lincoln, a Republican, and his successors, Democrat Andrew Johnson and then Republican Grant, made the process of reintegrating the nation, which was dubbed Reconstruction, a top priority of their presidencies. All three leaders emphasized the need for a moderate approach to allowing the states of the former Confederacy back into the Union. This moderate position angered politicians on the two extremes of the debate.

The controversy about how Reconstruction should take place was made more complicated by the issue of how to deal with the collapse of the largest slave system in the world. The Thirteenth Amendment, ratified on December 6, 1865, officially ended slavery in the United States. In so doing, it created approximately four million new citizens. These new African American citizens were concentrated in the South of the country, in the states of the former Confederacy, where they were viewed with suspicion and fear by the majority white population.

In every Southern state, local governments suppressed the rights bestowed on African Americans by the Thirteenth Amendment. Local ordinances restricting the freedom of African Americans, the so-called Black Codes, sprang up all throughout the former Confederacy. Pro-Confederate paramilitary groups, such as the newly formed Ku Klux Klan, used terrorist tactics against African Americans who tried to assert their rights, as well as white citizens who supported the Republican Party.

In the decade after the Civil War, the federal government took a series of steps aimed at protecting the rights of free African Americans. Congress overcame a veto by President Johnson to pass the Civil Rights

Act of 1866, which made all persons within the territory of the United States American citizens unless they were subjects of other nations or members of American Indian tribes. The Fourteenth Amendment, ratified in 1868, reinforced the legal status of freed slaves as American citizens and affirmed their right to vote in elections. The Fifteenth Amendment, ratified in early 1870, further enforced the right of all adult male citizens to vote, regardless of race or previous condition of servitude. The Civil Rights Act of 1875 was a bold further step in asserting the equal rights of African Americans, attempting to undo the system of enforced racial segregation that had developed in the postwar South.

Author Biography

Charles Sumner was born to a modestly middle-class Boston family on January 6, 1811. He graduated from Harvard Law School in 1833 and began practicing law in Boston. Sumner spent 1837 to 1840 in Europe, studying different legal systems. When he returned to Boston, he was a committed abolitionist.

After working as a lawyer and lecturer on law in Boston, Sumner entered political life. He was a founding member of the Free Soil Party, which was briefly an important antislavery force in Northern politics. He was elected to the Senate as a Free Soiler in 1851 and later joined the newly formed Republican Party.

On May 19, 1856, Sumner delivered a speech called the "Crime against Kansas," in which he railed against proslavery activism in the state and personally insulted Senator Andrew Butler of South Carolina. On May 22, Butler's cousin, Representative Preston Brooks of South Carolina, assaulted Sumner with a cane in Senate chambers, beating him into unconsciousness.

Brooks claimed to be acting to defend his family's honor. He became a hero among proslavery Southerners. On the other side, sympathy for Sumner, who spent three years recovering from spinal and brain injuries, rallied many moderate Northerners to the abolitionist cause.

Until his death from a heart attack on March 11, 1874, Sumner was outspoken about the need for civil rights reform in the United States. He is remembered for his work against slavery and as an advocate for Radical Reconstruction, the political philosophy that the defeated Confederate states should have to make major changes in order to rejoin the Union.

HISTORICAL DOCUMENT

18 Stat. Part III, p. 335 (Act of Mar. 1, 1875).

Chap. 114. — An act to protect all citizens in their civil and legal rights. Whereas, it is essential to just government we recognize the equality of all men before the law, and hold that it is the duty of government in its dealings with the people to mete out equal and exact justice to all, of whatever nativity, race, color, or persuasion, religious or political; and it being the appropriate object of legislation to enact great fundamental principles into law:

Therefore, Be it enacted by the Senate and House of Representatives of the United States of America in Congress assembled, That all persons within the jurisdiction of the United States shall be entitled to the full and equal and enjoyment of the accommodations, advantages, facilities, and privileges of inns, public conveyances on land or water, theaters, and other places of public amusement; subject only to the conditions and limitations established by law, and applicable alike to citizens of every race and color, regardless of any previous condition of servitude.

Sec. 2. That any person who shall violate the foregoing section by denying to any citizen, except for reasons by law applicable to citizens of every race and color, and regardless of any previous condition of servitude, the full enjoyment of any of the accommodations, advantages, facilities, or privileges in said section enumerated, or by aiding or eliciting such denial, shall, for every offence, forfeit and pay the sum of five hundred dollars to the person aggrieved thereby, to be recovered in an action of debt, with full costs; and shall also, for every such offense, be deemed guilty of a misdemeanor, and, upon conviction thereof, shall be fined not less than five hundred nor more than one thousand dollars, or shall be imprisoned not less than thirty days nor more than one year:

Provided, that all persons may elect to sue for the State under their rights at common law and by State statutes; and having so elected to proceed in the one mode or the other, their right to proceed in the other jurisdiction shall be barred. But this proviso shall not apply to criminal proceedings, either under this act or the criminal law of any State: And provided further, That a judgment for the penalty in favor of the party aggrieved, or a judgment upon an indictment, shall be a bar to either prosecution respectively.

Sec. 3. That the district and circuit courts of the United States shall have, exclusively of the courts of the several States, cognizance of all crimes and offenses against, and violations of, the provisions of this act; and actions for the penalty given by the preceding section may be prosecuted in the territorial, district, or circuit courts of the United States wherever the defendant may be found, without regard to the other party; and the district attorneys, marshals, and deputy marshals of the United States, and commissioners appointed by the circuit and territorial courts of the United States, with powers of arresting and imprisoning or bailing offenders against the laws of the United States, are hereby specially authorized and required to institute proceedings against every person who shall violate the provisions of this act, and cause him to be arrested and imprisoned or bailed, as the case may be, for trial before such court of the United States, or territorial court, as by law has cognizance of the offense, except in respect of the right of action accruing to the person aggrieved; and such district attorneys shall cause such proceedings to be prosecuted to their termination as in other cases: Provided, That nothing contained in this section shall be construed to deny or defeat any right of civil action accruing to any person, whether by reason of this act or otherwise; and any district attorney who shall willfully fail to institute and prosecute the proceedings herein required, shall, for every such offense, forfeit and pay the sum of five hundred dollars to the person aggrieved thereby, to be recovered by an action of debt, with full costs, and shall, on conviction thereof, be deemed guilty of a misdemeanor, and be fined not less than one thousand nor more than five thousand dollars:

And provided further, That a judgment for the penalty in favor of the party aggrieved against any such district attorney, or a judgment upon an indictment against any such district attorney, shall be a bar to either prosecution respectively.

Sec. 4. That no citizen possessing all other qualification which are or may be prescribed by law shall be disqualified for service as grand or petit juror in any court of the United States, or of any State, on account of race, color, or previous condition of servitude; and any officer or other person charged with any duty in the selection or summoning of jurors who shall exclude or fail to summon any citizen for the cause aforesaid shall, on conviction thereof, be deemed guilty of a misdemeanor, and be fined not more than five thousand dollars.

GLOSSARY

aggrieved: legally harmed

grand or petit jury: a jury appointed to determine if laws have been violated (grand jury) or to render a verdict at trial (petit jury)

Document Analysis

The Civil Rights Act of 1875 was arguably the most aggressive piece of civil rights legislation created during the Reconstruction era. It began by making assertions that would have immediately aroused anger and suspicion among many in the vanquished South. In its first paragraph, the legislation says that "it is essential to just government we recognize the equality of all men before the law," and that government exists to "mete out equal and exact justice to all, of whatever nativity, race, color, or persuasion, religious or political." Such an introduction was certain to generate controversy, and the Civil

Rights Act of 1875 was bitterly contested until it was ultimately struck down by the Supreme Court in 1883.

In its second paragraph, the legislation becomes more specific. It says that all people within the jurisdiction of US law should have "full and equal enjoyment" of various forms of accommodation. It then specifies that it seeks to expand access to inns, modes of transportation, and places of amusement to all citizens, regardless of race or former slave status. This was a direct affront to the Black Codes springing up throughout the South, which were chiefly concerned with enforcing racial segregation. Many Southerners of the day were shocked that the Civil Rights Act of 1875 stipulated that African Americans were to have the right to mix with whites in theaters and inns and on trains and ships.

The law was serious about curtailing unequal access to accommodations, establishing stiff financial penalties for violators. It states that those individuals discriminated against were to be compensated up to $500. Those who denied access to protected forms of accommodation were to be charged with a misdemeanor crime, fined $500 to $1,000, or face thirty days to one year in prison. As $500 in 1875 was roughly equivalent to more than $10,000 in the early twenty-first century, the financial penalties for violators of the Civil Rights Act of 1875 and the compensation due to victims of such discrimination were quite serious. The other major achievement of the law was the stipulation that all adult men should have the right to sit on juries, regardless of race or former servitude. The law imposes even steeper fines on violators of this provision, up to $5,000.

The Civil Rights Act of 1875 also contained instructions for how the law should be handled by the courts, stating that federal district and circuit courts should try violations of its provisions. This was to circumvent local or state courts, which the law's drafters considered unlikely to be fair venues for cases involving racial discrimination.

Essential Themes

Many historians consider the Civil Rights Act of 1875 to be the boldest piece of legislation passed during the Reconstruction period. This interpretation is based in the fact that the law sought to eliminate segregation in a variety of day-to-day settings, in direct conflict with the various Black Codes passed throughout the South in the years after the Civil War. Ultimately, however, the Civil Rights Act of 1875 proved to be too far-reaching for its time.

There were a handful of cases prosecuted under the law. These included a few cases of innkeepers refusing rooms to African Americans in New York and San Francisco and another, in which a woman was refused a seat on a train because of her race. However, the law's effects fell far short of guaranteeing the reforms its Radical Republican supporters envisioned. The protections it outlined proved difficult to enforce, largely because few African American victims of discrimination had the resources or opportunities to pursue their cases in the federal court system.

By the time the Civil Rights Act of 1875 passed, it had lost much of its support from government officials. Its firebrand author, Sumner, died the year before it became law. The drive for Radical Reconstruction had slowed considerably as the former Confederate states were commercially and socially reintegrated into the Union.

In a series of decisions in 1883, known collectively as the Civil Rights Cases, the Supreme Court struck down most of the points of the Civil Rights Act of 1875 that dealt with equal access to accommodation. Interestingly, the Supreme Court of 1883 was dominated by Republican-appointed judges and might, therefore, have been expected to back aggressive civil rights reform. However, many of these judges came to feel that the Civil Rights Act of 1875 went beyond the intended powers of the federal government in its attempt to stop discrimination by private rather than just governmental entities. Justice Joseph Bradley summed up his opposition by stating that the law was in fact unfair in giving extra protections to African Americans, and it risked making them "the special favorites of the law" rather than equal citizens.

—*Adam J. Berger, PhD*

Bibliography and Additional Reading

Cimbala, Paul and Randall Miller. *The Great Task Remaining before Us: Reconstruction as America's Continuing Civil War.* New York: Fordham UP, 2010. Print.

Ferrell, Claudine. *Reconstruction.* Westport, CT: Greenwood, 2003. Print.

Lowery, Charles and John Marszalek. *Encyclopedia of African-American Civil Rights.* New York: Greenwood, 1992. Print.

Pohlmann, Marcus and Linda Whisenhunt. *Student's Guide to Landmark Congressional Laws on Civil Rights.* Westport, CT: Greenwood, 2002. Print.

AN AMBIGUOUS LEGACY

Reconstruction was not an unalloyed success, although the degree to which it did succeed—or failed—is still debated today. We have seen that paramilitary groups interfered with the electoral process and with the daily lives of African Americans. These attacks occurred despite the military occupation of much of the South by federal forces and the existence of a system of military justice. Although racism and the legacy of slavery and the Civil War were very much at issue in these postwar conflicts, they were also a manifestation of continued hostility in the South toward a "robust" federal system as a whole and the concomitant trampling of states' rights. At least that is what animated some of the more ardent believers in the "lost cause" of the Confederacy and the traditional political culture it represented.

In this final section we look at a number of developments unfolding at the tail-end of the Reconstruction era. The section opens with an examination of the U.S. Supreme Court decision *United States v. Cruikshank.* The *Cruikshank* decision effectively put a break on federal actions in the area of state elections, affirming the rule of states in such matters. The decision made it clear that if an election is disrupted—by, for example, a white militia—the federal government has no right to step in and pursue criminal charges against individuals alleged to have disrupted it; that, rather, is a matter for the states to pursue (or not). We hear a counterview from a black Republican of Mississippi, Blanche Bruce, who argues that whites in his state were attempting to

"redeem" themselves and their cause on the backs of free blacks.

Also supporting the promise of Reconstruction and its achievements to date are Frederick Douglass and Ulysses S. Grant. Douglass provides his inspiring remarks, in which he reflects back on President Abraham Lincoln, in the form of an address given on the occasion of the dedication of the Freedmen's Monument in Washington, D.C. Grant provides his comments in the form of a letter to (Republican) South Carolina governor Daniel Chamberlain. Grant writes that "a government that cannot give protection to life, property, and all guaranteed civil rights ... to the citizen ... is a failure, and every energy of the oppressed should be exerted ... to regain lost privileges and protections."

That was written in the summer of the same year, 1876, in which the landmark Hayes-Tilden presidential election occurred and the bargaining began to put Hayes in office and give to Tilden and his supporters in the South the deal of the century: the end of a federal presence there. Thus ended Reconstruction, after barely ten years. And so began the return of the South to its traditional roots, albeit absent slavery and the old plantation economy. Still, white supremacy was allowed to flourish under Jim Crow for the next hundred years. We end the present section with an example of a sharecropper's contract, a document that reflects the exploitation of black southerners seeking to support themselves by white landowners.

■ *United States v. Cruikshank*

Date: 1874
Author: Joseph P. Bradley
Genre: court case

Summary Overview

United States v. Cruikshank was an appeal to the United States Supreme Court, argued in 1875 and decided the following year, to overturn the conviction of several men arrested following a massacre in Colfax, Louisiana, on April 13, 1873. After the hotly contested election of 1872, a paramilitary group of white men overpowered and killed a group of black freemen and state militia members guarding the newly elected Republican government at the Grant Parish courthouse. Several of the white men were convicted of conspiracy under a federal act designed to enforce the US Constitution's Fourteenth and Fifteenth Amendment guarantees of equal rights regardless of color. The defendants challenged the conviction, arguing that Congress did not have the authority to criminalize individuals' behavior and could only legislate against government discrimination. In 1874, Supreme Court associate justice Joseph P. Bradley, serving as a circuit justice in the Louisiana circuit court, heard the defendants' appeal and ruled in their favor, thus sending the case on to the Supreme Court. The Supreme Court agreed with Bradley's ruling and overturned the convictions, paving the way for paramilitary white supremacist groups to control the Southern states through violence and intimidation against black men trying to exercise their rights.

Defining Moment

Racial tension in Louisiana was extremely high following the Civil War. The federal Reconstruction Act of 1867 required all states to grant black men the right to vote. Unfortunately, this led to violence and murder against those who attempted to exercise that right, as well as widespread election fraud on the part of whites who opposed black suffrage.

Initially, Louisiana governor Henry Clay Warmoth tried to provide racial balance in his community by appointing William Ward, a black Civil War veteran of the Union Army, to be a commanding officer of a black unit of the state militia. But shortly before the 1872 election Warmoth aligned with the Liberal Republicans, who sought to disenfranchise black citizens, and formed an alliance with the Democratic Party. This alliance supported Warmoth to become Louisiana's US senator and John McEnery to become the new governor of Louisiana.

Voter fraud was rampant, and the election board was split regarding which candidate had actually won. Much of the reelected board claimed that McEnery had won the governor's seat, but a minority of the board and the federal government claimed that Republican William Pitt Kellogg had won. McEnery and his party assumed control following the election, but with federal assistance, Kellogg was eventually certified as the Louisiana governor. When the newly elected Republicans took their offices in the Grant Parish courthouse, groups of free black citizens and the black state militia unit occupied the area outside the courthouse to protect the government against overthrow by white protestors. In late March of 1873, several white men formed an alliance to retake the courthouse and reinstate their preferred government. Supported by the Ku Klux Klan and armed with a cannon, approximately three hundred white men attacked the estimated one hundred black men surrounding the courthouse. Most of the black men were killed on the spot, many after surrendering, or else were executed later that night. The courthouse was burned.

In the weeks and months that followed, several members of the paramilitary group were tracked down and charged with criminal violations under the US Enforcement Act of 1870. This act was passed by Congress to enforce the newly ratified Fourteenth and Fifteenth Amendments guaranteeing black citizens equal rights and protection under the law. The defendants appealed the convictions on the grounds that the Enforcement Act was unconstitutional, and the appeal was heard by the US Supreme Court.

Author Biography

Joseph P. Bradley was born on March 14, 1813, in Berne, New York. At age twenty. he relocated to New Jersey to study divinity at Rutgers University, but eventually he decided to pursue law instead. He became a member of the New Jersey bar in 1839 and established a reputable and lucrative practice in the fields of patent and railroad law in the city of Newark. He earned a solid reputation for his trial work within the federal court system, and when the Judiciary Act of 1869 created a vacancy on the US Supreme Court, he secured a nomination from President Ulysses S. Grant. Justice Bradley took his oath of office and assumed his seat on March 21, 1870.

From April 4, 1870, to January 9, 1881, Justice Bradley served as the circuit justice for the US Circuit Court for the Fifth Circuit. While there, he wrote the opinion for the District of Louisiana case *United*

States v. Cruikshank et al., which narrowly construed Congress's authority under the Fourteenth and Fifteenth Amendments to the Constitution and sent the case on to the Supreme Court for judgment. The Supreme Court's decision ultimately paved the way for white supremacist groups to control the post–Civil War South. Bradley also became infamous for his concurring opinion in *Bradwell v. Illinois*, a Supreme Court case that held that the right of a woman to practice law was not constitutionally protected under the privileges and immunities clause of the Fourteenth Amendment. In writing separate from the majority, who had relied upon states' rights grounds to justify the decision, Bradley declared that "the paramount destiny and mission of women are to fulfill the noble and benign offices of wife and mother. This is the law of the Creator."

Justice Bradley also served in the Sixth Circuit, which covered Ohio, Kentucky, and Tennessee, from May 2 until May 17, 1881, and the Third Circuit, covering New Jersey, Delaware, and Pennsylvania, from January 10, 1881, until early 1892. His service in both the Supreme Court and the Third Circuit ended with his death in Washington, DC, on January 22, 1892, most likely of tuberculosis. Bradley was buried at the Mount Pleasant Cemetery in Newark, New Jersey.

HISTORICAL DOCUMENT

The main ground of objection is that the act is municipal in its character, operating directly on the conduct of individuals, and taking the place of ordinary state legislation; and that there is no constitutional authority for such an act, inasmuch as the state laws furnish adequate remedy for the alleged wrongs committed.

It cannot, of course, be denied that express power is given to congress to enforce by appropriate legislation the 13th, 14th and 15th amendments of the constitution, but it is insisted that this act does not pursue the appropriate mode of doing this. A brief examination of its provisions is necessary more fully to understand the form in which the questions arise. The first section provides that all citizens of the United States, otherwise qualified, shall be allowed to vote at all elections in any

state, county, city, township, etc., without distinction of race, color or previous condition of servitude, any constitution, law, custom or usage of any state or territory to the contrary notwithstanding. This is not quite the converse of the 15th amendment. That amendment does not establish the right of any citizens to vote; it merely declares that race, color or previous condition of servitude shall not exclude them.

This is an important distinction, and has a decided bearing on the questions at issue. The second section requires that equal opportunity shall be given to all citizens, without distinction of race, color or previous condition of servitude, to perform any act required as a prerequisite or qualification for voting, and makes it a penal offense for officers and others to refuse or omit to give such equal opportunity.

The third section makes the offer to perform such preparatory act, if not performed by reason of such wrongful act or omission of the officers or others, equivalent to performance; and makes it the duty of inspectors or judges of election, on affidavit of such offer being made, to receive the party's vote; and makes it a penal offense to refuse to do so. These three sections relate to the right secured by the 15th amendment. The fourth section makes it a penal offense for any person, by force, bribery, threats, etc., to hinder or prevent, or to conspire with others to hinder or prevent, any citizen from performing any preparatory act requisite to qualify him to vote, or from voting, at any election. This section does not seem to be based on the 15th amendment, nor to relate to the specific right secured thereby. It extends far beyond the scope of the amendment, as will more fully appear hereafter. The fifth section makes it a penal offense for any person to prevent or attempt to prevent, hinder or intimidate any person from exercising the right of suffrage, to whom it is secured by the 15th amendment, by means of bribery, threats, or threats of depriving of occupation, or of ejecting from lands or tenements, or of refusing to renew a lease, or of violence to such person or his family. The sixth section, under which the first sixteen counts of the indictment are framed, contains two distinct clauses. The first declares that "if two or more persons shall band or conspire together, or go in disguise upon the public highway, or upon the premises of another with intent (to violate any provision of this act), such persons shall be held guilty of felony." Of course this would include conspiracy to prevent any person from voting, or from performing any preparatory act requisite thereto. The next clause has a larger scope. Repeating the introductory and concluding words, it is as follows: "If two or more persons shall band or conspire together, or go in disguise upon the public highway, or upon the premises of another with intent to injure, oppress, threaten, or intimidate any citizen, with intent to prevent or hinder his free exercise and enjoyment of any right or privilege granted or secured to him by the constitution or laws of the United States, or because of his having exercised the same, such persons shall be held guilty of felony." Here it is made penal to enter into a conspiracy to injure or intimidate any citizen, with intent to prevent or hinder his exercise and enjoyment, not merely of the right to vote, but of any right or

privilege granted or secured to him by the constitution or laws of the United States.

The question is at once suggested, under what clause of the constitution does the power to enact such a law arise? It is undoubtedly a sound proposition, that whenever a right is guarantied by the constitution of the United States, congress has the power to provide for its enforcement, either by implication arising from the correlative duty of government to protect, wherever a right to the citizen is conferred, or under the general power (contained in *article 1, § 8. par. 18*) "to make all laws necessary and proper for carrying into execution the foregoing powers, and all other powers vested by this constitution in the government of the United States, or any department or officer thereof." It was on the principle first stated that the fugitive slave law was sustained by the supreme court of the United States. *Prigg v. Pennsylvania, 16 Pet. [41 U. S.] 539.* The constitution guarantied the rendition of fugitives held to labor or service in any state, and it was held that congress had, by implication, the power to enforce the guaranty by legislation. "They require," says Justice Story, delivering the opinion of the majority of the court, "the aid of legislation to protect the right, to enforce the delivery, and to secure the subsequent possession of the slave. If, indeed, the constitution guaranties the right, and if it requires the delivery upon the claim of the owner (as cannot well be doubted), the natural inference certainly is, that the national government is clothed with the appropriate authority and functions to enforce it. The fundamental principle applicable to all cases of this sort would seem to be, that where the end is required, the means are given; and, where the duty is enjoined, the ability to perform it is contemplated to exist on the part of the functionaries to whom it is entrusted. The clause is found in the national constitution and not in that of any state. It does not point out any state functionaries, or any state action to carry its provisions into effect. The state, therefore, cannot be compelled to enforce them, etc. The natural if not the necessary conclusion is, that the national government, in the absence of all positive provisions to the contrary, is bound, through its own departments, legislative, judicial, or executive, as the case may require, to carry into effect all the rights and duties imposed upon it by the constitution." To the objection that the power did not fall within the scope of the enumerated powers of legislation confided to congress, Justice Story answers: "Stripped of its artificial and technical structure, the argument comes to this, that, although rights are exclusively secured by, or duties are exclusively imposed upon, the national government, yet, unless the power to enforce these rights or to execute these duties can be found among the express powers of legislation enumerated in the constitution, they remain without any means of giving them effect by any act of congress, and they must operate solely proprio vigore, however defective may be their operation; nay, even although in a practical sense, they may become a nullity from the want of a proper remedy to enforce them, or to provide against their violation. If this be the true interpretation of the constitution, it must, in a great measure, fail to attain many of its avowed and positive objects as a security of rights and a recognition of duties. Such a limited construction of the constitution has never yet been adopted as correct, either in theory or practice." *[Prigg v. Pennsylvania] 16 Pet. [41 U. S.] 618. . . .*

Again, "the citizens of each state shall be entitled to all the privileges and immunities of citizens in the several states." But this does not authorize congress to pass a general system of municipal law for the security of person and property, to have effect in the several states for the protection of citizens of other states to whom the fundamental right is guarantied. It only authorizes appropriate and efficient remedies to be provided in case the guaranty is violated. Where affirmative legislation is required to give the citizen the right guarantied, congress may undoubtedly adopt it, as was done in the case of the fugitive slave law and as has been done in later times, to carry into full effect the 13th amendment of the constitution by the passage of the civil rights bill, as will be more fully noted hereafter. But with regard to mere constitutional prohibitions of state interference with established or acknowledged privileges and immunities, the appropriate legislation to enforce such prohibitions is that which may be necessary or proper for furnishing suitable redress when such prohibitions are disregarded or violated. Where no violation is attempted, the interference of congress would be officious, unnecessary, and inappropriate.

The bearing of these observations on the effect of the several recent amendments of the constitution, in conferring legislative powers upon congress, is next to be noticed. The 13th amendment declares that neither slavery nor involuntary servitude, except as a punishment for crime, shall exist within the United States or any place subject to its jurisdiction, and that congress shall have power to enforce this article by appropriate legislation. This is not merely a prohibition against the passage or enforcement of any law inflicting or establishing slavery or involuntary servitude, but it is a positive declaration that slavery shall not exist. It prohibits the thing. In the enforcement of this article, therefore, congress has to deal with the subject matter. If an amendment had been adopted that polygamy should not exist within the United States, and a similar power to enforce it had been given as in the case of slavery, congress would certainly have had the power to legislate for the suppression and punishment of polygamy. So, undoubtedly, by the 13th amendment congress has power to legislate for the entire eradication of slavery in the United States. This amendment had an affirmative operation the moment it was adopted. It enfranchised four millions of slaves, if, indeed, they had not previously been enfranchised by the operation of the Civil War. Congress, therefore, acquired the power not only to legislate for the eradication of slavery, but the power to give full effect to this bestowment of liberty on these millions of people. All this it essayed to do by the civil rights bill, passed April 9, 1866 *[14 Stat. 27]*, by which it was declared that all persons born in the United States, and not subject to a foreign power (except Indians, not taxed), should be citizens of the United States; and that such citizens, of every race and color, without any regard to any previous condition of slavery or involuntary servitude, should have the same right in every state and territory to make and enforce contracts, to sue, be parties, and give evidence, to inherit, purchase, lease, sell, hold, and convey real and personal property, and to full and equal benefit of all laws and proceedings for the security of persons and property, as is enjoyed by white citizens, and should be subject to like punishment, pains and penalties, and to none other, any law, etc., to the contrary notwithstanding.

It was supposed that the eradication of slavery and involuntary servitude of every form and description required that the slave should be made a citizen and placed on an entire equality before the law with the white citizen, and, therefore, that congress had the power, under the amendment, to declare and effectuate these objects. The form of doing this, by extending the right of citizenship and equality before the law to persons of every race and color (except Indians not taxed and, of course, excepting the white race, whose privileges were adopted as the standard), although it embraced many persons, free colored people and others, who were already citizens in several of the states, was necessary for the purpose of settling a point which had been raised by eminent authority, that none but the white race were entitled to the rights of citizenship in this country. As disability to be a citizen and enjoy equal rights was deemed one form or badge of servitude, it was supposed that congress had the power, under the amendment, to settle this point of doubt, and place the other races on the same plane of privilege as that occupied by the white race.

Conceding this to be true (which I think it is), congress then had the right to go further and to enforce its declaration by passing laws for the prosecution and punishment of those who should deprive, or attempt to deprive, any person of the rights thus conferred upon him. Without having this power, congress could not enforce the amendment. It cannot be doubted, therefore, that congress had the power to make it a penal offense to conspire to deprive a person of, or to hinder him in, the exercise and enjoyment of the rights and privileges conferred by the 13th amendment and the laws thus passed in pursuance thereof. But this power does not authorize congress to pass laws for the punishment of ordinary crimes and offenses against persons of the colored race or any other race. That belongs to the state government alone. All ordinary murders, robberies, assaults, thefts, and offenses whatsoever are cognizable only in the state courts, unless, indeed, the state should deny to the class of persons referred to the equal protection of the laws. Then, of course, congress could provide remedies for their security and protection. But, in ordinary cases, where the laws of the state are not obnoxious to the provisions of the amendment, the duty of congress in the creation and punishment of offenses is limited to those offenses which aim at the deprivation of the colored citizen's enjoyment and exercise of his rights of citizenship and of equal protection of the laws because

of his race, color, or previous condition of servitude. To illustrate: If in a community or neighborhood composed principally of whites, a citizen of African descent, or of the Indian race, not within the exception of the amendment, should propose to lease and cultivate a farm, and a combination should be formed to expel him and prevent him from the accomplishment of his purpose on account of his race or color, it cannot be doubted that this would be a case within the power of congress to remedy and redress. It would be a case of interference with that person's exercise of his equal rights as a citizen because of his race. But if that person should be injured in his person or property by any wrongdoer for the mere felonious or wrongful purpose of malice, revenge, hatred, or gain, without any design to interfere with his rights of citizenship or equality before the laws, as being a person of a different race and color from the white race, it would be an ordinary crime, punishable by the state laws only. To constitute an offense, therefore, of which congress and the courts of the United States have a right to take cognizance under this amendment, there must be a design to injure a person, or deprive him of his equal right of enjoying the protection of the laws, by reason of his race, color, or previous condition of servitude. Otherwise it is a case exclusively within the jurisdiction of the state and its courts. . . .

The real difficulty in the present case is to determine whether the amendment has given to congress any power to legislate except to furnish redress in cases where the states violate the amendment. Considering, as before intimated, that the amendment, notwithstanding its negative form, substantially guaranties the equal right to vote to citizens of every race and color, I am inclined to the opinion that congress has the power to secure that right not only as against the unfriendly operation of state laws, but against outrage, violence, and combinations on the part of individuals, irrespective of the state laws. Such was the opinion of congress itself in passing the law at a time when many of its members were the same who had consulted upon the original form of the amendment in proposing it to the states. And as such a construction of the amendment is admissible, and the question is one at least of grave doubt, it would be assuming a great deal for this court to decide the law, to the extent indicated, unconstitutional. But the limitations which are prescribed by the amendment must not be lost sight of. It is not the right to vote which is guarantied to all citizens. Congress cannot interfere with the regulation of that right by the states except to prevent by appropriate legislation any distinction as to race, color, or previous condition of servitude. The state may establish any other conditions and discriminations it pleases, whether as to age, sex, property, education, or anything else. Congress, so far as the 15th amendment is concerned, is limited to the one subject of discrimination—on account of race, color or previous condition of servitude. It can regulate as to nothing else. No interference with a person's right to vote, unless made on account of his race, color or previous condition of servitude, is subject to congressional animadversion. There may be a conspiracy to prevent persons from voting having no reference to this discrimination. It may include whites as well as blacks, or may be confined altogether to the latter. It may have reference to the particular politics of the parties. All such conspiracies are amenable to the state laws alone. To bring them within the scope of the amendment and of the powers of congress they must have for motive the race, color or previous condition of servitude of the party whose right is assailed.

According to my view the law on the subject may be generalized in the following proposition: The war of race, whether it assumes the dimensions of civil strife or domestic violence, whether carried on in a guerrilla or predatory form, or by private combinations, or even by private outrage or intimidation, is subject to the jurisdiction of the government of the United States; and when any atrocity is committed which may be assigned to this cause it may be punished by the laws and in the courts of the United States; but any outrages, atrocities, or conspiracies, whether against the colored race or the white race, which do not flow from this cause, but spring from the ordinary felonious or criminal intent which prompts to such unlawful acts, are not within the jurisdiction of the United States, but within the sole jurisdiction of the states, unless, indeed, the state, by its laws, denies to any particular race equality of rights, in which case the government of the United States may furnish remedy and redress to the fullest extent and in the most direct manner. Unless this distinction be made we are driven to one of two extremes—either that congress can never interfere where the state laws are unobjectionable, however remiss the state authorities may be in executing them, and however much a proscribed race may be oppressed; or that congress may pass an entire body of municipal law for the protection of person and property within the states, to operate concurrently with the state laws, for the protection and benefit of a particular class of the community. This fundamental principle, I think, applies to both the 13th and 15th amendments. . . .

GLOSSARY

amenable: answerable or liable to

animadversion: criticism

indictment: a formal charge filed against an individual for committing a crime

privileges and immunities: a collection of rights that US citizens possess that stem from the existence of a federal government

proprio vigore: by its own force

Document Analysis

The massacre at the Grant Parish courthouse in Colfax, Louisiana, took place on April 13, 1873. In the weeks and months that followed, several members of the white paramilitary group that organized the attack were tracked down and tried for murder and conspiracy to deprive black individuals of their constitutionally guaranteed equal protection under the law. Their conviction was based on legislation signed into law on May 31, 1870, entitled "An act to enforce the Rights of Citizens of the United States to vote in the several States of this Union, and for other Purposes," commonly referred to as the Enforcement Act of 1870. The purpose of this legislation was to enforce upon the states the newly established Fifteenth Amendment to the US Constitution, which states that US citizens cannot be denied the right to vote on the basis of their "race, color, or previous condition of servitude."

The Enforcement Act consists of twenty-three sections, the first three of which are directly related to the rights granted by the Fifteenth Amendment. Section 1 provides that all US citizens must be allowed to vote in any election regardless of race, color, or previous condition of servitude and regardless of any state or local law enacted to the contrary. Section 2 provides that if there are any prerequisites to being allowed to vote, such as owning property or completing registration papers, all citizens must have an equal opportunity to meet those prerequisites without regard to race, color, or previous condition of servitude. Section 3 extends this protection to situations where an individual offers or attempts to complete those prerequisites but is prevented from doing so; this means that a state cannot, for example, refuse to accept an individual's properly completed voting paperwork because of his color.

The next three sections address the behavior of private individuals rather than government actions. Section 4 makes it a criminal offense for any individual to use force, bribery, or threats to prevent any citizen from performing an act prerequisite to being able to vote. Section 5 further makes it a criminal offense to prevent or attempt to prevent a person from exercising his right to vote by threatening his job or home or by threatening violence against his family. Section 6 establishes a felony offense for involvement in a conspiracy to violate any of the provisions of the act or deprive a person of any of his constitutional rights by using threats, intimidation, or violence.

The defendants in *United States v. Cruikshank* were convicted under the sixth section of the Enforcement Act. They were not acting officially on behalf of the government to prevent the black freemen and militia members from exercising their constitutionally guaranteed rights, but instead had formed a paramilitary group to accomplish this privately. They were charged with both violating the rights of the black citizens occupying the courthouse and forming a conspiracy to deprive them of those rights. To appeal their convictions, the defendants challenged the constitutionality of this section of the Enforcement Act. They did not contest Con-

gress's authority to prevent states and municipalities from disenfranchising black voters, as those provisions are permissible under the necessary and proper clause of the US Constitution (article 1, section 8), which grants Congress the authority to pass any law deemed "necessary and proper" to carry out its constitutional mandates. This would include passing laws to enforce the rights guaranteed by the newly ratified Thirteenth, Fourteenth, and Fifteenth Amendments. However, the defendants argued that Congress lacked the authority to regulate the behavior of individuals acting in a non-official capacity, and therefore their convictions should be overturned because this portion of the law is invalid.

In his opinion for the US Circuit Court for the District of Louisiana, Justice Bradley writes that when a citizen has rights that are secured by the Constitution "only by a declaration that the state or the United States shall not violate or abridge them," then these rights are "not created or conferred by the constitution"; instead, it is only guaranteed that those rights "shall not be impaired by the state, or the United States." And since section 1 of the Fifteenth Amendment states that "the right of citizens of the United States to vote shall not be denied or abridged by the United States or by any State on account of race, color, or previous condition of servitude," Congress only has the power to ensure that neither the state nor federal government prevents such individuals from voting, as it is "not a guaranty against the commission of individual offenses." Any regulation of individuals' actions must fall to the state governments, which are responsible for establishing appropriate legislation. Bradley further notes that the privileges and immunities clause of the Constitution, which states that "the Citizens of each State shall be entitled to all the Privileges and Immunities of Citizens in the several States," also does not authorize Congress to pass a general system of laws within each individual state, only to regulate the states themselves.

Bradley contrasts the Enforcement Act, which is at the heart of *United States v. Cruikshank*, with the Civil Rights Act, which was passed on April 9, 1866, and established, as he says, "that all persons born in the United States . . . should be citizens of the United States; and that such citizens, of every race and color, without any regard to any previous condition of slavery or involuntary servitude," should have the same rights in all US states and territories. This law was passed in response to the ratification of the Thirteenth Amendment to the Constitution, which states that "neither slavery nor involuntary servitude . . . shall exist within the United States, or any place subject to their jurisdiction," and it establishes criminal penalties for individuals who violate the provisions of the law. Bradley states that because this is an affirmative prohibition of the condition of slavery, the Civil Rights Act is an appropriate exercise of Congress's power to enforce this amendment.

By contrast, the Fifteenth Amendment states that "the right of citizens of the United States to vote shall not be denied or abridged by the United States or by any State on account of race, color, or previous condition of servitude." Bradley holds that the difference in language between these two amendments means that in the case of the Fifteenth Amendment, Congress only has the authority to prevent the states from denying its citizens of color the right to vote; it cannot exercise any power over the actions of private individuals. Additionally, he emphasizes that federal jurisdiction over violations of the Civil Rights Act only exists if the deprivation of rights is racially motivated. In other words, if a person is murdered because he is black, then federal laws would apply, but if a person is murdered and it is merely a coincidence that he is black, state laws would govern.

Bradley notes that the Fifteenth Amendment is in some ways an extension of the Civil Rights Act and "is to be interpreted on the same general principles." However, he elaborates that "the right conferred and guarantied is not an absolute, but a relative one." In particular, the Fifteenth Amendment "does not confer the right to vote" but rather grants "a right not to be excluded from voting." As such, that is "all the right that congress can enforce." According to Bradley, it is the "prerogative of the state laws" to confer the right to vote, and the Fifteenth Amendment can only prevent states from interfering with that right.

The decision in *United States v. Cruikshank* was not unexpected in light of a number of other Supreme Court decisions around the same time. In *Prigg v. Pennsylvania*, the Supreme Court upheld the federal Fugitive Slave Act, which mandated the return of any fugitive slave found in a free state, when the act was challenged by a Pennsylvania law providing protection to escaped slaves who had taken up residence in the state. Additionally, in a group of cases known collectively as the Slaughter-House Cases, the Supreme Court held that regulation of slaughterhouses was a state matter, not a federal one, even if there was an alleged violation of the Fourteenth Amendment's guarantee of equal protection

under the law. The Supreme Court's decision in these cases established that the federal government would accept only limited involvement in enforcing the rights enshrined in the Thirteenth, Fourteenth, and Fifteenth Amendments. By later affirming the circuit court's decision in *United States v. Cruikshank*, the Supreme Court made it clear that it would likewise selectively determine when it would step in to enforce these rights and when it would leave that enforcement to the states.

Finally, in a section not reproduced above, Bradley addresses the specific counts of the defendants' convictions. The first count alleges that the defendants formed a conspiracy to interfere with the right of the black freemen and militia to peaceably assemble at the courthouse, in violation of the First Amendment to the Constitution. Bradley notes that the language of the First Amendment merely prevents Congress from making laws that interfere with this right but says nothing about Congress's authority to prevent private individuals from interfering with the rights of other individuals.

The second count contains a similar allegation of conspiracy to interfere with the right to bear arms. Bradley holds that this count suffers from the same problem as the first; namely, that the Second Amendment prohibits the government from interfering with an individual's right to bear arms but does not authorize Congress to prevent a private individual from doing the same to another individual.

The third count charges the defendants with forming a conspiracy to deprive a group of black citizens of their constitutionally guaranteed right to life and liberty without due process of the law. Bradley dismisses this count by reasoning that every murderer deprives his victim of the right to life, but this alone does not give the federal government the authority to make and enforce a law criminalizing murder in every state.

Bradley also dismisses the fourth, fifth, and eighth counts—which allege further deprivation of constitutional rights—by stating that such deprivation perpetrated by a private individual is only a federal offense if it is racially motivated, but the complaint does not explicitly allege racial motivation. He admits that the defendants' actions probably were racially motivated, and even describes the fourth count as alleging that defendants deprived "certain colored citizens of African descent, of the free exercise and enjoyment of the right and privilege to the full and equal benefit of all laws and proceedings for the security of persons and property which is enjoyed by the white citizens." However, he dismisses the count anyway, stating that the prosecution should have been more explicit in claiming racial motivation for the defendants' actions.

The sixth and seventh counts specifically reference deprivation of the right to vote guaranteed under the Fifteenth Amendment. Bradley dismisses these on the grounds that only the states, and not Congress, have the authority to make these actions a crime, as described earlier in the opinion. The final eight counts are dismissed by stating that they "are literal copies, respectively, of the first eight, so far as relates to the language on which their validity depends."

Ultimately, *Cruikshank* has been criticized for its seemingly inconsistent treatment of the Thirteenth, Fourteenth, and Fifteenth Amendments. Bradley puts forth several arguments as to why the law under which Cruikshank and his fellow defendants were charged should be declared unconstitutional and attempts to justify this reasoning by citing prior precedents. However, those arguments often seem contradictory. The opinion specifically states that "the war of race . . . is subject to the jurisdiction of the government of the United States" regardless of who commits the crime and that "this fundamental principle . . . applies to both the 13th and 15th Amendment." Yet when dismissing the actual charges against the defendants, Bradley ignores the clear racial motivation behind the defendants' actions and declares that there is no federal jurisdiction because "Congress surely is not vested with power to legislate for the suppression and punishment of all murders, robberies, and assaults committed within the states." While both may be true statements, the conclusion only makes sense if one ignores the racial motivation for the underlying crime.

Essential Themes

The circuit court's decision in *United States v. Cruikshank* ultimately hinges on the notion that the right to vote is not granted by the US Constitution itself but is instead provided by the states. According to Bradley's interpretation, the federal government only has the authority to prevent the states from disenfranchising its black citizens; it is powerless to act against private individuals who seek to accomplish the same end. Bradley's attempts to explain why Congress was allowed to criminalize private behavior in the Civil Rights Act but not in the Enforcement Act were met with skepticism and continue to be debated many years later.

This case, and others like it, highlighted the growing racial tension in the United States as the Civil War ended and the Reconstruction efforts began. The Northern states of the Union refused to help rebuild the Confederate states if those states would not ratify the equal protection amendments to the US Constitution. But the establishment in the Southern states strongly resented the forced change to their way of life, and their citizens found other ways to disenfranchise black voters, including murder, violence, and intimidation.

The Supreme Court's decision to uphold Bradley's ruling in *United States v. Cruikshank* was heavily criticized for its failure to protect the rights the government had supposedly granted to newly freed black citizens in the Southern states. The Enforcement Act of 1870 prohibited states from taking any official actions to prevent black citizens from voting, but *United States v. Cruikshank* left it in the hands of the states themselves to protect black voters from aggression perpetrated by private individuals. The Southern states had no desire to pass or enforce laws protecting black voters, and the so-called right to vote enshrined in the Fifteenth Amendment was one that could not be exercised without fearing for one's life and safety.

Ultimately, the Supreme Court's decision had the effect of encouraging the growth of paramilitary white supremacy groups in the South. Organizations such as the Ku Klux Klan knew that the states themselves would never charge them for violating a black man's rights and, in the wake of *United States v. Cruikshank*, they also knew that the federal government would not intervene on behalf of the states' black citizens. The Supreme Court reversed some parts of the decision in later years, but the impact on the Reconstruction efforts was enormous, and the status of black citizens in the Southern states was severely harmed by the federal government's refusal to intervene in racially motivated deprivations of rights.

Tracey DiLascio, JD

Bibliography and Additional Reading

Curtis, Michael Kent. *No State Shall Abridge: The Fourteenth Amendment and the Bill of Rights.* Durham: Duke UP, 1986. Print.

Goldstone, Lawrence. *Inherently Unequal: The Betrayal of Equal Rights by the Supreme Court, 1865–1903.* New York: Walker, 2011. Print.

Hoffer, Williamjames Hull. *Plessy v. Ferguson: Race and Inequality in Jim Crow America*. Lawrence: UP of Kansas, 2012. Print

Keith, LeeAnna. *The Colfax Massacre: The Untold Story of Black Power, White Terror, and the Death of Reconstruction*. New York: Oxford UP, 2008. Print.

Lane, Charles. *The Day Freedom Died: The Colfax Massacre, the Supreme Court, and the Betrayal of Reconstruction*. New York: Holt, 2008. Print.

Stuntz, William J. *The Collapse of American Criminal Justice*. Cambridge: Belknap P of Harvard UP, 2012. Print.

■ Blanche Bruce: Speech in the Senate

Date: March 31, 1876
Author: Blanche K. Bruce
Genre: address, speech

Summary Overview

Blanche Bruce was one of the many courageous and determined African Americans who held a position in the federal government during Reconstruction. In fact, he was the only black American to complete an entire session in the US Senate before the 1960s (Patler 24). Unfortunately for him and his goals of achieving a fair playing field for Southern blacks, he was in office at the very end of the period and even for a few years after Reconstruction officially ended in early 1877. Yet, his protestations in this document—concerning the intimidation used by whites in the 1875 Mississippi state elections, which led to the Democrats "redeeming" the state—showed that African Americans at all levels were active in the attempt to change the South after the Civil War. In addition, the fact that Bruce was elected to the US Senate in 1874—when a number of other Southern states had already shed any remaining attachment to Reconstruction—and remained in office until early 1881 revealed that in some parts of the South, Reconstruction had positive effects that lasted longer than the official end of the era itself.

Defining Moment

The context surrounding Bruce's speech is very important to keep in mind when analyzing it. Mississippi was one of the Southern states in which the Democratic "redemption" came later, and this meant that there was still a relatively strong Republican Party there in 1874 to elect Bruce to the United States Senate. Within a year, however, the events he protested in his speech had occurred, when Democrats took over the Mississippi government again using voter fraud and intimidation. This had happened in several other Southern states already and Northern interest in reconstruct-ing the South and supporting black civil and political rights was clearly fading away by the mid-1870s, especially owing to the Panic of 1873, which distracted many Northerners and made them focus on labor issues instead of the plight of African Americans in the South. Indeed, Bruce's speech came earlier in the very year that a disputed presidential election would signal the death knell of Reconstruction officially, although Reconstruction had already become relatively ineffective in most areas of the South by that time. Yet Bruce still believed that he had to try to convince the federal government, and in effect Northerners, to investigate white Southern violence against African Americans and the violation of black rights.

Elected by the Mississippi Legislature to the Senate in 1874, when that body was still controlled by white and black Republicans, Bruce perhaps recognized his own precarious position after the 1875 Democratic victory in Mississippi and, therefore, tried to help out his friend P.B.S. Pinchback, an African American from Louisiana who had been fairly elected in 1873 to the US Senate, but who had been blocked from assuming his seat (Patler 36). Shortly thereafter, Bruce gave his more famous speech, in order to achieve his goal of a federal investigation into the 1875 elections in Mississippi and, while he did convince the Senate to pass a bill that would do so, the House of Representatives, which was again controlled by Democrats, did not likewise pass the bill ("Bruce, Blanche Kelso"). Therefore, it was in the context of flagging Northern support for Reconstruction and black rights in the South, the Democratic "redemption" of Mississippi, and an overall atmosphere of intimidation of any remaining African American legislators from the South that Bruce stood up and delivered his speech.

Author Biography

Bruce was born in 1841, the child of a white master and female slave, and lived in several states until he ran away to freedom in 1861 (Patler 29–30). During and immediately after the Civil War, Bruce worked in several places, trying to enhance educational opportunities for African Americans before he traveled to Mississippi in 1868 to begin a political career in the Republican Party at the height of Reconstruction (Patler 30). Rising through the party ranks, he achieved election to the US Senate in February 1874 and served his term fully until early 1881. After he left Congress, Bruce twice received votes at Republican conventions to be the party's vice presidential candidate, and he remained in various federal government positions under both parties, even providing advice to presidents on various issues, although he only actively supported Republican candidates (Patler 38–40). After a long and distinguished public career, he died in 1898 from diabetes (Patler 40). His ongoing attempts to help African Americans and other minorities led one of the best scholars of his lifetime, Nicholas Patler, to note that Bruce exhibited "skillful and strategic uses of power by a leader under some of the most formidable conditions in American history" (Patler 40).

HISTORICAL DOCUMENT

Speech by Senator Blanche Bruce, Introducing a Resolution to Appoint a Committee to Investigate Election Practices in Mississippi

The conduct of the late election in Mississippi affected not merely the fortunes of partisans—as the same were necessarily involved in the defeat or success of the respective parties to the contest—but put in question and jeopardy the sacred rights of the citizens; and the investigation contemplated in the pending resolution has for its object not the determination of the question whether the offices shall be held and the public affairs of that State be administered by democrats or republicans, but the higher and more important end, the protection in all their purity and significance of the political rights of the people and the free institutions of the country.

The evidence in hand and accessible will show beyond peradventure that in many parts of the State corrupt and violent influences were brought to bear upon the registrars of voters, thus materially affecting the character of the voting or poll lists; upon the inspectors of election, prejudicially and unfairly thereby changing the number of votes cast; and, finally, threats and violence were practiced directly upon the masses of voters in such measures and strength as to produce grave apprehensions for their personal safety and as to deter them from the exercise of their political franchises.

It will not accord with the laws of nature or history to brand colored people a race of cowards. On more than one historic field, beginning in 1776 and coming down to this centennial year of the Republic, they have attested in blood their courage as well as a love of liberty. I ask Senators to believe that no consideration of fear or personal danger has kept us quiet and forbearing under the provocations and wrongs that have so sorely tried our souls. But feeling kindly toward our white fellow-citizens, appreciating the good purposes and politics of the better classes, and, above all, abhorring a war of races, we determined to wait until such time as an appeal to the good sense and justice of the American people could be made.

The sober American judgment must obtain in the South as elsewhere in the Republic, that the only distinction upon which parties can be safely organized and in harmony with our institutions are differences of opinion relative to principles and policy of government, and that differences of religion nationality, or race can neither with safety nor propriety be permitted for a moment to enter into the party contests of the day. The unanimity with which the colored voters act with a party is not referable to any race prejudice on their part. On the contrary, they invite the political cooperation of their white brethren, and vote as a unit because proscribed as such. They deprecate the establishment of the color line by the opposition, not only because the act is unwise and wrong in principle, but because it isolates them from the white men of the South, and forces them, in sheer self-protection and against their inclination, to act seemingly upon the basis of a race prejudice that they neither respect nor entertain. As a class they are free from prejudices, and have no uncharitable suspicions against their white fellow-citizens, whether native born or settlers from the Northern States. They not only recognize the equality of citizenship and the right of every man to hold, without proscription any position of honor and trust to which the confidence of the people may elevate him; but owing nothing to race, birth, or surroundings, they, above all other classes in the community, are interested to see prejudices drop out of both politics and the business of the country, and success in life proceed only upon the integrity and merit of the man who seeks it. . . . But withal, as they progress in intelligence and appreciation of the dignity of their prerogatives as citizens, they, as an evidence of growth begin to realize the significance of the proverb, "When thou doest well for thyself, men shall praise thee"; and are disposed to exact the same protection and concession of rights that are conferred upon other citizens by the Constitution, and that, too, without the humiliation involved in the enforced abandonment of their political convictions.

I have confidence, not only in this country and her institutions, but in the endurance, capacity, and destiny of my people. We will, as opportunity offers and ability serves, seek our places, sometimes in the field of letters, arts, sciences, and the professions. More frequently mechanical pursuits will attract and elicit our efforts; more still of my people will find employment and livelihood as the cultivators of the soil. The bulk of this people—by surroundings, habits, adaptation, and choice—will continue to find their homes in the South, and constitute the masses of its yeomanry. We will there probably, of our own volition and more abundantly than in the past, produce the great staples that will contribute to the basis of foreign exchange, aid in giving the nation a balance of trade, and minister to the wants and comfort and build up the prosperity of the whole land. Whatever our ultimate position in the composite civilization of the Republic and whatever varying fortunes attend our career, we will not forget our instincts for freedom nor our love of country.

GLOSSARY

franchise: privilege or right

late: most recent

peradventure: chance, uncertainty

withal: despite that, nevertheless

Document Analysis

Bruce's purpose in giving his speech was to bolster Northern support, which was ebbing rapidly away by 1876, for Reconstruction and black rights in the South and, in this instance, he wanted that support to come in the form of a committee to investigate the fraudulent elections of 1875 that allowed the Democrats to "redeem" Mississippi that year. As noted above, this was particularly important to Bruce and other African Americans because other Southern states had already effectively suppressed black voting and civil rights, and Reconstruction certainly appeared to be ending. Bruce, of course, argued that black Southerners held certain rights based on natural law and the Constitution, yet he also argued for the support of black rights based on their racial egalitarianism, their military service, and their contribution to America's international economic strength.

Bruce was keen enough to understand that, although white Southerners employed race-based intimidation to keep African Americans from voting in 1875, he himself could not appear to be focused solely on race, for fear of being labeled as a man who just wanted to stir up Southern black anger against whites. Bruce was well aware of the fear of whites, both in the North and the South, of slave rebellions during the pre-Civil War era, and he knew that if he presented an image of blacks organizing solely by themselves politically, this image would be raised in the minds of whites. Therefore, he was very careful in his speech to emphasize that black Southerners wanted to work with whites and were only forced to organize in the Republican Party in the South due to Southern white pressure and abandonment of blacks. He continually claimed that parties should not be drawn along racial lines, and he emphasized the colorblindness of black Americans. Amid the sad reality that whites could oppress blacks and then charge blacks with organizing solely along racial lines, Bruce had to tread a very precarious middle ground.

Bruce then went on to invoke the military and economic service that African Americans had provided and would provide to the nation. He eloquently noted that black Americans had served in both the American Revolution and, in much higher numbers, in the Civil War when he stated, "On more than one historic field, beginning in 1776 and coming down to this centennial year of the Republic, they have attested in blood their courage as well as a love of liberty." After the Civil War, as well as after both World War I and World War II in the twentieth century, African Americans tried to remind the nation that they had patriotically served their country and, thus, deserved to enjoy all the political, civil, and economic rights that belonged to normal citizens.

Bruce also noted that African Americans would "produce the great staples that will contribute to the basis of foreign exchange, aid in giving the nation a balance of trade, and minister to the wants and comfort and build up the prosperity of the whole land." He was aware of the very real national and international economic benefits that the rest of the United States received due to the labor of black Southerners. Overall, while Bruce argued that African Americans deserved rights based both on their status as humans and on the Constitution alone, he was also savvy enough to realize that he would have to employ other arguments to make his case, including the racial egalitarianism of blacks, their military service, and their contribution to national economic strength.

Essential Themes

Bruce's actions clearly showed that African Americans were actively involved in trying to create a better society in the post-Civil War South. For decades after Reconstruction, historians debated whether or not the North and African Americans had oppressed the South, which was the Southern view most often, or whether the for-

mer slaves had become victims yet again at the hands of Southern whites, which was often the African American and then Northern white view. However, in more recent decades, and particularly because of Eric Foner's excellent 1988 *Reconstruction: America's Unfinished Revolution: 1863–1877*, African Americans have been portrayed as active participants in the events of Reconstruction, which has enhanced their value as historical subjects. Bruce's speech, his career in Congress, and, indeed, his whole life, were part of the black American attempts to shape the context in which blacks found themselves.

Relatedly, the fact that Bruce was elected to Congress in 1874, near the very end of Reconstruction and after a number of other Southern states had been "redeemed" by white Democrats, showed that in some parts of the South, African American and Republican political strength remained strong up until the very end of the period. In fact, it took a massive, widespread campaign of voter fraud and intimidation in 1875 for the Democrats to triumph, which only reveals just how popular and strong Reconstruction was in Mississippi among white Republicans and African Americans. Were it not for the North's abandonment of Southern African Americans, Reconstruction may have succeeded and altered Southern society many decades before lasting changes finally occurred. In addition, the fact that Bruce remained in Congress until his term as senator ended in early 1881 showed that—as was also the case in one North Carolina district that elected African Americans to Congress until 1901—there were some areas of the South where the political strength of African Americans and Republicans lasted many years after Reconstruction officially ended in early 1877.

—*Kevin Grimm, PhD*

Bibliography and Additional Reading

Foner, Eric. *Reconstruction: America's Unfinished Revolution, 1863–1877.* New York: Harper & Row, 1988. Print.

"Bruce, Blanche Kelso." *US House of Representatives: History, Art & Archives.* US House of Representatives, Office of the Historian, n.d. Web. 09 Apr. 2014.

Patler, Nicholas. "The Black 'Consummate Strategist': Blanche Kelso Bruce and the Skillful Use of Power in the Reconstruction and Post-Reconstruction Eras." *Before Obama: A Reappraisal of Black Reconstruction Era Politicians*, Vol. 1: Legacies Lost. Ed. Matthey Lynch. Santa Barbara, CA: Praeger, 2012. Print.

■ Freedmen's Monument Speech

Date: April 14, 1876
Author: Frederick Douglass
Genre: speech

Summary Overview

Eleven years after the assignation of Abraham Lincoln, the first public memorial to him was unveiled in Lincoln Park in Washington, D.C. The Freedmen's Memorial Monument was the result of the African-American community raising the necessary money for the creation of a statue commemorating Lincoln's role in the freeing of the slaves. As the preeminent African-American orator, Frederick Douglass delivered this speech as the central address of the day. All the national political leaders, from President Grant on down, were in attendance, as were Mrs. Lincoln and leaders of the African-American community. Douglass had the ability and freedom to speak his mind regarding Lincoln's views on slavery and his actions, but also to examine what had transpired since the adoption of the 13th Amendment prohibiting slavery. In this speech, Douglass gave a realistic picture of Lincoln and American society.

Defining Moment

By 1876, the Reconstruction Era in American history was drawing to a close. The hope for equality by African Americans living in the Southern states was still a distant dream. Even those who lived in other regions of the United States had not seen the fulfillment of their hopes. And yet, even in the midst of the ongoing struggle, the fact that slavery had been abolished was still a landmark in the lives of former slaves. The Emancipation Proclamation and the 13th Amendment guaranteed that there was no going back. Thus many in the African-American community sought to recognize this landmark and the president who had made it possible. As stated on the monument's plaque, when Charlotte Scott, a former slave living in Virginia, heard about Lincoln's death, she made a "contribution of five dollars... .her first earnings in freedom . . . to build a monu-

ment to his memory." An agency run by white men to help former slaves, soon took control of the collection effort and commissioned the statue in accordance to their viewpoint, rather than that of the freed slaves who made the donations.

For those organizing the unveiling, Frederick Douglass was the obvious choice as the keynote speaker. He had been born a slave and once free, he had campaigned vigorously for slavery's abolition. In all regions and among all races, Douglass was a leader in the African-American community. He had been both a supporter and critic of President Lincoln, advising him on African-American issues, but supporting the Democratic candidate in the 1864 election when Lincoln was not willing to promise to make voting rights for Blacks a priority after the war. It was with great anticipation that the large crowd gathered on that day to hear his speech. His realistic portrayal of Lincoln garnered him accolades from the crowd. His skills as a speech writer, orator, and analyst of Lincoln and the political crisis which he had faced, demonstrated that African Americans were not inherently inferior to whites. However, just as the statue demonstrated an outdated view of the relationship between the races, Douglass' speech was unable to move American society forward in the area of race relations. The Civil War was not that many years removed, and hard feelings still predominated in both North and South. While Douglass would live for almost two more decades, actively pushing for racial and gender equality, this speech, and others like it, have made him an enduring symbol of the struggle in the decades since his death.

Author Biography

Frederick Douglass believed he had been born in February, 1818, although since he was a slave, there were no records of his birth. At his birth in Maryland, his mother, Harriet Bailey named him Frederick Augustus Washington Bailey, later telling him that his father was white. Frederick took the name Douglass after he escaped from slavery in 1838. He married Anna Murray, a free Black woman, less than two weeks after she helped him escape. They had five children. Anna died in 1882. Two years later he married Helen Pitts, who was white. Frederick died on February 20, 1895.

He taught himself to read while a slave, and his reading created a foundation for his later view of what society should be. After gaining his freedom, he became a church leader and was then asked to speak at anti-slavery meetings. In 1845 he wrote his first autobiography, and traveled in Europe and the United States, speaking out against slavery, and working for equality. During and after the Civil War, he held a variety of governmental positions, as well as publishing a newspaper.master—to

do as he is told to do. Learning will spoil [original emphasis] the best [slave] in the world. Now…if you teach that [slave] (speaking of myself) how to read, there would be no keeping him. It would forever unfit him to be a slave. He would at once become unmanageable, and of no value to his master. As to himself, it could do him no good, but a great deal of harm. It would make him discontented and unhappy (177).

Fortunately in this case, we know just how well educated Douglass eventually became.

Douglass' personal life led him to become both a husband and a father. He and his first wife, Anna, whom he married in 1838 at the approximate age of 20, had five children together. Frederick and Anna were married for roughly forty-four years, and he remarried—to a white woman, Helen Pitts—following Anna's death in 1882. Helen was at his side until his own passing in 1895.

HISTORICAL DOCUMENT

Friends and Fellow-citizens:

I warmly congratulate you upon the highly interesting object which has caused you to assemble in such numbers and spirit as you have today. This occasion is in some respects remarkable. Wise and thoughtful men of our race, who shall come after us, and study the lesson of our history in the United States; who shall survey the long and dreary spaces over which we have traveled; who shall count the links in the great chain of events by which we have reached our present position, will make a note of this occasion; they will think of it and speak of it with a sense of manly pride and complacency.

I congratulate you, also, upon the very favorable circumstances in which we meet today. They are high, inspiring, and uncommon. They lend grace, glory, and significance to the object for which we have met. Nowhere else in this great country, with its uncounted towns and cities, unlimited wealth, and immeasurable territory extending from sea to sea, could conditions be found more favorable to the success of this occasion than here.

We stand today at the national center to perform something like a national act — an act which is to go

into history; and we are here where every pulsation of the national heart can be heard, felt, and reciprocated. A thousand wires, fed with thought and winged with lightning, put us in instantaneous communication with the loyal and true men all over the country.

Few facts could better illustrate the vast and wonderful change which has taken place in our condition as a people than the fact of our assembling here for the purpose we have today. Harmless, beautiful, proper, and praiseworthy as this demonstration is, I cannot forget that no such demonstration would have been tolerated here twenty years ago. The spirit of slavery and barbarism, which still lingers to blight and destroy in some dark and distant parts of our country, would have made our assembling here the signal and excuse for opening upon us all the flood-gates of wrath and violence. That we are here in peace today is a compliment and a credit to American civilization, and a prophecy of still greater national enlightenment and progress in the future. I refer to the past not in malice, for this is no day for malice; but simply to place more distinctly in front the gratifying and glorious change which has come both to our white fellow-citizens and ourselves, and to congratulate all upon the contrast between now and then, the new dispensation of freedom with its thousand blessings to both races, and the old dispensation of slavery with its ten thousand evils to both races — white and black. In view, then, of the past, the present, and the future, with the long and dark history of our bondage behind us, and with liberty, progress, and enlightenment before us, I again congratulate you upon this auspicious day and hour.

Friends and fellow-citizens, the story of our presence here is soon and easily told. We are here in the District of Columbia, here in the city of Washington, the most luminous point of American territory; a city recently transformed and made beautiful in its body and in its spirit; we are here in the place where the ablest and best men of the country are sent to devise the policy, enact the laws, and shape the destiny of the Republic; we are here, with the stately pillars and majestic dome of the Capitol of the nation looking down upon us; we are here, with the broad earth freshly adorned with the foliage and flowers of spring for our church, and all races, colors, and conditions of men for our congregation — in a word, we are here to express, as best we may, by appropriate forms and ceremonies, our grateful sense of the vast, high, and preeminent services rendered to ourselves, to our race, to our country, and to the whole world by Abraham Lincoln.

The sentiment that brings us here to-day is one of the noblest that can stir and thrill the human heart. It has crowned and made glorious the high places of all civilized nations with the grandest and most enduring works of art, designed to illustrate the characters and perpetuate the memories of great public men. It is the sentiment which from year to year adorns with fragrant and beautiful flowers the graves of our loyal, brave, and patriotic soldiers who fell in defense of the Union and liberty. It is the sentiment of gratitude and appreciation, which often, in the presence of many who hear me, has filled yonder heights of Arlington with the eloquence of eulogy and the sublime enthusiasm of poetry and song; a sentiment which can never die while the Republic lives.

For the first time in the history of our people, and in the history of the whole American people, we join in this high worship, and march conspicuously in the line of this time-honored custom. First things are always interesting, and this is one of our first things. It is the first time that, in this form and manner, we have sought to do honor to an American great man, however deserving and illustrious. I commend the fact to notice; let it be told in every part of the Republic; let men of all parties and opinions hear it; let those who despise us, not less than those who respect us, know that now and here, in the spirit of liberty, loyalty, and gratitude, let it be known everywhere, and by everybody who takes an interest in human progress and in the amelioration of the condition of mankind, that, in the presence and with the approval of the members of the American House of Representatives, reflecting the general sentiment of the country; that in the presence of that august body, the American Senate, representing the highest intelligence and the calmest judgment of the country; in the presence of the Supreme Court and Chief-Justice of the United States, to whose decisions we all patriotically bow; in the presence and under the steady eye of the honored and trusted President of the United States, with the members of his wise and patriotic Cabinet, we, the colored people, newly emancipated and rejoicing in our blood-bought freedom, near the close of the first century in the life of this Republic, have now and here unveiled, set apart, and dedicated a monument of enduring granite and bronze, in every line, feature, and figure of which the men of this generation may read, and those of aftercoming generations may read, something of the exalted character and great works of Abraham Lincoln, the first martyr President of the United States.

Fellow-citizens, in what we have said and done today, and in what we may say and do hereafter, we disclaim everything like arrogance and assumption. We claim for ourselves no superior devotion to the character, history, and memory of the illustrious name whose monument we have here dedicated today. We fully comprehend the relation of Abraham Lincoln both to ourselves and to the white people of the United States. Truth is proper and beautiful at all times and in all places, and it is never more proper and beautiful in any case than when speaking of a great public man whose example is likely to be commended for honor and imitation long after his departure to the solemn shades, the silent continents of eternity. It must be admitted, truth compels me to admit, even here in the presence of the monument we have erected to his memory, Abraham Lincoln was not, in the fullest sense of the word, either our man or our model. In his interests, in his associations, in his habits of thought, and in his prejudices, he was a white man.

He was preeminently the white man's President, entirely devoted to the welfare of white men. He was ready and willing at any time during the first years of his administration to deny, postpone, and sacrifice the rights of humanity in the colored people to promote the welfare of the white people of this country. In all his education and feeling he was an American of the Americans. He came into the Presidential chair upon one principle alone, namely, opposition to the extension of slavery. His arguments in furtherance of this policy had their motive and mainspring in his patriotic devotion to the interests of his own race. To protect, defend, and perpetuate slavery in the states where it existed Abraham Lincoln was not less ready than any other President to draw the sword of the nation. He was ready to execute all the supposed guarantees of the United States Constitution in favor of the slave system anywhere inside the slave states. He was willing to pursue, recapture, and send back the fugitive slave to his master, and to suppress a slave rising for liberty, though his guilty master were already in arms against the Government. The race to which we belong were not the special objects of his consideration. Knowing this, I concede to you, my white fellow-citizens, a preeminence in this worship at once full and supreme. First, midst, and last, you and yours were the objects of his deepest affection and his most earnest solicitude. You are the children of Abraham Lincoln. We are at best only his step-children; children by adoption, children by forces of circumstances and necessity. To you it especially belongs to sound his praises, to preserve and perpetuate his memory, to multiply his statues, to hang his pictures high upon your walls, and commend his example, for to you he was a great and glorious friend and benefactor. Instead of supplanting you at his altar, we would exhort you to build high his monuments; let them be of the most costly material, of the most cunning workmanship; let their forms be symmetrical, beautiful, and perfect, let their bases be upon solid rocks, and their summits lean against the unchanging blue, overhanging sky, and let them endure forever! But while in the abundance of your wealth, and in the fullness of your just and patriotic devotion, you do all this, we entreat you to despise not the humble offering we this day unveil to view; for while Abraham Lincoln saved for you a country, he delivered us from a bondage, according to Jefferson, one hour of which was worse than ages of the oppression your fathers rose in rebellion to oppose.

Fellow-citizens, ours is no new-born zeal and devotion — merely a thing of this moment. The name of Abraham Lincoln was near and dear to our hearts in the darkest and most perilous hours of the Republic. We were no more ashamed of him when shrouded in clouds of darkness, of doubt, and defeat than when we saw him crowned with victory, honor, and glory. Our faith in him was often taxed and strained to the uttermost, but it never failed. When he tarried long in the mountain; when he strangely told us that we were the cause of the war; when he still more strangely told us that we were to leave the land in which we were born; when he refused to employ our arms in defense of the Union; when, after accepting our services as colored soldiers, he refused to retaliate our murder and torture as colored prisoners; when he told us he would save the Union if he could with slavery; when he revoked the Proclamation of Emancipation of General Fremont; when he refused to remove the popular commander of the Army of the Potomac, in the days of its inaction and defeat, who was more zealous in his efforts to protect slavery than to suppress rebellion; when we saw all this, and more, we were at times grieved, stunned, and greatly bewildered; but our hearts believed while they ached and bled. Nor was this, even at that time, a blind and unreasoning superstition. Despite the mist and haze that surrounded him; despite the tumult, the hurry, and confusion of the hour, we were able to take a comprehensive view of Abraham Lincoln, and to make reasonable allowance for the circumstances of his position. We saw him, measured him, and estimated him; not by stray utterances to injudicious and tedious delegations, who often tried his patience; not by isolated facts torn from their connection; not by any partial and imperfect glimpses, caught at inopportune moments; but by a broad survey, in the light of the stern logic of great events, and in view of that divinity which shapes our ends, rough hew them how we will, we came to the conclusion that the hour and the man of our redemption had somehow met in the person of Abraham Lincoln. It mattered little to us what language he might employ on special occasions; it mattered little to us, when we fully knew him, whether he was swift or slow in his movements; it was enough for us that Abraham Lincoln was at the head of a great movement, and was in living and earnest sympathy with that movement, which, in the nature of things, must go on until slavery should be utterly and forever abolished in the United States.

When, therefore, it shall be asked what we have to do with the memory of Abraham Lincoln, or what Abraham Lincoln had to do with us, the answer is ready, full, and complete. Though he loved Caesar less than Rome, though the Union was more to him than our freedom or our future, under his wise and beneficent rule we saw ourselves gradually lifted from the depths of slavery to the heights of liberty and manhood; under his wise and beneficent rule, and by measures approved and vigorously pressed by him, we saw that the handwriting of ages, in the form of prejudice and proscription, was rapidly fading away from the face of our whole country; under his rule, and in due time, about as soon after all as the country could tolerate the strange spectacle, we saw our brave sons and brothers laying off the rags of bondage, and being clothed all over in the blue uniforms of the soldiers of the United States; under his rule we saw two hundred thousand of our dark and dusky people responding to the call of Abraham Lincoln, and with muskets on their shoulders, and eagles on their buttons, timing their high footsteps to liberty and union under the national flag; under his rule we saw the independence of the black republic of Haiti, the special object of slave-holding aversion and horror, fully recognized, and her minister, a colored gentleman, duly received here in the city of Washington; under his rule we saw the internal slave-trade, which so long disgraced the nation, abolished, and slavery abolished in the District of Columbia; under his rule we saw for the first time the law enforced against the foreign slave trade, and the first slave-trader hanged like any other pirate or murderer; under his rule, assisted by the greatest captain of our age, and his inspiration, we saw the Confederate States, based upon the idea that our race must be slaves, and slaves forever, battered to pieces and scattered to the four winds; under his rule, and in the fullness of time, we saw Abraham Lincoln, after giving the slave-holders three months' grace in which to save their hateful slave system, penning the immortal paper, which, though special in its language, was general in its principles and effect, making slavery forever impossible in the United States. Though we waited long, we saw all this and more.

Can any colored man, or any white man friendly to the freedom of all men, ever forget the night which followed the first day of January, 1863, when the world was to see if Abraham Lincoln would prove to be as good as his word? I shall never forget that memorable night, when in a distant city I waited and watched at a public meeting, with three thousand others not less anxious than myself, for the word of deliverance which we have heard read today. Nor shall I ever forget the outburst of joy and thanksgiving that rent the air when the lightning brought to us the emancipation proclamation. In that happy hour we forgot all delay, and forgot all tardiness, forgot that the President had bribed the rebels to lay down their arms by a promise to withhold the bolt which would smite the slave-system with destruction; and we were thenceforward willing to allow the President all the latitude of time, phraseology, and every honorable device that statesmanship might require for the achievement of a great and beneficent measure of liberty and progress.

Fellow-citizens, there is little necessity on this occasion to speak at length and critically of this great and good man, and of his high mission in the world. That ground has been fully occupied and completely covered both here and elsewhere. The whole field of fact and fancy has been gleaned and garnered. Any man can say things that are true of Abraham Lincoln, but no man can say anything that is new of Abraham Lincoln. His personal traits and public acts are better known to the American people than are those of any other man of his age. He was a mystery to no man who saw him and heard him. Though high in position, the humblest could approach him and feel at home in his presence. Though deep, he was transparent; though strong, he was gentle; though decided and pronounced in his convictions, he was tolerant towards those who differed from him, and patient under reproaches. Even those who only knew him through his public utterance obtained a tolerably clear idea of his character and personality. The image of the man went out with his words, and those who read them knew him.

I have said that President Lincoln was a white man, and shared the prejudices common to his countrymen towards the colored race. Looking back to his times and to the condition of his country, we are compelled to admit that this unfriendly feeling on his part may be safely set down as one element of his wonderful success in organizing the loyal American people for the tremendous conflict before them, and bringing them safely through that conflict. His great mission was to accomplish two things: first, to save his country from dismemberment and ruin; and, second, to free his country from the great crime of slavery. To do one or the other, or both, he must have the earnest sympathy and the powerful cooperation of his loyal fellow-countrymen. Without this primary and essential condition to success his efforts must have been vain and utterly fruitless. Had he put the abolition of slavery before the salvation of the Union, he would have inevitably driven from him a powerful class of the American people and rendered resistance to rebellion impossible. Viewed from the genuine abolition ground, Mr. Lincoln seemed tardy, cold, dull, and indifferent; but measuring him by the sentiment of his country, a sentiment he was bound as a statesman to consult, he was swift, zealous, radical, and determined.

Though Mr. Lincoln shared the prejudices of his white fellow-countrymen against the Negro, it is hardly necessary to say that in his heart of hearts he loathed and hated slavery. The man who could say, "Fondly do we hope, fervently do we pray, that this mighty scourge of war shall soon pass away, yet if God wills it continue till all the wealth piled by two hundred years of bondage shall have been wasted, and each drop of blood drawn by the lash shall have been paid for by one drawn by the sword, the judgments of the Lord are true and righteous altogether," gives all needed proof of his feeling on the subject of slavery. He was willing, while the South was loyal, that it should have its pound of flesh, because he thought that it was so nominated in the bond; but farther than this no earthly power could make him go.

Fellow-citizens, whatever else in this world may be partial, unjust, and uncertain, time, time! is impartial, just, and certain in its action. In the realm of mind, as well as in the realm of matter, it is a great worker, and often works wonders. The honest and comprehensive statesman, clearly discerning the needs of his country, and earnestly endeavoring to do his whole duty, though covered and blistered with reproaches, may safely leave his course to the silent judgment of time. Few great public men have ever been the victims of fiercer denuncia-

tion than Abraham Lincoln was during his administration. He was often wounded in the house of his friends. Reproaches came thick and fast upon him from within and from without, and from opposite quarters. He was assailed by Abolitionists; he was assailed by slave-holders; he was assailed by the men who were for peace at any price; he was assailed by those who were for a more vigorous prosecution of the war; he was assailed for not making the war an abolition war; and he was bitterly assailed for making the war an abolition war.

But now behold the change: the judgment of the present hour is, that taking him for all in all, measuring the tremendous magnitude of the work before him, considering the necessary means to ends, and surveying the end from the beginning, infinite wisdom has seldom sent any man into the world better fitted for his mission than Abraham Lincoln. His birth, his training, and his natural endowments, both mental and physical, were strongly in his favor. Born and reared among the lowly, a stranger to wealth and luxury, compelled to grapple single-handed with the flintiest hardships of life, from tender youth to sturdy manhood, he grew strong in the manly and heroic qualities demanded by the great mission to which he was called by the votes of his countrymen. The hard condition of his early life, which would have depressed and broken down weaker men, only gave greater life, vigor, and buoyancy to the heroic spirit of Abraham Lincoln. He was ready for any kind and any quality of work. What other young men dreaded in the shape of toil, he took hold of with the utmost cheerfulness.

> "A spade, a rake, a hoe,
> A pick-axe, or a bill;
> A hook to reap, a scythe to mow,
> A flail, or what you will."

All day long he could split heavy rails in the woods, and half the night long he could study his English Grammar by the uncertain flare and glare of the light made by a pine-knot. He was at home in the land with his axe, with his maul, with gluts, and his wedges; and he was equally at home on water, with his oars, with his poles, with his planks, and with his boat-hooks. And whether in his flat-boat on the Mississippi River, or at the fireside of his frontier cabin, he was a man of work. A son of toil himself, he was linked in brotherly sympathy with the sons of toil in every loyal part of the Republic. This very fact gave him tremendous power with the American people, and materially contributed not only to selecting him to the Presidency, but in sustaining his administration of the Government.

Upon his inauguration as President of the United States, an office, even when assumed under the most favorable condition, fitted to tax and strain the largest abilities, Abraham Lincoln was met by a tremendous crisis. He was called upon not merely to administer the Government, but to decide, in the face of terrible odds, the fate of the Republic.

A formidable rebellion rose in his path before him; the Union was already practically dissolved; his country was torn and rent asunder at the center. Hostile armies were already organized against the Republic, armed with the munitions of war which the Republic had provided for its own defense. The tremendous question for him to decide was whether his country should survive the crisis and flourish, or be dismembered and perish. His predecessor in office had already decided the question in favor of national dismemberment, by denying to it the right of self-defense and self-preservation — a right which belongs to the meanest insect.

Happily for the country, happily for you and for me, the judgment of James Buchanan, the patrician, was not the judgment of Abraham Lincoln, the plebeian. He brought his strong common sense, sharpened in the school of adversity, to bear upon the question. He did not hesitate, he did not doubt, he did not falter; but at once resolved that at whatever peril, at whatever cost, the union of the States should be preserved. A patriot himself, his faith was strong and unwavering in the patriotism of his countrymen. Timid men said before Mr. Lincoln's inauguration, that we have seen the last President of the United States. A voice in influential quarters said, "Let the Union slide." Some said that a Union maintained by the sword was worthless. Others said a rebellion of 8,000,000 cannot be suppressed; but in the midst of all this tumult and timidity, and against all this, Abraham Lincoln was clear in his duty, and had an oath in heaven. He calmly and bravely heard the voice of doubt and fear all around him; but he had an oath in heaven, and there was not power enough on earth to make this

honest boatman, backwoodsman, and broad-handed splitter of rails evade or violate that sacred oath. He had not been schooled in the ethics of slavery; his plain life had favored his love of truth. He had not been taught that treason and perjury were the proof of honor and honesty. His moral training was against his saying one thing when he meant another. The trust that Abraham Lincoln had in himself and in the people was surprising and grand, but it was also enlightened and well founded. He knew the American people better than they knew themselves, and his truth was based upon this knowledge.

Fellow-citizens, the fourteenth day of April, 1865, of which this is the eleventh anniversary, is now and will ever remain a memorable day in the annals of this Republic. It was on the evening of this day, while a fierce and sanguinary rebellion was in the last stages of its desolating power; while its armies were broken and scattered before the invincible armies of Grant and Sherman; while a great nation, torn and rent by war, was already beginning to raise to the skies loud anthems of joy at the dawn of peace, it was startled, amazed, and overwhelmed by the crowning crime of slavery — the assassination of Abraham Lincoln. It was a new crime, a pure act of malice. No purpose of the rebellion was to be served by it. It was the simple gratification of a hell-black spirit of revenge. But it has done good after all. It has filled the country with a deeper abhorrence of slavery and a deeper love for the great liberator.

Had Abraham Lincoln died from any of the numerous ills to which flesh is heir; had he reached that good old age of which his vigorous constitution and his temperate habits gave promise; had he been permitted to see the end of his great work; had the solemn curtain of death come down but gradually — we should still have been smitten with a heavy grief, and treasured his name lovingly. But dying as he did die, by the red hand of violence, killed, assassinated, taken off without warning, not because of personal hate — for no man who knew Abraham Lincoln could hate him — but because of his fidelity to union and liberty, he is doubly dear to us, and his memory will be precious forever.

Fellow-citizens, I end, as I began, with congratulations. We have done a good work for our race today. In doing honor to the memory of our friend and liberator, we have been doing highest honors to ourselves and those who come after us; we have been fastening ourselves to a name and fame imperishable and immortal; we have also been defending ourselves from a blighting scandal. When now it shall be said that the colored man is soulless, that he has no appreciation of benefits or benefactors; when the foul reproach of ingratitude is hurled at us, and it is attempted to scourge us beyond the range of human brotherhood, we may calmly point to the monument we have this day erected to the memory of Abraham Lincoln.

GLOSSARY

Arlington: reference to the military cemetery

colored people: a common term (not derogatory) for African Americans at the time

guilty masters: reference to the fact that some states seceded prior to Lincoln's inauguration as president

Document Analysis

Frederick Douglass understood the dual purpose of the celebration which was taking place in Lincoln Park. The statue was the Freedmen's Memorial Monument to Abraham Lincoln, and, for Douglass, the celebration lifted up the accomplishments of Lincoln and of freedmen. He was able to eloquently depict Lincoln both as a man of his time and as one who had a vision which went beyond many others. Douglass asserted creating the monument demonstrated that former slaves were the equals of whites.

Depicting the setting in terms of an ancient temple, Douglass set forth a picture of all the people gathered to celebrate the civic religion of the United States. He stated that just "twenty years ago" riot police would have broken up such a gathering, rather than the president and civic leaders joining with the freedmen to remember what had been accomplished during Lincoln's administration. However, Douglass was not blind to the problems of the last few decades or the ones which continued at that time. He believed the day was important because it demonstrated to all types of people, nationwide, that the African-American community was the equal of all others and that their aspirations were the same as those of whites.

As regarded Lincoln, Douglass thought the best way to praise him and to illustrate his accomplishments was to follow the ideal that one should always speak the truth. Thus, Douglass asserted that Lincoln was a "white man" and "devoted to the welfare of white men." Douglass understood that, unlike many, Lincoln opposed slavery, even though this was not the focus to his actions in the first months of the Civil War. As Douglass recalled, Lincoln wanted to preserve the Union and was willing to let slavery continue in the South to do so. As president, Lincoln was not a radical. However, Douglass pointed out, it was this very moderate stance which allowed Lincoln to accomplish so much. Douglass stated that "sharing prejudices with his fellow white-countrymen," allowed Lincoln not only to relate to them, but allowed them to support his actions which ultimately led to the freeing of the slaves. Lincoln moved slower than the staunch abolitionists would have liked, but he was able to push the issue forward in such a way that slavery ended far sooner than might otherwise have been the case. Douglass praised Lincoln for this ability and his accomplishments, even while wishing more could have been done. Douglass understood that while Lincoln's violent death kept him from accomplishing all he intended, it did make certain that pro-slavery forces could never again gain widespread support.

Essential Themes

Frederick Douglass' speech was a major step forward for African Americans, as was the Freedmen's Memorial Monument. Being invited to be the principal speaker, rather than President Grant, demonstrated Douglass' stature. Just as he seemed to be the right man for the occasion, one of the main points of his speech was that Lincoln was the right man to lead the United States during the crisis which resulted in the Civil War. To Douglass, Lincoln was a man of the people. This meant that he held some of the prejudices of his time, but it also meant that Lincoln could relate to the struggles of many Americans. Even though from Douglass' perspective, Lincoln was not perfect, Douglass recognized that Lincoln held strong beliefs about the evils of slavery and was slowly working toward its eradication. For Douglass, being a man of one's time did not mean that one had to go along with all the current beliefs and not to push for changes which would improve the condition of people and society. In Lincoln, Douglass saw just such a man, who went beyond the norms of the day.

Though it seemed to be a slow pace of change, Douglass understood that in terms of governmental action, Lincoln was "swift" in pushing for the changes which freed the slaves. The changes which Douglass had witnessed in recent decades were monumental. Douglass understood that Lincoln had to make the preservation of the Union his top priority, and ending slavery second, in order to get the necessary support from the northern population. The fact that for the first few years of the war, the president offered reconciliation and slavery to the South, if it ended the war, was ultimately less important to Douglass than the fact that in the end Lincoln did free the slaves. The Emancipation Proclamation, which, in the statue, Lincoln holds in one hand, was, for Douglass, a brave act which could never be diminished. Because many saw the monument, with the freedman kneeling at the feet of Lincoln, as racist,

as do many today, its significance and that of Frederick Douglass' speech have often been overlooked. However, Douglass' speech was a brilliant exposition of the struggle for freedom and the vital role which Lincoln had played. Douglass' straightforward, yet lofty, approach in his speeches, has often been compared to speeches made by Martin Luther King Jr. in the 1960s.

Donald A. Watt, Ph.D

Bibliography and Additional Reading

Douglass, Frederick. *The Life and Times of Frederick Douglass.* [Copy of the, Boston: De Wolfe & Fiske Co., 1892, edition.] Mineola, New York: Dover Publications, 2003. Print.

Frederick Douglass Institute. University of Rochester: Frederick Douglass Project, Rochester, New York: Frederick Douglass Project. Web. 20 March 2014.

Inaugural Ceremonies of the Freedmen's Memorial Monument to Abraham Lincoln. Saint Louis: Levison & Blythe, Printers, Stationers and Blank Book Manufacturers, 1876. Digitized, San Francisco: Internet Archive, 2001. Web. 20 March 2014.

Myers, Peter C. "Frederick Douglass's America: Race, Justice, and the Promise of the Founding." Washington, D.C.: The Heritage Foundation, 2011. Web. 20 March 2014.

■ Ulysses S. Grant: Letter to Daniel H. Chamberlain

Date: July 26, 1876
Author: Ulysses S. Grant
Genre: letter

Summary Overview

As both president and army general, Ulysses S. Grant played a significant role in keeping the Union together, completely eradicating slavery, and making sure that blacks in America obtained and exercised equal rights despite the salience of white supremacists and vigilantes using violence for obstruction. Grant had predicted that slavery would collapse prior to the Civil War, and the Union victory and passage of the Thirteenth Amendment confirmed his prediction. Throughout the Reconstruction period immediately following the war, Grant served as president Andrew Johnson's general-in-chief where he constantly had to deal with the problem of white terrorism against former slaves. As president, the racial hostilities as well as violence heightened, but Grant was hesitant to provide federal intervention in the South because of party politics. A letter written to South Carolina Governor Daniel Chamberlain in response to the governor's report on an incident of racial violence highlights Grant's hesitance. He uses colorful and blunt rhetoric to call for all Americans to accept the end of slavery in order for the nation to progress forward.

Furthermore, Grant's letter conveys a feeling of resignation that racial tensions would continue to plague the South and prevent it from moving forward. The letter indicates a sense of frustration that its author had failed to obtain and protect equal rights for blacks throughout the nation despite the passage of several laws that granted blacks social and political rights. While blacks made some progress during Reconstruction, the rise of white terrorism scaled back those gains and rendered African Americans second-class citizens for decades to follow.

Defining Moment

At the beginning of the Civil War in 1861, Union Army General Ulysses S. Grant predicted the destruction of slavery because the toll of military action would render the institution unviable. Although he hesitated to attack the institution of slavery because doing so would exacerbate the resistance of white Southerners, Grant concluded in 1862 that the collapse of slavery was a crucial component of the Union's war effort. Furthermore, the enlistment of black soldiers after their emancipation in 1863 became vital to the Union's eventual victory. Even though Grant embraced black liberation, the preservation of the Union remained the sole indication of victory.

Shortly after the Civil War ended in 1865, President Abraham Lincoln was assassinated. Vice president Andrew Johnson took charge in quickly putting in place a Reconstruction plan known as Presidential Reconstruction. Johnson desperately tried to repair the nation by convincing the Southern states to rejoin the Union. He pardoned the Confederate war generals, but stipulated that white Southerners living in Confederate states take loyalty oaths to the Union. Unlike the majority of Congress members, Johnson showed little regard for the status of former slaves because he believed that white Southerners should control them. In December 1865, however, the Thirteenth Amendment was passed and made slavery illegal throughout the United States.

Tensions grew between U.S. Congress and Johnson because he vetoed legislation that enumerated certain rights to former slaves. As a result, Congress took control of Reconstruction in 1867. A Republican Congress redrew the South into five military districts and subjected them to martial law, which upset many white Southerners. They passed the Fourteenth Amendment to the U.S. Constitution, which granted citizenship the African Americans and ensured that they would be counted in the population for the representative purposes in the House of Representatives. New state constitutions were drawn up in the Southern states. In 1867, the Freedmen's Bureau, a bureau intended to help African Americans adjust to free life by helping them find jobs and a suitable place to live, strengthened in the South. The bureau not only helped African Americans find jobs and homes, it also established the first public schools funded by the government in the South. The literacy of African Americans became necessary in order for them assimilate and successfully transition from the status of slave to U.S. citizen. In 1868, Grant was elected president. The Fifteenth Amendment was needed to give vote to blacks in all states, which the Fourteenth Amendment had not sought to do. Ratified in 1870, the Fifteenth Amendment granted blacks in the Union the right to vote. As a result, massive rioting by whites throughout the country occurred.

Grant pleaded to the American public to accept the freedom of blacks and called for them to treat blacks as equals. However, the presence of white terror groups such as the Ku Klux Klan made Grant's pleas futile. The Klan and other vigilante groups targeted both whites and African American men and their families who belonged to the Republican Party as well as white and African American school teachers. They also attacked black landowners and other blacks who did not act in deference to whites. Mob violence and lynching served as effective tools to control black behavior as well as prevent them from exercising their rights as citizens. White supremacists systematically waged violence against Republicans and African Americans in order to persuade the North to return control of the South to the Democrats. Through such interactions with white Southerners, African Americans realized that their freedom despite emancipation would come after a long, arduous struggle.

Author Biography

Ulysses S. Grant was born on April 27, 1822 in Point Pleasant, Ohio, to Jesse Root Grant and Hannah Simpson Grant. As a child his parents expected him to fulfill all duties young men were expected to do such as collecting firewood, which developed his skills in dealing with horses. At the age of seventeen, a congressman nominated Grant for a position at the U.S. Military Academy at West Point, where he eventually attended. At West Point, although he did not excel in his academ-

ics, Grant developed a reputation as a dexterous and fearless horseman. He graduated in 1843 and remarked that leaving West Point was one of the best moments of his life; he intended to resign after serving out his minimum obligated term in the military. The army failed to notice how skilled he was with horses and instead commissioned him as a second lieutenant in an infantry division. Grant resigned from the army in 1854 but struggled for the subsequent seven years in various civilian jobs.

In 1861, Grant served as a military commander who eventually rose in the ranks to become a general in chief of the armies of the Union during the Civil War and helped collapse slavery and preserve the Union. As a general he was widely respected for his ability to remain calm and collected under fire as well as for his talent for improvising under difficult circumstances. He also knew how to properly interact with superior officers and understood both tactics in waging war and strategies used in order to win. He waged several successful military campaigns, including the capture of Vicksburg, Mississippi and its thirty thousand Confederate soldiers on the fourth of July in 1863 and his victory at Chattanooga in November that same year. Because of his success Grant was chosen to lead the military campaigns in 1864 in which he saw great success. Union military victories ultimately secured the reelection of President Abraham Lincoln.

Grant served as general in chief during Reconstruction where he sought to preserve justice for the nearly four million freed slaves in the South. He witnessed the severity of white terrorism against African Americans and their allies and sought to stop the racial violence. He supported extending suffrage to African Americans as a means of protecting themselves and becoming equal citizens in the nation. In 1868, Grant ran for president as a Republican in order to make sure that the Union would be preserved and to protect African Americans from becoming re-enslaved. As president, Grant ratified the Fifteenth Amendment which enfranchised African Americans. He initially favored using federal force to protect African Americans from white terrorism and halt white Southerners from staging coups against Republican state governments. While his policies were successful to an extent, a combination of factors such as apathy in the North and the dominance of Democrats in Southern states constrained what Grant could do to thwart white supremacy. Ultimately, by the end of his presidency in 1876 Grant was powerless to stop the recoiling from Reconstruction.

HISTORICAL DOCUMENT

Executive Mansion, Washington, D.C.
Governor Daniel Chamberlain

Dear Sir: I am in receipt of your letter of the 22d of July, and all the enclosures enumerated therein, giving an account of the late barbarous massacre at the town of Hamburg, S.C. The views which you express as to the duty you owe to your oath of office and to citizens to secure to all their civil rights, including the right to vote according to the dictates of their own consciences, and the further duty of the Executive of the nation to give all needful aid, when properly called on to do so, to enable you to ensure this inalienable right, I fully concur in. The scene at Hamburg, as cruel, blood-thirsty, wanton, unprovoked, and uncalled for, as it was, is only a repetition of the course which has been pursued in other Southern States within the last few years, notably in Mississippi and Louisiana. Mississippi is governed to-day by officials chosen through fraud and violence, such as would scarcely be accredited to savages, much less to a civilized and Christian people. How long these things are to continue, or what is to be the final remedy, the Great Ruler of the universe only knows; but I have an abiding faith that the remedy will come, and come speedily, and I earnestly hope that it will come peacefully. There has never been a desire on the part of the North to humiliate the South. Nothing is claimed for one State that is not fully accorded to all the others, unless it may be the right to kill negroes and Republicans without fear of punishment and without loss of caste or reputa-

tion. This has seemed to be a privilege claimed by a few States. I repeat again, that I fully agree with you as to the measure of your duties in the present emergency, and as to my duties. Go on—and let every Governor where the same dangers threaten the peace of his State go on—in the conscientious discharge of his duties to the humblest as well as the proudest citizen, and I will give every aid for which I can find law or constitutional power. A government that cannot give protection to life, property, and all guaranteed civil rights (in this country the greatest is an untrammeled ballot) to the citizen is, in so far, a failure, and every energy of the oppressed should be exerted, always within the law and by constitutional means, to regain lost privileges and protections. Too long denial of guaranteed rights is sure to lead to revolution—bloody revolution, where suffering must fall upon the innocent as well as the guilty.

Expressing the hope that the better judgment and co-operation of citizens of the State over which you have presided so ably may enable you to secure a fair trial and punishment of all offenders without distinction of race or color or previous condition of servitude, and without aid from the Federal Government but with the promise of such aid on the conditions named in the foregoing, I subscribe myself, very respectfully, your obedient servant,

U.S. Grant.

GLOSSARY

caste: social group

dictates: authoritative commands or orders

Daniel Chamberlain: Republican governor of South Carolina during Grant's presidency

Massacre at...Hamburg: a racially charged outbreak of violence in Hamburg, South Carolina, on the fourth of July in 1876

wanton: unjust, unprovoked

Document Analysis

In 1868, Republican presidential candidate Ulysses S. Grant, the renowned general who led the Union army to victory, was sworn into office. Although he lacked political experience, Grant took office in order to advocate for and preserve the rights of African Americans as equal citizens to their white counterparts. He pushed through the Fifteenth Amendment in order to extend suffrage for African Americans. However, segregation and discrimination against African Americans prevailed, and an age of violence and lynching commenced during Reconstruction and for decades to follow. These lynchings were motivated by racism and racial stereotypes that developed during the antebellum period. Such violence occurred outside the due process of law and, indeed, law enforcement officials themselves often participated in the atrocities. President Grant wrote this letter in response to a report of violence against Republicans written by Republican South Carolina Governor Daniel H. Chamberlain in his state. His language indicates a level of frustration that the government has failed because it cannot protect its own citizens as well as a sense of resignation that he cannot stop the white supremacists from taking control over the South through the use of violence. This personal and collective discipline waged by white Southerners through the use of unlawful and heinous violence functioned to control the political and economic position of African Americans and to protect whites from the danger African Americans posed according to the prevailing stereotypes of the period.

On July 4, 1876, a black militia went to Hamburg, South Carolina, to celebrate the nation's centennial. South Carolina was the center of the South's Reconstruction as well as the burgeoning black power movement, such as it was. A white farmer came to the celebration and demanded that the militia move to the side of the road so that his carriage could pass through. The militia conceded, but on the following day the farmer told a state justice that the head of that militia be arrested because he got in the way of his road. The next day the militia returned to Hamburg but encountered a large group of white men who captured the twenty-five militia members, murdering five of them immediately. African American shops and homes were also destroyed. This massacre widened the chasm between the Republican governor and Democrats in the state, paving the way for a Democratic challenger to oust the incumbent in the election in November. At the national level, Democrats considered the event a prime example of why Republicans should not control the South; such violent events occurred in states such as South Carolina, Louisiana, and Mississippi because Republicans were in charge. The South wanted autonomy rather than the federal government interfering in their affairs. The prevalence of such violence led Northerners to feel more apathetic about maintaining Reconstruction efforts. As a result, Grant showed a reluctance to authorize federal intervention in the South because he knew that Northerners grew weary of reports of violence and desired peace if that meant giving Democrats back control of the South. He assured the governor that the North did not intend to humiliate the South and thus he would not send troops to intervene in state affairs.

Grant expresses that he took issue with the senseless murder of African Americans in the South and asserts that no citizens have the right to kill them with impunity. The age of lynchings began in the post-Civil War era and reveals underlying stereotypes and myths perpetuated about African Americans to ensure that they did not enjoy their newfound freedom or become part of the U.S. polity. The victims of lynchings endured horrific violence such as being hung, dragged by a wagon, or having parts of their body disfigured or dismembered. The perpetrators engaged in such acts with impunity, as local and state courts did relatively little to pursue or punish them because of the prevailing idea that African Americans were somehow less than fully human. Lynchings were often big public affairs with thousands of white men, women, and children observing, indicating that lynching functioned as a quasi-legal means to contain and discipline blacks as well as to consolidate a dominant concept of "whiteness" that crossed gender, class, and generational lines. Such violence signaled the growing chasm between the Democrats and Republicans as a result of Reconstruction and the fact that Southern Democrats would not accept African Americans as equal citizens.

Despite these salient stereotypes, Grant conveys a hope that he can appeal to the greater sense of the American people to accept the outcome of the Civil War and recognize African Americans as equal citizens. Furthermore, he views white supremacists as the violent, dangerous, and subhuman caste, thereby subverting the prevailing stereotypes of black men and white men. Grant's language suggests that he does not want to intervene in Southern affairs but hopes that Southerners will move forward and adopt a progressive attitude rather then hold on to antebellum attitudes and ideas about African Americans. His frustrations are further evident when he appeals to "the Great Ruler of the universe" to produce the "final remedy" for fixing the inhumane treatment of African Americans in the South. Grant's tone indicates that he was dubious over whether Americans were ready for African Americans to be treated as equal citizens under the law; while the Union proved victorious in the Civil War and reconsolidated the nation and outlawed slavery, the meaning of freedom for American citizens was still unclear. Grant laments the inability of the government to protect the rights and lives of its own citizens. His lamentations reveal his lack of experience in American politics especially with regards to African Americans and race relations.

The language Grant uses to describe the massacre and its perpetrators invokes the salient stereotypes of African Americans in public discourse in order to depict the perpetrators and fellow white Southerners as embodying the worst of those they claim to fear. His depiction of Southern Democratic politicians as "savages" and uncivilized and unchristian implies that they should not be granted any political clout and do not deserve any legal authority because it is they who pose a threat to the well-being of postwar American society. By doing so, Grant subverts the image of the African American as a dangerous, subhuman savage and rather argues that the white supremacists themselves are subhuman and present a danger to American society and the ideals it represents. Although he uses vivid language that conveys his frustration and anger over the current condition of race relations in the South, his tone is subdued because he has very little control over what is happening at the local level in the southern United States. He addresses the governor in very deferential language, calling himself an "obedient servant" in order to appease him as well as encourage him to protect the rights of African American citizens in his state. While such language offers support to the Republican efforts in the Southern states, it becomes clear that Grant knows that the Democrats would prevail through their tactics of unapologetic violence and murder.

Grant concludes his letter with a resigned tone and expresses unrealistic hopes that white Southerners would accept African Americans as equal citizens. His hope to "secure a fair trial and punishment of all offenders without distinction of race" highlights his advocacy for African American rights and desire to minimize lawlessness in the South. The resignation evident in Grant's letter was merited. After his presidency, Reconstruction came to an end and Democrats dominated politics--and no subsequent president during the nineteenth and early twentieth century would advocate for African Americans as much as Grant did.

Essential Themes

Although scholars believe Grant weakened the office of the presidency, it is undisputed that he advocated for African American rights more than any other U.S. president did in the nineteenth century. He intended his presidency to serve all American citizens and tried to avoid the party politics that had so plagued American society. He greatly wanted to extend and protect African Americans' right to vote through the ratification of the Fifteenth Amendment. Unfortunately, the country turned its back on African Americans and opened itself instead to discrimination and segregation.

Grant's letter to the governor clearly conveys a strong sense of resignation over the fact that he could not protect blacks from white terrorism and a sense of frustration about blacks not being treated as equal citizens. He felt that a government that could not protect the rights of its own citizens was a failure. This sentiment reflects the dark reality that throughout American history, the standard for fitness of U.S. citizenship was related to one's race: one must be white to be considered fit for citizenship. The ideal citizen according to conventional republican ideology possessed rationality and self-possession; however, historically African Americans were not self-possessed because the institution of slavery rendered them unfit to rule themselves. Thus, racial assumptions are ingrained in the republican ideology on which the United States was founded and suggests that a link between race and citizenship has existed since the nation's inception. Even after full citizenship was extended to blacks with the Fourteenth Amendment in 1868, minority groups outside of the black-white paradigm sued courts for citizenship by attempting to prove their whiteness and disproving their blackness, given the historical disadvantages that the concept of blackness has for achieving full political status in the United States. These cases implicate the sad reality of the noncitizenship of blackness and the birth of the alien citizen. Thus, as Grant laments in his letter, even though blacks legally acquired full citizenship, they never received the protections and guarantees of full citizenship because of entrenched racism within U.S. politics and society.

In addition, institutionalized segregation in the form

of the Jim Crow laws that were passed at the end of the nineteenth and early twentieth century further crippled the black population by forcing them to live in low-cost housing and by preventing them from access to social services provided by the state. The Supreme Court case decision known as *Plessy vs. Ferguson* in 1896 established the principle of "separate but equal" and institutionalized Jim Crow laws in the South. Segregation became a reality in the South and would define race relations there well into the twentieth century. The political status of blacks as full, legal citizens did little to alter the perceived inferiority of blacks in the eyes of the white population; furthermore, they were still viewed as a racial Other that threatened to destroy the purity of the white race well into the twentieth century. Grant's doubts that Americans were not prepared to make equality under the law for all citizens a reality thus became confirmed by the establishment of Jim Crow.

Madeline Weissman, MA.

Bibliography and Additional Reading

"Black Codes." *History.com.* A&E Television Networks, n.d. Web. 04 Oct. 2013.

Foner, Eric. *Reconstruction: America's Unfinished Revolution, 1863-1877.* New York: Harper & Row, 1988. Print.

Jacobson, Matthew Frye. *Whiteness of a Different Color: European Immigrants and the Alchemy of Race* . Cambridge, Massachusetts: Harvard UP, 1999. Print.

Kelley, Robin D. G., and Earl Lewis. *To Make Our World Anew: A History of African Americans.*

McPherson, James M. *Ordeal by Fire: the Civil War and Reconstruction.* Boston:

McGraw-Hill, 2001. Print.

McFeely, William S. *Grant: A Biography.* New York: Norton, 1981. Print.

Oxford: Oxford UP, 2000. Print.

Perret, Geoffrey. *Ulysses S. Grant: Soldier & President.* New York: Random House, 1997. Print.

Simpson Brooks D. *Let Us Have Peace: Ulysses S. Grant the Politics of War & Reconstruction, 1861-1868.* Chapel Hill: U of North Carolina P, 1991. Print.

Smith, Page. *Trial by Fire: A People's History of the Civil War and Reconstruction.* New York:

McGraw-Hill, 1982. Print.

Ngai, Mae M. *Impossible Subjects: Illegal Aliens and the Making of Modern America.* Princeton,

New Jersey: Princeton UP, 2004. Print.

Randall, J. G., and David Herbert Donald. *The Civil War and Reconstruction.* Boston: Heath, 1961. Print.

■ Sharecropping Contract

Date: January 18, 1879
Author: Solid South
Genre: contract

Summary Overview

The period after the Civil War was a time of uncertainty and chaos for both Southern landowners and former slaves. Agricultural land was devastated by the effects of neglect and war damage, and the new terms of labor in a racially-charged environment were uncertain. Former slaves believed initially that they would be granted land as part of their emancipation, but by the end of the 1860s, it was clear that this would not happen. For poor blacks and landless whites with only farming experience, the options were few. Landowners devised systems of land rental that returned many former slaves to a position of complete dependence. Sharecropping contracts, such as the one between the company Solid South and John Dawson, set terms on things, like equipment use and seed prices, which ensured that the tenant would always be in debt to the landowner and could be removed from the land at any time. It was a very precarious existence.

Defining Moment

By 1880, over half of black farmers in the deep South worked on farms that operated on a sharecropping system. When the Civil War ended with no widespread land grants to freed slaves, landowners who once owned slaves were left with land that was difficult to work with free-market labor. At the same time, many former slaves were left with very limited skills, except for agricultural work, but were unable to secure farmland. The system of sharecropping was a way for poor people, who owned very little, to be able to have access to equipment, seed, and a piece of farmland. During Reconstruction, the Freedman's Bureau saw the need for former slaves to be able to rent parcels of land on plantations, actively encouraged the sharecropping system, and became nominally responsible for the enforcement of freedmen's contracts. One Freedman's Bureau official, M. R. Delany, devised a model sharecropping contract that was equitable and spelled out the duties and obligations of the landowner as well as the tenant. Unfortunately, the Freedman's Bureau did not see the need to institute standardized contracts and, thus, dismissed Delany's concept in favor of allowing landowners and sharecroppers to write their own.

When this contract was written in 1879, sharecropping contracts gave the tenant no rights and exclusively protected the interest of the landowner. Sharecroppers were obligated by the terms of their contract to rent nearly everything, including housing, seed, equipment, and draft animals. They did not control the crops that were grown, how they were sold, or the price paid for those crops. They were often bound to plots of land insufficient to raise the quantity of crops that would be necessary just to pay the rent on the land and equipment, so they were kept desperately poor and in mounting debt.

Many sharecroppers rented land that they or their families had once worked as slaves, and they were extremely vulnerable to exploitation by landowners, who resented their new status as freedmen. Many sharecroppers were illiterate, meaning that they were easily cheated, as the landowner was the keeper of accounts and records, and the farmer simply had to pay what he was told was due. There was no recourse if theft or fraud occurred, or if the terms of the contract were violated, since the contract stipulated that a sharecropper could be removed from the land for any reason. The sharecropper was also obligated to pay for the upkeep and improvement of land that could be taken away at any time.

Most sharecroppers lived from harvest to harvest, going into debt each year and then hoping that the crop would be sufficient to settle the debt when it was sold. If the crop failed for any reason, the farmer still owed the full amount of the debt, which could be carried over from year to year at exorbitant interest rates set by the landowner and merchant, who were often the same entity. Even in successful years, these farmers often ended up with little to nothing after their debts were paid. Were the sharecropper to fall sick or become injured even temporarily, additional fees could be levied for missed work. If sharecroppers left the land while in debt, they could be jailed, but a landowner could remove tenants at any time and for any reason, including age, injury, or illness.

Author Biography

Little is known about John Dawson other than his lease of fifteen acres of Waterford Plantation in Madison Par-ish, Louisiana. As was the case with many sharecroppers, he could neither read nor write, as evidenced by his mark on the contract rather than a signature. The author of the contract is a company called Solid South, which is an intriguing choice of name. Solid South is the nickname for the results of the Compromise of 1877, which effectively ended Reconstruction by removing federal troops from the former Confederacy. Without the monitoring of the federal government, discriminatory practices were put in place to ensure that Democratic candidates would win elections, establishing the Democratic "Solid South" and ensuring that laws could be passed that effectively disenfranchised black people and stripped them of their rights. It was in such an environment that contracts, such as this one, which was clearly exploitative and discriminatory, were allowed to stand.

HISTORICAL DOCUMENT

Agreement between Landlord and Sharecropper

This agreement, made and entered into this 18th day of January, 1879, between Solid South, of the first part, and John Dawson, of the second part.

Witnesseth: that said party of the first part for and in consideration of eighty-eight pounds of lint cotton to be paid to the said Solid South, as hereinafter expressed, hereby leases to said Dawson, for the year A. D. 1879, a certain tract of land, the boundaries of which are well understood by the parties hereto, and the area of which the said parties hereby agree to be fifteen acres, being a portion of the Waterford Plantation, in Madison Parish, Louisiana.

The said Dawson is to cultivate said land in a proper manner, under the general superintendence of the said Solid South, or his agent or manager, and is to surrender to said lessor peaceable possession of said leased premises at the expiration of this lease without notice to quit. All ditches, turn-rows, bridges, fences, etc. on said land shall be kept in proper condition by said Dawson, or at his expense. All cotton-seed raised on said land shall be held for the exclusive use of said plantation, and no goods of any kind shall be kept for sale on any said land unless by consent of said lessor.

If said Solid South shall furnish to said lessee money or necessary supplies, or stock, or material, or either or all of them during this lease, to enable him to make a crop, the amount of said advances, not to exceed $475 (of which $315 has been furnished in two mules, plows, etc.), the said Dawson agrees to pay for the supplies and advances so furnished, out of the first cotton picked and saved on said land from the crop of said year, and to deliver said cotton of the first picking to the said Solid South, in the gin on said plantation, to be by him bought or shipped at his option, the proceeds to be applied to payment of said supply bill, which is to be fully paid on or before the 1st day of January, 1880.

After payment of said supply bill, the said lessee is to pay to said lessor, in the gin of said plantation, the rent cotton herein before stipulated, said rent to be fully paid on or before the 1st day of January, 1880. All cotton raised on said land is to be ginned on the gin of said lessor, on said plantation, and said lessee is to pay $4 per bale for ginning same.

To secure payment of said rent and supply bill, the said Dawson grants unto said Solid South a special privilege and right of pledge on all the products raised on said land, and on all his stock, farming implements, and personal property, and hereby waives in favor of said Solid South the benefit of any and all homestead laws and exemption laws now in force, or which may be in force, in Louisiana, and agrees that all his property shall be seized and sold to pay said rent and supply bill in default of payment thereof as herein agreed. Any violation of this contract shall render the lease void

[signed]

Solid South

John Dawson

X (his mark)

GLOSSARY

first part, second part: legal parties; persons or entities party to a contract

gin: cotton gin

said party: the party named previously

Document Analysis

This document lays out the terms under which an illiterate man may rent a parcel of land on a former slave plantation in Louisiana. Its primary goal was to control every aspect of John Dawson's business, from the rent he paid to the seed he bought, and to ensure that he remained in the debt of the landowner, Solid South. Dawson had no control over the land he was contracted to farm, and his rent of eighty-eight pounds of lint cotton (deseeded and cleaned) was just the beginning of his obligations to Solid South. Dawson's relationship to the landowner is spelled out clearly in the second paragraph: "All cotton-seed raised on said land shall be held for the exclusive use of said plantation, and no goods of any kind shall be kept for sale on any said land unless by consent of said lessor." In other words, no matter how much cotton John Dawson managed to raise, it could only be sold to the landowner, at his prices, and seed could also only be bought from him. The cotton could only be processed at the cotton gin owned by the landlord at the sharecropper's expense. It was a closed system.

In addition to owning the land and any cotton grown on it, Solid South also sold or rented tools, equipment, draft animals (in this case, a pair of mules), and housing. John Dawson was under obligation to pay first for the cleaning and processing of his cotton (he needed to pay his rent with cleaned cotton, so this was not optional); but since the payment of any debts and his rent were to come out of his crop before he was allowed to sell any (to the plantation, on their terms), there was no way to avoid significant debt. The eighty-eight pounds of cotton that Dawson was to pay in rent would cost him an additional four dollars per bale to clean before he made a penny from any of his other cotton.

Everything that John Dawson owned was surety on his rent: "Dawson grants unto said Solid South a special privilege and right of pledge on all the products raised on said land, and on all his stock, farming implements, and personal property." Under Louisiana law, he was also liable to imprisonment if he failed to pay the debt, but only after "all his property shall be seized and sold to pay said rent and supply bill." John Dawson signed away any rights to laws protecting him from such exploitation in this contract as well. Since he was in perpetual debt, Dawson's land, tools, equipment, and all of his other property were liable to be taken from him at any time and without notice.

Essential Themes

This contract highlights the exploitative and discriminatory environment that existed for landless freedmen after the Civil War and the end of Reconstruction. John Dawson agreed to a relationship with a landowner that was, in many ways, a form of continued slavery. Sharecroppers were tied to the land and its owner by debt and obligation, while the landowner did not have to worry about paying wages or providing living quarters. In the end, the owner of the land had no obligation to the sharecroppers and could remove them from the property they and their families had worked.

There was no real ability to go outside this system. The legal system did not offer effective recourse for sharecroppers, as they had signed contracts that were binding, and the courts were often biased in favor of white landowners. Moreover, in some states, a black claimant could be penalized with fines or jail time if found to have brought "false suit" against a white landowner. From seed to finished product, nearly every aspect of sharecropping was controlled by the landowner-merchant, who could ensure that the families who worked their land could never leave it and could not own it either.

—*Bethany Groff, MA*

Bibliography and Additional Reading

Alexander, Danielle. "Forty Acres and a Mule: *The Ruined Hope of Reconstruction." Humanities* 25.1 (2004): 26–29. Print.

Du Bois, W. E. B. *Black Reconstruction in America, 1860–1880.* New York: Simon, 1935. Print.

Feldman, Glenn. *The Irony of the Solid South: Democrats, Republicans, and Race, 1865–1944.* Tuscaloosa: U of Alabama P, 2013. Print.

Foner, Eric. *Reconstruction: America's Unfinished Revolution, 1863–1877.* New York: HarperCollins, 2002. Print.

Ransom, Roger L. and Richard Sutch. *One Kind of Freedom: The Economic Consequences of Emancipation.* 2nd ed. Cambridge: Cambridge UP, 2001. Print.

Sterling, Dorothy, ed. *The Trouble They Seen: The Story of Reconstruction in the Words of African Americans.* New York: Da Capo, 1994. Print.

APPENDIXES

Chronological List

Web Resources

civilwar.org

The Civil War Trust: Saving America's Civil War Battlefields site is dedicated to preserving battlefields of the American Civil War for educational and historical value. More than 34,000 acres of battlefield land at 110 battlefields in 20 states have been preserved. The online resource is rich in documentation and multi-media on the major battles of the war.

civil-war.net

Provides a wide selection of primary source documents and images of the Civil War. The website is also provides detailed information on the armies serving from each of the north and south states.

housedivided.dickinson.edu

House Divided: The Civil War Research Engine is a resource for primary source documents and images of the Civil War. House Divided is dedicated to building a continually growing collection through several digitization projects at Dickinson College.

americanjourneys.org

Chronicles American exploration through over 18,000 pages of firsthand accounts of North American exploration. Visitors can read through the views of various historical figures from America's lively and momentous past.

docsouth.unc.edu

A digital publishing project that reflects the southern perspective of American history and culture. It offers a wide collection of titles that students, teachers, and researchers of all levels can utilize.

teachinghistory.org

A project funded by the US Department of Education that aims to assist teachers of all levels to augment their efforts in teaching American history. It strives to amplify student achievement through improving the knowledge of teachers.

ushistory.org/us

Contains an outline that details the entire record of American history. This resource offers historical insight and stories that demonstrate what truly an American truly is from a historical perspective.

teachingamericanhistory.org

Allows visitors to learn more about American history through original source documents detailing the broad spectrum of American history. The site contains document libraries, audio lectures, lesson plans, and more.

history.com/topics/american-history

Tells the story of America through topics of interest such as the Declaration of Independence, major wars, and notable Americans.

loc.gov/topics/americanhistory.php

Covers the various eras and ages of American history in detail, including resources such as readings, interactive activities, multimedia, and more.

si.edu/encyclopedia_si/nmah/timeline.htm

Details the course of American history chronologically. Important dates and significant events link to other pages within the Smithsonian site that offer more details.

docsteach.org

Centered on teaching through the use of primary source documents. This online resource provides activities for many different historical eras dating to the American Revolution as well as thousands of primary source documents.

smithsonianeducation.org

An online resource for educators, families, and students offering lesson plans, interactive activities, and more.

edsitement.neh.gov

An online resource for teachers, students, and parents seeking to further their understanding of the humanities. This site offers lesson plan searches, student resources, and interactive activities.

digitalhistory.uh.edu

Offers an online history textbook, Hypertext History, which chronicles the story of America, along with interactive timelines. This online source also contains handouts, lesson plans, e-lectures, movies, games, biographies, glossaries, maps, music, and much more.

havefunwithhistory.com

An online, interactive resource for students, teachers, and anybody who has an interest in American history.

history.org

Offers an array of resources for visitors, including information on people, places, and culture. There are also resources for teachers including e-newsletters and electronic field trips.

gilderlehrman.org

Offers many options in relation to the history of America. The History by Era section provides detailed explanations of specific time periods while the primary sources present firsthand accounts from a historical perspective.

masshist.org

Home to millions of rare and distinctive documents that are crucial to the course of American history, many of them being irreplaceable national treasures. Online collections, exclusive publications, and teacher resources are included.

historymatters.gmu.edu

An online resource from George Mason University that provides links, teaching materials, primary documents, and guides for evaluating historical records.

Bibliography

"Address of a Convention of Negroes Held in Alexandria, Virginia August 1865." *American History from Revolution to Reconstruction and Beyond*. University of Groningen, 2012. Web. 29 Mar. 2014.

Adeleke, Tunde. *Without Regard to Race: the Other Martin Robison Delany*. Jackson: UP of Mississippi, 2003. Print.

Alexander, Danielle. "Forty Acres and a Mule: The Ruined Hope of Reconstruction." Humanities 25.1 (2004): 26–29. Print.

Alexander, Thomas B. *Political Reconstruction in Tennessee*. Nashville: Vanderbilt UP, 1950. Print.

"America's Reconstruction: People and Politics After the Civil War." *Digital History*. Eds. S. Mintz & S. McNeil. University of Houston, 2013. Web. 6 Apr. 2014.

Bauer, Craig A. *A Leader among Peers: The Life and Times of Duncan Farrar Kenner*. Lafayette: U of Southwestern Louisiana, 1993. Print.

Beckel, Deborah. *Radical Reform: Interracial Politics in Post-Emancipation North Carolina*. Charlottesville: U of Virginia P, 2011. Print.

Bell, Malcolm, Jr. *Major Butler's Legacy: Five Generations of a Slaveholding Family*. Athens: U of Georgia P, 1987. Print.

Benedict, Michael Less. "Preserving the Constitution: The Conservative Basis of Radical Reconstruction." *Journal of American History* 61.1 (1974): 65–90. Print.

Bergeron, Paul H., Stephen V. Ash, and Jeanette Keith. *Tennesseans and Their History*. Knoxville: U of Tennessee P, 1999. Print.

Bergesen, Albert, "Nation-Building and Constitutional Amendments: The Role of the Thirteenth, Fourteenth, and Fifteenth Amendments in the Legal Reconstitution of the American Polity Following the Civil War." *Pacific Sociological Review* 24.1 (1981): 3–15. Print.

Berry, Stephen W. "Butler Family." *New Georgia Encyclopedia*. Georgia Humanities Council and the University of Georgia Press, 16 Dec. 2013. Web. 29 Jan. 2014.

"Black Americans in Congress." *History, Art & Archives*. US House of Representatives, n.d. Web. 8 Jan. 2014.

"Black Codes." *History.com*. A&E Television Networks, n.d. Web. 04 Oct. 2013.

"Black History, American History." *The Atlantic*. The Atlantic Monthly, 12 Feb. 1997. Web. 9 Jan. 2014.

"Black Legislators: Primary Sources." *American Experience: Reconstruction, The Second Civil War*. PBS Online/WGBH, 12 Dec. 2003. Web. 19 Jan. 2014.

Blight, David W. "Frederick Douglass, 1818–1895." *Documenting the American South*. U of North Carolina at Chapel Hill, 2004. Web. 9 Jan. 2014.

Blight, David W. *Frederick Douglass' Civil War: Keeping Faith in Jubilee*. Baton Rouge: Louisiana State UP, 1989. Print.

Blight, David W. *Race and Reunion: The Civil War in American Memory*. Cambridge: Harvard UP, 2001. Print.

Bradley, Mark L. *Bluecoats and Tar Heels: Soldiers and Civilians in Reconstruction North Carolina*. Lexington: UP of Kentucky, 2009. Print.

Brodie, Fawn. *Thaddeus Stevens: Scourge of the South*. New York: Norton, 1959. Print.

Brown, William Wells. *The Negro in the American Rebellion: His Heroism and His Fidelity*. Boston: Lee, 1867. Print.

"Bruce, Blanche Kelso." *US House of Representatives: History, Art & Archives*. US House of Representatives, Office of the Historian, n.d. Web. 09 Apr. 2014.

Bryant, James K. *The 36th Infantry United States Colored Troops in the Civil War: A History and Roster*. Jefferson, NC: McFarland, 2012. Print.

Bryant, Jonathan M. "Ku Klux Klan in the Reconstruction Era." *New Georgia Encyclopedia*. Georgia Humanities Council, 9 May 2013. Web. 22 Jan. 2014.

Bryant, Jonathan M. "The Freedman's Struggle for Power in Greene County, Georgia, 1865–1874" *Georgia in Black and White: Explorations in Race Relations of a Southern State, 1865–1950*. Ed. John C. Inscoe. Athens, GA: University of Georgia Press, 2009. Print.

Budiansky, Stephen. *The Bloody Shirt: Terror after Appomattox*. New York: Viking, 2008. Print.

Bullard, Sara. *The Ku Klux Klan: A History of Racism and Violence*. 4th ed. Montgomery: Klanwatch Project of the Southern Poverty Law Center, 1991. Print.

Butchart, Ronald E. "Edmonia G. and Caroline V. Highgate: Black Teachers, Freed Slaves, and the Betrayal of Black Hearts." *Portraits of African American Life Since 1865*. Ed. Nina Mjagkij. Wilmington:

Scholarly Resources, 2003. Print.

Butchart, Ronald E. *Northern Schools, Southern Blacks, and Reconstruction: Freedmen's Education, 1862–1875.* Westport: Greenwood, 1980. Print.

Butchart, Ronald E. *Schooling the Freed People: Teaching, Learning, and the Struggle for Black Freedom, 1861–1876.* Chapel Hill: U of North Carolina P, 2010. Print.

Cannon, Clarence. *Cannon's precedents of the House of Representatives of the United States.* Washington, DC: GPO, 1945. Print.

"Carl Schurz, German American." *Watertown History.* Watertown Historical Society. 2013. Web. 28 Dec. 2013.

Carlson, Peter. "Abraham Lincoln Meets Frederick Douglass," *American History* 45 6 (Feb. 2011), p. 28-29. Print.

Cimbala, Paul and Randall Miller. *The Great Task Remaining before Us: Reconstruction as America's Continuing Civil War.* New York: Fordham UP, 2010. Print.

"Civil Rights Act of 1866." *A Century of Lawmaking for a New Nation: U.S. Congressional Documents and Debates, 1774–1875.* Washington, DC: Library of Congress, 2003. Web. 20 March 2014.

Clark Hine, Darlene and Kathleen Thompson. *A Shining Thread of Hope: The History of Black Women in America.* New York: Broadway Books, 1998. Print.

Clark-Lewis, Elizabeth. *First Freed: Washington, D.C. in the Emancipation Era.* Washington, DC: Howard UP, 2002. Print.

Click, Patricia C. *The Roanoke Island Freedmen's Colony.* 2001. Web. 17 Jan. 2014.

Click, Patricia C. *Time Full of Trial: The Roanoke Island Freedmen's Colony, 1862–1867.* Chapel Hill: U of North Carolina P, 2001. Print.

Cohen, William. *At Freedom's Edge: Black Mobility and the Southern White Quest for Racial Control, 1861–1915.* Baton Rouge: Louisiana State UP, 1991. Print.

"Constitution of the United States: Amendments 11–27." *National Archives.* National Archives and Records Administration. Web. 29 March, 2014.

Coulter, E. Merton. *William G. Brownlow: Fighting Parson of the Southern Highlands.* Chapel Hill: U of North Carolina P, 1937. Print.

Currie, David P. "The Reconstruction Congress." *University of Chicago Law Review* 75.1 (2008): 383–495. Print.

Curtis, Michael Kent. *No State Shall Abridge: The Fourteenth Amendment and the Bill of Rights.* Durham: Duke UP, 1986. Print.

Donald, David H. *Charles Sumner and the Coming of the Civil War.* 1960. Naperville: Sourcebooks, 2009. Print.

Donald, David Herbert, Jean Baker, and Michael Holt. *Civil War and Reconstruction.* New York: Norton, 2001. Print.

"Douglass Biography." *Frederick Douglass Papers Edition, Institute for American Thought.* Indiana University–Purdue University Indianapolis, n.d. Web. 9 Jan. 2014.

Douglass, Frederick. *The Life and Times of Frederick Douglass.* 1892. Mineola, New York: Dover Publications, 2003. Print.

Douglass, Frederick. *My Bondage and My Freedom.* New Haven: Yale UP, 2014. Print.

DuBois, W. E. B. *Black Reconstruction in America: Toward a History of the Part of Which Black Folk Played in the Attempt to Reconstruct Democracy in America, 1860–1880.* Rev. ed. New Brunswick, NH: Transaction, 2012. Print.

Duncan, Russell. "Rufus Bullock (1834–1907)." *New Georgia Encyclopedia.* Georgia Humanities Council and the U of Georgia P, 2004. Web. 28 Dec. 2013.

Duncan, Russell. *Entrepreneur for Equality: Governor Rufus Bullock, Commerce, and Race in Post–Civil War Georgia.* Athens: U of Georgia P, 1994. Print.

Elliott, Mark. *Color-Blind Justice: Albion Tourgée and the Quest for Racial Equality: From the Civil War to Plessy v. Ferguson.* New York: Oxford UP, 2006. Print.

Enoch, Jessica. *Refiguring Rhetorical Education: Women Teaching African American, Native American, and Chicano/a Students, 1865–1911.* Carbondale: Southern Illinois UP, 2008. Print.

Epps, Garrett. *Democracy Reborn: The Fourteenth Amendment and the Fight for Equal Rights in Post–Civil War America.* New York: Holt, 2006. Print.

Escott, Paul D., ed. *North Carolinians in the Era of the Civil War and Reconstruction.* Chapel Hill: U of North Carolina P, 2008. Print.

Exman, Eugene. *The House of Harper.* New York: Harper, 1967. Print.

Feldman, Glenn. *The Irony of the Solid South: Democrats, Republicans, and Race, 1865–1944.* Tuscaloosa: U of Alabama P, 2013. Print.

Ferrell, Claudine. *Reconstruction.* Westport, CT: Greenwood, 2003. Print.

Foner, Eric. *Forever Free: The Story of Emancipation*

and Reconstruction. New York: Knopf, 2005. Print.

Foner, Eric. *Reconstruction: America's Unfinished Revolution, 1863–1877*. New York: HarperCollins, 2011. Print.

Foner, Eric. "The Strange Career of the Reconstruction Amendments." *Yale Law Journal* 108.8 Symposium: Moments of Change: Transformation in American Constitutionalism (1999): 2003–9. Print.

Foner, Philip S. and Robert James Branham, eds. *Lift Every Voice: African American Oratory, 1787–1900*. Tuscaloosa: U of Alabama P, 1998. Print.

Foner, Philip S. *The Life and Writings of Frederick Douglass, IV, Reconstruction and After*. New York: International Publishers, 1955. Print.

"Frances Butler Leigh, 1838–1910." *Documenting the American South*. University Library, University of North Carolina at Chapel Hill, 2004. Web. 29 Jan. 2014.

Franklin, John Hope and Eric Foner. *Reconstruction after the Civil War*. Chicago: University of Chicago Press, 2013. Print.

Frederick Douglass Project. Frederick Douglass Institute, University of Rochester, Feb. 2001. Web. 20 Mar. 2014.

"The Freedmen's Colony on Roanoke Island." *Fort Raleigh, North Carolina: National Historic Site*. National Park Service, US Department of the Interior, n.d. Web. 1 Dec. 2013.

Garner, James Wilford. *Reconstruction in Mississippi*. New York: Macmillan, 1902. Print.

"Georgia Governor Rufus Brown Bullock." *National Governors Association*. National Governors Association. n.d. Web. 28 Dec. 2013.

Goldberg, Barry M. *The Unknown Architects of Civil Rights Thaddeus Stevens, Ulysses S. Grant, and Charles Sumner*. Los Angeles: Critical Minds Press, 2011. Print.

Goldman, Robert M. *Reconstruction and Black Suffrage: Losing the Vote in Reese and Cruikshank*. Kansas: UP of Kansas, 2001. Print.

Goldstone, Lawrence. *Inherently Unequal: The Betrayal of Equal Rights by the Supreme Court, 1865–1903*. New York: Walker, 2011. Print.

Gordon-Reed, Annette. *Andrew Johnson*. New York: Times Books, 2011. Print.

Graf, LeRoy and Ralph W. Haskins, eds. *The Papers of Andrew Johnson*. Knoxville: U of Tennessee P, 1967-1999. Print.

"Green, John Patterson." *The Encyclopedia of Cleveland History*. Case Western Reserve, 16 Jul. 1997. Web. 27 Jan. 2014.

Gross, Theodore L. *Albion W. Tourgée*. New York: Twayne, 1963. Print.

Hacker, Louis M. and Benjamin Kendrick. *The United States Since 1865*. Rev. ed. New York: F. S. Crofts & Co., 1937. Print.

Heiny, Louisa M. A. "Radical Abolitionist Influence on Federalism and the Fourteenth Amendment." *American Journal of Legal History* 49.2 (2007): 180–96. Print.

Hodges, Graham Russell, ed. *African American History and Culture*. New York: Garland, 1998. Print.

Hoffer, William James Hull. *Plessy v. Ferguson: Race and Inequality in Jim Crow America*. Lawrence: UP of Kansas, 2012. Print

Horn, Stanley F. *Invisible Empire: The Story of the Ku Klux Klan, 1866–1871*. Cos Cob: Edwards, 1969. Print.

Hume, Richard L. "Carpetbaggers in the Reconstruction South: A Group Portrait of Outside Whites and the 'Black and Tan' Constitutional Conventions." *Journal of American History* 64.2 (1977): 313–30. Print.

Inaugural Ceremonies of the Freedmen's Memorial Monument to Abraham Lincoln. 1876. Internet Archive, 2001. Web. 20 March 2014.

Jacobson, Matthew Frye. *Whiteness of a Different Color: European Immigrants and the Alchemy of Race*. Cambridge, Massachusetts: Harvard UP, 1999. Print.

Katz, William L. *The Invisible Empire: The Ku Klux Klan Impact on History*. Seattle: Open Hand, 1987. Print.

Keith, LeeAnna. *The Colfax Massacre: The Untold Story of Black Power, White Terror, and the Death of Reconstruction*. New York: Oxford UP, 2008. Print.

Kelley, Robin D. G., and Earl Lewis. *To Make Our World Anew: A History of African Americans*. Oxford: Oxford UP, 2000. Print.

Kendrick, Benjamin B. *The Journal of the Joint Committee of Fifteen on Reconstruction*. New York: Columbia University, 1914. Google eBooks. n.d. Web. 20 March 2014.

Kennedy, Robert C. "On This Day: The Freedmen's Bureau." *HarpWeek*. The New York Times Company, 2001. Web. 3 April 2014.

Kennedy, Stetson. *Jim Crow Guide to the U.S.A.: The Laws, Customs and Etiquette Governing the Conduct of Nonwhites and Other Minorities as Second-Class*

Citizens. 2nd ed. Tuscaloosa, AL: University of Alabama Press, 2011. Print.

Kolchin, Peter. *American Slavery: 1619-1877.* London: Penguin Books, 1995. Print.

Lane, Charles. *The Day Freedom Died: The Colfax Massacre, the Supreme Court, and the Betrayal of Reconstruction.* New York: Holt, 2008. Print.

Lawson, Elizabeth. *The Gentleman From Mississippi: Our First Negro Representative, Hiram R. Revels.* New York: The Author, 1960. Print.

Lee, Maurice S. *The Cambridge Companion to Frederick Douglass.* Cambridge: Cambridge UP, 2009. Print.

Leibowitz, Arnold H. *An Historical-Legal Analysis of the Impeachments of Presidents Andrew Johnson, Richard Nixon, and William Clinton: Why the Process Went Wrong.* Lewiston, NY: Edwin Mellen Press, 2012. Print.

Leigh, Frances Butler. *Ten Years on a Georgia Plantation since the War, 1866–1876.* Savannah: Beehive Press, 1992. Print.

Levine, Robert S. *Martin R. Delany: A Documentary Reader.* Chapel Hill: U of North Carolina P, 2003. Print.

Levine, Robert S. *Martin Delany, Frederick Douglass and the Politics of Representative Identity.* Chapel Hill: U of North Carolina P, 1997. Print.

Library of Congress. *American Memory: A Century of Lawmaking for a New Nation.* U.S. Congressional Documents and Debates, n.d. Web. 8 Apr. 2014.

"Lincoln and Douglass Shared Uncommon Bond." *NPR Books.* NPR, 16 Feb. 2009. Web. 9 Jan. 2014.

Lincoln Institute. "Frederick Douglass." Mr. Lincoln and Freedom [project]. Web.

Linder, Douglas O. "The Andrew Johnson Impeachment Trial, 1868." *Famous American Trials.* University of Missouri–Kansas City Law School, 1999. Web. 8 Apr. 2014.

Lowery, Charles and John Marszalek. *Encyclopedia of African-American Civil Rights.* New York: Greenwood, 1992. Print.

Lynch, Matthew, ed. *Legacies Lost.* Santa Barbara: Praeger, 2012. Print.

Mardock, Robert Winston. *The Reformers and the American Indians.* Columbia: University of Missouri Press, 1971. Print.

Martinez, J. Michael. *Carpetbaggers, Cavalry, and the Ku Klux Klan: Exposing the Invisible Empire during Reconstruction.* Lanham: Rowman, 2007. Print.

Mathews, John M. *Legislative and Judicial History of the Fifteenth Amendment.* New York: Da Capo, 1971. Print.

Matthews, John M. "Negro Republicans in the Reconstruction of Georgia." *The Politics of Freedom: African Americans and the Political Process During Reconstruction.* Ed. Donald G. Nieman. New York: Garland, 1994. 253–268. Print.

McCaleb, Edwin H. "Letter to T.P. Chandler." 1865. *Digital History.* Eds. S. Mintz & S. McNeil. University of Houston, 2012. Web. 29 Mar. 2014.

McConnell, John Preston. *Negroes and their Treatment in Virginia from 1865–1867.* Pulaski, VA: B.D.

McFeely, William S. *Frederick Douglass.* New York: Norton, 1995. Print.

McFeely, William S. *Grant: A Biography.* New York: Norton, 1981. Print. Oxford: Oxford UP, 2000. Print.

McIver, Stuart. "The Murder of a Scalawag." *American History Illustrated* 8 (1973): 12–18. Print.

McKitrick, Eric L. *Andrew Johnson and Reconstruction.* Chicago: U of Chicago P, 1960. Print.

McPherson, James M. *Battle Cry of Freedom: The Civil War Era.* New York: Ballantine, 1989. Print.

McPherson, James M. *Ordeal by Fire: the Civil War and Reconstruction.* Boston: McGraw-Hill, 2001. Print.

Meyer, Howard N. *The Amendment That Refused to Die: Equality and Justice Deferred: The History of the Fourteenth Amendment.* Lanham: Madison, 2000. Print.

Milner, Clyde A. and Floyd A. O'Neil, eds. *The Churchmen and the Western Indians, 1820–1920.* Norman: University of Oklahoma Press, 1985. Print.

Mjagkij, Nina. "Introduction." *Portraits of African American Life Since 1865.* Ed. Nina Mjagkij. Wilmington: Scholarly Resources, 2003. Print.

Morsman, Amy Feely. *The Big House after Slavery: Virginia Plantation Families and Their Postbellum Domestic Experiment.* Charlottesville: U of Virginia P, 2010.

Myers, Peter C. "Frederick Douglass's America: Race, Justice, and the Promise of the Founding." *First Principles Series Report #35 on Political Thought.* The Heritage Foundation, 11 Jan. 2011. Web. 20 March 2014.

Nelson, Michael, ed. *The Evolving Presidency: Landmark Documents, 1787–2010.* Washington, DC: CQ Press, 2012. Print.

Newkirk, Vann R. *Lynchings in North Carolina: A History, 1865–1941.* Jefferson: McFarland, 2009. Print.

Newton, Michael. *The Ku Klux Klan: History, Organization, Language, Influence and Activities of America's Most Notorious Secret Society.* Jefferson: McFarland, 2007. Print.

Ngai, Mae M. *Impossible Subjects: Illegal Aliens and the Making of Modern America.* Princeton, New Jersey: Princeton UP, 2004. Print.

Nye, Russel B. "Judge Tourgée and Reconstruction." Ohio *Archaeological and Historical Quarterly 50* (1941): 101–14. Print.

Oakes, James. *The Radical and the Republican: Frederick Douglass, Abraham Lincoln, and the Triumph of Antislavery Politics.* New York: Norton, 2008. Print.

Office of the Historian. "The Civil Rights Bill of 1866." *Historical Highlights.* Washington: United States House of Representatives, n.d. Web. 20 March 2014.

Olsen, Otto H. *Carpetbagger's Crusade: The Life of Albion Winegar Tourgée.* Baltimore: Johns Hopkins UP, 1965. Print.

Onion, Rebecca. "Threats from a Ghost: An 1868 Intimidation Letter Sent by the KKK." *Slate.* TheSlateGroup, 8 Apr. 2013. Web. 22 Jan. 2014.

Parsons, Elaine Frantz. "Midnight Rangers: Costume and Performance in the Reconstruction-Era Ku Klux Klan." *Journal of American History* 92.3 (2005): 811–36. Print.

Patler, Nicholas. "The Black 'Consummate Strategist': Blanche Kelso Bruce and the Skillful Use of Power in the Reconstruction and Post-Reconstruction Eras." *Before Obama: A Reappraisal of Black Reconstruction Era Politicians, Vol. 1: Legacies Lost.* Ed. Matthey Lynch. Santa Barbara, CA: Praeger, 2012. Print.

Patton, James Welch. *Unionism and Reconstruction in Tennessee 1860–1869.* Chapel Hill: U of North Carolina P, 1980. Print.

Perret, Geoffrey. *Ulysses S. Grant: Soldier & President.* New York: Random House, 1997. Print.

Perry, Michael J. *We the People: The Fourteenth Amendment and the Supreme Court.* New York: Oxford UP, 1999. Print.

Pohlmann, Marcus and Linda Whisenhunt. *Student's Guide to Landmark Congressional Laws on Civil Rights.* Westport: Greenwood, 2002. Print.

Potts, Kenneth. "Hiram Rhoades Revels." *Notable Black American Men.* Ed. Jessie Carney Smith. Farmington Hills: Gale, 1999. Print.

Prucha, Francis Paul. *The Great Father: The United States Government and the American Indian.* 2 vols. Lincoln: University of Nebraska Press, 1984. Print.

Queener, Verton M. "A Decade of East Tennessee Republicanism, 1867–1876." *East Tennessee Historical Society's Publications* 14 (1942): 59–85. Print.

Rable, George C. *But There Was No Peace: The Role of Violence in the Politics of Reconstruction.* Athens: U of Georgia P, 2007. Print.

Randall, J. G., and David Herbert Donald. *The Civil War and Reconstruction.* Boston: Heath, 1961. Print.

Randel, William P. *The Ku Klux Klan: A Century of Infamy.* Philadelphia: Chilton, 1965. Print.

Ransom, Roger L. and Richard Sutch. *One Kind of Freedom: The Economic Consequences of Emancipation.* 2nd ed. Cambridge: Cambridge UP, 2001. Print.

"Reconstruction." *The Columbia Encyclopedia.* New York: Columbia University Press, 2013. Credo Reference. Web. 29 March 2014.

"Reconstruction: The Second Civil War." *The American Experience.* PBS Online, 2005. Web. 20 March 2014.

Republican National Convention. *Proceedings of the First Three Republican National Conventions of 1856, 1860 and 1864.* Minneapolis: C.W. Johnson, 1893. Print.

"Revels, Hiram Rhodes." *US House of Representatives: History, Art & Archives.* US House of Representatives, Office of the Historian, n.d. Web. 10 Oct. 2013.

Richards, David A. J. *Conscience and the Constitution: History, Theory, and Law of the Reconstruction Amendments.* Princeton: Princeton UP, 1993. Print.

Richter, William L. *The ABC-CLIO Companion to American Reconstruction, 1862–1877.* Santa Barbara, CA: ABC-CLIO, 1996. Print.

Rollin, Frank A. *Life and Public Services of Martin R. Delany.* New York: Arno Press and the New York Times, 1969. Print.

Rubin, Anne Sarah. "Stone, Sarah Katherine 'Kate' (1841–1907)." *Encyclopedia of the American Civil War: A Political, Social, and Military History.* Santa Barbara: ABC-CLIO, 2000. Credo Reference. Web. 6 Apr. 2014.

Rutherglen, George A. *Civil Rights in the Shadow of Slavery: The Constitution, Common Law, and the Civil Rights Act of 1866.* Oxford: Oxford UP, 2012. Print.

Sawrey, Robert D. *Dubious Victory: The Reconstruction Debate in Ohio.* Lexington: UP of Kentucky, 1992. Print.

Saxon, Rufus. "Testimony before Congress's Joint Committee on Reconstruction." *History of St. Augustine.*

Ed. Gil Wilson. Dr. Bronson Tours. n.d. Web. 20 March 2014.

Scaturro, Frank J. *President Grant Reconsidered.* Latham, MD: Rowman & Littlefield, 1999. Print.

Schott, Thomas E. *Alexander H. Stephens of Georgia: A Biography.* Baton Rouge: Louisiana State UP, 1988. Print.

Schultz, Kevin. *HIST2.* 2nd ed. Vol. 1. Boston, MA: Wadsworth-Cengage Learning, 2012. Print.

Schurz, Carl. *The Reminiscences of Carl Schurz.* 3 vols. New York: McClure, 1907–1908. Print.

Schurz, Carl. *Report on the Condition of the South.* New York: Arno, 1969 Print.

Sernett, Milton C. *North Star Country: Upstate New York and the Crusade for African American Freedom.* Syracuse: Syracuse UP, 2002. Print.

Severance, Ben H. *Tennessee's Radical Army: The State Guard and Its Role in Reconstruction, 1867–1869.* Knoxville: U of Tennessee P, 2005. Print.

Simpson Brooks D. *Let Us Have Peace: Ulysses S. Grant the Politics of War & Reconstruction, 1861-1868.* Chapel Hill: U of North Carolina P, 1991. Print.

Smith, Jean Edward. *Grant.* New York: Simon and Schuster, 2001. Print.

Smith, John David. *A Just and Lasting Peace: A Documentary History of Reconstruction.* New York: Signet Classics, 2013. Print.

Smith, Page. *Trial by Fire: A People's History of the Civil War and Reconstruction.* New York: McGraw-Hill, 1982. Print.

"The Southern Black Codes of 1865–66." *Constitutional Rights Foundation: Bill of Right in Action.* Constitutional Rights Foundation. Spring 1999. Web. 29 Mar. 2014.

Stauffer, John. *The Black Hearts of Men: Radical Abolitionists and the Transformation of Race.* Cambridge, MA: Harvard UP, 2001. Print.

"Stephens, Alexander Hamilton (1812–1883)." *Biographical Directory of the United States Congress.* US Congress, n.d. Web. 8 Jan. 2014.

Stephens, George E. and Donald Yacovone. *A Voice of Thunder: A Black Soldier's Civil War.* Champaign: U of Illinois P, 1999. Print.

Sterling, Dorothy. *The Making of an Afro-American: Martin Robison Delany 1812–1885.* Garden City: Doubleday, 1971. Print.

Sterling, Dorothy, ed. *The Trouble They Seen: The Story of Reconstruction in the Words of African Americans.* New York: Da Capo, 1994. Print.

Sterling, Dorothy, ed. *We Are Your Sisters: Black Women in the Nineteenth Century.* New York: Norton, 1984. Print.

Stone, Kate. "All Have Suffered" *Reconstruction: America's Second Civil War.* PBS.org. 19 Dec. 2003. Web. 6 Apr. 2014.

Stuntz, William J. *The Collapse of American Criminal Justice.* Cambridge: Belknap P of Harvard UP, 2012. Print.

Summers, Mark W. *A Dangerous Stir: Fear, Paranoia, and the Making of Reconstruction.* Chapel Hill: U of North Carolina P, 2009. Print.

Sumner, Charles. "Charles Sumner on Reconstruction and the South, 1866." *Gilder Lehrman Institute of American History.* Gilder Lehrman Institute of American History, n.d. Web. 22 Jan. 2014.

Sumner, Charles. *The One Man Power vs. Congress! Address of Hon. Charles Sumner, at the Music Hall, Boston, October 2, 1866.* Boston: Wright and Potter, 1866. Internet Archive. Web. 22 Jan. 2014.

Taylor, Joe Gray. *Louisiana Reconstructed, 1863–1877.* Baton Rouge: Louisiana State UP, 1974. Print.

Teele, Arthur Earle. "Education of the Negro in North Carolina, 1862–1872." Diss. Cornell U, 1953. Print.

Tourgée, Albion W. "Letter to Senator Joseph C. Abbott (1870)." *Undaunted Radical: The Selected Writings and Speeches of Albion W. Tourgée.* Ed. Mark Elliott and John David Smith. Baton Rouge: Louisiana State UP, 2010. 47–51. Print.

Trefousse, Hans Louis. *Carl Schurz: A Biography.* New York: Fordham UP, 1998. Print.

Trefousse, Hans Louis. *Thaddeus Stevens: Nineteenth-Century Egalitarian.* Chapel Hill: U of North Carolina P, 1997. Print.

Trelease, Allen W. *White Terror: The Ku Klux Klan Conspiracy and Southern Reconstruction.* 1971. Baton Rouge: Louisiana State UP, 1995. Print.

Ullman, Victor. *Martin R. Delany: The Beginnings of Black Nationalism.* Boston: Beacon Press, 1971. Print.

United States Congress Joint Committee on Reconstruction. *Report.* Washington: Government Printing Office, 1866. Online University of Pittsburgh Library System. 28 Feb. 2009. Web. 20 March 2014.

Weidman, Budge. "The Fight for Equal Rights: Black Soldiers in the Civil War." *National Archives.* National Archives and Records Administration, 1997. Web. 28 Nov. 2013.

White, Horace. *Life of Lyman Trumbull.* New York:

Houghton Mifflin, 1913. Print.

"White Men Unite: Primary Sources." *American Experience: Reconstruction*. WGBH: PBS Online, 19 Dec. 2003. Web. 5 Apr. 2014.

Wilson, Theodore B. *The Black Codes of the South*. Tuscaloosa: U of Alabama P, 1965. Print.

Wright, David. *Fire on the Beach: Recovering the Lost Story of Richard Etheridge and the Pea Island Lifesavers*. New York: Oxford UP, 2002. Print.

Wynne, Ben. *Mississippi's Civil War: A Narrative History*. Macon, GA: Mercer UP, 2006. Print.

Zuczek, Richard. "The Federal Government's Attack on the Ku Klux Klan: A Reassessment." *South Carolina Historical Magazine* 97.1 (1996): 47–64. Print.

Index